WORKERS OF ALL COUNTRIES, UNITE!

SELECTED WORKS

OF

MAO TSE-TUNG

Volume IV

FOREIGN LANGUAGES PRESS
PEKING 1969

First Edition   1961
Second Printing   1967
Third Printing   1969

The present volume is an English translation of the first Chinese edition of the fourth volume of the *Selected Works of Mao Tse-tung*, published by the People's Publishing House, Peking, in September 1960.

Printed in the People's Republic of China

CONTENTS

THE THIRD REVOLUTIONARY CIVIL WAR PERIOD

THE SITUATION AND OUR POLICY AFTER THE VICTORY IN THE WAR OF RESISTANCE AGAINST JAPAN ... 11

CHIANG KAI-SHEK IS PROVOKING CIVIL WAR ... 27

TWO TELEGRAMS FROM THE COMMANDER-IN-CHIEF OF THE EIGHTEENTH GROUP ARMY TO CHIANG KAI-SHEK ... 33

ON A STATEMENT BY CHIANG KAI-SHEK'S SPOKESMAN ... 41

ON PEACE NEGOTIATIONS WITH THE KUOMINTANG – CIRCULAR OF THE CENTRAL COMMITTEE OF THE COMMUNIST PARTY OF CHINA ... 47

ON THE CHUNGKING NEGOTIATIONS ... 53

THE TRUTH ABOUT THE KUOMINTANG ATTACKS ... 65

RENT REDUCTION AND PRODUCTION ARE TWO IMPORTANT MATTERS FOR THE DEFENCE OF THE LIBERATED AREAS ... 71

POLICY FOR WORK IN THE LIBERATED AREAS FOR 1946 ... 75

BUILD STABLE BASE AREAS IN THE NORTHEAST ... 81

SOME POINTS IN APPRAISAL OF THE PRESENT INTERNATIONAL SITUATION ... 87

SMASH CHIANG KAI-SHEK'S OFFENSIVE BY A WAR OF SELF-DEFENCE ... 89

TALK WITH THE AMERICAN CORRESPONDENT ANNA LOUISE STRONG ... 97

CONCENTRATE A SUPERIOR FORCE TO DESTROY THE ENEMY FORCES ONE BY ONE ... 103

THE TRUTH ABOUT U.S. "MEDIATION" AND THE FUTURE OF THE CIVIL WAR IN CHINA ... 109

A THREE MONTHS' SUMMARY ... 113

GREET THE NEW HIGH TIDE OF THE CHINESE REVOLUTION ... 119

5

ON THE TEMPORARY ABANDONMENT OF YENAN AND THE
DEFENCE OF THE SHENSI-KANSU-NINGSIA BORDER REGION –
TWO DOCUMENTS ISSUED BY THE CENTRAL COMMITTEE OF
THE COMMUNIST PARTY OF CHINA   129

THE CONCEPT OF OPERATIONS FOR THE NORTHWEST WAR
THEATRE   133

THE CHIANG KAI-SHEK GOVERNMENT IS BESIEGED BY THE
WHOLE PEOPLE   135

STRATEGY FOR THE SECOND YEAR OF THE WAR OF LIBERATION   141

MANIFESTO OF THE CHINESE PEOPLE'S LIBERATION ARMY   147

ON THE REISSUE OF THE THREE MAIN RULES OF DISCIPLINE
AND THE EIGHT POINTS FOR ATTENTION – INSTRUCTION OF
THE GENERAL HEADQUARTERS OF THE CHINESE PEOPLE'S
LIBERATION ARMY   155

THE PRESENT SITUATION AND OUR TASKS   157

ON SETTING UP A SYSTEM OF REPORTS   177

ON SOME IMPORTANT PROBLEMS OF THE PARTY'S PRESENT
POLICY   181

THE DEMOCRATIC MOVEMENT IN THE ARMY   191

DIFFERENT TACTICS FOR CARRYING OUT THE LAND LAW IN
DIFFERENT AREAS   193

CORRECT THE "LEFT" ERRORS IN LAND REFORM PROPAGANDA   197

ESSENTIAL POINTS IN LAND REFORM IN THE NEW LIBERATED
AREAS   201

ON THE POLICY CONCERNING INDUSTRY AND COMMERCE   203

ON THE QUESTION OF THE NATIONAL BOURGEOISIE AND THE
ENLIGHTENED GENTRY   207

ON THE GREAT VICTORY IN THE NORTHWEST AND ON THE
NEW TYPE OF IDEOLOGICAL EDUCATION MOVEMENT IN THE
LIBERATION ARMY   211

A CIRCULAR ON THE SITUATION   219

SPEECH AT A CONFERENCE OF CADRES IN THE SHANSI-SUIYUAN
LIBERATED AREA   227

A TALK TO THE EDITORIAL STAFF OF THE *SHANSI-SUIYUAN
DAILY*   241

TELEGRAM TO THE HEADQUARTERS OF THE LOYANG FRONT
AFTER THE RECAPTURE OF THE CITY   247

TACTICAL PROBLEMS OF RURAL WORK IN THE NEW LIBERATED AREAS 251

THE WORK OF LAND REFORM AND OF PARTY CONSOLIDATION IN 1948 253

THE CONCEPT OF OPERATIONS FOR THE LIAOHSI-SHENYANG CAMPAIGN 261

ON STRENGTHENING THE PARTY COMMITTEE SYSTEM 267

ON THE SEPTEMBER MEETING – CIRCULAR OF THE CENTRAL COMMITTEE OF THE COMMUNIST PARTY OF CHINA 269

THE CONCEPT OF OPERATIONS FOR THE HUAI-HAI CAMPAIGN 279

REVOLUTIONARY FORCES OF THE WORLD UNITE, FIGHT AGAINST IMPERIALIST AGGRESSION! 283

THE MOMENTOUS CHANGE IN CHINA'S MILITARY SITUATION 287

THE CONCEPT OF OPERATIONS FOR THE PEIPING-TIENTSIN CAMPAIGN 289

MESSAGE URGING TU YU-MING AND OTHERS TO SURRENDER 295

CARRY THE REVOLUTION THROUGH TO THE END 299

ON THE WAR CRIMINAL'S SUING FOR PEACE 309

STATEMENT ON THE PRESENT SITUATION BY MAO TSE-TUNG, CHAIRMAN OF THE CENTRAL COMMITTEE OF THE COMMUNIST PARTY OF CHINA 315

COMMENT BY THE SPOKESMAN FOR THE COMMUNIST PARTY OF CHINA ON THE RESOLUTION OF THE NANKING EXECUTIVE YUAN 321

ON ORDERING THE REACTIONARY KUOMINTANG GOVERNMENT TO RE-ARREST YASUJI OKAMURA, FORMER COMMANDER-IN-CHIEF OF THE JAPANESE FORCES OF AGGRESSION IN CHINA, AND TO ARREST THE KUOMINTANG CIVIL WAR CRIMINALS – STATEMENT BY THE SPOKESMAN FOR THE COMMUNIST PARTY OF CHINA 325

PEACE TERMS MUST INCLUDE THE PUNISHMENT OF JAPANESE WAR CRIMINALS AND KUOMINTANG WAR CRIMINALS – STATEMENT BY THE SPOKESMAN FOR THE COMMUNIST PARTY OF CHINA 333

TURN THE ARMY INTO A WORKING FORCE 337

WHY DO THE BADLY SPLIT REACTIONARIES STILL IDLY CLAMOUR FOR "TOTAL PEACE"? 341

THE KUOMINTANG REACTIONARIES TURN FROM AN "APPEAL
    FOR PEACE" TO AN APPEAL FOR WAR   347

ON THE KUOMINTANG'S DIFFERENT ANSWERS TO THE QUESTION
    OF RESPONSIBILITY FOR THE WAR   351

REPORT TO THE SECOND PLENARY SESSION OF THE SEVENTH
    CENTRAL COMMITTEE OF THE COMMUNIST PARTY OF CHINA   361

METHODS OF WORK OF PARTY COMMITTEES   377

WHITHER THE NANKING GOVERNMENT?   383

ORDER TO THE ARMY FOR THE COUNTRY-WIDE ADVANCE   387

PROCLAMATION OF THE CHINESE PEOPLE'S LIBERATION ARMY   397

ON THE OUTRAGES BY BRITISH WARSHIPS – STATEMENT BY THE
    SPOKESMAN OF THE GENERAL HEADQUARTERS OF THE
    CHINESE PEOPLE'S LIBERATION ARMY   401

ADDRESS TO THE PREPARATORY MEETING OF THE NEW POLIT-
    ICAL CONSULTATIVE CONFERENCE   405

ON THE PEOPLE'S DEMOCRATIC DICTATORSHIP   411

CAST AWAY ILLUSIONS, PREPARE FOR STRUGGLE   425

FAREWELL, LEIGHTON STUART!   433

WHY IT IS NECESSARY TO DISCUSS THE WHITE PAPER   441

"FRIENDSHIP" OR AGGRESSION?   447

THE BANKRUPTCY OF THE IDEALIST CONCEPTION OF HISTORY   451

THE THIRD
REVOLUTIONARY CIVIL WAR
PERIOD

THE SITUATION AND OUR POLICY AFTER THE VICTORY IN THE WAR OF RESISTANCE AGAINST JAPAN*

August 13, 1945

These are days of tremendous change in the situation in the Far East. The surrender of Japanese imperialism is now a foregone conclusion. The decisive factor for Japan's surrender is the entry of the Soviet Union into the war. A million Red Army troops are entering China's Northeast; this force is irresistible. Japanese imperialism can no longer continue the fight.[1] The Chinese people's hard and bitter War of Resistance is crowned with victory. As a historical stage, the War of Resistance Against Japan is now over.

In these circumstances, what are the relations among the different classes in China and what are the relations between the Kuomintang and the Communist Party at present? What will they be like in the future? What is the policy of our Party? These are questions of great concern to the people of the whole country and to all members of our Party.

What about the Kuomintang? Look at its past, and you can tell its present; look at its past and present, and you can tell its future. In the past, this party carried on a counter-revolutionary civil war for ten whole years. During the War of Resistance it launched three large-scale anti-Communist campaigns,[2] in 1940, 1941 and 1943, each time attempting to develop the attack into a country-wide civil war. It was only because of the correct policy adopted by our Party and the opposition of the people of the whole country that its attempts failed. As everyone knows, Chiang Kai-shek, the political representative of China's big landlords and big bourgeoisie, is a most brutal and treacherous fellow. His policy has been to look on with folded arms, wait for victory, conserve his forces and prepare for civil war. Indeed, the victory he has been waiting for has arrived, and now

11

this "generalissimo" is about to "come down from the mountain".[3]
In the past eight years we have changed places with Chiang Kai-shek –
formerly we were on the mountain and he was by the water;[4] during
the War of Resistance we were behind the enemy lines and he went up
the mountain.   Now he is coming down from the mountain, coming
down to seize the fruits of victory.

During the past eight years the people and army of our Liberated
Areas, receiving no aid whatsoever from outside and relying solely
on their own efforts, liberated vast territories and resisted and pinned
down the bulk of the Japanese invading forces and practically all
the puppet troops.   Only by our determined resistance and heroic
struggle were the 200 million people in the Great Rear Area[5] saved
from being trampled underfoot by the Japanese aggressors and the
regions inhabited by these 200 million people saved from Japanese
occupation.   Chiang Kai-shek hid on Mount Omei with guards in
front of him – the guards were the Liberated Areas, the people and
army of the Liberated Areas.   In defending the 200 million people
of the Great Rear Area, we protected this "generalissimo" as well
and gave him both the time and the space to sit around waiting for
victory with folded arms.   Time – eight years one month.   Space – an
area inhabited by 200 million people.   These conditions we provided
for him.   But for us, he could not have stood by looking on.   Is
the "generalissimo" grateful to us, then?   No, not he!   This fellow has
never known what it is to be grateful.   How did Chiang Kai-shek
climb to power?   By the Northern Expedition,[6] by the first period
of co-operation between the Kuomintang and the Communist Party,[7]
by the support given him by the people, who had not yet seen
through him.   Once in power, Chiang Kai-shek, far from being

---

* This speech was delivered by Comrade Mao Tse-tung at a meeting of cadres
in Yenan.   Based on the Marxist-Leninist method of class analysis, it presented a
penetrating study of the fundamental political situation in China after victory in the
War of Resistance Against Japan and set forth the revolutionary tactics of the proletariat.
As Comrade Mao Tse-tung had pointed out in his opening address at the Seventh
National Congress of the Communist Party of China in April 1945, China after defeating
Japanese imperialism still faced two destinies, two futures – either to become a new
China or to remain the old China.   The big landlords and big bourgeoisie of China,
represented by Chiang Kai-shek, wanted to wrest the fruits of victory in the War of
Resistance from the hands of the people and to keep China a semi-colonial and semi-
feudal country under their dictatorship.   The Communist Party of China, representing
the interests of the proletariat and the masses of the people, on the one hand strove
for peace and opposed civil war with all its strength.   On the other hand, it had to
prepare fully against Chiang Kai-shek's counter-revolutionary plot of launching a

grateful to the people, knocked them down and plunged them into the bloodbath of ten years of civil war.   You comrades are familiar with this segment of history.   During the present War of Resistance the Chinese people again defended him.   This war is now ending in victory and Japan is on the point of surrender, but he is not at all grateful to the people.   On the contrary, thumbing through the records of 1927, he wants to act in the same old way.[8]   He says there has never been any "civil war" in China, only "bandit suppression".   Whatever he likes to call it, the fact is he wants to start a civil war against the people, he wants to slaughter the people.

Until a civil war breaks out all over the country, many of the people and many of our Party comrades will not have a very clear understanding of this question.   Since civil war is not yet here on a large scale, since it is not yet widespread or out in the open and since the battles are not yet numerous, many people think, "Well, there may not be a civil war after all!"   Many others are afraid of civil war.   Their fear is not without reason.   There were ten years of fighting and then another eight years of the War of Resistance; if the fighting keeps on, where will it all end?   It is quite natural that such fears should arise.   With regard to Chiang Kai-shek's plot to launch a civil war, our Party's policy has been clear and consistent, that is, resolutely to oppose civil war, be against civil war and prevent civil war.   In the days to come, we shall continue, with the utmost effort and greatest patience, to lead the people in preventing civil war.   Nevertheless, it is necessary to be soberly aware that the danger of civil war is extremely serious because Chiang Kai-shek's policy is already set.   Chiang Kai-shek's policy is civil war.   Our policy, the policy of the people, is against civil war.   The opponents of civil war

---

country-wide civil war and had to adopt the correct policy, that is to say, to harbour no illusions about imperialism and reaction, to have no fear of their threats, to resolutely safeguard the fruits of the people's struggle and strive to build a new China – a new-democratic China of the broad masses of the people under the leadership of the proletariat.   The decisive struggle between the two destinies, the two futures facing China, constituted the content of the historical period from the conclusion of the War of Resistance Against Japan to the founding of the People's Republic of China, the historical period of the Chinese People's War of Liberation or Third Revolutionary Civil War.   After the War of Resistance, Chiang Kai-shek, supported by U.S. imperialism, tore up peace agreements again and again and launched a gigantic counter-revolutionary civil war without parallel in history in an attempt to wipe out the people's forces.   Because of the correct leadership of the Communist Party of China, it took the Chinese people only four years of struggle to win a great country-wide victory – the overthrow of Chiang Kai-shek and the creation of a new China.

consist only of the Chinese Communist Party and the Chinese people –
it is a pity that they do not include Chiang Kai-shek and the Kuomintang. Here one side does not want to fight and the other does. If both
did not want it, there would be no fighting. Now, since only one side
is against it and this side is not yet strong enough to check the other,
the danger of civil war is extremely grave.

Our Party pointed out in good time that Chiang Kai-shek would
stick to his reactionary policy of dictatorship and civil war. Before,
during and after the Seventh Party Congress,[9] we did fairly adequate
work to call the people's attention to the danger of civil war, so
that the whole people, our Party members and our troops should be
mentally prepared well in advance. This is a very important point,
and it makes a world of difference whether or not there is such preparedness. In 1927 our Party was still in its infancy and was mentally
wholly unprepared for Chiang Kai-shek's counter-revolutionary surprise attack. Consequently the fruits of victory won by the people
were soon lost, the people had to undergo long suffering, and a
bright China was plunged into darkness. This time things are
different; our Party has acquired the rich experience of three revolutions[10] and a much higher degree of political maturity. Time and
again, the Central Committee of the Party has clearly explained the
danger of civil war, and so the whole people, all Party members and
the troops led by our Party are in a state of preparedness.

Chiang Kai-shek always tries to wrest every ounce of power and
every ounce of gain from the people. And we? Our policy is to
give him tit for tat and to fight for every inch of land. We act
after his fashion. He always tries to impose war on the people,
one sword in his left hand and another in his right. We take up
swords, too, following his example. We found this method only
after investigation and study. Such investigation and study are very
important. When we see the other fellow holding something in his
hands, we should do some investigating. What does he hold in his
hands? Swords. What are swords for? For killing. Whom does
he want to kill with his swords? The people. Having made these
findings, investigate further – the Chinese people, too, have hands
and can take up swords, they can forge a sword if there is none
handy. The Chinese people have discovered this truth after long
investigation and study. Warlords, landlords, local bullies and bad
gentry and the imperialists all have swords in their hands and are
out to kill. The people have come to understand this and so act

after the same fashion.   Some of us often neglect such investigation
and study.   Chen Tu-hsiu,[11] for example, did not understand that
with swords one can kill people.   Some say, this is a plain everyday
truth; how can a leader of the Communist Party fail to know it?
But you never can tell.   Chen Tu-hsiu made no investigation and
study and so did not understand this, hence we called him an opportunist.   He who makes no investigation and study has no right to
speak, and accordingly we deprived Chen Tu-hsiu of that right.   We
have adopted a course different from Chen Tu-hsiu's and enabled the
people suffering from oppression and slaughter to take up swords.
If ever again anybody wants to kill us, we will act after his fashion.
Not long ago, the Kuomintang sent six divisions to attack our Kuanchung sub-region, and three of them drove in and seized an area
measuring 20 by 100 *li*.   We acted after their fashion and wholly,
thoroughly and completely wiped out the Kuomintang troops in this
area of 20 by 100 *li*.[12]   Our policy is to give tit for tat and fight
for every inch of land; we will never let the Kuomintang easily
seize our land and kill our people.   Of course, to fight for every
inch of land does not mean following the old "Left" line of "not
abandoning a single inch of land in the base area".[13]   This time we
abandoned an area of 20 by 100 *li*.   Abandoned late in July, it was
retaken early in August.   After the Southern Anhwei Incident of
1941,[14] the Kuomintang liaison staff officer once asked me what we
intended to do.   I answered, "You are here in Yenan all the time
and you don't know?   If Ho goes for us, we'll go for him.   If Ho
stops, we'll stop too."[15]   At that time Chiang Kai-shek was not named,
only Ho Ying-chin.   Today we say, "If Chiang goes for us, we'll go
for him.   If Chiang stops, we'll stop too."   We will act after his fashion.
As Chiang Kai-shek is now sharpening his swords, we must sharpen
ours too.

     The rights the people have won must never be lightly given up
but must be defended by fighting.   We don't want civil war.   However, if Chiang Kai-shek insists on forcing civil war on the Chinese
people, the only thing we can do is to take up arms and fight him
in self-defence to protect the lives and property, the rights and well-
being of the people of the Liberated Areas.   This will be a civil
war he forces on us.   If we do not win, we will blame neither
heaven nor earth but only ourselves.   However, let no one think
that the people can be easily robbed or defrauded of the rights they
have won; that is impossible.   Last year an American correspondent

asked me, "Who has given you the power to act?" I replied, "The people." Who else indeed, if not the people? The ruling Kuomintang hasn't given us any power. It doesn't recognize us. We take part in the People's Political Council in the capacity of a "cultural organization"[16] as stipulated by its rules. But we are not a "cultural organization", we say, we have an army and are a "military organization". On March 1 this year Chiang Kai-shek stated that the Communist Party would have to turn over its army before it could acquire legal status. Chiang Kai-shek's statement still stands. We have not turned over our army, and so we have no legal status and are "defying laws human and divine". Our duty is to hold ourselves responsible to the people. Every word, every act and every policy must conform to the people's interests, and if mistakes occur, they must be corrected – that is what being responsible to the people means. Comrades! The people want liberation and therefore entrust power to those who can represent them and work faithfully for them, that is, to us Communists. As representatives of the people, we must represent them well and not act like Chen Tu-hsiu. Confronted by counter-revolutionary attacks against the people, Chen Tu-hsiu did not adopt the policy of giving tit for tat and fighting for every inch of land; as a result, in 1927, within the space of a few months, he forfeited all the rights the people had won. This time we must be on our guard. Our policy is absolutely different from Chen Tu-hsiu's; no trickery can fool us. We must be clearheaded and have a correct policy; we must not make mistakes.

To whom should the fruits of victory in the War of Resistance belong? It is very obvious. Take a peach tree for example. When the tree yields peaches they are the fruits of victory. Who is entitled to pick the peaches? Ask who planted and watered the tree. Chiang Kai-shek squatting on the mountain did not carry a single bucket of water, and yet he is now stretching out his arm from afar to pick the peaches. "I, Chiang Kai-shek, own these peaches," he says, "I am the landlord, you are my serfs and I won't allow you to pick any." We have refuted him in the press.[17] We say, "You never carried any water, so you have no right to pick the peaches. We the people of the Liberated Areas watered the tree day in day out and have the most right to gather the fruit." Comrades! The victory of the War of Resistance has been won by the people with bloodshed and sacrifice, it should be the victory of the people and it is to the people that the fruits of the War of Resistance should go.

As for Chiang Kai-shek, he was passive in resisting Japan but active in anti-communism. He was a stumbling-block in the people's War of Resistance. Now this stumbling-block is coming forward to monopolize the fruits of victory, wants China after victory to relapse into her old pre-war state and does not tolerate the slightest change. This gives rise to struggle. Comrades! It is a most serious struggle.

That the fruits of victory of the War of Resistance should go to the people is one thing, but who will eventually get them and whether it will be the people is another. Don't be too sure that all the fruits of victory will fall into the hands of the people. Chiang Kai-shek will grab a lot of big peaches, such as Shanghai, Nanking, Hangchow and other big cities. He has ganged up with U.S. imperialism and in those places they have the upper hand, while so far the revolutionary people can by and large occupy only the rural areas. Another bunch of peaches will be contested by both sides. These are the medium and small towns situated along the section of the Tatung-Puchow Railway north of Taiyuan, the middle section of the Peiping-Suiyuan Railway, the Peiping-Liaoning Railway, the section of the Peiping-Hankow Railway north of Chengchow, the Chengting-Taiyuan Railway, the Paikuei-Chincheng Railway,[18] the Tehchow-Shihchiachuang Railway, the Tientsin-Pukow Railway, the Tsingtao-Tsinan Railway and the section of the Lunghai Railway east of Chengchow. These medium and small towns must be contested; they are the medium and small peaches watered by the people of the Liberated Areas with their sweat and blood. It is difficult to say now whether these places will fall into the people's hands. Only two words can be said now: struggle hard. Are there places which are sure to fall into the hands of the people? Yes, there are. They are the vast rural areas and the numerous towns in the provinces of Hopei, Chahar and Jehol,[19] most of Shansi, Shantung and the northern part of Kiangsu, with villages linked together and with about a hundred towns in one area, seventy to eighty in another, forty to fifty in a third – altogether three, four, five or six such areas, big and small. What sort of towns? Medium and small towns. We are sure of them, we have the strength to pick these fruits of victory. In the history of the Chinese revolution this will be the first time that we have got such a bunch of fruit. Historically, it was only after we smashed the enemy's third "encirclement and suppression" campaign[20] in the latter half of 1931 that we had altogether as many as twenty-one county towns[21] in the Central Base Area in Kiangsi

Province, but there was not a single medium-sized town among them. With twenty-one small towns linked together, the total population at its height reached 2,500,000. Relying on this base, the Chinese people were able to continue the struggle for such a long time, win such big victories and smash such big "encirclement and suppression" campaigns. Later we were defeated, for which we should blame, not Chiang Kai-shek, but ourselves for not fighting well enough. This time, if scores of big and small towns are linked in a single contiguous area and if there are three, four, five or six such areas, then the Chinese people will have three, four, five or six revolutionary bases, each larger than the Central Base Area in Kiangsi Province, and the situation for the Chinese revolution will be very promising indeed.

If one looks at the situation as a whole, the stage of the War of Resistance Against Japan is over and the new situation and task is domestic struggle. Chiang Kai-shek talks about "building the country". From now on the struggle will be, build what sort of country? To build a new-democratic country of the broad masses of the people under the leadership of the proletariat? Or to build a semi-colonial and semi-feudal country under the dictatorship of the big landlords and the big bourgeoisie? This will be a most complicated struggle. At present it takes the form of a struggle between Chiang Kai-shek who is trying to usurp the fruits of victory of the War of Resistance and ourselves who oppose his usurpation. If there is any opportunism during this period, it will lie in failing to struggle hard and in making a voluntary gift to Chiang Kai-shek of the fruits which should go to the people.

Will an open and total civil war break out? That depends on internal and international factors. The internal factors consist chiefly of our strength and the degree of our political consciousness. Given the general trend of the international and internal situation and the feelings of the people, is it possible, through our own struggles, to localize the civil war or delay the outbreak of a country-wide civil war? There is this possibility.

Chiang Kai-shek will face many difficulties if he tries to let loose a civil war. First, in the Liberated Areas there are a hundred million people, a million troops and over two million people's militia. Second, the politically conscious people in the Kuomintang areas are against civil war, and this is some kind of check on Chiang Kai-shek. Third, inside the Kuomintang also there is a section which is not in favour of civil war. The situation today is vastly different from that in 1927. In particular, the condition of our Party today is vastly different from what it was in 1927. In those days our Party was still in its infancy and did not have a clear head or experience in armed struggle or the policy of giving tit for tat. Today the level of political consciousness in our Party is very much higher.

Apart from our own political consciousness, the political conscious-ness of the vanguard of the proletariat, there is the question of the political consciousness of the masses of the people. When the people are not yet politically conscious, it is entirely possible that their revolutionary gains may be handed over to others. This happened in the past. Today the level of political consciousness of the Chinese people is likewise very much higher. The prestige of our Party among the people has never been so great. Nevertheless, among the people, and chiefly among those living in the Japanese-occupied and Kuomintang areas, there are still a good many who believe in Chiang Kai-shek and have illusions about the Kuomintang and the United States of America, illusions which Chiang Kai-shek is working hard to spread. The fact that a section of the Chinese people is not yet politically conscious shows that much remains to be done in our propaganda and organizational work. The political awakening of the people is not easy. It requires much earnest effort on our part to rid their minds of wrong ideas. We should sweep backward ideas from the minds of the Chinese people, just as we sweep our rooms. Dust never vanishes of itself without sweeping. We must carry on extensive propaganda and education among the masses, so they will understand the real situation and trend in China and have confidence in their own strength.

It is up to us to organize the people. As for the reactionaries in China, it is up to us to organize the people to overthrow them. Everything reactionary is the same; if you don't hit it, it won't fall. It is like sweeping the floor; where the broom does not reach, the dust never vanishes of itself. There is a river called the Chieh-tse, south of the Shensi-Kansu-Ningsia Border Region. South of the river is Lochuan County and north of it, Fuhsien County. North and south of the river are two different worlds. The south is under the Kuomintang; since we have not reached there, the people are unorganized, and there is much filth and rottenness. Some of our comrades put their faith only in political influence, fancying that problems can be solved merely by influence. That is blind faith. In

1936, we were in Pao-an.[22] Forty to fifty *li* away, there was a fortified village held by a landlord despot. The Central Committee of the Party was then in Pao-an and our political influence could be considered very great indeed, but the counter-revolutionaries in this village obstinately refused to surrender. We swept to the south, we swept to the north, all in vain. Not until our broom swept right into the village did the landlord cry out, "Ow, I give up!"[23] That is how things are in this world. Bells don't ring till you strike them. Tables don't move till you shift them. Japan would not surrender until after the Red Army of the Soviet Union entered northeastern China. The enemy and puppet troops never handed over their arms until our troops fought them. Only where the broom reaches can political influence produce its full effect. Our broom is the Communist Party, the Eighth Route Army and the New Fourth Army. Broom in hand, you must learn to sweep; don't lie in bed, fancying that a gust of wind will somehow rise and blow all the dust away. We Marxists are revolutionary realists and never indulge in idle dreams. There is an old saying in China, "Rise at dawn and sweep the court-yard."[24] Dawn is the breaking of a new day. Our forefathers told us to rise and start sweeping at the very break of day. They were setting us a task. Only by thinking and acting in this way will we benefit and find work to do. China has a vast territory, and it is up to us to sweep it clean inch by inch.

On what basis should our policy rest? It should rest on our own strength, and that means regeneration through one's own efforts. We are not alone; all the countries and people in the world opposed to imperialism are our friends. Nevertheless, we stress regeneration through our own efforts. Relying on the forces we ourselves organize, we can defeat all Chinese and foreign reactionaries. Chiang Kai-shek, on the contrary, relies entirely on the aid of U.S. imperialism, which he looks upon as his mainstay. The trinity of dictatorship, civil war and selling out the country has always been the basis of his policy. U.S. imperialism wants to help Chiang Kai-shek wage civil war and turn China into a U.S. dependency, and this policy, too, was set long ago. But U.S. imperialism while outwardly strong is inwardly weak. We must be clear-headed, that is, we must not believe the "nice words" of the imperialists nor be intimidated by their bluster. An American once said to me, "You should listen to Hurley and send a few men to be officials in the Kuomintang government."[25] I replied: "It is no easy job to be an official bound hand and foot; we won't do it. If we become officials, our hands and feet must be unfettered, we must be free to act, that is, a coalition government must be set up on a democratic basis." He said, "It will be bad if you don't." I asked him, "Why bad?" He said, "First, the Americans will curse you; secondly, the Americans will back Chiang Kai-shek." I replied: "If you Americans, sated with bread and sleep, want to curse people and back Chiang Kai-shek, that's your business and I won't interfere. What we have now is millet plus rifles, what you have is bread plus cannon. If you like to back Chiang Kai-shek, back him, back him as long as you want. But remember one thing. To whom does China belong? China definitely does not belong to Chiang Kai-shek, China belongs to the Chinese people. The day will surely come when you will find it impossible to back him any longer." Comrades! This American was trying to scare people. Imperialists are masters at this sort of stuff, and many people in the colonial countries do get scared. The imperialists think that all people in the colonial countries can be scared, but they do not realize that in China there are people who are not afraid of that sort of stuff. In the past we have openly criticized and exposed the U.S. policy of aiding Chiang Kai-shek to fight the Communists; it was necessary, and we shall continue to do so.

The Soviet Union has sent its troops, the Red Army has come to help the Chinese people drive out the aggressor; such an event has never happened before in Chinese history. Its influence is immeasurable. The propaganda organs of the United States and Chiang Kai-shek hoped to sweep away the Red Army's political influence with two atom bombs.[26] But it can't be swept away; that isn't so easy. Can atom bombs decide wars? No, they can't. Atom bombs could not make Japan surrender. Without the struggles waged by the people, atom bombs by themselves would be of no avail. If atom bombs could decide the war, then why was it necessary to ask the Soviet Union to send its troops? Why didn't Japan surrender when the two atom bombs were dropped on her and why did she surrender as soon as the Soviet Union sent troops? Some of our comrades, too, believe that the atom bomb is all-powerful; that is a big mistake. These comrades show even less judgement than a British peer. There is a certain British peer called Lord Mountbatten. He said the worst possible mistake is to think that the atom bomb can decide the war.[27] These comrades are more backward than Mountbatten. What influence has made these comrades look upon the atom bomb as something miraculous? Bourgeois influence. Where does it come from? From their education in bourgeois schools, from the bourgeois press and news agencies. There are two world outlooks and two methodologies, the proletarian world outlook and methodology and the bourgeois world outlook and methodology. These comrades often cling to the bourgeois world outlook and methodology and often forget the proletarian world outlook and methodology. The theory that "weapons decide everything", the purely military viewpoint, a bureaucratic style of work divorced from the masses, individualist thinking, and the like – all these are bourgeois influences in our ranks. We must constantly sweep these bourgeois things out of our ranks just as we sweep out dust.

The entry of the Soviet Union into the war has decided Japan's surrender and the situation in China is entering a new period. Between the War of Resistance and the new period there is a transitional stage. The struggle during this transitional stage is to oppose Chiang Kai-shek's usurpation of the fruits of victory in the War of Resistance. Chiang Kai-shek wants to launch a country-wide civil war and his policy is set; we must be prepared for this. No matter when this country-wide civil war breaks out, we must be well prepared. If it comes early, say, tomorrow morning, we should also be prepared. That is point one. In the present international and domestic situation it is possible that for a time the civil war may be kept restricted in scale and localized. That is point two. Point one is what we should prepare for, point two is what has existed for a long time. In short, we must be prepared. Being prepared, we shall be able to deal properly with all kinds of complicated situations.

NOTES

[1] On August 8, 1945, the Soviet government declared war on Japan. On August 10 the Mongolian government declared war on Japan. The Soviet Red Army moved by land and sea into China's Northeast and into Korea and swiftly routed the Japanese Kwantung Army. The joint Soviet-Mongolian armies crossed the Inner Mongolian desert and entered Jehol and Chahar Provinces. On August 10 the Japanese government was compelled to send a note begging to surrender and on the 14th it formally announced its unconditional surrender. The Kwantung Army was the cream of the main force of the Japanese army and constituted Japan's general strategic reserve. The Japanese imperialists had dreamed of relying on this force to carry on a long-drawn-out war from their favourable strategic position in China's Northeast and in

Korea. This scheme was completely wrecked by the entry of the Soviet Union into the war, and the Japanese government had to admit defeat and surrender.

[2] For details, see "A Comment on the Eleventh Plenary Session of the Kuomintang's Central Executive Committee and the Second Session of the Third People's Political Council", *Selected Works of Mao Tse-tung*, Vol. III.

[3] "Mountain" here refers to Mount Omei in Szechuan Province and more generally to the mountainous areas in southwestern and northwestern China. After Wuhan was occupied by the Japanese army in 1938, Chiang Kai-shek and the main force under his command took refuge in these mountainous areas and sat there watching the bitter struggle against the Japanese aggressors which was being waged behind the enemy lines by the army and people of the Liberated Areas.

[4] Prior to the War of Resistance Against Japan, most of the revolutionary base areas led by the Communist Party of China were in mountainous regions. At that time Chiang Kai-shek's rule was centred in the large cities along the big rivers and the coast. Accordingly, Comrade Mao Tse-tung said "we were on the mountain and he was by the water".

[5] During the War of Resistance the front lines were in northern, eastern, central and southern China. People usually referred to the Kuomintang areas in southwestern and northwestern China which were not occupied by the Japanese invaders as the Great Rear Area.

[6] The Northern Expedition was the punitive war against the Northern warlords launched by the revolutionary army which marched north from Kwangtung Province in May-July 1926. The Northern Expeditionary Army, with the Communist Party of China taking part in its leadership and under the Party's influence (the political work in the army was at that time mostly under the charge of Communist Party members), gained the warm support of the broad masses of workers and peasants. In the second half of 1926 and the first half of 1927 it occupied most of the provinces along the Yangtse and Yellow Rivers and defeated the Northern warlords. In April 1927 this revolutionary war failed as a result of betrayal by the reactionary clique under Chiang Kai-shek within the revolutionary army.

[7] In 1924, with the help of the Communist Party of China, Sun Yat-sen reorganized the Kuomintang and effected co-operation between the Kuomintang and the Communist Party. The Revolutionary War of 1924-27 was launched on the basis of this co-operation. This first co-operation between the Kuomintang and the Communist Party was wrecked as a result of betrayals by Chiang Kai-shek and Wang Ching-wei in 1927.

[8] This refers to Chiang Kai-shek's betrayal of the revolution in 1927. After betraying the revolution, Chiang Kai-shek massacred great numbers of Communists, workers, peasants and revolutionary intellectuals and unleashed a counter-revolutionary war against the revolutionary masses.

[9] This Congress was held in Yenan in April 1945. It was there that Comrade Mao Tse-tung delivered the political report "On Coalition Government" (see *Selected Works of Mao Tse-tung*, Vol. III).

[10] The first revolution was the anti-imperialist, anti-feudal revolutionary struggle waged from 1924 to 1927 by the Chinese people under the leadership of the Communist Party of China; the Northern Expedition was the main content of this revolution. The second revolution was the revolutionary struggle from 1927 to 1937 to create and develop Red political power. The third revolution was the War of Resistance Against Japan from 1937 to 1945.

[11] Chen Tu-hsiu was originally a professor at Peking University and became famous as an editor of *New Youth*. He was one of the founders of the Communist

Party of China. Owing to his reputation at the time of the May 4th Movement and owing to the Party's immaturity in its initial period, he became General Secretary of the Party. In the last period of the revolution of 1924-27, the Rightist thinking in the Party represented by Chen Tu-hsiu developed into a line of capitulationism. In "The Present Situation and Our Tasks", Comrade Mao Tse-tung said that the capitulationists at that time "voluntarily gave up the Party's leadership of the peasant masses, urban petty bourgeoisie and middle bourgeoisie, and in particular gave up the Party's leadership of the armed forces, thus causing the defeat of the revolution" (p. 171 of this volume). After the defeat in 1927 Chen Tu-hsiu and a handful of other capitulationists lost faith in the future of the revolution and became liquidationists. They took the reactionary Trotskyist stand and together with the Trotskyites formed a small anti-Party group. Consequently Chen Tu-hsiu was expelled from the Party in November 1929. He died in 1942. With reference to Chen Tu-hsiu's Right opportunism, see the introductory notes to "Analysis of the Classes in Chinese Society" and to "Report on the Investigation into the Peasant Movement in Hunan", *Selected Works of Mao Tse-tung*, Vol. I, and "Introducing *The Communist*", *Selected Works of Mao Tse-tung*, Vol. II.

[12] On July 21, 1945, the Provisional 59th Division and 2nd Cavalry Division under Hu Tsung-nan, Commander of the Kuomintang's 1st War Zone, suddenly attacked Yehtai Mountain in Chunhua County in the Kuanchung sub-region of the Shensi-Kansu-Ningsia Border Region. On July 23 Hu Tsung-nan sent his 3rd Reserve Division to join in the attack. On July 27 our forces withdrew on their own initiative from Yehtai Mountain and forty-one villages west of it. The Kuomintang forces continued their attacks on Hsunyi, Yaohsien and other points. On August 8 our forces struck back at the invading Kuomintang troops and recovered the Yehtai mountain area.

[13] This slogan was raised by the "Left" opportunists during the period from October 1933 to October 1934 when the Red Army of the Central Base Area was repulsing the Kuomintang's fifth encirclement campaign. The slogan was diametrically opposed to the strategy formulated by Comrade Mao Tse-tung, which was to lure the enemy deep into our territory, concentrate a superior force and select the enemy's weak points in order to wipe him out in mobile warfare.

[14] In January 1941, as demanded by Chiang Kai-shek, the Headquarters of the New Fourth Army led by the Communist Party of China and the units under the direct command of this headquarters moved north from southern Anhwei Province to cross the Yangtse River. While on the march they were encircled and ambushed by Chiang Kai-shek's troops and lost more than 9,000, killed, wounded and captured. Subsequently Chiang Kai-shek announced the cancellation of the designation of the New Fourth Army and ordered attacks against its other units. The event was called the Southern Anhwei Incident.

[15] During the War of Resistance the Kuomintang kept a staff officer in Yenan for liaison. "Ho" refers to Ho Ying-chin, Chief of the Kuomintang General Staff. On October 19 and December 8, 1940, Chiang Kai-shek sent two telegrams in the names of Ho Ying-chin and Pai Chung-hsi, Deputy Chief of the Kuomintang General Staff, outrageously slandering the Eighth Route Army and the New Fourth Army, which were fighting stubbornly behind the Japanese lines, and arbitrarily ordering the people's anti-Japanese armed forces operating south of the Yellow River to withdraw north of the river within a definite time-limit. The Kuomintang reactionaries then launched a sudden attack on units of the New Fourth Army which were moving north and thus created the Southern Anhwei Incident. At that time the Communist Party of China pointed to Ho Ying-chin as the representative of the Kuomintang reactionaries who

had launched the large-scale anti-Communist campaign, but actually Chiang Kai-shek was meant.

[16] The "People's Political Council" was an advisory body set up by the Kuomintang government after the start of the War of Resistance. Its members were all "selected" by the Kuomintang government; the majority belonged to the Kuomintang, and only a very few belonged to the Communist Party of China and other political parties. Moreover, the Kuomintang government did not recognize the equal and legal status of the parties which were opposed to Japanese aggression, nor did it allow their members to sit in the "People's Political Council" as representatives of their parties. One of the stipulations of the "Organic Rules of the People's Political Council" promulgated by the Kuomintang government was that those persons might become members of the Council "who have served in important cultural or economic organizations for three years or more and enjoy prestige, or those who devote themselves to affairs of state and have long enjoyed prestige". It was on the basis of this stipulation that the Kuomintang "selected" some councillors from the Communist Party of China.

[17] This refers to the commentary, "Chiang Kai-shek Is Provoking Civil War", written by Comrade Mao Tse-tung for the Hsinhua News Agency, pp. 27-31 of this volume.

[18] An unfinished railway line in southeastern Shansi Province, between Paikuei in Chihsien County and Chincheng.

[19] The province of Chahar was abolished in 1952. The province of Jehol was abolished in 1955. The territories originally under their jurisdiction were transferred to Hopei, Shansi and Liaoning Provinces and the Inner Mongolian Autonomous Region.

[20] From July to September 1931 Chiang Kai-shek personally held the post of commander-in-chief and moved 300,000 reactionary troops in an encirclement campaign against the Kiangsi Red Base Area. The Red Army smashed this encirclement campaign and won a great victory. For details, see "Strategic Problems of the Chinese Revolutionary War", Chapter 5, Section 5, *Selected Works of Mao Tse-tung*, Vol. I.

[21] The twenty-one county towns here referred to were Juichin, Huichang, Hsunwu, Anyuan, Hsinfeng, Yutu, Hsingkuo, Ningtu, Kuangchang, Shihcheng and Lichuan in Kiangsi Province, and Chienning, Taining, Ninghua, Chingliu, Kueihua, Lungyen, Changting, Liencheng, Shanghang and Yungting in Fukien Province.

[22] Pao-an was a county in the northwestern part of Shensi Province. It is now called Chihtan County. The Central Committee of the Communist Party of China had its headquarters there from early July 1936 to January 1937. Later it moved to Yenan.

[23] The fortified village referred to was Tanpachai in the southwest of Pao-an County. There were over two hundred households in the village, which occupied a highly strategic position. Tsao Chun-chang, a landlord despot who headed a reactionary local armed band of over a hundred men, had long entrenched himself in this village. The Chinese Red Army repeatedly besieged the village but failed to capture it. In August 1936 the Red Army, while surrounding Tanpachai with the local armed forces, proceeded to win over the basic masses in the village and disintegrate the enemy from within. In December of the same year the bandit Tsao fled with a handful of his men, and Tanpachai was liberated.

[24] From *Maxims for the Good Household*, written by Chu Po-lu in the 17th century.

[25] The American referred to was Colonel David D. Barrett, head of the U.S. Army Observer Group in Yenan. With the consent of the Communist Party of China, this group was sent to Yenan in 1944 by the U.S. forces fighting against Japan. Patrick J. Hurley, a reactionary politician of the Republican Party, came to China in September 1944 as the personal representative of the U.S. president and at the end of the year became U.S. ambassador to China. See "The Foolish Old Man Who Removed the Mountains", Note 1, *Selected Works of Mao Tse-tung*, Vol. III.

[26] The United States dropped an atom bomb on Hiroshima on August 6, 1945, and another on Nagasaki on August 9. The propaganda organs of the United States and of the Kuomintang made much of the event, alleging that the Japanese government had surrendered because it was afraid of the U.S. atom bombs. By such propaganda they hoped to belittle the decisive role played by the entry of the Soviet Union into the war in compelling Japan to surrender.

[27] Mountbatten, then Supreme Commander of Allied Forces in Southeast Asia, made a statement on August 9, 1945, welcoming the entry of the Soviet Union into the war against Japan. He also said that the worst possible mistake would be to believe that the atom bomb could end the war in the Far East.

CHIANG KAI-SHEK IS PROVOKING CIVIL WAR*

August 13, 1945

A spokesman for the Propaganda Department of the Kuomintang Central Executive Committee has made a statement describing as "a presumptuous and illegal act" the order[1] setting a time-limit for the surrender of the enemy and the puppets,[2] which was issued by Chu Teh, Commander-in-Chief of the Eighteenth Group Army, on August 10 from the General Headquarters in Yenan. This comment is absolutely preposterous. Its logical implication is that it was wrong of Commander-in-Chief Chu Teh to act in accordance with the Potsdam Declaration[3] and with the enemy's declared intention of surrendering and to order his troops to effect the surrender of the enemy and the puppets, and that on the contrary it would have been right and legitimate to advise the enemy and puppets to refuse to surrender.   No wonder that even before the enemy's actual surrender, Chiang Kai-shek, China's fascist ringleader, autocrat and traitor to the people, had the audacity to "order" the anti-Japanese armed forces in the Liberated Areas to "stay where they are, pending further orders", that is, to tie their own hands and let the enemy attack them.   No wonder this selfsame fascist ringleader dared to "order" the so-called underground forces (who are, in fact, puppet troops "saving the nation by a devious path"[4] and Tai Li's[5] secret police collaborating with the Japanese and puppets) as well as other puppet troops to "be responsible for maintaining local order", while forbidding the anti-Japanese armed forces in the Liberated Areas to "take presumptuous action on their own" against enemy and puppet forces.   This transposition of the enemy and the Chinese is in truth a confession by Chiang Kai-shek; it gives a vivid picture of his whole psychology, which is one of consistent collusion with the enemy and puppets and of liquidation of all those not of his ilk. However, the people's anti-Japanese armed forces in China's Liberated Areas will never be taken in by this venomous scheme.   They know

27

that Commander-in-Chief Chu Teh's order is precisely the resolute fulfilment of the provision in paragraph 2 of the Potsdam Declaration, "prosecute the war against Japan until she ceases to resist". On the other hand, Chiang Kai-shek's so-called "orders" are precisely violations of the Potsdam Declaration which he himself signed. One has only to make the comparison to see at once who is not "adhering faithfully to the provisions of the common agreements of the Allies".

Both the comment by the spokesman for the Propaganda Department of the Kuomintang Central Executive Committee and Chiang Kai-shek's "orders" are from beginning to end provocations to civil war; at this moment, when attention at home and abroad is focussed on Japan's unconditional surrender, their aim is to find a pretext for switching to civil war as soon as the War of Resistance ends. In reality, the Kuomintang reactionaries are pitifully stupid. They have sought their pretext in Commander-in-Chief Chu Teh's order for the surrender and disarming of the enemy and puppet troops. Can this be considered a clever pretext? No. That they seek a pretext in this way proves only that the Kuomintang reactionaries are fonder of the enemy and puppets than of their fellow-countrymen and that they hate their fellow-countrymen more than they do the enemy and puppets. The Chunhua Incident[6] was plainly an invasion of the Shensi-Kansu-Ningsia Border Region by Hu Tsung-nan's troops to provoke civil war, and yet the Kuomintang reactionaries said it was a "rumour offensive" by the Communist Party of China. The Kuomintang reactionaries found their long-sought-for pretext in the Chunhua Incident, but Chinese and foreign public opinion saw through it at once. So now they are saying that the Eighth Route Army and the New Fourth Army should not demand that the enemy and puppet troops surrender their guns. In the eight years of the War of Resistance, the Eighth Route Army and the New Fourth Army have suffered enough from the attacks and encirclements of both Chiang Kai-shek and the Japanese. And now, with the War of Resistance coming to an end, Chiang Kai-shek is hinting to the Japanese (and to his beloved puppet troops) that they should not surrender their guns to the Eighth Route Army and the New Fourth Army but "only to me, Chiang Kai-shek". One thing, however, Chiang Kai-shek has left unsaid, ". . . so that I can use these guns to kill the Communists and wreck the peace of China

---

* This was a commentary written by Comrade Mao Tse-tung for the Hsinhua News Agency.

and the world." Isn't this the truth? What will be the result of telling the Japanese to hand over their guns to Chiang Kai-shek and telling the puppet troops to "be responsible for maintaining local order"? The result can only be that a merger of the Nanking and Chungking regimes[7] and co-operation between Chiang Kai-shek and the puppets will take the place of "Sino-Japanese collaboration" and of co-operation between the Japanese and the puppets, and that Chiang Kai-shek's "anti-communism and national reconstruction" will take the place of the "anti-communism and national reconstruction" of the Japanese and Wang Ching-wei.[8] Isn't this a violation of the Potsdam Declaration? Can there be any doubt that the grave danger of civil war will confront the people of the whole country the moment the War of Resistance is over? We now appeal to all our fellow-countrymen and to the Allied countries to take action, together with the people of the Liberated Areas, resolutely to prevent a civil war in China, which would endanger world peace.

After all, who has the right to accept the surrender of the Japanese and puppets? Relying solely on their own efforts and the support of the people, the anti-Japanese armed forces in China's Liberated Areas, to whom the Kuomintang government refused all supplies and recognition, have succeeded by themselves in liberating vast territories and more than 100 million people and have resisted and pinned down 56 per cent of the invading enemy troops in China and 95 per cent of the puppet troops. If not for these armed forces, the situation in China would never have been what it is today! To speak plainly, in China only the anti-Japanese armed forces of the Liberated Areas have the right to accept the surrender of the enemy and puppet troops. As for Chiang Kai-shek, his policy has been to look on with folded arms and sit around and wait for victory; indeed he has no right at all to accept the surrender of the enemy and the puppets.

We declare to all our fellow-countrymen and to the people of the whole world: The Supreme Command in Chungking cannot represent the Chinese people and those Chinese armed forces which have really fought Japan; the Chinese people demand the right of the anti-Japanese armed forces of China's Liberated Areas under Commander-in-Chief Chu Teh to send their representatives directly in order to participate in the acceptance of Japan's surrender and in the military control over Japan by the four Allied Powers and also to participate in the future peace conference. If this is not done, the Chinese people will deem it most improper.

NOTES

[1] On August 10, 1945, Commander-in-Chief Chu Teh issued an order from the General Headquarters in Yenan to all armed forces in the Liberated Areas concerning the surrender of the Japanese invaders. The order reads as follows:

Japan has announced her unconditional surrender, and the Allies will meet to discuss measures for accepting the surrender on the basis of the Potsdam Declaration. I hereby issue the following order to all our armed forces in the Liberated Areas:

(1) In accordance with the provisions of the Potsdam Declaration, any anti-Japanese armed forces in the Liberated Areas may serve notice on enemy troops and headquarters in cities and towns or along communication lines in the vicinity, requiring them to hand over all their arms to our fighting forces within a given time; when they have handed over their arms, our forces will protect their lives in accordance with our regulations on the lenient treatment of prisoners of war.

(2) Any anti-Japanese armed forces in the Liberated Areas may serve notice on all the puppet troops and puppet government organs in the vicinity, requiring them to come over with their troops to our side before the signing of the surrender by the Japanese invaders and to wait for reorganization and disbandment; those who fail to comply within the time allowed shall hand over all their arms.

(3) All anti-Japanese armed forces in the Liberated Areas should resolutely wipe out all those enemy and puppet armed forces which refuse to surrender and hand over their arms.

(4) Our armed forces have full authority to send their units to take over and occupy any city, town or communication line held by the enemy and the puppets, to set up military control, to maintain order and to appoint commissioners to take charge of all administrative matters there; in case of any act of sabotage or resistance, the culprits shall be punished as traitors.

Then, on August 11 the General Headquarters in Yenan issued six successive orders, under which the armed forces of the Shansi-Suiyuan Liberated Area (led by Comrade Ho Lung), the Shansi-Chahar-Hopei Liberated Area (led by Comrade Nieh Jung-chen) and the Hopei-Jehol-Liaoning Liberated Area were to march on Inner Mongolia and the Northeast; the armed forces of the Shansi Liberated Area were to mop up the Japanese and puppet troops along the Tatung-Puchow Railway and in the Fenho River valley; and the armed forces of all the Liberated Areas were to launch vigorous offensives on all the main communication lines under enemy control to compel the Japanese and puppet troops to surrender. The units of the People's Liberation Army in all the Liberated Areas resolutely carried out these orders and won important victories.

[2] Here "enemy" refers to the Japanese invading forces, and "puppets" refers to the puppet governments set up by the Japanese invaders and to the troops of these puppet governments, consisting largely of former Kuomintang officials and of troops who had surrendered to Japan.

[3] This refers to the declaration made by China, Britain and the United States at the Potsdam conference on July 26, 1945, requiring Japan to surrender. The main points of the declaration were that Japanese militarism must be eliminated for good and all; Japan's military forces must be completely disarmed; Japan's war industries must be dismantled; Japanese war criminals must be tried; the Cairo Declaration must be carried out, that is, Japan must renounce the territories she had stolen, such

as Korea and China's Manchuria, Taiwan and the Penghu Islands, and Japan's territory must be limited to the islands of Honshu, Hokkaido, Kyushu, Shikoku and various minor islands; and that the armed forces of the Allies were to occupy Japan until the establishment of a democratic Japanese government. The Soviet Union also signed the Potsdam Declaration after it declared war on Japan on August 8, 1945.

[4] This refers to the dastardly practice of capitulating to Japan and fighting communism followed by the Kuomintang reactionaries during the War of Resistance Against Japan. The Kuomintang reactionaries directed part of their troops and government officials to surrender to the Japanese invaders and then, as puppet troops and officials, to join the Japanese troops in attacking the Liberated Areas; this was what they cunningly named "saving the nation by a devious path".

[5] Tai Li was the Director of the Bureau of Investigation and Statistics of the Military Council of the Kuomintang, one of the Kuomintang's huge secret service agencies.

[6] The invasion by Kuomintang troops of Chunhua, Hsunyi and Yaohsien in the Kuanchung sub-region of the Shensi-Kansu-Ningsia Border Region in July 1945. See "The Situation and Our Policy After the Victory in the War of Resistance Against Japan", Note 12, p. 24 of this volume.

[7] Wang Ching-wei's puppet regime was in Nanking and Chiang Kai-shek's regime was in Chungking. The "merger of the Nanking and Chungking regimes" was a political plot hatched by Japanese imperialism and the pro-Japanese elements within the Kuomintang.

[8] Wang Ching-wei was a notorious Kuomintang leader and pro-Japanese traitor. He openly surrendered to the Japanese invaders in December 1938 when he was vice-chairman of the Kuomintang and chairman of its People's Political Council. In March 1940 he became president of the puppet central government then formed in Nanking. He died in Japan in November 1944.

TWO TELEGRAMS
FROM THE COMMANDER-IN-CHIEF OF
THE EIGHTEENTH GROUP ARMY
TO CHIANG KAI-SHEK*

August 1945

I. TELEGRAM OF AUGUST 13

We have received through the Chungking radio two Central News Agency dispatches, one carrying the order you sent us and the other your order to the officers and men in various war zones. Your order to us reads, "All units of the Eighteenth Group Army should stay where they are, pending further orders." In addition, it talks about such things as forbidding us to take over the enemy's arms. Your order to the officers and men in various war zones was reported as follows in the Central News Agency dispatch from Chungking, dated August 11: "The Supreme Command today sent telegrams to the officers and men in various war zones, ordering them to step up the war effort and in accordance with existing military plans and orders actively to push forward without the slightest relaxation." We hold that these two orders contradict each other. According to the first, our units should "stay where they are, pending further orders" and should no longer attack or fight. Why do you tell us not to fight at this moment when the Japanese aggressors have not yet actually surrendered, when every hour and every minute they are killing Chinese people and fighting Chinese troops as well as Soviet, U.S. and British troops, and when, in their turn, the Soviet, U.S. and British troops are fighting the Japanese aggressors every hour and every minute? As to the second order, we consider it very good. "Step up the war effort and actively push forward without the slightest relaxation" – that's more like it! But what a pity you have given this order only to your own troops, and not to us,

33

and that you have given us something quite different. Chu Teh issued an order on August 10 to all anti-Japanese armed forces in China's Liberated Areas[1] precisely to the effect that they should "step up the war effort". His order said further that while stepping up their war effort they must order the Japanese aggressors to surrender to them and must take over the arms and other equipment of the enemy and puppet troops. Isn't this very good? Undoubtedly it is very good; undoubtedly it is in the interest of the Chinese nation. But to "stay where they are, pending further orders" is definitely not in the national interest. We hold that you have given a wrong order, an order so wrong that we have to inform you we firmly reject it. For your order to us is not only unjust but also runs counter to China's national interest and benefits only the Japanese aggressors and the traitors to the motherland.

II. TELEGRAM OF AUGUST 16

At a time when our common enemy, the Japanese government, has accepted the terms of the Potsdam Declaration and already announced its surrender but has not yet actually surrendered, I hereby address to you the following statement and demands on behalf of all the anti-Japanese armed forces and all the 260 million people in China's Liberated Areas and Japanese-occupied areas.

---

* These telegrams were written by Comrade Mao Tse-tung for the Commander-in-Chief of the Eighteenth Group Army. At that time, when the Japanese aggressors had announced their surrender but had not yet actually surrendered, the Chiang Kai-shek government, with the armed assistance of U.S. imperialism, monopolized the right to accept the Japanese surrender and was actively preparing a counter-revolutionary civil war by sending large forces to advance on the Liberated Areas on the pretext of accepting the Japanese surrender. Comrade Mao Tse-tung's purpose in writing the first telegram was to unmask the counter-revolutionary face of Chiang Kai-shek and teach the whole people to be on guard against his civil war plot. The second telegram further exposed the plot of the Chiang Kai-shek clique for preparing civil war and put forward the six-point proposal of the Communist Party of China for preventing civil war. For the same purpose, Comrade Mao Tse-tung wrote for the Hsinhua News Agency two commentaries, "Chiang Kai-shek Is Provoking Civil War" and "On a Statement by Chiang Kai-shek's Spokesman", which are included in this volume. Owing to the firm, determined stand of the Communist Party of China in refusing to be cowed by Chiang Kai-shek's reactionary bluster, both the Liberated Areas and the Liberation Army expanded quickly; and, under strong political pressure from the forces at home and abroad opposed to civil war in China, Chiang Kai-shek had to change his tactics, assume a posture of peace and invite Comrade Mao Tse-tung to Chungking for peace negotiations.

With the War of Resistance Against Japan coming to a victorious close, I call your attention to this fact in the China war theatre today, namely, that in the vast occupied areas abandoned by you and seized by the enemy and puppets we have, against your will, by our eight years of bitter fighting recaptured nearly 1,000,000 square kilometres of territory; liberated over 100,000,000 people; organized over 1,000,000 regular troops and over 2,200,000 people's militia; established nineteen large Liberated Areas in the nineteen provinces of Liaoning, Jehol, Chahar, Suiyuan, Hopei, Shansi, Shensi, Kansu, Ningsia, Honan, Shantung, Kiangsu, Anhwei, Hupeh, Hunan, Kiangsi, Chekiang, Fukien and Kwangtung;[2] and encircled most of the cities and towns, vital communication lines and sections of the sea coast seized by the enemy and puppets since the July 7th Incident of 1937,[3] except in a few areas. In addition, in China's Japanese-occupied areas (with a population of 160 million) we have organized extensive underground forces to strike at the enemy and puppets. In the fighting we are continuing to resist and encircle 69 per cent of the Japanese troops invading China (not counting those in the Northeast) and 95 per cent of the puppet troops. Your government and armed forces, on the contrary, have all along followed a policy of looking on with folded arms, sitting around and waiting for victory, conserving your forces and preparing for civil war, and have not only refused recognition and supplies to our Liberated Areas and armies but encircled and attacked us with a huge force of 940,000 men. Although all the troops and civilians in China's Liberated Areas have suffered enough from being attacked by the enemy and puppet forces on the one side and by your troops on the other, we have never in the least weakened in our determination to persevere in the War of Resistance, in unity and in democracy. The people of China's Liberated Areas and the Communist Party of China have proposed many times to you and your government that a conference of all parties be convened and that a democratic coalition government of the whole country be formed in order to stop internal strife, mobilize and unite the people's anti-Japanese forces throughout China, lead the War of Resistance to victory and ensure peace after the war. But our proposals have invariably been rejected by you and your government. We are extremely dissatisfied with all this.

The enemy country will soon sign its surrender, but you and your government have continued to ignore our opinions, issued a most outrageous order to me on August 11 and ordered your troops to press against the Liberated Areas on a large scale under the pretext of disarming the enemy; the danger of civil war is therefore more serious than ever. All of which compels us to make the following demands on you and your government:

1. I demand that you consult with us, so that we may reach common views before you, your government and your Supreme Command accept the surrender of the Japanese and the puppets and conclude any post-surrender agreements or treaties. For you and your government have aroused the dissatisfaction of the people and cannot represent the broad masses or any of the people's anti-Japanese armed forces in China's Liberated Areas and Japanese-occupied areas. We reserve our right to speak out, if the agreements or treaties include, without our prior consent, anything that concerns the people's anti-Japanese armed forces in China's Liberated Areas and Japanese-occupied areas.

2. All the people's anti-Japanese armed forces in China's Liberated Areas and Japanese-occupied areas have the right, in accordance with the Potsdam Declaration and the measures laid down by the Allies for accepting the enemy surrender,[4] to accept the surrender of the Japanese and puppet troops encircled by us, take over their arms and matériel and assume the responsibility for carrying out all stipulations laid down by the Allies after Japan's surrender has been accepted. On August 10 I ordered the armed forces of China's Liberated Areas to make all efforts to attack the enemy troops and be prepared to accept their surrender. On August 15, I ordered the enemy commander-in-chief, Yasuji Okamura, to surrender with his troops;[5] this order, however, applies only to the sphere of operations of the armed forces of the Liberated Areas, and not to any other. I consider my orders very reasonable and very much in the common interest of China and the Allies.

3. The broad masses and all the anti-Japanese armed forces in China's Liberated Areas and Japanese-occupied areas have the right to send their representatives to participate in the Allies' acceptance of the enemy surrender and in the work of dealing with the enemy country after its surrender.

4. China's Liberated Areas and all the anti-Japanese armed forces have the right to select their own delegation to participate in the future peace conference concerned with Japan and any United Nations meetings.

5. I ask you to prevent civil war. The way to do this is for the armed forces of the Liberated Areas to accept the surrender of the

enemy and puppet troops they have encircled, while your armed forces accept the surrender of the enemy and puppet troops you have encircled. Not only is this the established practice in all wars, it is particularly imperative in order to avert civil war. If you act otherwise, it will lead to adverse consequences. I am now giving you a serious warning on this matter and I ask you not to treat this warning casually.

6. I ask you immediately to abolish the one-party dictatorship, call a conference of all parties to set up a democratic coalition government, dismiss corrupt officials and all reactionaries from their posts, punish the traitors, abolish the secret services, recognize the legal status of the various parties (the Communist Party of China and all democratic parties have up to now been regarded as illegal by you and your government), annul all reactionary laws and decrees that suppress the liberties of the people, recognize the popularly elected governments and the anti-Japanese armed forces of China's Liberated Areas, withdraw the troops encircling the Liberated Areas, release political prisoners and carry out economic and other democratic reforms.

Apart from this, I sent you a telegram on August 13 in reply to your order to me of August 11, and presumably you have received it. I now declare again, your order was completely wrong. On August 11 you ordered my troops to "stay where they are, pending further orders" and not to attack the enemy any more. However, not only was it true on August 11, but it is equally true even today (August 16) that the Japanese government has surrendered only in words, and not in deeds; no instrument of surrender has been signed, no actual surrender has taken place. My view is completely in accord with that of the Allies, Britain, the United States and the Soviet Union. On August 11, the very day you issued your order to me, the British Army Command on the Burma front announced that the war with Japan was still in progress. Nimitz,[6] the commander of the U.S. forces, declared that not only did a state of war continue but the war with all its devastating consequences must be carried on. The Far Eastern Command of the Red Army of the Soviet Union announced, "The enemy must be ruthlessly smashed." On August 15, Colonel-General Antonov, Chief of the General Staff of the Red Army, made the following statement:

> The message concerning Japan's surrender issued by the Japanese Emperor on August 14 is only a general declaration concerning unconditional surrender. The order to the armed forces to cease hostilities has not yet been issued and the Japanese troops are

continuing their resistance. Hence there is still no actual surrender by the armed forces of Japan. The surrender of the armed forces of Japan can be considered to have taken place only from the moment the Japanese Emperor orders his armed forces to discontinue hostilities and lay down their arms and when this order is carried out in practice. In view of the above, the armed forces of the Soviet Union in the Far East will continue their offensive operations against Japan.

It can be seen that you alone, of all the high commanders of the Allied forces, have given an absolutely wrong order. I consider that your error stems from your self-seeking and is of an extremely serious nature; that is to say, your order serves the interest of the enemy. Therefore, taking my stand on the common interest of China and the Allies, I shall firmly and completely oppose your order so long as you do not openly admit your error and countermand this wrong order. At present I am still ordering the armed units under my command to make determined attacks on the enemy, in co-ordination with the armed forces of the Soviet Union, the United States and Britain, until the enemy actually stops hostilities and surrenders his arms and all the territory of the motherland has been fully recovered. I declare to you, I am a patriotic soldier, I cannot act otherwise.

With regard to the above I request your early reply.

NOTES

[1] See "Chiang Kai-shek Is Provoking Civil War", Note 1, p. 30 of this volume.

[2] The nineteen Liberated Areas were: Shensi-Kansu-Ningsia, Shansi-Suiyuan, Shansi-Chahar-Hopei, Hopei-Jehol-Liaoning, Shansi-Hopei-Honan, Hopei-Shantung-Honan, Shantung, Northern Kiangsu, Central Kiangsu, Southern Kiangsu, Huai River North, Huai River South, Central Anhwei, Chekiang, Kwangtung, Chiungyai (Hainan Island), Hunan-Hupeh-Kiangsi, Hupeh-Honan-Anhwei and Honan.

[3] On July 7, 1937, Japanese invading forces attacked the Chinese garrison at Lukouchiao, ten kilometres southwest of Peking. Under the influence of the ardent anti-Japanese movement of the whole people, the Chinese troops there put up resistance. This incident marked the beginning of the Chinese people's heroic War of Resistance Against Japan which lasted for eight years.

[4] On August 10, 1945, the Japanese government notified the Soviet Union, China, the United States and Britain of its desire to surrender. On August 11 the governments of the four countries replied that "all the Japanese military, naval and air authorities" and "all the forces under their control wherever located" must "cease active operations" and "surrender their arms".

[5] Yasuji Okamura was then commander-in-chief of the Japanese invading forces in China. The order from Commander-in-Chief Chu Teh to Yasuji Okamura reads as follows:

(1) The Japanese government has formally accepted the terms of the Potsdam Declaration and announced its surrender.

(2) You are to order all the troops under your command to cease all military operations; all of them, except those encircled by the troops of the Kuomintang government, must surrender to us upon orders from the Eighth Route Army, New Fourth Army and Southern China Anti-Japanese Column of China's Liberated Areas.

(3) With regard to the surrender of the Japanese troops in northern China, you are to order General Sadamu Shimomura to appoint a representative to go to the Eighth Route Army's Fuping area to receive orders from General Nieh Jung-chen; with regard to the surrender of the Japanese troops in eastern China, you yourself are to appoint a representative to go to the Tienchang area, where the Headquarters of the New Fourth Army is located, to receive orders from General Chen Yi; with regard to the surrender of the Japanese troops in Hupeh and Honan Provinces, you are to order your representative in Wuhan to go to the Tapieh mountain area of the 5th Division of the New Fourth Army to receive orders from General Li Hsien-nien; with regard to the surrender of the Japanese troops in Kwangtung, you are to instruct your representative in Canton to go to the Tungkuan area of the Southern China Anti-Japanese Column to receive orders from General Tseng Sheng.

(4) All the Japanese troops in northern, eastern, central and southern China (except those encircled by the Kuomintang troops) must keep all arms and matériel intact, pending our army's acceptance of their surrender, and must not take orders except from the Eighth Route Army, the New Fourth Army or the Southern China Anti-Japanese Column.

(5) All the aircraft and vessels in northern and eastern China are to stay where they are, but the vessels anchored along the Chinese coast of the Yellow Sea and the Pohai Gulf should be assembled at Lienyunkang, Tsingtao, Weihaiwei and Tientsin.

(6) There must be no destruction of any matériel or installations.

(7) You and the commanders of the Japanese army in northern, eastern, central and southern China will be held completely responsible for the execution of this order.

[6] Chester W. Nimitz was then Commander-in-Chief of the U.S. Pacific Fleet and Pacific War Theatre.

ON A STATEMENT
BY CHIANG KAI-SHEK'S SPOKESMAN*

August 16, 1945

A spokesman for Chiang Kai-shek, commenting on the alleged violation by the Communist Party of Generalissimo Chiang Kai-shek's order to Commander-in-Chief Chu Teh, said at a press conference in Chungking on the afternoon of August 15, "The orders of the generalissimo must be obeyed" and "Those who violate them are enemies of the people." A Hsinhua News Agency correspondent states: This is an open signal by Chiang Kai-shek for all-out civil war. On August 11, at the critical moment when the Japanese invaders were being finally wiped out, Chiang Kai-shek issued an order of national betrayal forbidding the Eighth Route Army, the New Fourth Army and all the other armed forces of the people to fight the Japanese and the puppet troops. Of course, this order absolutely cannot and should not be accepted. Soon afterwards, Chiang Kai-shek through his spokesman proclaimed the armed forces of the Chinese people to be "enemies of the people". This shows that Chiang Kai-shek has declared civil war against the Chinese people. Chiang Kai-shek's plotting of civil war did not of course begin with his order of August 11; it has been his consistent plan throughout the eight years of the War of Resistance. During those eight years, Chiang Kai-shek launched three large-scale anti-Communist campaigns, in 1940, 1941 and 1943,[1] each time attempting to develop the attack into a country-wide civil war, and only the opposition of the Chinese people and of public figures in the Allied countries prevented its occurrence, much to Chiang's regret. Thus he was forced to postpone the country-wide civil war until the end of the War of Resistance Against Japan, and so came the order of August 11 and the statement of August 15. For the purpose of unleashing civil war, Chiang Kai-shek had already invented many terms, such as "alien party", "traitor party", "traitor army", "rebel army", "traitor

41

areas", "bandit areas", "disobedience to military and government
orders", "feudal separatism", "undermining the War of Resistance"
and "endangering the state"; and he had alleged that, since in the past
there had been only "suppression of Communists" in China and not
"civil war", there would be no "civil war" in the future either, and
so on and so forth.   The slight difference this time is the addition of
a new term, "enemy of the people".   But people will perceive that this
is a foolish invention.   For whenever the term, "enemy of the people",
is used in China, everyone knows who is meant.   There is a person
in China who betrayed Sun Yat-sen's Three People's Principles[2] and
the Great Revolution of 1927.   He plunged the Chinese people into
the bloodbath of ten years of civil war and thereby invited aggression
by Japanese imperialism.   Then, scared out of his wits, he took to
his heels and led a flock of people in a flight all the way from Heilungkiang to Kweichow Province.   He became an onlooker and sat around,
waiting with folded arms for victory to come.   Now that victory has
come, he tells the people's armies to "stay where they are, pending
further orders" and tells the enemy and the traitors to "maintain
order" so that he can swagger back to Nanking.   One need only mention
these facts for the Chinese people to know that this person is Chiang
Kai-shek.   After all he has done, can there be any dispute as to
whether Chiang Kai-shek is an enemy of the people?   Dispute there
is.   The people say "Yes".   The enemy of the people says "No".   And
that is the only dispute.   Among the people it is becoming less and
less a matter of dispute.   The problem now is that this enemy of the
people wants to start a civil war.   What are the people to do?   The
Hsinhua News Agency correspondent says: The policy of the Communist Party of China in regard to Chiang Kai-shek's launching a civil
war is clear and consistent, namely, to oppose it.   As far back as the
time when Japanese imperialism began to invade China, the Communist Party of China demanded an end to civil war and unity against
foreign aggression.   In 1936-37 the Party made tremendous efforts,
forced Chiang Kai-shek to accept its proposal and so carried out
the War of Resistance Against Japan.   During the eight years of
resistance, the Communist Party of China never once relaxed its
efforts to alert the people to check the danger of civil war.   Since last
year, the Communist Party has time and again called the people's
attention to the huge plot being hatched by Chiang Kai-shek to unleash

* This commentary was written by Comrade Mao Tse-tung for the Hsinhua
News Agency.

a country-wide civil war as soon as the War of Resistance ended. The Communist Party, like the rest of the Chinese people and all the people in the world concerned for peace in China, holds that a new civil war would be a calamity. But the Communist Party maintains that civil war can still be prevented and must be prevented. It is in order to prevent civil war that the Communist Party has advocated the formation of a coalition government. Now Chiang Kai-shek has rejected this proposal, and so civil war is touch-and-go. But there is definitely a way of checking this move of Chiang Kai-shek's. The people's democratic forces must strive to expand resolutely and rapidly; the people must liberate the big cities under enemy occupation and disarm the enemy and puppet troops; and if an autocrat and traitor to the people dares to attack them, the people must act in self-defence and resolutely strike back to frustrate the designs of the instigator of civil war. That is the way, the only way. The Hsinhua News Agency correspondent calls on the whole nation and the whole world to repudiate the utterly hypocritical and shameless lie which asserts that, on the contrary, civil war in China can be averted if Chiang Kai-shek forbids the Chinese people to liberate the enemy-occupied big cities, forbids them to disarm enemy and puppet forces and forbids them to establish democracy, and if he himself goes to these big cities to "inherit" (not to smash) the enemy and puppet regimes. This is a lie, the Hsinhua News Agency correspondent points out, and this lie obviously runs counter to the national and democratic interests of the Chinese people and also flies in the face of all the facts of modern Chinese history. It must always be remembered that it was not because the big cities were in the hands of the Communist Party rather than in his own hands that Chiang Kai-shek waged the ten-year civil war from 1927 to 1937; on the contrary, since 1927 none of the big cities has been in the hands of the Communist Party but all have been in Chiang's hands or have been yielded by him to the Japanese and the traitors, and this is the very reason why the civil war lasted for ten years on a country-wide scale and has continued on a local scale to this day. It must always be remembered that the ten-year civil war was stopped and that the three large-scale anti-Communist campaigns and countless other provocations during the War of Resistance were checked (up to and including Chiang Kai-shek's recent invasion of the southern part of the Shensi-Kansu-Ningsia Border Region[3]), not because Chiang Kai-shek was strong, but on the contrary because Chiang was relatively not strong enough, while the Communist Party and the people were relatively strong. The ten-

year civil war was stopped, not by the appeals of public figures throughout the country who desired peace and feared war (such as those of
the former "League for Banning Civil War"[4] and similar bodies), but
by the armed demand of the Communist Party of China and the
armed demands of the Northeastern Army under Chang Hsueh-liang
and the Northwestern Army under Yang Hu-cheng.[5] The three large-
scale anti-Communist campaigns and countless other provocations were
not beaten back by unlimited concessions and submission by the
Communist Party; they were beaten back by the Communist Party's
persistence in a just, stern attitude of self-defence – "We will not
attack unless we are attacked; if we are attacked, we will certainly
counter-attack."[6]   If the Communist Party had been utterly power-
less and spineless and had not fought to the finish for the interests of
the nation and the people, how could the ten-year civil war have been
ended? How could the War of Resistance Against Japan have started?
And even though started, how could it have been carried on resolutely
until victory today? How else could Chiang Kai-shek and his ilk be
alive now, issuing orders and making statements from a mountain
retreat so far from the front lines?   The Communist Party of China
is firmly opposed to civil war.   The Soviet Union, the United States
and Britain declared in the Crimea, "establish conditions of internal
peace" and "form interim governmental authorities broadly representative of all democratic elements in the population and pledged to the
earliest possible establishment through free elections of governments
responsive to the will of the people".[7] That is exactly what the Communist Party of China has persistently advocated – the formation of
a "coalition government".   The carrying out of this proposal can prevent civil war.   But there is one precondition – strength.   If all the
people unite and increase their strength, civil war can be prevented.

NOTES

[1] See "A Comment on the Eleventh Plenary Session of the Kuomintang's Central
Executive Committee and the Second Session of the Third People's Political Council",
Selected Works of Mao Tse-tung, Vol. III.

[2] The Three People's Principles were the principles and programmes put forward
by Sun Yat-sen on the questions of nationalism, democracy and people's livelihood
in the bourgeois democratic revolution in China.   In 1924, in the Manifesto of the
First National Congress of the Kuomintang, a congress characterized by co-operation

between the Kuomintang and the Communist Party, Sun Yat-sen restated the Three People's Principles, interpreted nationalism as opposition to imperialism and expressed active support for the movements of the workers and peasants. The old Three People's Principles thus developed into the new Three People's Principles with the Three Great Policies, that is, alliance with the Soviet Union, alliance with the Communist Party and assistance to the peasants and workers. The new Three People's Principles provided the political basis for the co-operation between the Communist Party of China and the Kuomintang during the First Revolutionary Civil War period.

[3] This refers to the attack in July 1945 by Kuomintang troops on Chunhua, Hsunyi and Yaohsien in the Kuanchung sub-region of the Shensi-Kansu-Ningsia Border Region. See "The Situation and Our Policy After the Victory in the War of Resistance Against Japan", Note 12, p. 24 of this volume.

[4] The "League for Banning Civil War" was formed in Shanghai in August 1932 with a mainly bourgeois membership. It issued a declaration calling for "ending the civil war and uniting to resist foreign aggression".

[5] In 1936 the Kuomintang's Northeastern Army headed by Chang Hsueh-liang and the Kuomintang's Northwestern Army headed by Yang Hu-cheng were stationed in and around Sian; they were charged with the task of attacking the Chinese Red Army which had arrived in northern Shensi. Influenced by the Chinese Red Army and the people's anti-Japanese movement, they agreed to the Anti-Japanese National United Front put forward by the Communist Party of China and demanded that Chiang Kai-shek unite with the Communist Party to resist Japan. Chiang Kai-shek turned down the demand, became even more active in his military preparations for the "suppression of the Communists" and massacred the anti-Japanese youth of Sian. Chang Hsueh-liang and Yang Hu-cheng took joint action and arrested Chiang Kai-shek. This was the famous Sian Incident of December 12, 1936. Chiang Kai-shek was forced to accept the terms of unity with the Communist Party and resistance to Japan and was then set free to return to Nanking.

[6] See "Talk with the Correspondents of the Central News Agency, the *Sao Tang Pao* and the *Hsin Min Pao*", *Selected Works of Mao Tse-tung*, Vol. II.

[7] From the communiqué of the Crimea (Yalta) conference of the Soviet Union, the United States of America and the United Kingdom, February 11, 1945.

ON PEACE NEGOTIATIONS
WITH THE KUOMINTANG
—CIRCULAR OF THE CENTRAL COMMITTEE
OF THE COMMUNIST PARTY OF CHINA*

August 26, 1945

The speedy surrender of the Japanese invaders has changed the whole situation. Chiang Kai-shek has monopolized the right to accept the surrender, and for the time being (for a stage) the big cities and important lines of communication will not be in our hands. Nevertheless, in northern China we should still fight hard, fight with all our might to take all we can. In the past two weeks our army has recovered fifty-nine cities of various sizes and vast rural areas, and including those already in our hands we now control 175 cities, thus winning a great victory. In northern China, we have recovered Weihaiwei, Yentai, Lungkou, Itu, Tsechuan, Yangliuching, Pikechi, Po-ai, Changchiakou, Chining and Fengchen. The might of our army has shaken northern China and, together with the sweeping advance of the Soviet and Mongolian forces to the Great Wall, has created a favourable position for our Party. In the coming period we should continue the offensive and do our best to capture the Peiping-Suiyuan Railway, the northern section of the Tatung-Puchow Railway and the Chengting-Taiyuan, Tehchow-Shihchiachuang, Paikuei-Chincheng and Taokou-Chinghua Railways; and also to cut up the Peiping-Liaoning, Peiping-Hankow, Tientsin-Pukow, Tsingtao-Tsinan, Lunghai and Shanghai-Nanking Railways. We should gain control of whatever we can, even though temporarily. At the same time, the necessary forces should be employed to take as many villages, county and higher administrative centres and small towns as possible. For example, a highly favourable situation has been created because the New Fourth Army has occupied many county towns lying between Nanking, Taihu Lake and the Tienmu Mountains and between the

47

Yangtse and the Huai Rivers, because our forces in Shantung have
occupied the whole of the Eastern Shantung Peninsula and because
our forces in the Shansi-Suiyuan Border Region have occupied many
cities and towns north and south of the Peiping-Suiyuan Railway. After another period of offensive operations, it will be possible
for our Party to control most of the areas north of the lower Yangtse
River and the Huai River, most of Shantung, Hopei, Shansi and
Suiyuan Provinces, all of Jehol and Chahar Provinces and a part of
Liaoning Province.

At present the Soviet Union, the United States and Britain all
disapprove of civil war in China;[1] at the same time our Party has
put forward the three great slogans of peace, democracy and unity[2]
and is sending Comrades Mao Tse-tung, Chou En-lai and Wang
Jo-fei to Chungking to discuss with Chiang Kai-shek the great issues
of unity and national reconstruction; thus it is possible that the civil
war plot of the Chinese reactionaries may be frustrated. The Kuomintang has now strengthened its position by recovering Shanghai,
Nanking and other places, reopening sea communications, taking
over the arms of the enemy and incorporating the puppet troops into
its own forces. Nevertheless, it is riddled with a thousand gaping
wounds, torn by innumerable inner contradictions and beset with
great difficulties. It is possible that after the negotiations the Kuomintang, under domestic and foreign pressure, may conditionally recognize
our Party's status. Our Party too may conditionally recognize the status
of the Kuomintang. This would bring about a new stage of co-
operation between the two parties (plus the Democratic League,[3]
etc.) and of peaceful development. In that event, our Party should

---

* This inner-Party circular was drafted by Comrade Mao Tse-tung for the Central
Committee of the Communist Party of China two days before he went to Chungking for peace negotiations with Chiang Kai-shek. Because the Chinese Communist
Party and the broad masses of the Chinese people firmly opposed Chiang Kai-shek's
civil war plot and because U.S. imperialism still had to pay some heed to world-wide
democratic public opinion, which unanimously condemned his policy of civil war and
dictatorship, Chiang sent three telegrams to Comrade Mao Tse-tung on August 14, 20
and 23, 1945, inviting him to Chungking for peace negotiations, and for the same
purpose Patrick J. Hurley, then U.S. ambassador to China, came to Yenan on
August 27. The Communist Party of China decided to send Comrades Mao Tse-tung,
Chou En-lai and Wang Jo-fei to Chungking for peace negotiations with the
Kuomintang in order to make every possible effort for peace and also, in the process of
struggling for peace, to show U.S. imperialism and Chiang Kai-shek in their true colours
and so help unite and educate the masses of the people. This circular drafted by
Comrade Mao Tse-tung analysed developments in China during the fortnight after
Japan announced her surrender. It set forth the policy of the Central Committee of

strive to master all methods of legal struggle and intensify its work in the Kuomintang areas in the three main spheres, the cities, the villages and the army (all weak points in our work there). During the negotiations, the Kuomintang is sure to demand that we drastically reduce the size of the Liberated Areas, cut down the strength of the Liberation Army and stop issuing currency. We on our side are prepared to make such concessions as are necessary and as do not damage the fundamental interests of the people. Without such concessions, we cannot explode the Kuomintang's civil war plot, cannot gain the political initiative, cannot win the sympathy of world public opinion and the middle-of-the-roaders within the country and cannot obtain in exchange legal status for our Party and a state of peace. But there are limits to such concessions; the principle is that they must not damage the fundamental interests of the people.

If the Kuomintang still wants to launch civil war after our Party has taken the above steps, it will put itself in the wrong in the eyes of the whole nation and the whole world, and our Party will be justified in waging a war of self-defence to crush its attacks. Moreover, our Party is powerful, and if anyone attacks us and if the conditions are favourable for battle, we will certainly act in self-defence to wipe him out resolutely, thoroughly, wholly and completely (we do not strike rashly, but when we do strike, we must win). We must never be cowed by the bluster of reactionaries. But we must at all times firmly adhere to, and never forget, these principles: unity, struggle, unity through struggle; to wage struggles with good reason, with advantage and with restraint; and to make use of contradictions, win over the many, oppose the few and crush our enemies one by one.[4]

the Communist Party of China on the peace negotiations, certain concessions the Party was prepared to make in the negotiations and policies for coping with the two possible outcomes of the negotiations. It contained directives concerning the principles to be followed in the struggles in the Liberated Areas of northern and eastern China and of central and southern China respectively. And it warned the whole Party that it must absolutely not relax its vigilance or its struggle against Chiang Kai-shek because negotiations were to take place. Comrade Mao Tse-tung and his colleagues arrived in Chungking on August 28 and held negotiations with the Kuomintang for forty-three days. Although the negotiations resulted only in the publication of the "Summary of Conversations Between the Representatives of the Kuomintang and the Communist Party of China" (also known as the "October 10th Agreement"), they were nevertheless successful in that politically they enabled the Chinese Communist Party to gain the initiative to a great extent and put the Kuomintang in a passive position. Comrade Mao Tse-tung returned to Yenan on October 11. Comrades Chou En-lai and Wang Jo-fei remained in Chungking to continue the negotiations. For the results see "On the Chungking Negotiations", the next article in this volume.

In Kwangtung, Hunan, Hupeh, Honan and some other provinces our Party forces are in a more difficult position than in northern China and the area between the Yangtse and the Huai Rivers. The comrades in those places are much in the thoughts of the Central Committee. But the Kuomintang has many weak spots and its areas are vast; our comrades will be fully able to deal with the situation, provided they make no big mistakes in military policy (movements and operations) and in the policy of uniting with the people, and provided they are modest and prudent, not conceited or rash. Besides receiving the necessary directives from the Central Committee, the comrades in these areas must use their own judgement to analyse the situation, solve their problems, surmount difficulties, maintain themselves and expand their forces. When the Kuomintang becomes unable to do anything with you, it may be compelled in the negotiations between the two parties to give your forces recognition and agree to arrangements advantageous to both sides. But you must definitely not rely on the negotiations, must definitely not hope that the Kuomintang will be kind-hearted, because it will never be kind-hearted. You must rely on your own strength, on correct guidance of activities, on brotherly unity within the Party and good relations with the people. Firmly rely on the people, that is your way out.

To sum up, our Party is confronted with many difficulties which must not be ignored, and all Party comrades must be well prepared mentally. But the general trend of the international and internal situation is favourable to our Party and to the people. So long as the whole Party is united as one, we shall be able to overcome all difficulties step by step.

NOTES

[1] Around the time of Japan's surrender, the Soviet Union, the United States and Britain for a period all expressed disapproval of civil war in China. Events soon demonstrated, however, that the U.S. statement about its so-called disapproval of civil war in China was only a screen for actively helping the reactionary Kuomintang government prepare for a counter-revolutionary civil war.

[2] The three great slogans of peace, democracy and unity were put forward in the "Declaration on the Current Situation" by the Central Committee of the Communist Party of China on August 25, 1945. The declaration pointed out that after the surrender of Japanese imperialism, "the important task confronting the whole nation is to consolidate unity in the country, safeguard domestic peace, bring about democracy and

improve the people's livelihood so as, on the basis of peace, democracy and unity, to achieve national unification and build a new China, independent, free, prosperous and powerful".

[3] The Democratic League was formed in 1941 under the name of the China Federation of Democratic Political Groups.   It was reorganized under the name of the China Democratic League in 1944.

[4] See "Problems of Tactics in the Present Anti-Japanese United Front" and "On Policy", *Selected Works of Mao Tse-tung*, Vol. II.

ON THE CHUNGKING NEGOTIATIONS*

October 17, 1945

Let us talk about the present situation. That is what our comrades are interested in. This time the negotiations between the Kuomintang and the Communist Party at Chungking have lasted forty-three days. The results have already been published in the newspapers.[1] The representatives of the two parties are continuing to negotiate. The negotiations have borne fruit. The Kuomintang has accepted the principles of peace and unity, recognized certain democratic rights of the people and agreed that civil war should be averted and that the two parties should co-operate in peace to build a new China. On these points agreement has been reached. There are other points on which there is no agreement. The question of the Liberated Areas has not been solved, and that of the armed forces has not really been solved either. The agreements reached are still only on paper. Words on paper are not equivalent to reality. Facts have shown that a very great effort must still be made before they can be turned into reality.

The Kuomintang is negotiating with us on the one hand, and is vigorously attacking the Liberated Areas on the other hand. Not counting the forces surrounding the Shensi-Kansu-Ningsia Border Region, 800,000 Kuomintang troops are already directly engaged in these attacks. Wherever there are Liberated Areas, fighting is going on or being prepared. The very first article of the "October 10th Agreement" is on "peace and national reconstruction"; don't these words on paper contradict reality? Yes, they do. That is why we say it still requires effort on our part to turn what is on paper into reality. Why does the Kuomintang mobilize so many troops to attack us? Because long ago it made up its mind to wipe out the people's forces, to wipe us out. Best of all, it would like to wipe us out quickly or, failing that, to worsen our situation and improve its own. Peace, though written into the agreement, has not in fact been realized. In

53

places like the Shangtang area in Shansi Province there is fighting on
a fairly large scale.   The Shangtang area, rimmed by the Taihang,
Taiyueh and Chungtiao Mountains, is like a tub.   This tub contains
fish and meat, and Yen Hsi-shan sent thirteen divisions to grab it.
Our policy also was set long ago – to give tit for tat, to fight for every
inch of land.   This time we gave tit for tat, fought and made a very
good job of it.   In other words, we wiped out all thirteen divisions.
Their attacking forces had 38,000 men, and we employed 31,000 men.
Of their 38,000 men, 35,000 were destroyed, 2,000 fled and 1,000
scattered.[2]   Such fighting will continue.   They want desperately to
grab our Liberated Areas.   This seems hard to explain.   Why are
they so anxious to grab?   Isn't it good for the Liberated Areas to
be in our hands, in the hands of the people?   Yes, but that is only
what we think, what the people think.   If they thought so too, there
would be unity and we would all be "comrades".   But they won't
think this way; they will oppose us stubbornly.   They can't see why
they shouldn't oppose us.   It is quite natural that they should attack
us.   For our part, we can't see why we should let them seize our
Liberated Areas.   It is also quite natural that we should counter-
attack.   When two "can't-see-whys" come together, they fight.   Since
there are two can't-see-whys, why have they negotiated?   And why
have they concluded the "October 10th Agreement"?   In this world,
things are complicated and are decided by many factors.   We should
look at problems from different aspects, not from just one.   In Chungking, some people think that Chiang Kai-shek is unreliable and deceitful and that negotiations with him can lead nowhere.   So I was told
by many people I met, including some members of the Kuomintang.
I told them that what they said was justified and well-founded and
that we were firmly convinced by eighteen years of experience[3] that
this would be the case.   The Kuomintang and the Communist Party
are sure to fail in their negotiations, sure to start fighting and sure to
break with each other, but that is only one aspect of the matter.
Another aspect is that many other factors are bound to make Chiang
Kai-shek have misgivings.   Among these factors, the three main ones
are the might of the Liberated Areas, the opposition to civil war by
the people in the Great Rear Area and the international situation.
In our Liberated Areas there are 100 million people, one million troops
and two million people's militia, a force no one dares to belittle.   Our

---

* This report was made by Comrade Mao Tse-tung to a meeting of cadres in
Yenan after his return from Chungking.

Party's place in the nation's political life is no longer what it was in 1927, nor what it was in 1937. The Kuomintang, which has always refused to recognize the equal status of the Communist Party, is now forced to do so. Our work in the Liberated Areas has already influenced all China and the whole world. The people in the Great Rear Area desire peace and need democracy. When in Chungking, I had a profound sense of the warm support given us by the broad masses of the people. They are dissatisfied with the Kuomintang government and place their hopes on us. I also met many foreigners, including Americans, who sympathize with us. The broad masses of the people in foreign countries are dissatisfied with the reactionary forces in China and sympathize with the Chinese people's forces. They also disapprove of Chiang Kai-shek's policies. We have many friends in all parts of the country and of the world; we are not isolated. Those who oppose civil war in China and stand for peace and democracy include not only the people in our Liberated Areas but also the masses in the Great Rear Area and throughout the world. The subjective desire of Chiang Kai-shek is to maintain his dictatorship and destroy the Communist Party, but many objective difficulties stand in his way. Therefore, he has to be a little realistic. He is being realistic, and we are realistic too. He was realistic in inviting us and we were realistic in going to negotiate with him. We arrived in Chungking on August 28. On the evening of the 29th, I told the Kuomintang representatives that the country had needed peace and unity ever since the September 18th Incident in 1931.[4] We had asked for peace and unity, but they had not materialized. Peace and unity materialized only after the Sian Incident of 1936[5] before the outbreak of the War of Resistance on July 7, 1937. During the eight years of that war we fought together against Japan. But civil war never stopped; there were continuous frictions, big and small. To say that there was no civil war is deception and does not square with facts. In the past eight years we repeatedly expressed our willingness to negotiate. At the Seventh Congress of our Party we declared that "we are willing to resume negotiations with the Kuomintang authorities as soon as they are willing to renounce their present erroneous policies and agree to democratic reforms".[6] In the negotiations we declared that, first, China needs peace and, second, China needs democracy. Chiang Kai-shek could find no reason to object and had to agree. On the one hand, the policy of peace and the agreements on democracy published in the "Summary of Conversations" are words

on paper and not yet reality; on the other hand, they have been determined by a variety of forces.   The forces of the people in the Liberated
Areas, the forces of the people in the Great Rear Area, the international
situation – the general trend has forced the Kuomintang to accept
these things.

How to give "tit for tat" depends on the situation.   Sometimes,
not going to negotiations is tit-for-tat; and sometimes, going to negotiations is also tit-for-tat.   We were right not to go before, and also
right to go this time; in both cases we have given tit for tat.   We
did well to go this time, for we exploded the rumour spread by the
Kuomintang that the Communist Party did not want peace and unity.
They sent three successive telegrams to invite us, and we went.   But
they were totally unprepared, and we had to make all the proposals.
As a result of the negotiations, the Kuomintang has accepted the
general policy of peace and unity.   That's fine.   If the Kuomintang
launches civil war again, it will put itself in the wrong in the eyes of
the whole nation and the whole world, and we shall have all the
more reason to smash its attacks by a war of self-defence.   Now
that the "October 10th Agreement" has been concluded, our task is to
uphold the agreement, to demand that the Kuomintang honour it and
to continue to strive for peace.   If they fight, we will wipe them out
completely.   This is the way things are: if they attack and we wipe
them out, they will have that satisfaction; wipe out some, some satisfaction; wipe out more, more satisfaction; wipe out the whole lot,
complete satisfaction.   China's problems are complicated, and our
brains must also be a little complicated.   If they start fighting, we fight
back, fight to win peace.   Peace will not come unless we strike hard
blows at the reactionaries who dare to attack the Liberated Areas.

Some comrades have asked why we should concede eight Liberated
Areas.[7]   It is a great pity to concede these eight areas, but it is better
to do so.   Why is it a pity?   Because these Liberated Areas have
been created and arduously built up by the people, with sweat and
blood.   Therefore, we must explain matters clearly to the people and
make appropriate arrangements in the areas we are going to concede.
Why should we concede those areas?   Because otherwise the Kuomintang will not feel easy.   They are going back to Nanking, but some
Liberated Areas in the south are right by their beds or in their corridor.
So long as we are there, they will not be able to sleep easily and will
therefore fight for those places at all costs.   Our concession on this
point will help frustrate the Kuomintang's plot for civil war and win

us the sympathy of the numerous middle elements at home and abroad. All the means of propaganda in China, except the Hsinhua News Agency, are now controlled by the Kuomintang. They are all rumour factories. Concerning the current negotiations, they have spread the rumour that the Communist Party just wants territory and will make no concessions. Our policy is to protect the fundamental interests of the people. Subject to the principle of not damaging the fundamental interests of the people, it is permissible to make certain concessions in exchange for peace and democracy, which the people of the whole country need. In our past dealings with Chiang Kai-shek we also made concessions, and even larger ones. In 1937, to bring about the nation-wide War of Resistance, we voluntarily dropped the name, "Workers' and Peasants' Revolutionary Government", changed the name of our Red Army to "National Revolutionary Army" and altered our policy of confiscating the land of the landlords to one of reducing rent and interest. This time, by conceding certain areas in the south, we have completely exploded the Kuomintang's rumours before the people of all China and the whole world. It is the same with the problem of armed forces. Kuomintang propaganda has been saying that the Communist Party is just scrambling for guns. But we have said we are ready to make concessions. First, we proposed cutting our present armed strength to 48 divisions. As the Kuomintang has 263 divisions, this means our strength would be about a sixth of the total. Later, we proposed a further reduction to 43 divisions, about a seventh of the total. The Kuomintang then said they would reduce to 120 divisions. We said we would reduce by the same proportion to 24 or even 20 divisions, which would still be only a seventh of the total. In the Kuomintang army the proportion of officers as compared to soldiers is unduly large and the complement of a division is under 6,000. By their standard, we could form 200 divisions out of our 1,200,000 men. But we are not going to do so. Therefore the Kuomintang can say nothing more and all their rumours are bankrupt. Does this mean that we are going to hand over our guns to the Kuomintang? Not that either. If we hand over our guns, won't the Kuomintang have too many? The arms of the people, every gun and every bullet, must all be kept, must not be handed over.

The above is what I want to say to the comrades about the present situation. Its development shows many contradictions. In the negotiations between the Kuomintang and our Party, why is there agreement on some questions and not on others? Why does the "Summary of Conversations" speak of peace and unity, while fighting is actually going on? Some comrades just can't understand such contradictions. What I have said is meant to answer these questions. Some comrades can't understand why we should be willing to negotiate with Chiang Kai-shek, who has always been anti-Communist and against the people. Was our Party right or wrong in deciding at its Seventh Congress that we were willing to negotiate with the Kuomintang, provided they changed their policy? It was absolutely right. The Chinese revolution is a long one and victory can only be won step by step. China's future depends on our exertions. The situation will remain in flux for six months or so. We must redouble our efforts to make it develop in a direction favourable to the people of the whole country.

Now, a few more words about our work. Some comrades present will be leaving for the front. Many, full of enthusiasm, are vying with each other for the opportunity to go to work there, and this active and fervent spirit is very valuable. But there are also a few comrades who have mistaken ideas, who don't think of the many difficulties to be overcome, but believe that everything will be plain sailing at the front and that they will have an easier time than in Yenan. Are there people who think that way? I believe there are. I advise such comrades to correct their ideas. If one goes, it is to work. What is work? Work is struggle. There are difficulties and problems in those places for us to overcome and solve. We go there to work and struggle to overcome these difficulties. A good comrade is one who is more eager to go where the difficulties are greater. The work in those places is hard. Hard work is like a load placed before us, challenging us to shoulder it. Some loads are light, some heavy. Some people prefer the light to the heavy; they pick the light and leave the heavy to others. That is not a good attitude. Some comrades are different; they leave ease and comfort to others and carry the heavy loads themselves; they are the first to bear hardships, the last to enjoy comforts. They are good comrades. We should all learn from their communist spirit.

Many local cadres will be leaving their native places for the front. And many southern-born cadres who came to Yenan are also going to the front. All comrades going to the front should be mentally prepared, once there, to take root, blossom and bear fruit. We Communists are like seeds and the people are like the soil. Wherever we go, we must unite with the people, take root and blossom among them.

Wherever our comrades go, they must build good relations with the masses, be concerned for them and help them overcome their difficulties. We must unite with the masses; the more of the masses we unite with, the better. We must go all out to mobilize the masses, expand the people's forces and, under the leadership of our Party, defeat the aggressor and build a new China. This is the policy laid down by the Party's Seventh Congress.[8] We must strive to carry it out. China depends on the Communist Party and the people to run her affairs. We have the will and the way to achieve peace and democracy. Provided we unite even more closely with the whole people, China's affairs can be run well.

The world after World War II has a bright future. This is the general trend. Does the failure of the Five Power Conference of Foreign Ministers in London[9] mean that a third world war is about to break out? No. Just think, how is it possible for a third world war to break out right after the end of World War II? The capitalist and the socialist countries will yet reach compromises on a number of international matters, because compromise will be advantageous.[10] The proletariat and the people of the whole world are firmly opposed to an anti-Soviet and anti-Communist war. In the past thirty years two world wars have been fought. Between World Wars I and II there was an interval of more than twenty years. In the half million years of human history, it is only in the last thirty years that world wars have been fought. After World War I the world made great progress. After World War II the world is sure to make even faster progress. Following World War I the Soviet Union was born and scores of Communist Parties were founded – they did not exist before. After the end of World War II the Soviet Union is much stronger, the face of Europe is changed, the political consciousness of the proletariat and the people of the world is much higher and the progressive forces throughout the world are more closely united. Our China is also undergoing rapid and drastic change. The general trend of China's development is certainly for the better, not the worse. The world is progressing, the future is bright and no one can change this general trend of history. We should carry on constant propaganda among the people on the facts of world progress and the bright future ahead so that they will build their confidence in victory. At the same time, we must tell the people and tell our comrades that there will be twists and turns in our road. There are still many obstacles and difficulties along the road of revolution. The Seventh

Congress of our Party assumed that the difficulties would be many, for
we preferred to assume there would be more difficulties rather than
less. Some comrades do not like to think much about difficulties.
But difficulties are facts; we must recognize as many difficulties as
there are and should not adopt a "policy of non-recognition". We
must recognize difficulties, analyse them and combat them. There are
no straight roads in the world; we must be prepared to follow a road
which twists and turns and not try to get things on the cheap. It
must not be imagined that one fine morning all the reactionaries will
go down on their knees of their own accord. In a word, while the
prospects are bright, the road has twists and turns. There are still
many difficulties ahead which we must not overlook. By uniting with
the entire people in a common effort, we can certainly overcome all
difficulties and win victory.

NOTES

[1] This refers to the "Summary of Conversations", also known as the "October 10th
Agreement", which was signed by representatives of the Kuomintang and the Communist Party of China on October 10, 1945. In the summary, Chiang Kai-shek had to
feign agreement with the "basic policy of peace and national reconstruction" put forward by the Communist Party of China and accept "long-term co-operation on the basis
of peace, democracy, solidarity and unity . . . resolute avoidance of civil war and the
building of a new China, independent, free, prosperous and powerful" and "democratization of political life, nationalization of troops and equality and legality of political
parties as ways and means absolutely essential for achieving peace and national reconstruction". He also had to agree to bring the Kuomintang's political tutelage to a
speedy conclusion, convene a political consultative conference, "guarantee the freedoms of person, belief, speech, the press, assembly and association as enjoyed by the
people in all democratic countries in peacetime, and abolish or amend existing laws and
decrees according to this principle", abolish the secret services, "strictly prohibit all
organs other than those of the judiciary and police from making arrests, conducting
trials and imposing punishment", "release political prisoners", "actively carry out
local self-government and conduct general elections from the lower level upward",
etc. The Chiang Kai-shek government, however, stubbornly refused to recognize
the legal status of the people's army and the democratic governments in the Liberated
Areas and, on the pretexts of "unifying the military command" and "unifying government administration", insolently tried to eliminate altogether the people's army and
the Liberated Areas led by the Communist Party of China; consequently no agreement
could be reached on this question. The following are excerpts from the "Summary
of Conversations" concerning the negotiations on the problem of the armed forces
and political power in the Liberated Areas; in the "Summary" the so-called "Government" refers to Chiang Kai-shek's Kuomintang government.

"On the nationalization of troops. The Communist Party of China proposed that with a view to unifying the military command the Government should effect an equitable and rational reorganization of the armed forces of the whole country, draw up a programme for carrying it out in stages, make a fresh delimitation of the military zones and establish a conscription and replenishment system. The Communist Party of China stated that, given such a programme, it was ready to reduce the anti-Japanese troops under its command to twenty-four divisions or to a minimum of twenty divisions and to take prompt action to demobilize its anti-Japanese troops now distributed in the eight areas of Kwangtung, Chekiang, southern Kiangsu, southern Anhwei, central Anhwei, Hunan, Hupeh and Honan (not including northern Honan). The troops to be reorganized would be gradually withdrawn from the above areas to assemble in the Liberated Areas north of the Lunghai Railway and in northern Kiangsu and northern Anhwei. The Government stated that the programme for the reorganization of troops on a country-wide basis was under way and that the Government was willing to consider the reorganization of the anti-Japanese troops led by the Communist Party of China into twenty divisions, if the issues coming up in the present negotiations could all be settled. As to the question of the stationing of these troops, it stated further that the Communist Party of China could submit plans for discussion and decision. The Communist Party of China proposed that the Communist Party and its local military personnel should participate in the work of the National Military Council and its various departments, that the Government should preserve the existing personnel system and commission the existing personnel as officers of various ranks in the reorganized units, that officers not receiving appointment after reorganization should be assigned to different areas for training and that a fair and reasonable system for filling vacancies and a plan for political education should be adopted. The Government indicated that it had no objection to these proposals and was willing to discuss details. The Communist Party of China proposed that all the militiamen in the Liberated Areas should be organized into local self-defence corps. The Government indicated that such organization could be considered only where local conditions would so require or permit. In order to formulate concrete plans in regard to all the questions mentioned in this section, both sides agreed that a sub-committee of three be formed, with one representative each from the Board of Military Operations of the National Military Council, the Ministry of War and the Eighteenth Group Army."

"On local governments in the Liberated Areas. The Communist Party of China proposed that the Government should recognize the legal status of the popularly elected governments at all levels in the Liberated Areas. The Government indicated that, since Japan had surrendered, the term 'Liberated Area' should have become obsolete and that government administration throughout the country should be unified. The initial formula advanced by the Communist Party of China was that the provincial and administrative areas were to be delimited afresh in the light of the existence of eighteen Liberated Areas and that, for the sake of unifying government administration, it would submit a list of all the popularly elected government personnel at various levels for reappointment by the Government. The Government indicated that, as Chairman Chiang had stated to Mr. Mao, the Central Government, after the unification of the military command and government administration throughout the country, would give consideration to the administrative personnel nominated by the Communist Party of China. The Government would consider retaining a due proportion of the administrative personnel who had served in the areas recovered during the War of Resistance, taking account of their record of ability and service, irrespective of party affiliation. Thereupon, a second formula was

proposed by the Communist Party of China, asking the Central Government to
appoint nominees of the Communist Party of China as chairmen and members of the
provincial governments of the Shensi-Kansu-Ningsia Border Region and the five
provinces of Jehol, Chahar, Hopei, Shantung and Shansi, and to appoint the Communist Party's nominees as deputy chairmen and members of the six provincial
governments of Suiyuan, Honan, Kiangsu, Anhwei, Hupeh and Kwangtung (because
in the aforesaid eleven provinces there were extensive Liberated Areas or sections
thereof). The Communist Party of China also requested the appointment of its
nominees as deputy mayors of the four special municipalities of Peiping, Tientsin,
Tsingtao and Shanghai and the participation of its nominees in the administration of
the northeastern provinces. After many discussions on this matter, the Communist
Party of China modified the aforesaid proposals by requesting the appointment of
its nominees as chairmen and members of the provincial governments of the Shensi-
Kansu-Ningsia Border Region and the four provinces of Jehol, Chahar, Hopei and
Shantung, as deputy chairmen and members of the two provincial governments of
Shansi and Suiyuan and as deputy mayors of the three special municipalities of
Peiping, Tientsin and Tsingtao. In reply the Government stated that while the
Communist Party of China might nominate those of its members who had rendered
distinguished service during the War of Resistance and who possessed administrative
ability to the Government for appointment, the Communist Party would not be
sincerely endeavouring to achieve unity of military command and government
administration if it should insist upon nominating a chairman or deputy chairman or
members of any specific provincial government. The Communist Party of China
then said it would withdraw its second suggestion and proposed a third formula. It
suggested that general elections be held under the existing popularly elected governments at all levels in the Liberated Areas, and members of all other political parties
as well as people in different walks of life would be welcome to return to their native
places to take part in the elections to be held under the supervision of persons
designated by the Political Consultative Conference. A popular election was to
be held in any county where more than half the districts and townships had already
held popular elections. Likewise, a popular election was to be held in any province
or administrative area where more than half the counties had already held popular
elections. In the interest of unity of government administration, the names of all
the officials so elected in the provincial, administrative area and county governments
should be submitted to the Central Government for appointment by confirmation.
The Government replied that this formula of government confirmation of appointments in provinces and areas was not in the interest of unity of government
administration. The Government might, however, consider holding popular elections
for county officials, but popular elections for the provincial governments could be
held only after the promulgation of a national constitution, when the status of the
province would have been defined. For the time being, only those provincial government officials who had been appointed by the Central Government should proceed
to take up their posts so that conditions in the recovered areas might be restored to
normal at the earliest possible moment. At this point, a fourth formula was proposed
by the Communist Party of China, namely, that the *status quo* in all the Liberated
Areas should temporarily be maintained until the constitutional provision for the
popular election of provincial governments had been adopted and put into effect and
that, for the time being, an interim arrangement be worked out in order to guarantee
the restoration of peace and order. The Communist Party of China stated that meanwhile this particular problem might be submitted to the Political Consultative
Conference for settlement. The Government insisted that unity of government

administration must be carried out first, because this problem, if left unsolved, might become an obstacle to peace and reconstruction, and it expressed the hope that a concrete formula with regard to this matter could be agreed upon soon. The Communist Party of China agreed to hold further discussions."

2 Shangtang was an ancient name for the southeastern part of Shansi Province with Changchih as its centre. Its mountainous sections were the base of the 129th Division of the Eighth Route Army during the War of Resistance Against Japan and formed part of the Shansi-Hopei-Shantung-Honan Liberated Area. In September 1945 the Kuomintang warlord, Yen Hsi-shan, mustered thirteen divisions and, in co-ordination with Japanese and puppet troops, moved in successively from Linfen, Fushan and Yicheng and from Taiyuan and Yutse to invade Hsiangyuan, Tunliu and Lucheng in the Southeastern Shansi Liberated Area. In October the army and people of this Liberated Area counter-attacked this invading force, wiped out 35,000 men and captured several high-ranking officers, including corps and division commanders.

3 This refers to the experience gained by the Communist Party of China in its struggles with the Kuomintang from 1927, when the Kuomintang betrayed the revolution, to 1945.

4 On September 18, 1931, the Japanese "Kwantung Army" quartered in northeastern China seized Shenyang. Under Chiang Kai-shek's order of "absolute non-resistance", the Chinese troops at Shenyang and elsewhere in the Northeast (the Northeastern Army) withdrew to the south of the Great Wall, and consequently the Japanese forces rapidly occupied the provinces of Liaoning, Kirin and Heilungkiang. The Chinese people called this act of aggression committed by the Japanese invaders the "September 18th Incident".

5 See "On a Statement by Chiang Kai-shek's Spokesman", Note 5, p. 45 of this volume.

6 Quoted from "On Coalition Government", Part IV, Section "Our Specific Programme", Item 2, Selected Works of Mao Tse-tung, Vol. III.

7 This refers to the bases of the people's army scattered over Kwangtung, Chekiang, southern Kiangsu, southern Anhwei, central Anhwei, Hunan, Hupeh and Honan (not including northern Honan).

8 See "China's Two Possible Destinies" and "The Foolish Old Man Who Removed the Mountains", Selected Works of Mao Tse-tung, Vol. III.

9 From September 11 to October 2, 1945, the Foreign Ministers of the Soviet Union, China, the United States, Britain and France met in London to discuss peace treaties with Italy, Rumania, Bulgaria, Hungary and Finland, countries which had taken part in the war of aggression started by fascist Germany, and to discuss the disposal of the Italian colonies. No agreement was reached because the United States, Britain and France rejected the reasonable proposals put forward by the Soviet Union and persisted in their imperialist policy of aggression aiming at overthrowing the people's governments set up in Rumania, Hungary and Bulgaria after victory in the anti-fascist war.

10 See "Some Points in Appraisal of the Present International Situation", pp. 87-88 of this volume.

THE TRUTH ABOUT
THE KUOMINTANG ATTACKS*

November 5, 1945

In a dispatch from Chungking, dated November 3, the United Press reported that Wu Kuo-chen, Director of the Propaganda Department of the Kuomintang Central Executive Committee, had declared that "the government is entirely on the defensive in this war" and had proposed measures for "restoring communications".[1] A Hsinhua News Agency reporter asked the spokesman for the Communist Party of China about this.

The spokesman for the Communist Party of China replied to the reporter as follows: What Wu Kuo-chen said about being "on the defensive" is a complete lie. The Kuomintang, besides occupying the five Liberated Areas evacuated by our troops in eastern Chekiang, southern Kiangsu, central and southern Anhwei and Hunan and trampling on the people there, has moved more than seventy divisions of its regular troops into or close to most of the other Liberated Areas – for example, those in Kwangtung, Hupeh, Honan, northern Kiangsu, northern Anhwei, Shantung and Hopei – and has been oppressing the people there and attacking or preparing to attack our troops. Furthermore, scores of other Kuomintang divisions are heading for the Liberated Areas. Can this be described as being on the defensive? Of the eight Kuomintang divisions which reached the Hantan area in their drive northward from Changteh, two opposed civil war and favoured peace, while the other six (including three U.S.-equipped divisions) were compelled to lay down their arms after the troops and people of the Liberated Areas counter-attacked in self-defence. Many officers of these Kuomintang troops, including war-zone deputy commanders, corps commanders and deputy corps commanders, are now in the Liberated Areas[2] and can confirm the whole truth about where they came from and how they were ordered to attack. Can

this, too, be described as being on the defensive? Our troops in the
Liberated Areas in Honan and Hupeh Provinces are now completely
encircled by more than twenty Kuomintang divisions from the 1st, 5th
and 6th War Zones, with Liu Chih as field commander in charge of
the "suppression of Communists". Our Liberated Areas in western
and central Honan and southern, eastern and central Hupeh have all
been invaded and occupied by the Kuomintang forces, which burned
and killed so wantonly that our troops commanded by Li Hsien-nien
and Wang Shu-sheng could find no shelter and had to seek quarters
on the Honan-Hupeh border in order to survive. But there again
they have been closely pursued and attacked by Kuomintang troops.[3]
Can this, too, be described as being on the defensive? It is the
same in the three provinces of Shansi, Suiyuan and Chahar. In early
October, Yen Hsi-shan ordered thirteen divisions to attack the
Hsiangyuan-Tunliu sector in the Shangtang Liberated Area. Fighting
in self-defence, our troops and the people there disarmed them all,
and several commanders of corps and divisions were among the captured. They are now in the Taihang Liberated Area, every one alive,
and can confirm the whole truth about where they came from and
how they were ordered to attack. In Chungking recently, Yen Hsi-
shan told all sorts of lies about how he had been attacked and how
he had merely been "on the defensive". Probably he had forgotten
all about his generals: Shih Tse-po, Commander of the 19th Corps;
Kuo Jung, Commander of the Provisional 46th Division; Chang Hung,
Commander of the Provisional 49th Division; Li Pei-ying, Commander
of the 66th Division; Kuo Tien-hsing, Commander of the 68th Division and Yang Wen-tsai, Commander of the Provisional 37th Division.[4]
They are now living in our Liberated Areas and can refute any lies
told by Wu Kuo-chen, Yen Hsi-shan and all the other reactionary
instigators of civil war. General Fu Tso-yi, under orders, has been
attacking our Liberated Areas in Suiyuan, Chahar and Jehol for over
two months and on one occasion pushed right to the gates of Changchiakou and occupied our entire Suiyuan Liberated Area and western
Chahar. Can this, too, be described as being on the defensive and
not firing "the first shot"? Our troops and people in Chahar and
Suiyuan rose in self-defence and in their counter-attacks also captured

---

* This statement prepared by Comrade Mao Tse-tung was issued in the name
of the spokesman for the Communist Party of China. By this time Chiang Kai-shek
had already torn up the "October 10th Agreement", and the civil war against the
Liberated Areas was expanding daily.

large numbers of officers and men who can all testify where they came from, how they attacked, and so on.[5] In various battles of self-defence we have captured piles of "bandit suppression" and anti-Communist documents, among which are the *Handbook on Bandit Suppression*, orders for "bandit suppression"[6] and other anti-Communist documents issued by the highest Kuomintang authorities but dismissed as a "joke" by Wu Kuo-chen; these are now being forwarded to Yenan. All these documents are iron-clad proofs that Kuomintang troops have attacked the Liberated Areas.

The Hsinhua News Agency reporter went on to ask the spokesman for the Communist Party of China about his views on the measures proposed by Wu Kuo-chen for restoring communications. The spokesman replied: These are nothing but stalling tactics. The Kuomintang authorities are mustering large forces and are trying to swamp all the Liberated Areas as in a great flood. Following the failure of several attacks in September and October, they are preparing new attacks on an even larger scale. And one way to obstruct these attacks and effectively check the civil war is not to let them transport their troops by rail. Like everybody else, we advocate speedy restoration of the lines of communication, but this can be done only after the settlement of the three problems of accepting the Japanese surrender, disposing of the puppet troops and realizing self-government in the Liberated Areas. Which should be settled first, the problem of communications or these three problems? Why are the troops of the Liberated Areas, which fought strenuously and bitterly against Japan for eight years, not qualified to accept the Japanese surrender? And why should other troops be put to the trouble of coming from afar to accept it? Every citizen has the right to punish the puppet troops; why are they all being incorporated into the "national army" and ordered to attack the Liberated Areas? Local self-government is explicitly stipulated in the "October 10th Agreement", and Dr. Sun Yat-sen long ago advocated the popular election of provincial governors; why does the Kuomintang government still insist on dispatching local officials? The problem of communications should be speedily settled, but even more so, the three major problems should be speedily settled. To talk of restoring communications without first settling the three major problems can only serve to spread and prolong the civil war and help its instigators achieve their purpose of swamping the Liberated Areas. In order quickly to stop the anti-popular and anti-democratic civil war which has now spread all over the country, we advocate the following:

(1)   All the Kuomintang government forces that have entered the Liberated Areas in northern China, northern Kiangsu, northern Anhwei, central China and nearby regions to accept the Japanese surrender and to attack us should be withdrawn immediately to their original positions; the troops of the Liberated Areas should accept the Japanese surrender and garrison the cities and lines of communication; and the Liberated Areas which have been invaded and occupied should be restored.

(2)   All puppet troops should be immediately disarmed and disbanded, and in northern China, northern Kiangsu and northern Anhwei the Liberated Areas should take charge of such disarming and disbanding.

(3)   The people's democratic self-government in all the Liberated Areas should be recognized; the Central Government should not appoint and send out local officials; the provisions of the "October 10th Agreement" should be carried out.

The spokesman said: Only in this way can civil war be averted; otherwise there is absolutely no safeguard against it. The documents captured during the three battles we fought in self-defence in Suiyuan, Shangtang and Hantan and such concrete actions as massive troop movements and attacks all give the lie to the claim of the Kuomintang authorities that the so-called restoration of communications is for the sake of the people and not of civil war. The Chinese people have been fooled long enough and can be fooled no longer. At present, the central problem is for the people of the whole country to mobilize to stop the civil war by every means.

NOTES

[1] At the end of the War of Resistance Against Japan, most of China's railways were either under the control of the army and people of the Liberated Areas or surrounded by them. Under the pretext of "restoring communications", the Kuomintang reactionaries tried to utilize these railways to cut the Liberated Areas apart, transport millions of Kuomintang troops to northeastern, northern, eastern and central China, attack the Liberated Areas and grab the big cities.

[2] In September 1945, Kuomintang troops from the region of Chengchow and Hsinhsiang advanced along the Peiping-Hankow Railway to attack the Shansi-Hopei-Shantung-Honan Liberated Area. In late October their vanguard, comprising three corps, invaded the region of Tsehsien and Hantan. The army and people of the

Liberated Area rose bravely in self-defence, and after a week's bitter fighting General Kao Shu-hsun, Deputy Commander of the Kuomintang's 11th War Zone and concurrently Commander of the New 8th Corps, revolted against the Kuomintang at Hantan and came over to us with the New 8th Corps and one column, totalling over ten thousand men. The other two corps retreated in confusion but were surrounded and disarmed. Many high-ranking officers were compelled to surrender, including Ma Fa-wu, another Deputy Commander of the Kuomintang's 11th War Zone and concurrently Commander of the 40th Corps, Liu Shih-jung, its Deputy Commander, Li Hsu-tung, its Chief of Staff, Liu Shu-sen, a Deputy Division Commander.

[3] After Japan's surrender the Kuomintang gathered more than twenty divisions from three war zones to launch large-scale attacks on the Liberated Areas in Honan and Hupeh Provinces. Part of the forces of Hu Tsung-nan, Commander of the Kuomintang's 1st War Zone, advanced from the northwest to the east along both sides of the Lunghai Railway to invade the Liberated Areas in western Honan; the forces of Liu Chih, Commander of the 5th War Zone, advanced from the north to the south along both sides of the Peiping-Hankow Railway to invade the Liberated Areas in central Honan and central and eastern Hupeh; the forces of the 6th War Zone advanced from southern Hupeh to the north in concert. Most of these Kuomintang forces were under the command of Liu Chih. The people's army of the Liberated Areas in Honan and Hupeh put up a stubborn fight against the invaders, conserved its strength and moved in late October 1945 to an area on the Honan-Hupeh border in the Tahung and the Tungpai Mountains and around Tsaoyang. The army later shifted to Hsuanhuatien, east of the Peiping-Hankow Railway, because the Kuomintang continued to pursue and attack.

[4] About the Shangtang battle, see "On the Chungking Negotiations", Note 2, p. 63 of this volume. The captured Kuomintang officers here mentioned were all high-ranking generals in Yen Hsi-shan's army.

[5] The province of Suiyuan was abolished on March 6, 1954, and became part of the Inner Mongolian Autonomous Region. General Fu Tso-yi was in 1945 Commander of the Kuomintang's 12th War Zone. His troops had been stationed at and around Wuyuan and Linho in western Suiyuan during the War of Resistance Against Japan. After Japan's surrender he was ordered to attack the Liberated Areas in Suiyuan, Jehol and Chahar Provinces. In August 1945 he occupied Kueisui (now Huhehot), Chining and Fengchen. In early September he occupied Hsingho, Shangyi, Wuchuan, Taolin, Hsintang and Liangcheng, launched massive attacks on the Liberated Areas in Chahar and pushed to the neighbourhood of Changchiakou. In self-defence our army repulsed these attacks and captured large numbers of his officers and men.

[6] The *Handbook on Bandit Suppression* was a counter-revolutionary pamphlet compiled by Chiang Kai-shek in 1933 dealing exclusively with methods of attacking the Chinese people's forces and the revolutionary bases. In 1945, after the conclusion of the War of Resistance, Chiang Kai-shek had it reprinted and issued to Kuomintang officers together with a confidential order, saying: "The present campaign for the suppression of the bandits, on which the happiness of the people depends, must be speedily completed. You should urge your officers and men to do their utmost to suppress the bandits in the spirit of the resistance against Japanese aggression and in accordance with the *Handbook on Bandit Suppression* which I have compiled. Any meritorious action in the service of the state shall be richly rewarded, and those responsible for delays or mistakes shall be court-martialled. This order should be made known to and obeyed by all officers and men under your command engaged in suppressing the bandits."

RENT REDUCTION AND PRODUCTION ARE TWO IMPORTANT MATTERS FOR THE DEFENCE OF THE LIBERATED AREAS*

November 7, 1945

1. The Kuomintang, aided by the United States, is mobilizing all its forces to attack our Liberated Areas. Country-wide civil war is already a fact. Our Party's present task is to mobilize all forces, take the stand of self-defence, smash the attacks of the Kuomintang, defend the Liberated Areas and strive for the realization of peace. To achieve this aim the following have become very urgent tasks. See to it that in the Liberated Areas the peasants generally get the benefits of rent reduction and that the workers and other labouring people benefit by appropriate wage increases and improved conditions; at the same time, see to it that the landlords can still make a living and that the industrial and commercial capitalists can still make profits. Unfold a large-scale production drive next year, increase the output of food and daily necessities, improve the people's livelihood, provide relief for victims of famine and for refugees and meet the needs of the army. Only when the two important matters of rent reduction and production are well handled can we overcome our difficulties, support the war and win victory.

2. As the scale of the war is now very large, many leading comrades are in command at the front and cannot divert their attention to rent reduction and production. Hence there must be division of labour. Those leading comrades who remain in the rear areas, in addition to doing a great deal of work in direct support of the front, must not miss the opportune time for organizing these two important tasks of rent reduction and production. In the next few months of the winter and spring, they must launch large-scale rent reduction campaigns and carry out rent reduction universally in all the Liberated Areas, and particularly in the vast newly liberated areas, so as to arouse

71

the revolutionary fervour of the great majority of the peasant masses. Meanwhile they must see to it that there is a new development of agricultural and industrial production in all the Liberated Areas in 1946. Do not neglect rent reduction and production because of the new large-scale war; on the contrary, it is precisely in order to defeat the Kuomintang offensive that rent reduction and production must be stepped up.

3. Rent reduction must be the result of mass struggle, not a favour bestowed by the government. On this depends the success or failure of rent reduction. In the struggle for rent reduction, excesses can hardly be avoided; as long as it is really a conscious struggle of the broad masses, any excesses that have occurred can be corrected afterwards. Only then can we persuade the masses and enable them to understand that it is in the interest of the peasants and the people as a whole to allow the landlords to make a living so that they will not help the Kuomintang. The present policy of our Party is still to reduce rents, not to confiscate land. During and following rent reduction we must help the great majority of the peasants to organize themselves into peasant associations.

4. The key to victory in the production drive is to organize the great majority of the producers into mutual-aid production groups. An indispensable measure is to provide government credits for agriculture and industry. It is also very important to do farm work in the right season and reduce loss of working time. At present we must mobilize civilian manpower to support the war; on the other hand, we must so far as possible not miss any season for farming; hence we should study methods of adjustments. Army units, government organs and schools should continue to take part in production to an appropriate extent, provided it does not interfere with the war, with work and with study. Only thus can they better their livelihood and lighten the burden on the people.

5. We already hold some large and many medium cities. It has become an important task for our Party to take control of the economy of these cities and to develop their industry, commerce and finance. For this purpose, it is very necessary to use all the qualified persons available and persuade Party members to co-operate with them and learn technique and methods of management from them.

---

* This inner-Party directive was drafted by Comrade Mao Tse-tung for the Central Committee of the Communist Party of China.

6. Tell all Party members to stand firmly together with the people, to have concern for their economic difficulties and to regard the carrying out of the two important tasks of rent reduction and production as the key to helping the people overcome their difficulties; by so doing, we shall win the heartfelt support of the people and be able to defeat attacks by any reactionaries. Everything must still be considered from the standpoint of a long-term effort, manpower and material resources must be used sparingly, everything must be planned on a long-term basis; thus we will be sure to win victory.

POLICY FOR WORK
IN THE LIBERATED AREAS
FOR 1946*

December 15, 1945

In the past few months our Party has gained great successes in leading the people in fierce struggles to clean up the Japanese and puppet forces and smash the attacks of the Kuomintang on the Liberated Areas. All our Party comrades have worked as one man and made marked achievements in every field. The year 1945 will soon be over, and in 1946 we must pay attention to the following points in the work in all the Liberated Areas:

1. Smash new attacks. Since our army smashed the large-scale attacks on our Liberated Areas in Suiyuan, Shansi and southern Hopei, the Kuomintang has been moving up larger forces and making preparations for new attacks. If no new development makes the Kuomintang stop its civil war quickly, the fighting in the spring of 1946 will be intense. Therefore, the central task of all the Liberated Areas is still to take a stand of self-defence and do their utmost to smash the Kuomintang attacks.

2. Spread the Kao Shu-hsun movement.[1] In order to smash the Kuomintang attacks our Party must work to disintegrate the Kuomintang troops which are preparing to attack or are already attacking. On the one hand, our army must carry on extensive, open political propaganda and political offensives to undermine the will to fight of the Kuomintang troops engaged in the civil war. On the other hand, we must prepare and organize uprisings within the Kuomintang army and spread the Kao Shu-hsun movement so that, at crucial moments in the fighting, large numbers of Kuomintang troops will follow Kao Shu-hsun's example and come over to the people, oppose the civil war and take a stand for peace. In order to do this work in a practical way and produce speedy results, every

area must, in compliance with the Central Committee directive, set up a special department and assign a large number of cadres to devote themselves to it whole-heartedly and exclusively. The leading bodies of each area must give this work close direction.

3. Train the troops. The field armies of the Liberated Areas have already been formed in the main, and the regional troops are also quite numerous. Hence, for the time being, we should generally stop expanding the number of troops and should make use of the intervals between battles to stress the training of troops. This applies to field armies, regional troops and people's militia. As for the training courses, the main objective should still be to raise the level of technique in marksmanship, bayoneting, grenade-throwing and the like and the secondary objective should be to raise the level of tactics, while special emphasis should be laid on night operations. As for the method of training, we should unfold the mass training movement in which officers teach soldiers, soldiers teach officers and the soldiers teach each other. During 1946 we must further improve the political work in the army, overcome any dogmatic and formalist working styles existing in the army and strive to unite officers and soldiers, unite the army and the people, unite with friendly troops, disintegrate the enemy troops and ensure that the tasks of training, supply and fighting are accomplished. The local people's militia should be reorganized in accordance with present conditions. The army's rear services should be readjusted. Everything possible should be done to organize and expand the artillery and engineer units in all areas. The military academies should continue their work, with stress on the training of technical personnel.

4. Reduce rent. In accordance with the November 7, 1945 directive of the Central Committee,[2] all areas must launch movements in 1946 for the reduction of rent and interest in their newly liberated areas, movements on a large scale, of a mass character, but with leadership. As for the workers, their wages should be appropriately raised. Through these movements the broad masses should be able to emancipate themselves, organize, and become the conscious masters of the Liberated Areas. Without these determined measures, the masses in the newly liberated areas will not be able to tell which of the two parties, the Communist Party or the Kuomintang, is good and which is bad; they will waver and will not

* This inner-Party directive was drafted by Comrade Mao Tse-tung for the Central Committee of the Communist Party of China.

give firm support to our Party. In the old Liberated Areas the work of rent and interest reduction should be rechecked in order to consolidate those areas further.

5. Production. All areas must follow the directive of November 7 and promptly make every preparation to ensure that in 1946 both public and private production in all Liberated Areas should surpass any previous year in scale and in achievements. The feeling of weariness which has appeared among the people can be overcome only after the two tasks of rent reduction and production are carried out in earnest and with marked success. Whether or not these two tasks are fulfilled will finally decide victory or defeat in the political and military struggles of the Liberated Areas. They must not be neglected in any area.

6. Finance. In 1946 the financial burden, which has become heavier to cover the intensive work of the recent period, must be brought back to normal in a planned and systematic way. There must be appropriate reductions for those whose burdens are too heavy. In the interest of the long-term effort, the number of people diverted from production in any area must not exceed the limits of local financial capacity. Troops are valued for quality rather than for number; in building the army this remains one of our principles. To develop production, ensure supply, centralize leadership, decentralize management, give consideration to both army and people and to both public and private interests, and stress both production and economy – all these are still the proper guiding principles for solving our financial and economic problems.

7. Support the government and cherish the people; support the army and give preferential treatment to the families of the armymen who fought in the War of Resistance.[3] In 1946 we must perform these two tasks better than in the past few years. This will be of great significance for smashing the Kuomintang attacks and consolidating the Liberated Areas. In the army it should be handled through the ideological education of every commander and fighter, so that all thoroughly understand the importance of supporting the government and cherishing the people. As long as the army on its part does this job well, the local government and the people will also improve their relations with the army.

8. Relief. In the Liberated Areas there are many victims of natural disasters, refugees, unemployed and partially unemployed, who urgently need relief. Whether this problem is solved well or

badly has a great and widespread influence. Relief should depend mainly on mutual aid by the masses themselves, in addition to government measures. The Party and the government should encourage the masses to organize relief through mutual aid.

9. Take good care of local cadres. In every Liberated Area today there are large numbers of cadres from other areas doing the leading work at all levels. This is especially true in the northeastern provinces. The leading bodies of each area must tirelessly counsel these cadres to take good care of the local cadres and treat them with great warmth and goodwill. Cadres from outside should make the selection, training and promotion of local cadres an important task for themselves. Only thus can our Party take root in the Liberated Areas. The working style of people from outside who look down on local people should be criticized.

10. Calculate everything on a long-term basis. No matter how the situation develops, our Party must always calculate on a long-term basis, if our position is to be invincible. At present, our Party on the one hand persists in its stand for self-government and self-defence in the Liberated Areas, firmly opposes attacks by the Kuomintang and consolidates the gains won by the people of these areas. On the other hand, we support the democratic movement now developing in the Kuomintang areas (as marked by the student strike in Kunming[4]) in order to isolate the reactionaries, win numerous allies for ourselves and expand the national democratic united front under our Party's influence. Moreover, a delegation of our Party will soon attend the Political Consultative Conference of various parties and public figures without party affiliation, reopen negotiations with the Kuomintang and strive for peace and democracy throughout the country. However, there may yet be twists and turns. Ahead of us lie many difficulties. For example, our new areas and our new troops are still not consolidated, and we have problems in finance. We must face all these difficulties squarely and overcome them, arrange all our work on a long-term basis, pay the closest attention to the economical use of manpower and material resources and guard against any wishful thinking about easy success through good luck.

These ten points should receive special attention in our work in 1946, and particularly in the first half of the year. It is hoped that comrades in different places will carry out these policies flexibly in the light of local conditions. As for the work in various areas, such as building local political authority, doing united front work, spreading education on current affairs inside and outside the Party and doing work in cities and towns near the Liberated Areas – all this is important but we shall not dwell on it here.

NOTES

[1] On October 30, 1945, Kao Shu-hsun, Deputy Commander of the Kuomintang's 11th War Zone, revolted at the civil war front in Hantan, southern Hopei Province, and came over to our side with one corps and one column. This had a great influence throughout the country. In order to intensify the work of dividing and disintegrating the Kuomintang troops and arousing them to revolt, the Central Committee of the Communist Party of China decided to start a propaganda campaign calling upon other Kuomintang officers and men to follow the example of Kao Shu-hsun and his troops, refuse to attack the Liberated Areas, sabotage the civil war at the front, fraternize with the People's Liberation Army, rise in revolt and come over to the side of the people. This was known as the Kao Shu-hsun movement.

[2] See "Rent Reduction and Production Are Two Important Matters for the Defence of the Liberated Areas", pp. 71-73 of this volume.

[3] "Support the government and cherish the people" was a slogan of the People's Liberation Army, while "Support the army and give preferential treatment to the families of the armymen who fought in the War of Resistance" was a slogan of the Party organizations, government bodies, people's organizations and the masses of the people in the Liberated Areas. The second slogan was later changed into "Support the army and give preferential treatment to the families of the revolutionary armymen".

[4] On the evening of November 25, 1945, more than six thousand college and middle school students in Kunming, capital of Yunnan Province, assembled at the Southwest Associated University to discuss current affairs and protest against the civil war. The Kuomintang reactionaries sent troops who surrounded the assembly, fired on the students with light artillery, machine-guns and rifles and placed guards around the university to prevent teachers and students from going home. Subsequently, students from Kunming's schools and colleges joined in a strike. On December 1 the Kuomintang reactionaries dispatched a large number of soldiers and secret agents to the Southwest Associated University and the Teachers College where they threw hand-grenades, killing four people and wounding over ten. This incident was known as the "December 1st Massacre".

BUILD STABLE BASE AREAS
IN THE NORTHEAST*

December 28, 1945

1. Our Party's present task in the Northeast is to build base areas, stable military and political base areas in eastern, northern and western Manchuria.[1] To build such base areas is no easy job; it requires hard and bitter struggle. Three or four years are needed to build such base areas. But a solid preliminary groundwork must be laid in the year 1946. Otherwise we may not be able to stand our ground.

2. It should now be made clear that these base areas are not to be built in the big cities or along the main communication lines that are or will be occupied by the Kuomintang; under present conditions this is not practicable. Nor are they to be built in regions close to big cities or main communication lines held by the Kuomintang. The reason is that the Kuomintang, having seized the big cities and the main communication lines, will not let us build stable base areas in regions very close to them. Our Party should do adequate work and set up our first line of military defence in these regions, which must never be lightly abandoned. But they will be guerrilla zones for both parties and not our stable base areas. Therefore, the regions in which to build stable bases are the cities and vast rural areas comparatively remote from the centres of Kuomintang occupation. Those regions should now be designated so that we can dispose our forces accordingly and lead the whole Party towards this goal.

3. After we have decided on the location of our stable base areas and disposed our forces and after our army's numerical strength has greatly increased, mass work will be the centre of gravity of our Party's work in the Northeast. All cadres must be made to understand that the Kuomintang will be stronger than our Party in the

Northeast for some time and that unless our starting point is to arouse
the masses to struggle, solve their problems and rely on them in every
way and unless we mobilize all forces to work painstakingly among
the masses and lay a solid preliminary foundation within a year, and
particularly in the next few critical months, we shall become isolated
in the Northeast, be unable to build stable base areas or defeat the
attacks of the Kuomintang and indeed may encounter immense difficulties or even fail.   Conversely, if we rely firmly on the masses, we
shall overcome all difficulties and reach our goal step by step.   Mass
work consists in arousing the masses for struggles to settle accounts
with traitors and in launching campaigns for rent reduction and wage
increases and campaigns for production.   In these struggles we should
form various kinds of mass organizations, set up Party nuclei, build
armed units of the masses and organs of people's political power,
speedily raise mass economic struggles to the level of political struggles
and lead the masses to take part in building the base areas.   The
directive on arousing mass struggles recently issued by the Jehol
Provincial Party Committee[2] may be applied in the Northeast.   Our
Party must bring tangible material benefits to the people in the
Northeast; only then will the masses support us and oppose the

---

* This directive, drafted by Comrade Mao Tse-tung for the Central Committee
of the Communist Party of China, was addressed to its Northeast Bureau.   As soon
as the Soviet Union declared war on Japan and the Soviet Red Army entered the
Northeast, the Central Committee of the Communist Party of China and the Chinese
People's Liberation Army sent large numbers of cadres and troops to the Northeast
to lead the people in wiping out the remnants of the Japanese invaders and the
puppet "Manchukuo" regime, cleaning out traitors, eradicating bandits and establishing democratic local governments at various levels.   But at the same time the Kuomintang reactionaries, bent on exclusive control over the entire Northeast, transported
large numbers of troops there by land, sea and air with the aid of U.S. imperialism
and seized key places like Shanhaikuan and Chinchow which had already been
liberated by the People's Liberation Army.   A stern struggle was already inevitable
in the Northeast, and this struggle was obviously going to be of special significance
for the situation in the whole country.   In this directive Comrade Mao Tse-tung
foresaw how arduous the struggle in the Northeast would be and pointed out in good
time that the centre of gravity of the work there should be in the cities and vast
rural areas comparatively remote from the centres of Kuomintang occupation; that
is, we should "leave the high road alone and seize the land on both sides" in order to
arouse the masses in earnest, build stable base areas, gradually accumulate strength
and prepare for the future shift to the counter-offensive.   This correct policy of the
Central Committee and Comrade Mao Tse-tung was effectively carried out by the
Northeast Bureau headed by Comrade Lin Piao; hence the great victory, the liberation
of the entire Northeast three years later in November 1948.

Kuomintang attacks. Otherwise, the masses will be unable to see clearly which of the two parties, the Kuomintang or the Communist Party, is good and which is bad, may be taken in for a time by deceitful Kuomintang propaganda and may even turn against our Party, and thus an extremely unfavourable situation would be created for us in the Northeast.

4. At present there is a subjective difficulty for our Party in the Northeast. Large numbers of our cadres and armed forces in the Northeast are newcomers, unfamiliar with the place and the people. Cadres are dissatisfied because we cannot occupy large cities and they are impatient with the arduous work of arousing the masses and building base areas. These circumstances are in contradiction with the present situation and the tasks of the Party. Again and again we must teach all cadres from other areas to pay attention to investigation and study, to acquaint themselves with the place and the people and to resolve to become one with the people of the Northeast; and we must train large numbers of activists and cadres from among the masses. We should explain to the cadres that although the big cities and the communication lines are in the hands of the Kuomintang, the situation in the Northeast is nevertheless favourable to us. So long as we spread among all cadres and soldiers the idea of arousing the masses and of building our base areas and so long as we mobilize all forces and quickly undertake the great struggle to build these base areas, we shall be able to establish ourselves firmly in the Northeast and in Jehol and be sure of victory. We must tell the cadres that they should on no account underestimate the strength of the Kuomintang or become impatient with arduous work because they think the Kuomintang is going to attack eastern and northern Manchuria anyhow. Of course, in making these explanations we should not lead the cadres to believe that the Kuomintang is terribly strong and that its attacks cannot be smashed. It should be pointed out that the Kuomintang has no deep, organized foundation in the Northeast and that its attacks can be smashed; it is therefore possible for our Party to build base areas. But the Kuomintang troops are now attacking the Jehol-Liaoning border, and if no blows are dealt them, they will attack eastern and northern Manchuria before long. All our Party members must therefore resolve to undertake the most difficult tasks, swiftly arouse the masses, build our base areas and smash the Kuomintang attacks in western Manchuria and Jehol

resolutely and in a planned way. In eastern and northern Manchuria we should quickly prepare the conditions for smashing the Kuomintang attacks. We must thoroughly clear away all ideas among our cadres of winning easy victories through good luck, without hard and bitter struggle, without sweat and blood.

5. Promptly delimit military areas and sub-areas in western, eastern and northern Manchuria and divide our forces into field armies and regional troops. Distribute a considerable part of the regular troops among the military sub-areas to arouse the masses, wipe out bandits, set up organs of political power, organize guerrillas, people's militia and self-defence forces so as to make our areas secure, co-ordinate with the field armies and smash the Kuomintang attacks. All troops must be assigned to specific areas and specific tasks; only in this way can they quickly unite with the people and build stable base areas.

6. This time over 100,000 of our troops have entered the Northeast and Jehol; the army there has recently expanded by more than 200,000, and the trend is to keep on expanding. Adding Party and government workers, we estimate that the total will exceed 400,000 within a year. A situation in which such a large number of personnel, divorced from production, depends solely on the people of the Northeast for supplies certainly cannot last long and is very dangerous. Therefore, all army units and government organs must take part in production when not fighting or doing their regular work, except for those field armies which are concentrated and charged with major military actions. The year 1946 must not pass without results; the entire Northeast must promptly make plans accordingly.

7. In the Northeast the direction in which the workers and intellectuals move is vitally important to building our base areas and winning future victories. Our Party should therefore give its full attention to work in the big cities and along the main communication lines and especially to winning over the workers and intellectuals. In view of the fact that in the early years of the War of Resistance our Party did not pay sufficient attention to winning over the workers and intellectuals to come to the base areas, the Party organizations in the Northeast should now do everything possible to draw workers and intellectuals into our army and into the various construction tasks in the base areas, besides paying attention to underground work in the Kuomintang areas.

NOTES

[1] The eastern Manchuria base area included Kirin, Hsi-an, Antu, Yenchi, Tunhua and other places east of the Shenyang-Changchun section of the Chinese Changchun Railway. The northern Manchuria base area included Harbin, Mutankiang, Pei-an and Kiamusze, among others. The western Manchuria base area included Tsitsihar, Tao-an, Kailu, Fuhsin, Chengchiatun, Fuyu and other places west of the Shenyang-Changchun section of the Chinese Changchun Railway. The Party also built a base area in southern Manchuria. It included Antung, Chuangho, Tunghua, Linchiang and Chingyuan and other places east of the Shenyang-Talien section of the Chinese Changchun Railway and Liaochung, southwest of Shenyang. The persistent struggle against the enemy in southern Manchuria played an important role in the building of base areas in the Northeast.

[2] This refers to the "Directive on Arousing the Masses" issued by the Jehol Provincial Committee of the Chinese Communist Party in December 1945. It pointed out that the central task in arousing the masses then was to launch a mass campaign of accusation and retribution to settle accounts with traitors and secret agents, that through the campaign the enthusiasm of the masses should be heightened, their social, political and economic status should be raised, and that trade unions, peasant associations and other mass organizations should be organized and that preparations should be made to proceed, when this campaign was over, to a mass campaign for the reduction of rent and interest. In arousing the masses in the cities, we had to arouse the workers first so that they could play the vanguard and leading role in the campaign to settle accounts with traitors and secret agents. The directive also called for learning the entire work of city administration, for making economical use of manpower and for planning everything on a long-term basis.

SOME POINTS IN APPRAISAL OF
THE PRESENT INTERNATIONAL SITUATION*

April 1946

1. The forces of world reaction are definitely preparing a third world war, and the danger of war exists. But the democratic forces of the people of the world have surpassed the reactionary forces and are forging ahead; they must and certainly can overcome the danger of war. Therefore, the question in the relations between the United States, Britain and France and the Soviet Union is not a question of compromise or break, but a question of compromise earlier or compromise later. "Compromise" means reaching agreement through peaceful negotiation. "Earlier or later" means several years, or more than ten years, or even longer.

2. The kind of compromise mentioned above does not mean compromise on all international issues. That is impossible so long as the United States, Britain and France continue to be ruled by reactionaries. This kind of compromise means compromise on some issues, including certain important ones. But there will not be many such compromises in the near future. There is, however, a possibility that the trade relations of the United States, Britain and France with the Soviet Union will expand.

3. Such compromise between the United States, Britain and France and the Soviet Union can be the outcome only of resolute, effective struggles by all the democratic forces of the world against the reactionary forces of the United States, Britain and France. Such compromise does not require the people in the countries of the capitalist world to follow suit and make compromises at home. The people in those countries will continue to wage different struggles in accordance with their different conditions. The principle of the reactionary forces in dealing with the democratic forces of the people is definitely to destroy all they can and to prepare to destroy later whatever they

cannot destroy now. Face to face with this situation, the democratic forces of the people should likewise apply the same principle to the reactionary forces.

* This document was written to counter a pessimistic appraisal of the international situation at that time. In the spring of 1946, imperialism headed by the United States of America, together with the reactionaries in various countries, was daily intensifying its anti-Soviet, anti-Communist and anti-popular activities and trumpeting that "war between the United States and the Soviet Union is inevitable" and that "the outbreak of a third world war is inevitable". In these circumstances, since some comrades overestimated the strength of imperialism, underestimated the strength of the people, feared U.S. imperialism and feared the outbreak of a new world war, they showed weakness in the face of the armed attacks of the U.S.-Chiang Kai-shek reactionary gang and dared not resolutely oppose counter-revolutionary war with revolutionary war. In this document Comrade Mao Tse-tung was combating such erroneous thinking. He pointed out that if the forces of the people throughout the world waged resolute, effective struggles against the forces of world reaction, they could overcome the danger of a new world war. At the same time, he pointed out that it was possible for the imperialist countries and the socialist countries to reach certain compromises but that such compromises do "not require the people in the countries of the capitalist world to follow suit and make compromises at home", and that "the people in those countries will continue to wage different struggles in accordance with their different conditions". This document was not made public at the time and was circulated only among some leading comrades of the Central Committee. It was distributed at the meeting of the Central Committee of the Communist Party of China in December 1947. Since the comrades present unanimously agreed with its contents, the full text was later included in "A Circular on the Decisions Made at the Central Committee Meeting of December 1947", issued by the Central Committee in January 1948.

SMASH CHIANG KAI-SHEK'S OFFENSIVE
BY A WAR OF SELF-DEFENCE*

July 20, 1946

1.   Chiang Kai-shek, after violating the truce agreement,[1] violating the resolutions of the Political Consultative Conference[2] and occupying Szepingkai, Changchun and other cities of ours in the Northeast, is now launching another large-scale offensive against us in eastern and northern China; later, he may again attack the Northeast. Only after completely smashing Chiang's offensive in a war of self-defence can the Chinese people regain peace.

2.   Our Party and our army are making every preparation to smash Chiang Kai-shek's offensive and thus to win peace.   Although Chiang Kai-shek has U.S. aid, the feelings of the people are against him, the morale of his troops is low, and his economy is in difficulty. As for us, although we have no foreign aid, the feelings of the people are for us, the morale of our troops is high, and we can handle our economy.   Therefore, we can defeat Chiang Kai-shek.   The whole Party should be fully confident of this.

3.   For defeating Chiang Kai-shek the general method of fighting is mobile warfare.   Therefore, the temporary abandonment of certain places or cities is not only unavoidable but also necessary.   Certain places or cities are temporarily abandoned in order to win final victory, which would otherwise be impossible.   We must make all Party members and all the people in the Liberated Areas understand this so that they will be mentally prepared.

4.   In order to smash Chiang Kai-shek's offensive we must co-operate closely with the masses of the people and win over all who can be won over.   In the rural areas, on the one hand, we should resolutely solve the land problem, rely firmly on the farm labourers and poor peasants and unite with the middle peasants; on the other hand, when solving the land problem, we should distinguish the

ordinary rich peasants and middle and small landlords from the traitors, bad gentry and local tyrants. We should be more strict in our
treatment of the traitors, bad gentry and local tyrants, and more
lenient in our treatment of the rich peasants and middle and small
landlords. In places where the land problem has already been solved,
we should change to a moderate attitude towards the landlord class
as a whole, with the exception of a few reactionaries. In order to
reduce the number of hostile elements and to consolidate the Liberated Areas, we should help all those landlords who have difficulty
in making a living and induce runaway landlords to return and give
them an opportunity to earn a living. In the cities, besides uniting
with the working class, the petty bourgeoisie and all progressives, we
should take care to unite with all the middle elements and isolate
the reactionaries. Among the Kuomintang troops, we should win
over all the possible opponents of civil war and isolate the bellicose
elements.

5. In order to smash Chiang Kai-shek's offensive we must plan
on a long-term basis. We must use our manpower and material

---

* This inner-Party directive was drafted by Comrade Mao Tse-tung for the
Central Committee of the Communist Party of China. Chiang Kai-shek tore up the
"October 10th Agreement" in the winter of 1945, but his preparations for an all-out
civil war were not complete, mainly because large numbers of Kuomintang troops
had not yet been moved to the civil war fronts. Consequently, in January 1946, under
the pressure of the demand of the entire people for peace and democracy, the Kuomintang government had to convene the Political Consultative Conference with the
participation of the Communist Party of China and other democratic parties. The
Conference adopted a series of resolutions favourable to peace and democracy, and
on January 10 the Kuomintang government issued an order to cease fire. Chiang
Kai-shek was not willing to observe the resolutions of the Political Consultative Conference and the cease-fire order. In the first half of 1946 the Kuomintang troops
continued to attack the Liberated Areas at many points, the attack in the Northeast
being on a particularly large scale, and a situation was created with small-scale
fighting south of the Great Wall and large-scale fighting north of it. Meanwhile
the United States made very great efforts to transport and equip the Kuomintang
troops. By the end of June 1946 Chiang Kai-shek and his U.S. masters thought that
they were fully prepared and could wipe out the whole People's Liberation Army
in three to six months. Accordingly, they launched an all-out offensive against the
Liberated Areas, which began on June 26 with a massive encircling attack on the
Central Plains Liberated Area. Between July and September the Kuomintang troops
started successive large-scale attacks against the Liberated Areas of Kiangsu-Anhwei,
Shantung, Shansi-Hopei-Shantung-Honan, Shansi-Chahar-Hopei and Shansi-Suiyuan.
In October they launched another large-scale attack on the Northeast Liberated Area.
At the same time they continued to encircle the Shensi-Kansu-Ningsia Liberated Area
with large numbers of troops. When the country-wide civil war broke out, the
Kuomintang employed 193 brigades (divisions), or some 1,600,000 of its regular troops,

resources with the utmost economy and do everything possible to avoid waste. We must investigate and clean up the petty graft which has appeared in some places. We must work hard in production in order to become completely self-sufficient in all necessities and first of all in grain and cloth. We must promote the extensive planting of cotton and encourage every family to spin and every village to weave. We should start to promote this even in the Northeast. In the spheres of finance and supplies, we must meet the material needs of the war of self-defence and at the same time lighten the burden on the people, so that there will be some improvement in the livelihood of the people in our Liberated Areas even under war-time conditions. To sum up, we rely entirely on our own efforts, and our position is invincible; this is the very opposite of Chiang Kai-shek who depends entirely on foreign countries. We live plainly and work hard, we take care of the needs of both the army and the people; this is the very opposite of the situation in Chiang Kai-shek's areas, where those at the top are corrupt and degenerate, while the people under them are destitute. Under these circumstances, we shall surely be victorious.

---

to attack the Liberated Areas; they constituted 80 per cent of its total strength of 248 regular brigades (divisions), or 2,000,000 men. Under the leadership of the Central Committee of the Party and its bureaus and sub-bureaus, the army and people in the Liberated Areas fought heroically against the offensive of Chiang Kai-shek's troops. At that time there were six major theatres of war in the Liberated Areas. These six theatres of war and the forces of the People's Liberation Army fighting there were:

The Shansi-Hopei-Shantung-Honan Liberated Area with People's Liberation Army forces led by Liu Po-cheng, Teng Hsiao-ping and other comrades.

The Eastern China Liberated Area (including the Shantung and the Kiangsu-Anhwei Liberated Areas) with People's Liberation Army forces led by Chen Yi, Su Yu, Tan Chen-lin and other comrades.

The Northeast Liberated Area with People's Liberation Army forces led by Lin Piao, Lo Jung-huan and other comrades.

The Shansi-Chahar-Hopei Liberated Area with People's Liberation Army forces led by Nieh Jung-chen and other comrades.

The Shansi-Suiyuan Liberated Area with People's Liberation Army forces led by Ho Lung and other comrades.

The Central Plains Liberated Area with People's Liberation Army forces led by Li Hsien-nien, Cheng Wei-san and other comrades.

The People's Liberation Army, then totalling about 1,200,000 troops, was outnumbered by the enemy. It correctly carried out the strategy laid down by Comrade Mao Tse-tung and struck incessant, powerful blows at the invading enemy. After wiping out 66 regular brigades and some irregular units of the enemy, totalling more than 710,000 men, in about eight months, the People's Liberation Army halted the enemy's all-out offensive. Then, step by step, it unfolded its strategic counter-offensive.

6.   Difficulties lie ahead of us but they can and must be overcome. All Party comrades and all the troops and people in the Liberated Areas must unite as one, completely smash Chiang Kai-shek's offensive and build an independent, peaceful and democratic new China.

NOTES

[1] The "truce agreement" was the agreement concluded on January 10, 1946 between representatives of the Communist Party of China and Chiang Kai-shek's Kuomintang government. It stipulated that the troops of both parties should cease military operations from their respective positions as of midnight, January 13. But in fact Chiang Kai-shek used this agreement as a smoke-screen behind which he made arrangements for a major war; at the very time the cease-fire order was being transmitted, he ordered the Kuomintang troops "to seize strategic points" and from then on moved up troops continuously to attack the Liberated Areas. By July Chiang Kai-shek had openly torn up the truce agreement and launched an all-out offensive against the Liberated Areas.

[2] The Political Consultative Conference was attended by representatives of the Kuomintang, the Communist Party of China and other political parties, and by personages without party affiliation and was held in Chungking from January 10 to 31, 1946. The Conference adopted five agreements:

(1)   Agreement on Government Organization. This agreement affirmed that "the Organic Law of the National Government shall be revised with a view to strengthening the National Government Council". It increased the number of National Government Councillors and provided that "the National Government Councillors shall be chosen by the President of the National Government from both Kuomintang and non-Kuomintang members"; that "the appointment of members of various parties as National Government Councillors by the President of the National Government shall be made on the recommendation of the parties concerned, which, in case of the President's disapproval, shall make new recommendations"; that "when the President of the National Government nominates as Government Councillor any personage without party affiliation, whose appointment is opposed by one-third of the Councillors already appointed, the President must reconsider the matter and make a new nomination for appointment"; and that "half the National Government Councillors shall be Kuomintang members and the other half members of other political parties and public personages". The National Government Council was nominally defined as "the supreme government organ in charge of state affairs", with powers to discuss and decide legislative principles, administrative policies and major military measures, financial plans and the budget as well as matters submitted by the President of the National Government for consideration; yet at the same time the President of the National Government was vested with great powers, including the power of nominating persons for office, the power of veto (which, though nominally limited, was virtually absolute, for it required a majority of three-fifths to override a veto, while the President's own party, the Kuomintang, had half the seats) and emergency powers. The agreement also provided that "seven or eight members

of the Executive Yuan shall be non-Kuomintang members who shall either hold the portfolios of existing ministries or hold the proposed posts of ministers of state without portfolio".

(2) The Programme for Peace and National Reconstruction. This programme was composed of nine sections, namely, General Principles, Rights of the People, Political Affairs, Military Affairs, Foreign Relations, Economic and Financial Affairs, Education and Culture, Relief and Rehabilitation, and Overseas Chinese Affairs. The section on "General Principles" provided that all political parties of the country shall "unite closely to build a new China, united, free and democratic"; that there shall be "political democratization, nationalization of troops, and equality and legality for all political parties"; and that "political disputes shall be settled by political means in order to ensure peace and national development". The section on "Rights of the People" provided that "the freedoms of person, thought, religious belief, speech, the press, assembly, association, residence, movement and correspondence shall be guaranteed to the people" and that "any organ or person other than the judiciary and the police is strictly forbidden to arrest, try and punish people, and anyone who violates this provision shall be punished". The section on "Political Affairs" provided that "all levels of the administration shall be overhauled, their powers and responsibilities unified and clearly defined, all duplicated agencies abolished, administrative procedures simplified and each level of administration charged with definite responsibilities"; that "competent office-holders shall be protected, appointments to government posts based not on party affiliation but on competency and seniority, and the holding of concurrent posts and the practice of favouritism forbidden"; that "the supervisory system shall be strictly enforced, corruption severely punished and facilities given to the people freely to lodge accusations against corrupt officials"; that "local self-government shall be actively promoted and elections from the lower level upwards through universal suffrage carried out"; and that "the powers of the central and local governments shall be defined according to the principle of fair distribution of powers, that the local governments may take such measures as are suitable to local circumstances, but those enacted by a province or county must not contradict those of the central government". The section on "Military Affairs" provided that "the military organizations shall be adapted to the needs of national defence, the military system reformed in line with a democratic system of government and the conditions in the country, military power separated from political parties, military authority separated from civil authority, military education improved, equipment be adequate and personnel and financial systems be improved in order to build a modernized national army" and that "the numerical strength of the nation's troops shall be effectively reduced and reorganized in accordance with the provisions of the Military Reorganization Plan". The section on "Economic and Financial Affairs" provided that "the development of bureaucrat-capital shall be curbed and government officials strictly forbidden to make use of their official position and influence to engage in speculation, monopoly, tax evasion, smuggling, embezzlement of public funds and unlawful use of the means of transport"; that "rents and rates of interest shall be reduced, the rights of lessees protected, the payment of farm rents ensured, agricultural credits expanded, usury strictly prohibited in order to better the life of the peasants and an agrarian law to attain the objective of 'land to the tillers' shall be put into effect"; that "labour laws shall be put into effect to improve working conditions"; that "the administration of finance shall be made public, the

budget system and the system of financial reports strictly adhered to, budget expenditures drastically reduced, revenues and expenditures balanced, central and local government finances defined, the currency in circulation contracted and the monetary system stabilized and the raising of both domestic and foreign loans and their uses made public and subject to supervision by public bodies"; and that "the system of taxation shall be reformed and all exorbitant and miscellaneous levies and illegal exactions completely abolished". The section on "Education and Culture" provided that "academic freedom shall be guaranteed, and there shall be no interference with school and college administration for reasons of religious belief or political thought"; that "the proportion of the national budget allocated to education and culture shall be increased"; and that "the war-time censorship of the press, publications, motion pictures, the drama, posts and telegrams shall be abolished".

(3) Agreement on the National Assembly. This agreement provided that "there shall be added to the National Assembly seven hundred delegates from various parties and from among public personages" and that "the duty and power of the first National Assembly shall be to frame and adopt a constitution".

(4) Agreement on the Draft Constitution. This agreement provided for the establishment of a review committee to revise the draft constitution prepared by the Kuomintang and laid down the principles for revision. In addition to prescribing the principles governing the duties and powers of the National Assembly and government organizations, special provisions were made regarding "local government" and "the rights and duties of the people". With respect to "local government", it provided that "the province shall be the highest unit of local self-government"; that "the powers of the provincial government in relation to those of the central government shall be defined according to the principle of a fair distribution of powers"; that "the provincial governor shall be elected by the people"; and that "the province may have a provincial constitution which, however, must not contravene the provisions of the national constitution". With respect to "the rights and duties of the people", it provided that "all freedoms and rights which are generally enjoyed by the people of a democratic country shall be protected by the constitution against illegal violation"; that "if any provision is made by law regarding the freedom of the people, it shall be aimed at the protection of such freedom and not at its restriction"; that "drafting of labour may be provided for in local laws, but not in the national constitution"; and that "the right of self-government shall be guaranteed to minority nationalities who live together in specific communities".

(5) Agreement on Military Affairs. This agreement provided that "the military system shall be reformed in line with a democratic system of government and the conditions in our country"; that "military conscription shall be improved"; that "military education shall be conducted on the basis of the principles governing the building of the army and shall for ever be dissociated from political parties and personal relationships"; that "military power shall be separated from political parties" and "all political parties and individuals shall refrain from using the army as an instrument of political struggle"; and that "military authority shall be separated from civil authority" and "no soldier in active service may serve concurrently as a civil official". With regard to the reorganization of the Kuomintang troops and the troops of the Liberated Areas, it provided that "the three-man military sub-committee proceed as planned with all possible speed to reach an agreement on measures for reorganizing the troops of the Communist Party of China and to complete their reorganization"; that the Kuomintang troops shall

"be reorganized according to the plan already laid down by the Ministry of War into ninety divisions and this reorganization shall be completed at the highest possible speed within six months"; and that "when the above-mentioned two items of reorganization have been completed, all troops of the entire nation shall be unified and further reorganized into fifty or sixty divisions".

These Political Consultative Conference agreements were, in varying degrees, favourable to the people and unfavourable to Chiang Kai-shek's reactionary rule. While expressing his approval of these agreements in an attempt to use them to carry out his peace fraud, Chiang Kai-shek actively made military preparations for launching a country-wide civil war. These Political Consultative Conference agreements were soon torn up by him one after another.

TALK WITH THE AMERICAN CORRESPONDENT ANNA LOUISE STRONG*

August 1946

Strong: Do you think there is hope for a political, a peaceful settlement of China's problems in the near future?

Mao: That depends on the attitude of the U.S. government. If the American people stay the hands of the American reactionaries who are helping Chiang Kai-shek fight the civil war, there is hope for peace.

Strong: Suppose the United States gives Chiang Kai-shek no help, besides that already given,[1] how long can Chiang Kai-shek keep on fighting?

Mao: More than a year.

Strong: Can Chiang Kai-shek keep on that long, economically?

Mao: He can.

Strong: What if the United States makes it clear that it will give Chiang Kai-shek no more help from now on?

Mao: There is no sign yet that the U.S. government and Chiang Kai-shek have any desire to stop the war within a short time.

Strong: How long can the Communist Party keep on?

Mao: As far as our own desire is concerned, we don't want to fight even for a single day. But if circumstances force us to fight, we can fight to the finish.

Strong: If the American people ask why the Communist Party is fighting, what should I reply?

Mao: Because Chiang Kai-shek is out to slaughter the Chinese people, and if the people want to survive they have to defend themselves. This the American people can understand.

Strong: What do you think of the possibility of the United States starting a war against the Soviet Union?

Mao: There are two aspects to the propaganda about an anti-Soviet war. On the one hand, U.S. imperialism is indeed preparing

a war against the Soviet Union; the current propaganda about an
anti-Soviet war, as well as other anti-Soviet propaganda, is political
preparation for such a war.   On the other hand, this propaganda is
a smoke-screen put up by the U.S. reactionaries to cover many actual
contradictions immediately confronting U.S. imperialism.   These are
the contradictions between the U.S. reactionaries and the American
people and the contradictions of U.S. imperialism with other capitalist
countries and with the colonial and semi-colonial countries.   At
present, the actual significance of the U.S. slogan of waging an
anti-Soviet war is the oppression of the American people and the
expansion of the U.S. forces of aggression in the rest of the capitalist
world.   As you know, both Hitler and his partners, the Japanese
warlords, used anti-Soviet slogans for a long time as a pretext for
enslavement of the people at home and aggression against other
countries.   Now the U.S. reactionaries are acting in exactly the
same way.

To start a war, the U.S. reactionaries must first attack the
American people.   They are already attacking the American peo-
ple – oppressing the workers and democratic circles in the United
States politically and economically and preparing to impose fascism

---

* This is a very important statement made by Comrade Mao Tse-tung on the
international and domestic situation not long after the conclusion of World War II.
Here, Comrade Mao Tse-tung put forward his famous thesis, "All reactionaries are
paper tigers." This thesis armed the people of our country ideologically, strengthened
their confidence in victory and played an exceedingly great role in the People's War of
Liberation. Just as Lenin considered imperialism a "colossus with feet of clay", so
Comrade Mao Tse-tung regards imperialism and all reactionaries as paper tigers; both
have dealt with the essence of the matter.   This thesis is a fundamental strategic concept for the revolutionary people.   Since the period of the Second Revolutionary Civil
War, Comrade Mao Tse-tung has repeatedly pointed out: strategically, with regard
to the whole, revolutionaries must despise the enemy, dare to struggle against him
and dare to seize victory; at the same time, tactically, with regard to each part, each
specific struggle, they must take the enemy seriously, be prudent, carefully study and
perfect the art of struggle and adopt forms of struggle suited to different times, places
and conditions in order to isolate and wipe out the enemy step by step.   On December
1, 1958, at a meeting of the Political Bureau of the Central Committee of the Communist Party of China held at Wuchang, Comrade Mao Tse-tung stated:
       Just as there is not a single thing in the world without a dual nature (this is
    the law of the unity of opposites), so imperialism and all reactionaries have a dual
    nature – they are real tigers and paper tigers at the same time.   In past history,
    before they won state power and for some time afterwards, the slave-owning
    class, the feudal landlord class and the bourgeoisie were vigorous, revolutionary
    and progressive; they were real tigers.   But with the lapse of time, because their
    opposites – the slave class, the peasant class and the proletariat – grew in strength

there. The people of the United States should stand up and resist the attacks of the U.S. reactionaries. I believe they will.

The United States and the Soviet Union are separated by a vast zone which includes many capitalist, colonial and semi-colonial countries in Europe, Asia and Africa. Before the U.S. reactionaries have subjugated these countries, an attack on the Soviet Union is out of the question. In the Pacific the United States now controls areas larger than all the former British spheres of influence there put together; it controls Japan, that part of China under Kuomintang rule, half of Korea, and the South Pacific. It has long controlled Central and South America. It seeks also to control the whole of the British Empire and Western Europe. Using various pretexts, the United States is making large-scale military arrangements and setting up military bases in many countries. The U.S. reactionaries say that the military bases they have set up and are preparing to set up all over the world are aimed against the Soviet Union. True, these military bases are directed against the Soviet Union. At present, however, it is not the Soviet Union but the countries in which these military bases are located that are the first to suffer U.S. aggression. I believe it won't be long before these countries come

---

step by step, struggled against them and became more and more formidable, these ruling classes changed step by step into the reverse, changed into reactionaries, changed into backward people, changed into paper tigers. And eventually they were overthrown, or will be overthrown, by the people. The reactionary, backward, decaying classes retained this dual nature even in their last life-and-death struggles against the people. On the one hand, they were real tigers; they ate people, ate people by the millions and tens of millions. The cause of the people's struggle went through a period of difficulties and hardships, and along the path there were many twists and turns. To destroy the rule of imperialism, feudalism and bureaucrat-capitalism in China took the Chinese people more than a hundred years and cost them tens of millions of lives before the victory in 1949. Look! Were these not living tigers, iron tigers, real tigers? But in the end they changed into paper tigers, dead tigers, bean-curd tigers. These are historical facts. Have people not seen or heard about these facts? There have indeed been thousands and tens of thousands of them! Thousands and tens of thousands! Hence, imperialism and all reactionaries, looked at in essence, from a long-term point of view, must be seen for what they are – paper tigers. On this we should build our strategic thinking. On the other hand, they are also living tigers, iron tigers, real tigers which can eat people. On this we should build our tactical thinking.

For the necessity of despising the enemy strategically and taking full account of him tactically, see "Strategic Problems of China's Revolutionary War", Chapter 5, Section 6, *Selected Works of Mao Tse-tung*, Vol. I, and "On Some Important Problems of the Party's Present Policy", Section 1, pp. 181-82 of this volume.

to realize who is really oppressing them, the Soviet Union or the United States. The day will come when the U.S. reactionaries find themselves opposed by the people of the whole world.

Of course, I do not mean to say that the U.S. reactionaries have no intention of attacking the Soviet Union. The Soviet Union is a defender of world peace and a powerful factor preventing the domination of the world by the U.S. reactionaries. Because of the existence of the Soviet Union, it is absolutely impossible for the reactionaries in the United States and the world to realize their ambitions. That is why the U.S. reactionaries rabidly hate the Soviet Union and actually dream of destroying this socialist state. But the fact that the U.S. reactionaries are now trumpeting so loudly about a U.S.-Soviet war and creating a foul atmosphere, so soon after the end of World War II, compels us to take a look at their real aims. It turns out that under the cover of anti-Soviet slogans they are frantically attacking the workers and democratic circles in the United States and turning all the countries which are the targets of U.S. external expansion into U.S. dependencies. I think the American people and the peoples of all countries menaced by U.S. aggression should unite and struggle against the attacks of the U.S. reactionaries and their running dogs in these countries. Only by victory in this struggle can a third world war be avoided; otherwise it is unavoidable.

Strong: That is very clear. But suppose the United States uses the atom bomb? Suppose the United States bombs the Soviet Union from its bases in Iceland, Okinawa and China?

Mao: The atom bomb is a paper tiger which the U.S. reactionaries use to scare people. It looks terrible, but in fact it isn't. Of course, the atom bomb is a weapon of mass slaughter, but the outcome of a war is decided by the people, not by one or two new types of weapon.

All reactionaries are paper tigers. In appearance, the reactionaries are terrifying, but in reality they are not so powerful. From a long-term point of view, it is not the reactionaries but the people who are really powerful. In Russia, before the February Revolution in 1917, which side was really strong? On the surface the tsar was strong but he was swept away by a single gust of wind in the February Revolution. In the final analysis, the strength in Russia was on the side of the Soviets of Workers, Peasants and Soldiers. The tsar was just a paper tiger. Wasn't Hitler once considered very strong? But history proved that he was a paper tiger. So was Mussolini, so was Japanese imperialism. On the contrary, the strength of the Soviet Union and of the people in all countries who loved democracy and freedom proved much greater than had been foreseen.

Chiang Kai-shek and his supporters, the U.S. reactionaries, are all paper tigers too. Speaking of U.S. imperialism, people seem to feel that it is terrifically strong. Chinese reactionaries are using the "strength" of the United States to frighten the Chinese people. But it will be proved that the U.S. reactionaries, like all the reactionaries in history, do not have much strength. In the United States there are others who are really strong – the American people.

Take the case of China. We have only millet plus rifles to rely on, but history will finally prove that our millet plus rifles is more powerful than Chiang Kai-shek's aeroplanes plus tanks. Although the Chinese people still face many difficulties and will long suffer hardships from the joint attacks of U.S. imperialism and the Chinese reactionaries, the day will come when these reactionaries are defeated and we are victorious. The reason is simply this: the reactionaries represent reaction, we represent progress.

NOTES

[1] To help Chiang Kai-shek start civil war against the people, U.S. imperialism gave his government a very great amount of aid. By the end of June 1946 the United States had equipped 45 Kuomintang divisions. It had trained 150,000 Kuomintang military personnel – army, naval and air forces, secret agents, communications police, staff officers, medical officers, supply personnel, etc. U.S. warships and aircraft transported to the front against the Liberated Areas 14 Kuomintang corps (41 divisions) and 8 regiments of the communications police corps, or over 540,000 men in all. The U.S. government landed 90,000 of its marines in China and stationed them at such important cities as Shanghai, Tsingtao, Tientsin, Peiping and Chinwangtao. They guarded the lines of communication for the Kuomintang in northern China. According to data disclosed in *United States Relations with China* (The White Paper), released by the State Department on August 5, 1949, the total value of various kinds of U.S. aid given to the Chiang Kai-shek government from the time of the War of Resistance Against Japan to 1948 was more than 4,500 million dollars (the overwhelming bulk of U.S. aid given during the War of Resistance had been hoarded by the Kuomintang for the ensuing civil war against the people). But the actual amount of U.S. aid to Chiang Kai-shek far exceeded this total. The U.S. White Paper admitted that U.S. aid was equivalent to "more than 50 percent of the monetary expenditures" of the Chiang Kai-shek government and was of "proportionately greater magnitude in relation to the budget of that Government than the United States has provided to any nation of Western Europe since the end of the war".

CONCENTRATE A SUPERIOR FORCE
TO DESTROY THE ENEMY FORCES
ONE BY ONE*

September 16, 1946

1. The method of fighting by concentrating a superior force to destroy the enemy forces[1] one by one must be employed not only in the disposition of troops for a campaign but also in the disposition of troops for a battle.

2. With regard to the disposition for a campaign, when the enemy employs many brigades[2] (or regiments) and advances against our army from several directions, our army must concentrate an absolutely superior force – six, five, four or at least three times the enemy strength – and pick an opportune moment to encircle and wipe out one enemy brigade (or regiment) first. It should be one of the enemy's weaker brigades (or regiments), or one that has less support, or one stationed where the terrain and the people are most favourable to us and unfavourable to the enemy. We should tie down the rest of the enemy brigades (or regiments) with small forces in order to prevent them from rushing reinforcements to the brigade (or regiment) we are encircling and attacking so that we can destroy it first. When this has been achieved, we should, according to the circumstances, either wipe out one or several more enemy brigades or retire to rest and consolidate for further fighting. (Here are two examples of the former. Our troops under the command of Su Yu and Tan Chen-lin wiped out five thousand of the enemy's communications police corps[3] near Jukao on August 22, one enemy brigade on August 26 and one and a half brigades on August 27.[4] Our troops under Liu Po-cheng and Teng Hsiao-ping annihilated one enemy brigade near Tingtao between September 3 and 6, another in the afternoon of September 6 and two more on September 7-8.[5]) In the disposition for a campaign, we must reject the wrong method of fighting, which underrates

the enemy and therefore divides our forces to deal with all the enemy
detachments, for by this method we cannot destroy even one enemy
detachment but will land ourselves in a passive position.

3. In the disposition for a battle, when we have concentrated an
absolutely superior force and encircled one of the enemy detachments
(a brigade or regiment), our attacking formations (or units) should
not attempt to wipe out all the encircled enemy simultaneously at one
swoop and thus divide themselves and strike everywhere without
enough strength anywhere, losing time and making it hard to get results.
Instead, we should concentrate an absolutely superior force, that is to
say, a force six, five, four or at least three times that of the enemy,
concentrate the whole or the bulk of our artillery, select one (not two)
of the weak spots in the enemy's positions, attack it fiercely and be
sure to win. This accomplished, swiftly exploit the victory and destroy
the enemy forces one by one.

4. The effects of this method of fighting are, first, complete annihilation and, second, quick decision. Only complete annihilation
can deal the most telling blows to the enemy, for when we wipe out
one regiment, he will have one regiment less, and when we wipe out
one brigade, he will have one brigade less. This method is most
useful when employed against an enemy lacking second-line troops.
Only complete annihilation can replenish our own forces to the greatest possible extent. It is now not only the main source of our arms
and ammunition, but also an important source of our manpower.
Complete annihilation demoralizes the enemy's troops and depresses
his followers; it raises the morale of our troops and inspires our people.
A quick decision makes it possible for our troops either to wipe out
the enemy reinforcements one by one or evade them. Quick decision
in battle and campaign is a necessary condition for the strategy of a
protracted war.

5. Among our military cadres there are still many who, when
not in action, approve the principle of concentrating our forces to
wipe out the enemy forces one by one, but often fail to apply it in
action. That is due to underestimation of the enemy and to lack of
intensive education and study. It is necessary to cite detailed cases
of past battles to explain again and again the advantages of this
method of fighting and to point out that it is the chief method of

---

* This inner-Party directive was drafted by Comrade Mao Tse-tung for the
Revolutionary Military Commission of the Central Committee of the Communist Party
of China.

defeating Chiang Kai-shek's attacks. Using this method we shall win. Acting counter to it we shall lose.

6. The principle of concentrating our forces to wipe out the enemy forces one by one has been a fine tradition of our army ever since its founding more than a decade ago; this is not the first time it has been put forward. During the War of Resistance Against Japan, however, the dispersal of our forces for guerrilla warfare was primary, and the concentration of our forces for mobile warfare was supplementary. In the present civil war, as conditions have changed, so should the method of fighting. The concentration of our forces for mobile warfare should be primary, and the dispersal of our forces for guerrilla warfare should be supplementary. Now that Chiang Kai-shek's army has acquired more powerful weapons, it is necessary for our army to lay special stress on the method of concentrating a superior force to wipe out the enemy forces one by one.

7. When the enemy is on the offensive and we are on the defensive, this method must be employed. However, when the enemy is on the defensive and we are on the offensive, we should distinguish between two kinds of situations and adopt different methods. When our force is big and the enemy in that locality is rather weak, or when we are making a surprise attack on the enemy, we may strike at several of his units simultaneously. For example, between June 5 and 10, our troops in Shantung Province simultaneously attacked and captured more than ten towns on the Tsingtao-Tsinan and the Tientsin-Pukow Railways.[6] Or to take another example, between August 10 and 21, our troops under Liu Po-cheng and Teng Hsiao-ping attacked and captured more than ten towns along the section of the Lunghai Railway between Kaifeng and Hsuchow.[7] On the other hand, when we do not have enough forces, we should seize the enemy-occupied towns one by one and should not attack the enemy at several towns simultaneously. That was how our forces in Shansi Province took the towns along the Tatung-Puchow Railway.[8]

8. When the main force of our troops is concentrated to annihilate the enemy, it must co-ordinate its operations with vigorous activities by the regional formations, local guerrillas and people's militia. When regional formations (or troops) attack an enemy regiment, battalion or company, they should also adopt the principle of concentrating our forces to annihilate the enemy forces one by one.

9. The principle of concentrating our forces to wipe out the enemy forces one by one is aimed chiefly at annihilating the enemy's effective

strength, not at holding or seizing a place. In some circumstances, it is permissible to abandon certain places for the purpose of concentrating our forces to wipe out the enemy or of enabling our main force to avoid heavy enemy attacks and to facilitate rest and consolidation for further fighting. So long as we are able to wipe out the enemy's effective strength on a large scale, it will be possible to recover lost territory and seize new territory. Therefore, all those who succeed in destroying the enemy's effective strength should be commended. This applies not only to those who destroy the enemy's regular forces but also to those who destroy his peace preservation corps, home-going contingents[9] and other reactionary local armed bands. However, we must hold or seize territory wherever the relative strength of the enemy and our own forces makes this possible or wherever such territory is significant for our campaigns or battles; to do otherwise would be a mistake. Therefore, those who succeed in holding or seizing such territory should also be commended.

NOTES

[1] The expressions "to destroy the enemy", "to wipe out the enemy" and "to annihilate the enemy" are used as synonyms in this book. They all include enemy troops killed, wounded and captured. To wipe out (annihilate, destroy) an enemy force means either to wipe it out completely or to wipe out the major part of that force.

[2] A regular corps of the Kuomintang army originally consisted of three (sometimes two) divisions, each with three regiments. Beginning in May 1946 the Kuomintang regular troops south of the Yellow River were reorganized in stages; what had been a corps became a reorganized division and former divisions became brigades, each with three (sometimes two) regiments. Part of the Kuomintang troops north of the Yellow River were not reorganized, and their designations remained the same. Some of the reorganized divisions later reverted to their original designation of corps.

[3] The communications police corps of the Kuomintang was formed in March 1945. Following Japan's surrender, the corps was deployed along communication lines for "garrison duties" under the pretext of guarding the railways, but actually to carry on secret police activities. It was one of the forces the Kuomintang used for fighting the civil war.

[4] In July 1946 the Kuomintang forces began a large-scale invasion of the Kiangsu-Anhwei Liberated Area, and our army fought bravely in self-defence. The Kuomintang troops attacking the Central Kiangsu Liberated Area consisted of fifteen brigades with about 120,000 men under Tang En-po. From July 13 to August 27, eighteen regiments of the Eastern China People's Liberation Army, commanded by Su Yu, Tan Chen-lin and other comrades, concentrated superior forces and fought seven successive battles in the region of Taihsing, Jukao, Hai-an and Shaopai in central Kiangsu. Our forces

wiped out six enemy brigades and five battalions of the enemy's communications police corps. The text refers to the results of two of these battles.

[5] In August 1946 the Kuomintang forces advanced along two routes from the Hsuchow and Chengchow sectors and attacked the Shansi-Hopei-Shantung-Honan Liberated Area. The People's Liberation Army of this area, under the command of Liu Po-cheng, Teng Hsiao-ping and other comrades, concentrated superior forces to engage the enemy detachment advancing from Chengchow. Between September 3 and 8 they wiped out four enemy brigades in succession in the region of Hotse, Tingtao and Tsaohsien in Shantung Province.

[6] Early in June 1946 the Shantung People's Liberation Army sent an expedition against the puppet troops along the Tsingtao-Tsinan and Tientsin-Pukow Railways and liberated more than ten towns, including Chiaohsien, Changtien, Choutsun, Tehchow, Tai-an and Tsaochuang.

[7] From August 10 to 21, 1946, the Shansi-Hopei-Shantung-Honan People's Liberation Army, supporting the Central Plains and Eastern China People's Liberation Armies, moved by several routes and attacked the enemy troops stationed along the Kaifeng-Hsuchow section of the Lunghai Railway, capturing more than ten towns, including Tangshan, Lanfeng, Huangkou, Lichuang and Yangchi.

[8] In July 1946 the Kuomintang forces under Hu Tsung-nan and Yen Hsi-shan jointly attacked the Southern Shansi Liberated Area. The Taiyueh units of the Shansi-Hopei-Shantung-Honan People's Liberation Army and a part of the Shansi-Suiyuan People's Liberation Army counter-attacked and beat back the enemy in southern Shansi. In August they started an offensive against the enemy between Linfen and Lingshih along the Tatung-Puchow Railway and liberated the towns of Hungtung, Chaocheng, Huohsien, Lingshih and Fenhsi.

[9] During the People's War of Liberation some landlords and local tyrants in the Liberated Areas fled to the Kuomintang areas. They were organized by the Kuomintang into "home-going contingents", "home-going legions" and other reactionary armed bands to attack the Liberated Areas together with the Kuomintang troops. Everywhere they robbed, killed and committed all kinds of atrocities.

THE TRUTH ABOUT U.S. "MEDIATION" AND THE FUTURE OF THE CIVIL WAR IN CHINA

Talk with the American Correspondent A. T. Steele

September 29, 1946

Steele: Sir, do you consider that the U.S. effort to mediate in the Chinese civil war has failed? If the policy of the United States continues as at present, what will it lead to?

Mao: I doubt very much that the policy of the U.S. government is one of "mediation".[1] Judging by the large amount of aid the United States is giving Chiang Kai-shek to enable him to wage a civil war on an unprecedented scale, the policy of the U.S. government is to use the so-called mediation as a smoke-screen for strengthening Chiang Kai-shek in every way and suppressing the democratic forces in China through Chiang Kai-shek's policy of slaughter so as to reduce China virtually to a U.S. colony. The continuation of this policy will certainly arouse the firm resistance of all patriotic people throughout China.

Steele: How long will the Chinese civil war go on? What will be its outcome?

Mao: If the U.S. government abandons its present policy of aiding Chiang Kai-shek, withdraws its forces now stationed in China and carries out the agreement reached at the Moscow Conference of the Foreign Ministers of the Soviet Union, the United States and Britain,[2] the Chinese civil war is sure to end at an early date. Otherwise it may turn into a long war. This would of course bring suffering to the Chinese people, but on the other hand, the Chinese people would certainly unite, fight for survival and decide their own fate. Whatever

109

the difficulties and hardships, the Chinese people will certainly fulfil their task of achieving independence, peace and democracy. No forces of suppression, domestic or foreign, can prevent the fulfilment of this task.

Steele: Sir, do you consider Chiang Kai-shek the "natural leader" of the Chinese people? Is the Communist Party of China going to reject Chiang Kai-shek's five demands[3] in all circumstances? If the Kuomintang tries to convene a National Assembly without the participation of the Communist Party,[4] what action will the Communist Party take?

Mao: There is no such thing in the world as a "natural leader". If Chiang Kai-shek deals with the political, military, economic and other problems of China in accordance with the truce agreement[5] signed last January and the joint resolutions then adopted by the Political Consultative Conference,[6] and not in accordance with the so-called "five demands" or ten demands, which are one-sided and run counter to the agreement and joint resolutions, we will still be willing to work with him. The National Assembly must be convened jointly by various political parties, in line with the resolutions adopted by the Political Consultative Conference; otherwise we will firmly oppose it.

NOTES

[1] In December 1945 the U.S. government sent George C. Marshall to China as the president's special representative and used "mediation in the hostilities between the Kuomintang and the Communist Party of China" as a cover for strengthening the U.S. forces of aggression and the reactionary Kuomintang rule in various ways. To gain time to prepare for his civil war, Chiang Kai-shek, prompted by U.S. imperialism, pretended to accept the demand of the Chinese Communist Party and the Chinese people to stop the civil war. In January 1946 representatives of the Kuomintang government and the Chinese Communist Party signed a truce agreement, issued a cease-fire order and formed the "Committee of Three" and the "Peiping Executive Headquarters" with the participation of U.S. representatives. During the "mediation", Marshall resorted to all kinds of ruses to help the Kuomintang forces attack the Liberated Areas, first in northeastern China and later in northern, eastern and central China; he actively trained and equipped the Kuomintang troops and supplied Chiang Kai-shek with a vast amount of arms and other war matériel. By June 1946 Chiang Kai-shek had massed 80 per cent of his regular forces (which were about two million men) at the front for attacks on the Liberated Areas; more than 540,000 of these troops were transported directly by the warships and planes of the U.S. armed forces. In July, when the disposition of his troops had

been completed, Chiang Kai-shek launched a country-wide counter-revolutionary war. Subsequently, on August 10, Marshall and Leighton Stuart, U.S. ambassador to China, issued a joint statement declaring that "mediation" had failed in order to give Chiang Kai-shek a free hand to wage civil war.

[2] This refers to the agreement on China reached at the Moscow Conference of the Foreign Ministers of the Soviet Union, the United States and Britain in December 1945. In the conference communiqué the three foreign ministers "reaffirmed their adherence to the policy of non-interference in the internal affairs of China". The foreign ministers of the Soviet Union and the United States agreed that Soviet and U.S. forces should be withdrawn from China at the earliest possible time. The Soviet Union faithfully carried out the terms of this agreement. It was only because of repeated requests from the Kuomintang government that the Soviet forces postponed the date of withdrawal. On May 3, 1946, the armed forces of the Soviet Union completed their withdrawal from northeastern China. But the U.S. government broke its promise completely, refused to withdraw its troops and stepped up its interference in China's internal affairs.

[3] On two occasions, in June and August 1946, Chiang Kai-shek put forward his "five demands" to the Chinese Communist Party, declaring that only if the Communist Party accepted them would the Kuomintang consider stopping the civil war. The five demands stipulated that the Chinese People's Liberation Army withdraw from the following places: (1) all areas south of the Lunghai Railway; (2) the entire length of the Tsingtao-Tsinan Railway; (3) Chengteh and the area south of it; (4) most of northeastern China; and (5) all areas liberated since June 7, 1946, from the puppet troops in Shantung and Shansi Provinces by the people's armed forces of the Liberated Areas. The Chinese Communist Party categorically rejected all these counter-revolutionary demands.

[4] According to the resolution of the Political Consultative Conference held in January 1946, the National Assembly was to be an assembly of democracy and unity, in which various political parties would take part, and was to be convened under the auspices of a reorganized government after the terms of the agreements reached at the Political Consultative Conference had been carried out. On October 11, 1946, the Kuomintang troops occupied Changchiakou, and this "victory" turned the heads of the Chiang Kai-shek clique. On that very afternoon it openly violated the terms of the PCC resolution and ordered the convening of a divisive and dictatorial "National Assembly" controlled exclusively by the Kuomintang. Officially opened in Nanking on November 15, 1946, this "National Assembly" was firmly opposed and boycotted by the Chinese Communist Party, the democratic parties and the entire people.

[5] See "Smash Chiang Kai-shek's Offensive by a War of Self-Defence", Note 1, p. 92 of this volume.

[6] See the same article, Note 2, pp. 92-95 of this volume.

A THREE MONTHS' SUMMARY*

October 1, 1946

1. The Central Committee's directive of July 20 on the current situation[1] stated: "We can defeat Chiang Kai-shek. The whole Party should be fully confident of this." The fighting in July, August and September has proved this judgement to be correct.

2. Apart from the fundamental political and economic contradictions which Chiang Kai-shek cannot resolve and which are the basic cause rendering our victory certain and Chiang's defeat inevitable, a sharp contradiction has arisen in the military sphere between Chiang's over-extended battle lines and his shortage of troops. That contradiction is bound to be the direct cause of our victory and Chiang Kai-shek's defeat.

3. The total of Chiang Kai-shek's regular troops attacking the Liberated Areas, not counting the puppet troops, the peace preservation corps and communications police corps, is more than 190 brigades. Besides this total, the most he can do is again to move part of his troops from the south to the north as reinforcements; but after that it will be hard for him to send any more reinforcements. Of the 190 odd brigades, 25 have been wiped out by our army in the past three months. This does not include the forces we wiped out in the Northeast from February to June this year.

4. Of Chiang Kai-shek's more than 190 brigades, nearly half must perform garrison duties; only a little more than half can be put into the field. And when these field forces advance to certain regions, part or even a majority will have to switch over to garrison duty. The enemy's field forces are bound to dwindle as the fighting goes on because, first, they will be continually wiped out by us and, second, many will have to perform garrison duties.

5. Of the 25 brigades we destroyed in the past three months, 7 were under the command of Tang En-po (previously under Li Mo-an),

113

2 under Hsueh Yueh, 7 under Ku Chu-tung (previously under Liu Chih), 2 under Hu Tsung-nan, 4 under Yen Hsi-shan, 2 under Wang Yao-wu and 1 under Tu Yu-ming. Only the 4 groups under Li Tsung-jen, Fu Tso-yi, Ma Hung-kuei and Cheng Chien have not yet received crushing blows from our army; all the remaining 7 groups have received serious blows or initial blows. Those who have received serious blows are Tu Yu-ming (taking into account the fighting in the Northeast from February to June this year), Tang En-po, Ku Chu-tung and Yen Hsi-shan. Those who have received initial blows are Hsueh Yueh, Hu Tsung-nan and Wang Yao-wu. All this proves that our army can defeat Chiang Kai-shek.

6. In the coming period our task is to wipe out some 25 more enemy brigades. The completion of this task will make it possible to halt Chiang Kai-shek's offensive and recover part of our lost territory. It can be predicted that after wiping out this second batch of 25 brigades our army will certainly be able to seize the strategic initiative and go over from the defensive to the offensive. Our task then will be to destroy a third batch of 25 enemy brigades. If we achieve that, we can recover most or even all of the lost territory and expand the Liberated Areas. By that time a tremendous change will surely have taken place in the relative military strength of the Kuomintang and the Communist Party. To attain this we must follow up our great achievement of wiping out 25 brigades in the past three months and destroy about 25 more in the coming three months or so. This is the key to changing the situation as between the enemy and ourselves.[2]

7. In the past three months we have lost a few dozen medium and small towns, such as Huaiyin, Hotse, Chengteh and Chining. The abandonment of most of these towns was unavoidable and it was right to abandon them temporarily on our own initiative. Some others we were forced to abandon because we did not fight well. In any case, we shall be able to recover our lost territory, provided we fight

---

* This inner-Party directive was drafted by Comrade Mao Tse-tung for the Central Committee of the Communist Party of China. It summed up in detail the series of experiences in the three months of fighting beginning with the outbreak of the country-wide civil war in July 1946, set forth the strategy and fighting tasks of the People's Liberation Army from then on and pointed out that after overcoming a period of difficulties we were certain to win victory in the People's War of Liberation. The directive also explained in principle the problems which needed to be solved for the support of and in co-ordination with the People's War of Liberation, such as land reform, the development of production in the Liberated Areas, the strengthening of leadership in the mass struggles in the Kuomintang areas and other relevant problems.

well from now on.   In the future there may still be places we cannot prevent the enemy from taking, but we shall be able to recover all of them later.   All areas should critically review their past experience in fighting in order to draw lessons and avoid repeating mistakes.

8.   In the past three months our Central Plains Liberation Army has shown matchless stamina in overcoming difficulties and hardships and, aside from that part of the army which has moved into the old Liberated Areas, its main force has established two guerrilla bases in southern Shensi and western Hupeh.[3]   Moreover, in both eastern and central Hupeh our troops are persisting in guerrilla warfare. All this has greatly helped, and is still helping, the fighting in the old Liberated Areas, and it will play a greater role in the long war ahead.

9.   In the past three months of war we have pinned down south of the Great Wall several of Chiang Kai-shek's crack forces, which he had originally planned to send to the Northeast, and have thus gained time for resting and consolidating our troops and for arousing the masses in the Northeast.   This, too, is of great significance for our future struggles.

10.   To concentrate a superior force to wipe out the enemy forces one by one is the only correct method of fighting, the method we have used in the past three months to destroy 25 enemy brigades.   Only by concentrating a force six, five, four or at least three times as strong as the enemy's force can we be effective in wiping it out.   This must be done both in campaigns and in battles.   This method of fighting must be mastered not only by all high-ranking commanders but also by all middle and lower-ranking cadres.

11.   In the past three months, in addition to 25 regular brigades of the enemy, our army has destroyed considerable numbers of reactionary forces, such as puppet troops, peace preservation corps and communications police corps; this also is a great achievement.   We should continue to annihilate such troops in large numbers.

12.   The experience of the past three months has proved that in order to wipe out 10,000 enemy troops we have to pay a price of 2,000 to 3,000 casualties of our own.   This is unavoidable.   To cope with a long war (and everything, everywhere should be considered with such a war in mind) we must expand our army in a planned way, ensure that our main forces are always kept at full strength and train large numbers of military cadres.   We must develop production and regulate finances according to plan and firmly put into effect the principles of developing our economy and ensuring supply, of unified

leadership and decentralized management and of giving consideration to both the army and the people and to both public and private interests.

13.   The experience of these three months has proved that higher fighting efficiency was shown by all troops who, during the period of the truce from January to June, intensified their military training according to the directives of the Central Committee (which has repeatedly instructed the various areas to regard troop training, production and land reform as their three central tasks). It has also proved that all troops not so trained showed much lower fighting efficiency. From now on, all areas must utilize the intervals between battles for intensified military training. All army units must strengthen their political work.

14.   The experience of these three months has proved that the peasants stood with our Party and our army against the attacks of Chiang Kai-shek's troops wherever the Central Committee's directive of May 4[4] was carried out firmly and speedily and the land problem was solved radically and thoroughly. The peasants took a wait-and-see attitude wherever the "May 4th Directive" was not carried out firmly or the arrangements were made too late, or wherever this work was mechanically divided into stages or land reform was neglected on the excuse of preoccupation with the war. In the coming few months all areas, no matter how busy they are with the war, must resolutely lead the peasant masses to solve the land problem and, on the basis of the land reform, make arrangements for large-scale production work next year.

15.   The experience of these three months has proved that wherever the regional armed forces, including the people's militia, the guerrillas and the armed working teams,[5] are well organized, we can control vast rural areas even though many points and lines are temporarily occupied by the enemy. But wherever the regional armed forces are weak and the leadership is poor, the enemy is given a much easier time. From now on, in areas temporarily occupied by the enemy, we must strengthen the Party's leadership, develop the regional armed forces, persevere in guerrilla warfare, safeguard the interests of the masses and strike blows at the activities of the reactionaries.

16.   Three months of war have almost exhausted the reserve forces of the Kuomintang and seriously weakened its military strength in its own areas. At the same time, the Kuomintang's resumption of conscription and grain levies[6] has aroused popular discontent and created a situation favourable for the development of mass struggles.

The whole Party must strengthen its leadership of the mass struggles in the Kuomintang areas and intensify the work of disintegrating the Kuomintang army.

17. The Kuomintang reactionaries, under the direction of the United States, have violated the truce agreement and the resolutions of the Political Consultative Conference of January this year and are determined to wage the civil war in their attempt to destroy the people's democratic forces. All their fine words are nothing but humbug; we must expose all the plots of the United States and Chiang Kai-shek.

18. In these three months the broadest strata of the people in the Kuomintang areas, including the national bourgeoisie,[7] have quickly arrived at a better understanding of the fact that the Kuomintang and the United States government are working in collusion, have started the civil war and are oppressing the people. More and more people now realize the truth that Marshall's mediation is a fraud and that the Kuomintang is the arch-criminal of the civil war. The broad masses, disillusioned with the United States and the Kuomintang, now place their hopes on the victory of our Party. This domestic political situation is extremely favourable. The reactionary policy of U.S. imperialism is rousing increasing discontent among the broad masses of the people in all countries. The level of political consciousness of the people in all countries is rising every day. The people's democratic struggle is mounting in all capitalist countries, the strength of the Communist Parties in many countries has greatly increased, and it will be impossible for the reactionaries to reduce them to submission. The might of the Soviet Union and its prestige among the peoples are growing daily. The U.S. reactionaries and the reactionaries whom they support in other countries are bound to become more and more isolated. This international political situation is extremely favourable. The situation both at home and abroad differs greatly from that after World War I. The revolutionary forces have grown tremendously since World War II. We can defeat the Chinese and foreign reactionaries, no matter how rampant they are (this rampancy is historically inevitable and not at all strange). Leading comrades in all areas should explain this fully to those comrades in the Party who are gloomy about the future of the struggle owing to their inadequate understanding of the favourable situation at home and abroad. It must be made clear that the enemy still has strength, that we ourselves still have some weaknesses and that the struggle is still a long and cruel one. But we can certainly

win victory. This understanding and conviction must be firmly established throughout the Party.

19. The coming few months will be an important and difficult period. We must strenuously mobilize the whole Party, undertake meticulously planned military operations and radically change the military situation. All areas must resolutely carry out the above policies and strive for a radical change in the military situation.

NOTES

[1] See "Smash Chiang Kai-shek's Offensive by a War of Self-Defence", pp. 89-95 of this volume.

[2] Later developments showed that the situation between the enemy and ourselves began to change in July 1947, when the Shansi-Hopei-Shantung-Honan People's Liberation Army forced the Yellow River and marched towards the Tapieh Mountains. By then the People's Liberation Army had fought for twelve months and wiped out about a hundred enemy brigades, averaging eight a month. This exceeded the estimate made in this article because, with the support of U.S. imperialism, Chiang Kai-shek had used all his available forces in the offensive.

[3] At the end of June 1946 the Central Plains Liberation Army led by Li Hsien-nien, Cheng Wei-san and other comrades initiated a strategic shift of its forces and victoriously broke through an encirclement by 300,000 Kuomintang troops. The units mentioned by Comrade Mao Tse-tung as having moved into the old Liberated Areas were those led by Wang Chen and other comrades; they entered the Shensi-Kansu-Ningsia Border Region after breaking through the encirclement. The guerrilla base in southern Shensi was founded by a part of the main force of the Central Plains Liberation Army and included Lushih and Hsichuan in western Honan and Lonan and Shanyang in southern Shensi. The guerrilla base in western Hupeh was set up by another part of the same army with the Wutang Mountains in northwestern Hupeh as its centre.

[4] This refers to the "Directive on the Land Question" issued by the Central Committee of the Communist Party of China on May 4, 1946. After Japan's surrender, in view of the peasants' eager demand for land, the Central Committee decided to change the land policy of the period of the War of Resistance, that is, to change from the reduction of rent and interest to confiscation of the land of the landlords and its distribution among the peasants. The "May 4th Directive" marked this change.

[5] The armed working teams were small working teams which went deep into the enemy-occupied areas to organize the masses and strike blows at the enemy. Such a team consisted of cadres drawn from various organizations – the Communist Party, the governments in the Liberated Areas, the people's army and mass organizations – and was equipped with some weapons. This was a convenient form of organization for carrying out activities in the enemy-occupied areas.

[6] This refers to land taxes in kind.

[7] The national bourgeoisie is the section of the bourgeoisie which has little or no connection with imperialism, as distinguished from that section of the bourgeoisie which is closely dependent on imperialism and is comprador in character, that is, the big bourgeoisie or bureaucrat-capitalists.

GREET THE NEW HIGH TIDE OF
THE CHINESE REVOLUTION*

February 1, 1947

1. All circumstances now show that the situation in China is about to enter a new stage of development. This new stage is one in which the country-wide struggle against imperialism and feudalism will develop into a great new people's revolution. We are now on the eve of this revolution. The task of our Party is to struggle for the advent of this high tide and its triumph.

2. The military situation has now developed in a direction favourable to the people. In seven months of fighting, from last July to this January, we wiped out 56 brigades of Chiang Kai-shek's regular forces which invaded the Liberated Areas, a monthly average of 8 brigades, not counting the numerous puppet troops and the peace preservation corps which were wiped out and those of Chiang's regular forces which were routed. Although Chiang Kai-shek's offensive continues in southern and western Shantung, in the Shensi-Kansu-Ningsia Border Region, along the northern section of the Peiping-Hankow Railway and in southern Manchuria, it has become much feebler than it was last autumn. Chiang Kai-shek's army does not have enough troops to dispose and cannot fulfil its conscription quotas; this fact is in serious contradiction with its extended battle lines and the enormous drain on its manpower. The morale of Chiang's army is sinking lower every day. During the recent fighting in northern Kiangsu, southern and western Shantung and western Shansi, the morale of many of Chiang's forces sank to a very low level. On several fronts our armies are beginning to seize the initiative, while Chiang Kai-shek's armies are beginning to lose it. We can foresee that in the next few months we may achieve the objective of wiping out a grand total of 100 of Chiang's brigades, including those previously destroyed. Chiang Kai-shek has altogether 93 regular infantry and cavalry divisions

119

(corps), composed of 248 brigades (divisions), totalling 1,916,000 men, not counting the puppet troops, police, local peace preservation corps, communications police corps, rear services and technical arms. The forces attacking the Liberated Areas number 78 divisions (corps), composed of 218 brigades (divisions), totalling 1,713,000 men, or about 90 per cent of Chiang Kai-shek's regular troops. Only 15 divisions, with 30 brigades, totalling 203,000 men, or about 10 per cent of the total, remain in the Kuomintang rear areas. Therefore, Chiang Kai-shek can no longer send large combat-worthy reinforcements from his rear areas to attack the Liberated Areas. We have already wiped out more than a quarter of the 218 brigades attacking the Liberated Areas. Although some have been replenished and restored under their original designations after having been wiped out, their combat effectiveness is very low. Some have been wiped out a second time. Some have not been replenished at all. If our armies can wipe out another 40 to 50 brigades in the next few months and bring the grand total up to about 100, there will be an important change in the military situation.

3. Meanwhile, a great people's movement is unfolding in the Kuomintang areas. The riots of the people in Shanghai,[1] which began on November 30 of last year as a result of the Kuomintang's persecution of the street vendors, and the student movement in Peiping, which began last December 30 as a result of the rape of a Chinese girl student by U.S. soldiers,[2] both mark a new upsurge in the struggle of the people in the Chiang Kai-shek areas. The student movement which began in Peiping has spread to other big cities all over the country, with hundreds of thousands taking part and on a larger scale than the December 9th Student Movement against Japanese imperialism.[3]

4. The victories of the People's Liberation Army in the Liberated Areas and the development of the people's movement in the Kuomintang areas foretell that a great new people's revolution against imperialism and feudalism is surely approaching and can be victorious.

5. The circumstances in which this situation has arisen are that U.S. imperialism and its running dog Chiang Kai-shek have replaced Japanese imperialism and its running dog Wang Ching-wei and adopted the policies of turning China into a U.S. colony, launching a civil war and strengthening the fascist dictatorship. Confronted by these reactionary policies of U.S. imperialism and Chiang Kai-shek,

---

* This inner-Party directive was drafted by Comrade Mao Tse-tung for the Central Committee of the Communist Party of China.

the Chinese people have no way out except through struggle. The struggle for independence, peace and democracy still constitutes the basic demand of the Chinese people in the present period. As far back as April 1945, our Party's Seventh National Congress foresaw the possibility that U.S. imperialism and Chiang Kai-shek would carry out these reactionary policies and formulated a complete and fully correct political line to defeat them.

6. These reactionary policies of U.S. imperialism and Chiang Kai-shek have forced all strata of the Chinese people to unite for their own salvation. These strata include the workers, peasants, urban petty bourgeoisie, national bourgeoisie, enlightened gentry, other patriotic elements, the minority nationalities and overseas Chinese. This is a very broad united front of the whole nation. In comparison with the united front in the period of the War of Resistance Against Japan, it is not only as broad in scope but has even deeper foundations. All Party comrades must strive to consolidate and develop this united front. In the Liberated Areas the policy of the "three thirds system"[4] is to remain unchanged, on the condition that the policy of land to the tillers is carried out resolutely and unhesitatingly. In addition to Communists, we should continue to draw the broad ranks of progressives outside the Party and the middle elements (such as the enlightened gentry) into the organs of political power and into social undertakings. In the Liberated Areas, all citizens, irrespective of class, sex or belief, have the right to elect and stand for election, except traitors and those reactionaries who have opposed the interests of the people and incurred their bitter hatred. After the system of land to the tillers has been thoroughly carried out, the right to private property of the people in the Liberated Areas will continue to be guaranteed.

7. Because the Chiang Kai-shek government has pursued reactionary financial and economic policies for a long time and because Chiang Kai-shek's bureaucrat-comprador capital[5] has become linked with U.S. imperialist capital through the notorious and treasonable Sino-U.S. Treaty of Commerce,[6] malignant inflation has swiftly developed; the industry and commerce of China's national bourgeoisie are daily going bankrupt; the livelihood of the working masses, government employees and teachers is deteriorating every day; large numbers of middle class elements are losing their savings and becoming penniless; and therefore strikes of workers and students and other struggles are constantly occurring. An economic crisis more serious than China has ever faced before is threatening all strata of the people.

In order to carry on the civil war, Chiang Kai-shek has restored the extremely vicious system of conscription and grain levies of the period of the War of Resistance; this makes life impossible for the vast rural population, particularly the poverty-stricken peasants; as a result, peasant revolts have already started and will continue to spread. Hence, the reactionary Chiang Kai-shek ruling clique will become more and more discredited in the eyes of the broad masses of the people and be confronted with serious political and military crises. On the one hand, this situation is daily pushing forward the people's anti-imperialist, anti-feudal movement in the areas under Chiang Kai-shek's control; on the other hand, it is further demoralizing Chiang's troops and increasing the possibility of victory by the People's Liberation Army.

8. The illegal and divisive "National Assembly", which was convened by Chiang Kai-shek in order to isolate our Party and other democratic forces, and the bogus constitution fabricated by that body enjoy no prestige at all among the people. Instead of isolating our Party and other democratic forces, they have isolated the reactionary Chiang Kai-shek ruling clique itself. Our Party and other democratic forces adopted the policy of refusing to participate in the bogus National Assembly; this was perfectly correct. The reactionary Chiang Kai-shek ruling clique has brought over to its side the Youth Party[7] and the Democratic Socialist Party,[8] two small parties which never had the slightest prestige in Chinese society, as well as certain so-called "public personages",[9] and it can be foreseen that some of the middle-of-the-roaders may also go over to the side of reaction. The reason is that the democratic forces in China are getting stronger and stronger while the reactionary forces are becoming more and more isolated, and therefore the line between the enemy and ourselves has to be so sharply drawn. All elements which hide in the democratic front and deceive the people will eventually be revealed in their true colours and be cast aside by the people; and the people's anti-imperialist and anti-feudal ranks will grow even stronger because they have drawn a clear line of demarcation between themselves and these hidden reactionaries.

9. The development of the international situation is extremely favourable for the Chinese people's struggle. The growing might of the Soviet Union and the successes of its foreign policy, the growing radicalization of the peoples of the world and their ever-developing struggles against reactionary forces both at home and abroad – these

two great factors have forced U.S. imperialism and its running dogs in various countries into ever greater isolation and will continue to do so. If one adds the factor of an inevitable economic crisis in the United States, then U.S. imperialism and its running dogs will be forced into an even worse predicament. The power of U.S. imperialism and its running dog Chiang Kai-shek is only temporary; their offensives can be smashed. The myth that the offensives of the reactionaries cannot be smashed should have no place in our ranks. The Central Committee has pointed this out time and again, and the development of the international and domestic situation has increasingly borne out the correctness of this judgement.

10. In order to gain a respite in which to replenish his troops and launch a fresh offensive, to obtain new loans and munitions from the United States and to allay the indignation of the people, Chiang Kai-shek is perpetrating a new hoax by demanding the resumption of so-called peace negotiations with our Party.[10] Our Party's policy is not to refuse negotiations and in this way expose his deception.

11. In order to smash Chiang Kai-shek's offensive thoroughly, we must wipe out another forty to fifty of his brigades in the next few months; this is the key that will decide everything. To achieve this objective, we must put into full effect the Central Committee's directive of October 1 last year, "A Three Months' Summary",[11] and the Military Commission's directive of September 16 last year on concentrating our forces to destroy the enemy forces one by one.[12] Here, we are once again emphasizing a few points for the attention of the comrades in all areas:

(a) The Military Problem. In the past seven months of bitter fighting our army has proved that it can certainly smash Chiang Kai-shek's offensive and win final victory. Our army has improved in both equipment and tactics. From now on, the central task in building our armed forces is to make every effort to step up the building of our artillery and engineer corps. All military areas, big and small, and all field armies should solve the concrete problems involved in strengthening the artillery and engineer corps and, first of all, the two problems of training cadres and manufacturing ammunition.

(b) The Land Problem. In about two-thirds of the territory in each Liberated Area, the Central Committee's directive of May 4, 1946,[13] has been put into effect, the land problem has been solved and the policy of land to the tillers has been carried out; this is a great victory. There remains around one-third of the territory, however, where further efforts must be made to arouse the masses fully and put the policy of land to the tillers into effect. In places where the policy of land to the tillers has been carried out, there are still shortcomings insofar as the solution was not thorough – mainly because the masses were not fully aroused, so that the confiscation and the distribution of land were not thorough and the masses became dissatisfied. In such places, we must check carefully and must "even up"[14] to ensure that the peasants with little or no land obtain some and the bad gentry and local tyrants are punished. In the entire process of carrying out the policy of land to the tillers, we must unite firmly with the middle peasants, and it is absolutely impermissible to encroach on the interests of the middle peasants (including the well-to-do middle peasants); if cases occur where the interests of the middle peasants are encroached upon, there must be compensation and apology. Moreover, during and after the land reform, appropriate consideration in accordance with the will of the masses should be given to ordinary rich peasants and middle and small landlords, and it should be given in accordance with the "May 4th Directive". To sum up, in the land reform movement in the rural areas we must unite with the more than 90 per cent of the masses who support the reform and isolate the small number of feudal reactionaries who oppose it so that we can speedily realize the policy of land to the tillers.

(c) The Production Problem. All places must plan on a long-term basis, work hard at production, practise economy and correctly solve the financial problem on the basis of production and economy. The first principle here is to develop production and ensure supply. For this reason, we must oppose the wrong view which lays one-sided emphasis on finance and commerce and neglects agricultural and industrial production. The second principle is to give consideration to both the army and the people, to both public and private interests. Therefore, we must oppose the wrong view which takes only one side into account and neglects the other. The third principle is unified leadership and decentralized management. Therefore, except where conditions call for centralized management, we must oppose the wrong view which favours centralizing everything, regardless of circumstances, and which dares not give full rein to decentralized management.

12. Our Party and the Chinese people have every assurance of final victory; there is not the slightest doubt about it. But that does not mean there are no difficulties before us. China's anti-imperialist and anti-feudal struggle is protracted in nature, Chinese and foreign

reactionaries will continue to oppose the Chinese people with all their strength, fascist rule in the areas under Chiang Kai-shek's control will be intensified; certain parts of the Liberated Areas will temporarily become enemy-occupied areas or guerrilla zones, some of the revolutionary forces may suffer temporary losses, and there will be losses of manpower and material resources in a long war. The comrades throughout the Party must take all this fully into account and be prepared to overcome all difficulties with an indomitable will and in a planned way. The reactionary forces and we both have difficulties. But the difficulties of the reactionary forces are insurmountable because they are forces on the verge of death and have no future. Our difficulties can be overcome because we are new and rising forces and have a bright future.

NOTES

[1] Beginning in August 1946 the Kuomintang authorities in Shanghai forbade the street vendors in the Whangpoo and Louza districts to carry on their business. In late November nearly a thousand who were still operating were arrested. On November 30 three thousand street vendors demonstrated and surrounded the Whangpoo district police station. The Kuomintang authorities gave the order to fire; seven demonstrators were killed and a great many were wounded and arrested. On December 1, the street vendors continued their struggle. Despite the fact that ten more were killed and over a hundred wounded, the number taking part in the struggle grew to over five thousand. All shops in Shanghai closed down to show sympathy. Thus the incident developed into a city-wide mass movement against Chiang Kai-shek.

[2] This incident occurred in Peiping on December 24, 1946. A girl student of Peking University was raped by U.S. soldiers. Consequently, from December 30 through January 1947, students in scores of big and medium cities in the Kuomintang areas struck and demonstrated against the United States and Chiang Kai-shek, demanding the withdrawal of U.S. troops from China. More than half a million students took part in this movement.

[3] In 1935 a new upsurge began in the patriotic movement of the people of the whole country. Students in Peking, under the leadership of the Communist Party of China, were the first to hold a patriotic demonstration on December 9, putting forward such slogans as "Stop the civil war and unite to resist foreign aggression" and "Down with Japanese imperialism!" This movement broke open the long reign of terror imposed by the Kuomintang government in league with the Japanese invaders and soon won the support of the people throughout the country. It is known as the "December 9th Movement". As a consequence, new changes became manifest in the relations among various classes in the country, and the Anti-Japanese National United Front proposed by the Communist Party of China became the openly advocated policy of

all patriotic people. The Kuomintang government became very isolated with its traitorous policy.

⁴ The "three thirds system" was the Chinese Communist Party's policy for united front organs of political power in the Liberated Areas during the War of Resistance Against Japan. According to this policy, the proportion of personnel in the anti-Japanese democratic political organs was about one-third each for Communist Party members, for left progressives, and for middle elements and others.

⁵ See "The Present Situation and Our Tasks", Section 6, pp. 167-69 of this volume.

⁶ The "Sino-U.S. Treaty of Commerce" or "Sino-U.S. Treaty of Friendship, Commerce and Navigation" was concluded between the Chiang Kai-shek government and the U.S. government on November 4, 1946, in Nanking. This treaty, which sold out a large part of China's sovereignty to the United States, contains thirty articles, the main contents of which are as follows:

(1)   U.S. nationals shall enjoy in "the whole extent of . . . the territories" of China the rights to reside, travel, carry on commercial, manufacturing, processing, scientific, educational, religious and philanthropic activities, explore and exploit mineral resources, lease and hold land, and follow various occupations and pursuits. In regard to economic rights U.S. nationals in China shall be accorded the same treatment as Chinese.

(2)   In respect of taxation, sale, distribution and use in China, U.S. commodities shall be accorded treatment no less favourable than that accorded to the commodities of any third country or to Chinese commodities. "No prohibition or restriction shall be imposed" by China on the importation from the United States of any article grown, produced or manufactured in the United States, or on the exportation to the United States of any Chinese article.

(3)   U.S. vessels shall have the freedom of sailing in any of the ports, places or waters in China which are open to foreign commerce or navigation, and their personnel and freight shall have freedom of transit through Chinese territory "by the routes most convenient". On the pretext of "any . . . distress", U.S. vessels, including warships, can sail into "any of the ports, places or waters" of China which are "not open to foreign commerce or navigation".

Wellington Koo, then Chiang Kai-shek's ambassador to the United States, openly and shamelessly stated that this treaty meant "the opening of the entire territory of China to U.S. merchants".

⁷ The Youth Party was the shortened name of the Chinese Youth Party, also called the *Étatiste* Party; its predecessor was the Chinese *Étatiste* Youth League. This party was composed of a handful of fascist politicians. They made counter-revolutionary careers for themselves by opposing the Communist Party and the Soviet Union and therefore received subsidies from various groups of reactionaries in power and from the imperialists.

⁸ The Democratic Socialist Party was formed in August 1946 through the merger of the Democratic Constitutional Party and the National Socialist Party. It consisted mainly of reactionary politicians and feudal dregs from the time of the Northern warlords.

⁹ "Certain so-called public personages" refers to shameless politicians like Wang Yun-wu, Fu Sze-nien and Hu Cheng-chih, who posed as persons with no party affiliation and served as a window-dressing for Chiang Kai-shek's "National Assembly".

¹⁰ On January 16, 1947, because of repeated setbacks in its military offensives and because of its worsening military situation, the Kuomintang government, in an

attempt to gain a respite and prepare a fresh offensive, asked the Chinese Communist Party, through the U.S. ambassador to China, Leighton Stuart, for permission to send delegates to Yenan for "peace negotiations". This new U.S.-Chiang deception was promptly and thoroughly exposed by the Chinese Communist Party. The Chinese Communist Party pointed out that negotiations could be renewed only if two minimum conditions were fulfilled: (1) the bogus constitution framed and adopted by the Kuomintang in violation of the resolutions of the Political Consultative Conference had to be abolished, and (2) Kuomintang troops had to evacuate all the territory of the Liberated Areas they had occupied since the truce agreement went into effect on January 13, 1946; otherwise, there would be no guarantee that the Kuomintang would not again tear up any agreement reached in renewed negotiations. The Kuomintang government realized that the ruse of "peace" did not work and on February 27 and 28 it notified all the representatives of the Chinese Communist Party stationed in Nanking, Shanghai and Chungking for negotiations and liaison that they had to leave and announced the complete breakdown of the negotiations between the Kuomintang and the Communist Party.

[11] This refers to the article, "A Three Months' Summary", pp. 113-18 of this volume.

[12] This refers to the article, "Concentrate a Superior Force to Destroy the Enemy Forces One by One", pp. 103-07 of this volume.

[13] This refers to the "Directive on the Land Question" of the Central Committee of the Chinese Communist Party dated May 4, 1946. See "A Three Months' Summary", Note 4, p. 118 of this volume.

[14] "Evening up" was a policy adopted in the old Liberated Areas, where a comparatively thorough land reform had been carried out. The purpose was to solve the problem of insufficient land and other means of production among some of the poor peasants and farm labourers and other problems left over from the reform. The method was, on a limited scale, to take from those who had better and give to those who had worse, to take from those who had a surplus and give to those who had a shortage, so that the distribution of land and other means of production could be rationally readjusted.

ON THE TEMPORARY ABANDONMENT OF YENAN AND THE DEFENCE OF THE SHENSI-KANSU-NINGSIA BORDER REGION — TWO DOCUMENTS ISSUED BY THE CENTRAL COMMITTEE OF THE COMMUNIST PARTY OF CHINA*

November 1946 and April 1947

I.   DIRECTIVE OF NOVEMBER 18, 1946

Chiang Kai-shek is at the end of his rope.   He wants to strike at our Party and strengthen himself by two methods, by convening the "National Assembly" and by attacking Yenan.   Actually, he will accomplish the very opposite.   The Chinese people resolutely oppose the "National Assembly" stage-managed by Chiang Kai-shek to split the nation; the opening day of that assembly marked the beginning of the self-destruction of the Chiang Kai-shek clique.   Now that we have wiped out thirty-five brigades[1] of Chiang Kai-shek's troops and their offensive power is nearly exhausted, even if his troops should occupy Yenan by means of a sudden thrust, it would not damage the general prospect of victory in the People's War of Liberation, nor could it save Chiang Kai-shek from the doom awaiting him.   In short, Chiang Kai-shek has taken the road to ruin; as soon as he makes these two moves of convening the "National Assembly" and attacking Yenan, all his trickery will be exposed; this will help the progress of the People's War of Liberation.   In every area we should fully explain to people inside and outside the Party these two actions of Chiang Kai-shek, the convening of the "National Assembly" and the attack on Yenan, and unite the whole Party, the whole army and the whole people in the fight to smash Chiang Kai-shek's offensive and build a democratic China.

II.   CIRCULAR OF APRIL 9, 1947

In order to save its moribund regime, the Kuomintang, besides taking such steps as convening the bogus National Assembly, drawing up the bogus constitution, driving out the representative agencies of our Party from Nanking, Shanghai and Chungking and proclaiming a break between the Kuomintang and the Communist Party,[2] has taken the further step of attacking Yenan, the seat of our Party's Central Committee and the General Headquarters of the People's Liberation Army, and of attacking the Shensi-Kansu-Ningsia Border Region.

The fact that the Kuomintang has taken these steps does not in the least indicate that its regime is strong but rather that the crisis of the Kuomintang regime has become extremely deep.   Its attack on Yenan and the Shensi-Kansu-Ningsia Border Region is moreover a vain attempt to settle the Northwest question first, cut off our Party's right arm, drive our Party's Central Committee and the General Head-quarters of the People's Liberation Army from the Northwest, then move its troops to attack northern China and so achieve the objective of defeating our forces one by one.

In these circumstances, the Central Committee has decided as follows:

---

* The first of these two documents was drafted by Comrade Mao Tse-tung in Yenan in the winter of 1946 when Kuomintang troops were preparing to attack that city, and the second at Chingyangcha, Hengshan County, northern Shensi, twenty days after Kuomintang troops occupied Yenan on March 19, 1947.   After the bank-ruptcy of Chiang Kai-shek's plan for an all-out offensive against the Liberated Areas, he adopted frantic measures to save his dying regime, convened a bogus National Assembly, expelled the representatives of the Communist Party of China from the Kuomintang areas and launched an attack on Yenan, the seat of the Central Committee of the Communist Party of China.   As these documents pointed out, the outcome of Chiang Kai-shek's measures was his complete self-destruction politically.   Militarily, he concentrated his forces on the eastern and western flanks of the Liberated Areas, that is, the Shantung Liberated Area and the Shensi-Kansu-Ningsia Liberated Area, in an attempt to carry out "attacks against key sectors"; and again the outcome was complete failure.   The Kuomintang troops attacking the Shensi-Kansu-Ningsia Border Region were more than 230,000 strong, while the Northwest People's Liberation Army had only some 20,000 in that region.   Therefore the enemy forces were able to occupy Yenan and all the region's county towns, which we abandoned on our own initiative. The enemy, however, failed to achieve his objective of destroying the headquarters of the Central Committee of the Communist Party of China and the Northwest People's Liberation Army or of driving them east of the Yellow River.   On the contrary, he suffered many heavy blows from our army, lost about 100,000 men and finally had to flee in confusion from the Border Region, while our army triumphantly went

1.   We must defend and expand the Shensi-Kansu-Ningsia Border Region and the Liberated Areas in the Northwest with a firm fighting spirit; it is entirely possible to achieve this objective.

2.   The Central Committee of our Party and the General Headquarters of the People's Liberation Army must remain in the Shensi-Kansu-Ningsia Border Region. It is an area where we have a favourable mountainous terrain, a good mass base, plenty of room for manoeuvre, and full guarantee for security.

3.   At the same time, to facilitate our work, we have set up a Working Committee of the Central Committee to proceed to northwestern Shansi or some other suitable place to carry out the tasks entrusted to it by the Central Committee.

These three decisions were made last month and have already been put into effect. You are hereby notified.

---

over to the offensive for the liberation of the Great Northwest.   Moreover, our army in the Northwest theatre, employing a very small force, pinned down and destroyed large numbers of the enemy's main force, and thereby strongly supported the operations of our troops in other theatres, particularly in the Shansi-Hopei-Shantung-Honan theatre, and helped them go over more quickly to the offensive. Comrade Mao Tse-tung, the Central Committee of the Communist Party of China and the General Headquarters of the People's Liberation Army remained in the Shensi-Kansu-Ningsia Border Region the whole time from March 1947, when our army withdrew from Yenan, to a year later when we went over to the offensive in the Northwest theatre.   This fact was of great political significance.   It greatly inspired and strengthened the will to fight and the confidence in victory of the army and the people in the Shensi-Kansu-Ningsia Border Region and in other Liberated Areas throughout the country.   While in the Shensi-Kansu-Ningsia Border Region, Comrade Mao Tse-tung not only continued to direct the People's War of Liberation on all fronts throughout the country but also took personal command in the Northwest theatre and successfully achieved the aim set forth in the present document, "defend and expand the Shensi-Kansu-Ningsia Border Region and the Liberated Areas in the Northwest with a firm fighting spirit".   Concerning the operations in the Northwest theatre, see "The Concept of Operations for the Northwest War Theatre", pp. 133-34 and "On the Great Victory in the Northwest and on the New Type of Ideological Education Movement in the Liberation Army", pp. 211-17, of this volume.

NOTES

[1] The statistics were for the period from early July to November 13, 1946.

[2] On February 27-28, 1947, the representatives and personnel of the Chinese Communist Party stationed in Nanking, Shanghai and Chungking for negotiations and liaison were forced by the Kuomintang government to leave within a stated time. On March 15, 1947, the Central Executive Committee of the Kuomintang convened its third plenary session, at which Chiang Kai-shek proclaimed the Kuomintang's break with the Communist Party and his determination to fight the civil war to the finish.

THE CONCEPT OF OPERATIONS FOR
THE NORTHWEST WAR THEATRE*

April 15, 1947

1. The enemy is now quite tired, but not yet tired out. He is in considerable difficulties with his food supply, but not yet in extreme difficulties. Although our army has not destroyed any large number of the enemy's forces since wiping out his 31st Brigade,[1] in the last twenty days we have achieved the objective of tiring him and considerably reducing his food supplies, thus creating favourable conditions for tiring him out completely, cutting off all his food supplies and finally wiping him out.

2. At present, despite the enemy's fatigue and shortage of food, his policy is to drive our main force east across the Yellow River, then seal off Suiteh and Michih and divide his forces for "mopping-up" operations. The enemy troops reached Chingchien on March 31 but did not advance north immediately; their purpose was to leave us a clear passage. Their advance west towards Wayaopao was designed to drive us to Suiteh and Michih. Having discovered our troops, they are now veering to the south and west of Wayaopao and then they will again advance towards that town to drive us northward.

3. Our policy is to continue our former method, that is, to keep the enemy on the run in this area for a time (about another month); the purpose is to tire him out completely, reduce his food supplies drastically and then look for an opportunity to destroy him. There is no need for our main force to hurry north to attack Yulin or south to cut off the enemy's retreat. It should be made clear to the commanders and fighters and also to the masses that this method of our army is the necessary road to the final defeat of the enemy. Unless we reduce the enemy to extreme fatigue and complete starvation, we cannot win final victory. This may be called the tactics of "wear and

133

tear", that is, of wearing the enemy down to complete exhaustion and then wiping him out.

4. As you are now in localities east and north of Wayaopao, it would be best to induce the enemy to move to the north of Wayaopao; then you may attack the weaker part of Liao Ang's[2] forces and induce the enemy to move east; afterwards you may turn towards Ansai, and induce the enemy to move west again.

5. But within a few days you must order the entire 359th Brigade to complete its preparations for a southward drive, so that a week from now it can be sent southward to make a surprise attack on the area south of the Yenchang-Yenan line and north of the Yichuan-Lochuan line and cut the enemy's food transport line.

6. Please reply whether you consider the above views sound.

NOTES

[1] Having withdrawn from Yenan on its own initiative, the Northwest People's Liberation Army sent out a small force to lure the enemy's main force as far as Ansai, northwest of Yenan, while leaving its main force to ambush the enemy in the Chinghuapien sector, northeast of Yenan. On March 25, 1947, a Kuomintang regiment of the 31st Brigade of Hu Tsung-nan's Reorganized 27th Division, led by the brigade headquarters, walked right into this trap and was completely destroyed in a battle lasting just over an hour.

[2] Liao Ang, Commander of the Reorganized 76th Division of the Kuomintang forces under Hu Tsung-nan, was later captured in a battle at Chingchien on October 11, 1947.

* This telegram was sent by Comrade Mao Tse-tung to the Northwest Field Army, which was then composed of the People's Liberation Army forces of the Shensi-Kansu-Ningsia and Shansi-Suiyuan Liberated Areas and commanded by Peng Teh-huai, Ho Lung, Hsi Chung-hsun and other comrades.

THE CHIANG KAI-SHEK GOVERNMENT
IS BESIEGED
BY THE WHOLE PEOPLE*

May 30, 1947

The Chiang Kai-shek government, hostile to the whole people, now finds itself besieged by the whole people. On both the military and political fronts, it has met defeats, is now besieged by the forces it has declared to be its enemies and can find no way of escape.

The traitorous Chiang Kai-shek clique and its master, U.S. imperialism, have wrongly appraised the situation. They overestimated their own strength and underestimated the strength of the people. They regarded China and the world after World War II as being the same as in the past; they would permit nothing to change nor anyone to go against their will. After Japan's surrender they were determined to restore the old order in China. And having gained time by such deceptions as political consultation and military mediation, the traitorous Chiang Kai-shek government mustered two million troops and launched an all-out offensive.

There are now two battle fronts in China. The war between Chiang Kai-shek's invading troops and the People's Liberation Army constitutes the first front. Now a second front has emerged, that is, the sharp struggle between the great and righteous student movement and the reactionary Chiang Kai-shek government.[1] The slogan of the student movement is "Food, Peace, Freedom" or "Against Hunger, Against Civil War, Against Persecution". Chiang Kai-shek has promulgated the "Provisional Measures for the Maintenance of Public Order".[2] Everywhere his army, police, gendarmes and secret agents are clashing with the student masses. Chiang Kai-shek is using brute force against unarmed students, subjecting them to arrest, imprisonment, beating and slaughter; as a result the student movement is daily growing in strength. Public sympathy is all on the side of the students, Chiang Kai-shek and his running dogs are completely isolated, and his ferocious features have been completely unmasked. The student movement is part of the whole people's movement. The upsurge of the student movement will inevitably promote an upsurge of the whole people's movement. This is borne out by the historical experience of the May 4th Movement of 1919 [3] and the December 9th Movement of 1935.

Since U.S. imperialism and its running dog Chiang Kai-shek have taken the place of Japanese imperialism and its running dog Wang Ching-wei and adopted the policies of turning China into a U.S. colony, launching a civil war and strengthening the fascist dictatorship, they have declared themselves to be enemies of the entire Chinese people and driven all strata of the people to the brink of starvation and death. This has compelled all strata of the people to unite in a life-and-death struggle against the reactionary Chiang Kai-shek government and brought about the speedy development of that struggle. For the people there is no other way out. The strata of the Chinese people oppressed by the reactionary policies of the Chiang Kai-shek government and united for their own salvation include the workers, peasants, urban petty bourgeoisie, national bourgeoisie, enlightened gentry, other patriotic elements, the minority nationalities and overseas Chinese. This is a very broad national united front.

The extremely reactionary financial and economic policies long pursued by the Chiang Kai-shek government have now been aggravated by the Sino-U.S. Treaty of Commerce, the most treasonable treaty ever known. On the basis of this treaty, U.S. monopoly capital and Chiang Kai-shek's bureaucrat-comprador capital have become tightly intertwined and control the economic life of the whole country. The results are unbridled inflation, unparalleled soaring prices, ever-spreading bankruptcy of the industry and commerce of the national bourgeoisie and daily deterioration in the livelihood of the working masses, government employees and teachers. In these circumstances all strata of the people cannot but unite and fight for their very survival.

Military suppression and political deception have been the two main instruments by which Chiang Kai-shek maintains his reactionary

---

* This commentary was written by Comrade Mao Tse-tung for the Hsinhua News Agency. It pointed out that the march of events in China was faster than people had expected and called upon the people to prepare speedily all necessary conditions for the country-wide victory of the Chinese revolution. This prediction was soon confirmed. Both this commentary and "The Concept of Operations for the Northwest War Theatre" were written at Wangchiawan, Chingpien County, northern Shensi.

rule. People are now witnessing the rapid collapse of both these instruments.

On every battlefield Chiang Kai-shek's army has met with defeat. About ninety brigades of his regular troops alone have been wiped out in the eleven months since last July. His troops no longer display the overweening pride of last year when they occupied Chang-chun, Chengteh, Changchiakou, Hotse, Huaiyin and Antung, or even of this year when they occupied Linyi and Yenan.   Chiang Kai-shek and Chen Cheng made a wrong appraisal of the strength and fighting methods of the People's Liberation Army. Mistaking our retreats for cowardice and our abandonment of a number of cities for defeats, they had fondly hoped to finish us off south of the Great Wall in three months or at most six, and then proceed to finish us off in the Northeast.   But after ten months, all Chiang Kai-shek's invading troops are in desperate straits; they are completely besieged by the people of the Liberated Areas and the People's Liberation Army and find it very difficult to escape.

As more and more news of the defeats of Chiang Kai-shek's troops at the front reaches his rear areas, the broad masses of the people there, suffocating under the oppression of his reactionary government, see more and more hope of ending their sufferings and winning their emancipation. At this very time, all Chiang Kai-shek's political tricks are failing as fast as he plays them. Everything has gone against the expectations of the reactionaries. Such steps as convening a "National Assembly" to adopt a "constitution", reorganizing the one-party government into a "multi-party government" and what not, were originally aimed at isolating the Communist Party and other democratic forces. They have produced the opposite result; it is not the Communist Party or any other democratic forces that are isolated but the reactionaries themselves. After this the Chinese people know from their own experience what Chiang Kai-shek's "National Assembly", "constitution" and "multi-party government" really are. Previously, many Chinese people, mainly those of the middle strata, had illusions to a greater or lesser extent about these manoeuvres of Chiang Kai-shek. It is the same with his "peace negotiations". Now that Chiang Kai-shek has torn several solemn truce agreements to shreds and used bayonets against the student masses demanding peace and opposing civil war, nobody will any longer believe in his so-called peace negotiations except those bent on deceiving people or those absolutely inexperienced politically.

All events have proved our appraisal to be correct. We have repeatedly pointed out that the Chiang Kai-shek government is nothing but a government of treason, civil war and dictatorship. It seeks to wipe out the Chinese Communist Party and all other democratic forces by civil war in order to turn China into a U.S. colony and maintain its own dictatorial rule. Because it has adopted these reactionary policies, this government has lost all prestige and strength politically. The power of the Chiang Kai-shek government is only temporary and superficial; in fact, it is a government outwardly strong but inwardly weak. Its offensives can be smashed no matter where or on what fronts they are launched. Its inevitable end will be rebellion by the masses, desertion by its followers and the total destruction of its army. All events have borne out and will continue to bear out the correctness of this appraisal.

The march of events in China is faster than people expected. On the one hand, there are the victories of the People's Liberation Army; on the other, there is the advance of the people's struggle in the areas under Chiang Kai-shek's control; both are moving at high speed. The Chinese people should quickly prepare all the necessary conditions for the establishment of a peaceful, democratic and independent new China.

NOTES

[1] After December 1946 the democratic and patriotic movement of the broad masses of students in the Kuomintang areas against hunger, civil war and persecution gathered new momentum with the development of the People's War of Liberation and gradually became a second front in the struggle against Chiang Kai-shek's reactionary rule. In late December 1946 and early January 1947, more than 500,000 students in scores of big and medium cities, including Peiping, Tientsin, Shanghai and Nanking, went on strike and held demonstrations in protest against the atrocity of the raping of a Peking University girl student perpetrated by U.S. soldiers and demanded the withdrawal of U.S. armed forces from China. This struggle won the immediate support of workers, teachers and other people. On May 4, 1947, students in Shanghai demonstrated against the civil war. At the same time eight thousand workers and students besieged the Kuomintang police headquarters. The patriotic movement soon spread to Nanking, Peiping, Hangchow, Shenyang, Tsingtao, Kaifeng and many other cities. The Kuomintang reactionaries resorted to extremely brutal measures to suppress the students' patriotic and democratic movement. On May 20 more than a hundred students were wounded and arrested in Nanking and Tientsin in the notorious "Bloody Incident of May 20th". Nevertheless, the patriotic student movement, supported by the broad masses of the people, could not be quelled. The

students' strikes and demonstrations under the slogan, "Against Hunger, Against Civil War, Against Persecution", and the people's anti-U.S. and anti-Chiang Kai-shek struggles, such as strikes of workers and teachers, spread to more than sixty large and medium cities.   In May 1948 the students in Shanghai, together with cultural workers, journalists, and people from other walks of life, started a patriotic movement against the revival of the Japanese forces of aggression fostered by the United States, a movement which also spread rapidly to many other cities.   The patriotic struggles of the students never ceased until the country-wide victory; they struck heavy blows at the Kuomintang.

[2] Promulgated on May 18, 1947 by the Chiang Kai-shek government, these measures strictly prohibited the presentation of petitions by more than ten persons together and forbade all strikes by workers and students and all demonstrations. They also authorized the Kuomintang local authorities to take "necessary steps" and "emergency measures" for the sanguinary suppression of the patriotic and democratic movements of the people.

[3] On May 4, 1919, students in Peking demonstrated against the handing over to Japan of many of China's sovereign rights in Shantung by Britain, the United States, France, Japan, Italy and other imperialist countries then in conference in Paris.   This student movement evoked an immediate response throughout the country.   After June 3, it developed into a country-wide anti-imperialist and anti-feudal revolutionary movement embracing large numbers of the proletariat, the urban petty bourgeoisie and even the national bourgeoisie.

STRATEGY FOR THE SECOND YEAR
OF THE WAR OF LIBERATION*

September 1, 1947

1. In the first year's fighting (from July last year to June this year), we wiped out $97^1/_2$ regular brigades, or 780,000 men, and puppet troops, peace preservation corps and others totalling 340,000 – altogether 1,120,000 of the enemy. This was a great victory. It dealt the enemy a heavy blow, created profound defeatism in the whole enemy camp, elated the people throughout the country and laid the foundation for the complete annihilation of the enemy by our army and for final victory.

2. In the first year's fighting, the enemy launched a large-scale offensive against the Liberated Areas, using 218 of his 248 regular brigades, or more than 1,600,000 men, and nearly 1,000,000 men from the special arms (navy, air force, artillery, engineer corps and armoured units) and from the puppet troops, communications police corps and peace preservation corps. Our army rightly adopted the strategy of fighting on interior lines; and in order to hold the initiative at all times and places it did not balk at paying the price of over 300,000 casualties and of enemy occupation of large tracts of territory. Consequently, we succeeded in wiping out 1,120,000 enemy troops, forced the enemy to disperse his troops, steeled and strengthened our own forces, launched strategic counter-offensives in the Northeast, Jehol, eastern Hopei, southern Shansi and northern Honan, recovered large territories and liberated vast new areas.[1]

3. In the second year of fighting, our army's basic task is to launch a country-wide counter-offensive, that is, to use our main forces to fight our way to exterior lines, carry the war into the Kuomintang areas, wipe out large numbers of the enemy on the exterior lines and completely wreck the Kuomintang's counter-revolutionary strategy, which is, on the contrary, to continue to carry the war into the Liberated

141

Areas, further damage and drain our manpower and material resources and make it impossible for us to hold out very long.   In the
second year's fighting, a partial task of our army is to use a portion
of our main forces and large numbers of our regional troops to continue
fighting on interior lines, wipe out the enemy there and recover lost
territory.

4.   Our army will of course meet many difficulties in carrying out
the policy of fighting on exterior lines and bringing the war into the
Kuomintang areas.   For it takes time to build new bases in the Kuomintang areas and we can build stable bases only when we have wiped
out large numbers of the enemy in many back-and-forth mobile operations, aroused the masses, distributed land, established our political
power and built up the people's armed forces.   Until then, there will
be quite a few difficulties.   But they can and must be overcome.   For
the enemy will be forced to spread out even more, and vast territories
will be available to our army as battlefields for mobile operations, and
so we will be able to wage mobile warfare; the broad masses in those
territories hate the Kuomintang and support us; and though part of
the enemy forces still has a comparatively high combat effectiveness,

---

* This inner-Party directive was drafted by Comrade Mao Tse-tung for the Central
Committee of the Communist Party of China when he and the Central Committee
were at Chukuanchai, Chiahsien County, northern Shensi.   The directive formulated
the basic task for the second year of the War of Liberation.   This task was to carry
the war into the Kuomintang areas with our main forces and to switch from fighting
on interior lines to fighting on exterior lines, that is, to pass from the stage of the
strategic defensive to that of the strategic offensive.   In accordance with the strategic
plan laid down by Comrade Mao Tse-tung, the People's Liberation Army went over
to the offensive on a country-wide scale during July-September 1947.   The Shansi-
Hopei-Shantung-Honan Field Army forced the Yellow River in southwestern Shantung
on June 30, crossed the Lunghai Railway early in August and thrust into the Tapieh
Mountains.   The Taiyueh Army of the Shansi-Hopei-Shantung-Honan Field Army
forced the Yellow River from southern Shansi in late August and thrust into western
Honan.   The Eastern China Field Army thrust into southwestern Shantung early in
September after smashing a concentrated attack by the enemy.   In the same month
the Shantung Army of the Eastern China Field Army started an offensive against the
enemy in eastern Shantung.   The Northwest Field Army went over to the offensive
late in August.   The Shansi-Chahar-Hopei Field Army started an offensive against
the enemy along the northern section of the Peiping-Hankow Railway early in
September.   Immediately after its summer offensive throughout the Northeast, the
Northeast Field Army, beginning in September, launched a large-scale autumn offensive
in the Changchun-Kirin-Szepingkai region and in the Chinhsi-Ihsien sector along the
Peiping-Liaoning Railway.   The offensives in all these theatres of war constituted a
general offensive by the entire People's Liberation Army.   This large-scale offensive
led to a turning point in the War of Liberation, marking a radical change in the war
situation.   See "The Present Situation and Our Tasks", pp. 157-76 of this volume.

on the whole the enemy's morale and combat effectiveness are much lower than a year ago.

5. The keys to victory in fighting in the Kuomintang areas are, first, to be good at seizing the opportunities for fighting, to be brave and determined and win as many battles as possible; and, second, to carry out resolutely the policy of winning the masses and enable the broad masses to benefit so that they side with our army.   If these two points are carried out, we shall win victory.

6. Up to the end of August this year, the distribution of enemy forces, including those which had been wiped out or dealt crushing blows, was 157 brigades on the southern front, 70 on the northern front and 21 in the Kuomintang rear areas.   The total in the whole country was still 248 brigades and the actual number of troops was about 1,500,000.   Troops in the special arms, puppet troops, communications police and peace preservation corps numbered about 1,200,000. Non-combatants in the military institutions in the enemy rear were about 1,000,000.   The entire enemy forces totalled about 3,700,000 men. Of the troops on the southern front, 117 brigades belong to Ku Chu-tung's group, 7 to Cheng Chien's group and others, and 33 to Hu Tsung-nan's group.   Of the 117 brigades of Ku Chu-tung's group, 63 have been wiped out or have received crushing blows.   Of these, some have not been replenished; others, although they are being replenished, have few men and low combat effectiveness; and others, although their manpower and arms have been fairly well replenished and their combat effectiveness has to some extent been restored, are still far weaker than before.   There are only 54 brigades which have neither been wiped out nor received crushing blows.   Of Ku Chu-tung's entire forces, 82 to 85 brigades are employed for garrison duty and can be used only for local manoeuvres, and no more than 32 to 35 brigades can be used for strategic manoeuvres.   The 7 brigades of Cheng Chien's group and others can in the main be used only for garrison duty, and one has already received a crushing blow. Of the 33 brigades of Hu Tsung-nan's group (including those east of Lanchow, south of Ningsia and Yulin, and west of Linfen and Loyang), 12 have been wiped out or received crushing blows, only 7 can be used for strategic manoeuvres, and the rest are on garrison duty.   On the northern front the enemy has 70 brigades altogether. Of these, the Northeast group has 26 brigades, of which 16 have been wiped out or have received crushing blows; Sun Lien-chung's group has 19 brigades, of which 8 have been wiped out or received crushing

blows; Fu Tso-yi has 10 brigades, of which 2 have received crushing blows; and Yen Hsi-shan has 15 brigades, of which 9 have been wiped out or received crushing blows.   These enemy troops are now mainly on the defensive and only a small part is available for mobile operations.   In the Kuomintang rear areas there are only 21 brigades on garrison duty.   Of these, 8 brigades are in Sinkiang and western Kansu, 7 in Szechuan and Sikang, 2 in Yunnan, 2 in Kwangtung (that is, the 69th Division that was wiped out) and 2 in Taiwan.   There are no regular troops at all in the six provinces of Hunan, Kwangsi, Kweichow, Fukien, Chekiang and Kiangsi.   The Kuomintang is planning, with U.S. assistance, to draft 1,000,000 men this year to replenish the front and to train a number of new brigades and replacement regiments.   However, if our army can wipe out an average of 8 enemy brigades a month, as it did in the first year of fighting, and wipe out another 96 to 100 brigades in the second year (already in July and August $16^1/_2$ brigades were wiped out), then the enemy army will be further and greatly weakened, its strategic reserve will be reduced to the minimum, and it will be forced into a defensive position in all parts of the country and will be attacked by us everywhere.   Although the Kuomintang has this plan of drafting 1,000,000 men and training new brigades and replacement regiments, it will be of no avail.   Since its only methods of recruiting are pressganging and hiring, to reach a million will certainly be difficult and many will desert.   Moreover, by carrying out the policy of fighting on exterior lines our army will be able to reduce the enemy's manpower and material resources.

7.   The operational principles of our army are still the same as those laid down before:

Attack dispersed, isolated enemy forces first (this applies also to a large-scale campaign of annihilation directed against several brigades, such as the Laiwu campaign[2] in February and the Southwestern Shantung campaign[3] in July this year); attack concentrated, strong enemy forces later.

Take medium and small cities and extensive rural areas first; take big cities later.

Make wiping out the enemy's effective strength our main objective; do not make holding or seizing a place our main objective. Holding or seizing a place is the outcome of wiping out the enemy's effective strength, and often a place can be held or seized for good only after it has changed hands a number of times.

In every battle, concentrate an absolutely superior force, encircle the enemy forces completely, strive to wipe them out thoroughly and do not let any escape from the net. In special circumstances, use the method of dealing crushing blows to the enemy, that is, concentrate all our strength to make a frontal attack and also to attack one or both of his flanks, with the aim of wiping out one part and routing another so that our army can swiftly move its troops to smash other enemy forces.

On the one hand, be sure to fight no battle unprepared, fight no battle you are not sure of winning; make every effort to be well prepared for each battle, make every effort to ensure victory in the given set of conditions as between the enemy and ourselves. On the other hand, give full play to our fine style of fighting – courage in battle, no fear of sacrifice, no fear of fatigue, and continuous fighting (that is, fighting successive battles in a short time).

Strive to draw the enemy into mobile warfare, but at the same time lay great stress on learning the tactics of positional attack and on stepping up the building of the artillery and engineer corps in order to capture enemy fortified points and cities on a large scale.

Resolutely attack and seize all fortified points and cities which are weakly defended. Attack and seize at opportune moments all fortified points and cities defended with moderate strength, provided circumstances permit. For the time being, leave alone all fortified points and cities which are strongly defended.

Replenish our strength with all the arms and most of the soldiers captured from the enemy (80-90 per cent of the men and a small number of the junior officers). Seek replenishment chiefly from the enemy and from the Kuomintang areas and only partly from the old Liberated Areas; this applies especially to the armies on the southern front.

In all the new and old Liberated Areas, we must resolutely carry through the land reform (which is the most fundamental requirement for supporting a long war and winning country-wide victory), develop production, practise economy and strengthen the building of war industry – all for victory at the front. Only by doing this can we support a long war and win victory in the whole country. If we do so, we shall certainly be able to support a long war and win victory throughout the country.

8. The above sums up the year's fighting and sets forth the principles for future fighting. Leading comrades in all areas are requested

to pass the contents on to all cadres of regimental rank and above, of the level of prefectural Party committee and above and of the level of prefectural commissioner's office and above, so that everyone will understand his own task and carry it out resolutely and unwaveringly.

NOTES

[1] This strategic counter-offensive in the Northeast, Jehol and eastern Hopei was the 1947 summer offensive of the Northeast People's Liberation Army. On May 13 the People's Liberation Army began simultaneous offensives on these fronts and by July 1 had wiped out over 80,000 enemy troops and recovered more than 40 county towns. The enemy plan of cutting up the Liberated Areas in northeastern China was thus completely wrecked. The enemy troops, driven into two narrow corridors along the Chinese Changchun Railway and the Peiping-Liaoning Railway, were forced into the "defence of key points". This changed the whole situation in northeastern China. The strategic counter-offensive in southern Shansi and northern Honan comprised the offensives launched by the Shansi-Hopei-Shantung-Honan People's Liberation Army in northern Honan and on the flanks of the Tatung-Puchow Railway in southern Shansi between March and May 1947. Our army in northern Honan started attacking on March 23. After taking Yenchin, Yangwu, Puyang and Fengchiu one after another, our army turned north to exploit these successes. By May 28 it had captured Tsihsien, Chunhsien, Huahsien and Tangyin and wiped out over 45,000 enemy troops. Our troops in southern Shansi began offensive operations on April 4. By May 4 they had captured twenty-two county towns, including Chuwo, Hsinchiang and Yungtsi, and two important ferry crossings on the Yellow River, Yumenkou and Fenglingtu, and had wiped out over 18,000 enemy troops.

[2] The Laiwu campaign was a campaign of mobile warfare fought by the Eastern China People's Liberation Army in the Laiwu region, southeast of Tsinan, Shantung Province. Towards the end of January 1947 the Kuomintang troops launched an offensive against the Shantung Liberated Areas from both the north and the south. From the south, eight Kuomintang reorganized divisions drove northward by three routes along the Yiho and Shuho Rivers towards Linyi and from the north, in coordination with them, three Kuomintang corps belonging to the Li Hsien-chou group advanced southward on Laiwu and Hsintai from Mingshui, Tsechuan and Poshan, seeking to engage the main force of the Eastern China People's Liberation Army in a decisive battle in the Yi-Meng mountain area. Our army used part of its forces to block the enemy from the south but marched its main force north towards Laiwu to destroy the Li Hsien-chou group. All the enemy troops, over 60,000 men, were wiped out in a battle which started on February 20 and ended on the afternoon of February 23. Li Hsien-chou, Deputy Commander of the 2nd Pacification Zone of the Kuomintang's Hsuchow Pacification Headquarters, was captured, and thirteen towns were recovered.

[3] This Southwestern Shantung campaign was the campaign fought by the Shansi-Hopei-Shantung-Honan People's Liberation Army in July 1947 in the region of Hotse, Yuncheng, Chuyeh, Tingtao, Chinhsiang and Tsaohsien, in southwestern Shantung Province. In this campaign 4 Kuomintang division headquarters and 9½ brigades, totalling more than 56,000 men, were wiped out.

MANIFESTO OF THE CHINESE PEOPLE'S
LIBERATION ARMY*

October 1947

The Chinese People's Liberation Army, having smashed Chiang Kai-shek's offensive, has now launched a large-scale counter-offensive. Our armies on the southern front are advancing on the Yangtse River valley, our armies on the northern front are advancing on the Chinese Changchun Railway and the Peiping-Liaoning Railway. Wherever our troops go, the enemy flees pell-mell before us and the people give thunderous cheers. The whole situation between the enemy and ourselves has fundamentally changed as compared with a year ago.

The aim of our army in this war, as proclaimed time and again to the nation and the world, is the liberation of the Chinese people and the Chinese nation. And today, our aim is to carry out the urgent demand of the people of the whole country, that is, to overthrow the arch-criminal of the civil war, Chiang Kai-shek, and form a democratic coalition government in order to attain the general goal of liberating the people and the nation.

For eight long years the Chinese people fought heroically against Japanese imperialism for their own liberation and national independence. After the Japanese surrender the people longed for peace, but Chiang Kai-shek wrecked all their peace efforts and forced on them the disaster of an unprecedented civil war. Hence the people of all strata throughout the country were forced to unite to overthrow Chiang Kai-shek, having no other way out.

Chiang Kai-shek's present policy of civil war is no accident but is the inevitable outcome of the anti-popular policy which he and his reactionary clique have consistently followed. As far back as 1927, Chiang Kai-shek, devoid of all gratitude, betrayed the revolutionary alliance between the Kuomintang and the Communist Party[1] and betrayed the revolutionary Three People's Principles and the Three

Great Policies of Sun Yat-sen;[2] then he set up a dictatorship, capitulated to imperialism, fought ten years of civil war and brought on the aggression of the Japanese bandits. In the Sian Incident of 1936, the Communist Party of China returned good for evil and, acting together with Generals Chang Hsueh-liang and Yang Hu-cheng, set Chiang Kai-shek free in the hope that he would repent, turn over a new leaf and join in the fight against the Japanese aggressors. But once again he proved devoid of all gratitude; he was passive against the Japanese invaders, active in suppressing the people and extremely hostile to the Communist Party. The year before last (1945), Japan surrendered and the Chinese people once more forgave Chiang Kai-shek, demanding that he should stop the civil war he had already started, put democracy into practice and unite with all parties and groups for peace and national reconstruction. But no sooner had the truce agreement been signed, the resolutions of the Political Consultative Conference adopted and the four pledges[3] proclaimed than the utterly faithless Chiang Kai-shek went back on his word completely. Time and again the people showed themselves forbearing and conciliatory for the sake of the common good but, aided by U.S. imperialism, Chiang Kai-shek was determined to launch an unprecedented all-out offensive against the people, in utter disregard of the fate of the country and the nation. From January last year (1946), when the truce agreement was announced, up to the present, Chiang Kai-shek has mobilized more than 220 brigades of his regular troops and nearly a million miscellaneous troops[4] and launched large-scale attacks against the Liberated Areas which the Chinese people wrested from Japanese imperialism after bloody battles; he has seized successively the cities of Shenyang, Fushun, Penki, Szepingkai, Changchun, Yungchi, Chengteh, Chining, Changchiakou, Huaiyin, Hotse, Linyi, Yenan and Yentai and vast rural areas. Wherever Chiang Kai-shek's troops go, they murder and burn, rape and loot, carry out the policy of three atrocities[5] and behave exactly like the Japanese bandits. In November last year Chiang Kai-shek convened the bogus National Assembly and proclaimed the bogus constitution. In March this year he expelled the

---

* This political manifesto was drafted by Comrade Mao Tse-tung for the General Headquarters of the Chinese People's Liberation Army. It analysed the political situation in China at the time, raised the slogan "Overthrow Chiang Kai-shek and liberate all China!" and announced the eight basic policies of the Chinese People's Liberation Army, which were also those of the Communist Party of China. The manifesto was issued on October 10, 1947, and was known as the "October 10th Manifesto". It was drafted at Shenchuanpao, Chiahsien County, northern Shensi.

representatives of the Communist Party from the Kuomintang areas. In July he issued an order of general mobilization against the people.[6] Towards the just movement of the people in different parts of the country against civil war, against hunger and against U.S. imperialist aggression and towards the struggle for existence waged by the workers, peasants, students, townspeople, government employees and teachers, Chiang Kai-shek's policy is one of repression, arrest and massacre. Towards our country's minority nationalities, his policy is one of Han chauvinism, of persecution and repression by every possible means. In all the areas under Chiang Kai-shek's rule corruption is rife, secret agents run amuck, taxes are innumerable and crushing, prices are skyrocketing, the economy is bankrupt, all business languishes, conscription and the grain levy are imposed and voices of discontent are heard everywhere; all this has plunged the overwhelming majority of people throughout the country into an abyss of suffering. Meanwhile the financial oligarchs, corrupt officials, local bullies and bad gentry, all headed by Chiang Kai-shek, have amassed vast fortunes. Chiang Kai-shek and his like made these fortunes by using their dictatorial powers to extort taxes and levies and promote their private interests under the guise of serving the public. To maintain his dictatorship and carry on the civil war, Chiang Kai-shek has not hesitated to sell out our country's sovereign rights to foreign imperialism, to collude with the U.S. armed forces so that they should remain in Tsingtao and elsewhere and to procure advisers from the United States to take part in directing the civil war and training troops to slaughter his own fellow-countrymen. Aircraft, tanks, guns and ammunition for the civil war are shipped from the United States in great quantities. Funds for the civil war are borrowed from the United States on a large scale. In return for its favours, Chiang Kai-shek has presented U.S. imperialism with military bases and the rights of air flight and navigation and concluded with it a commercial treaty of enslavement[7] – acts of treason many times worse than those of Yuan Shih-kai.[8] In a word, Chiang Kai-shek's twenty-year rule has been traitorous, dictatorial and against the people. Today, the overwhelming majority of the people throughout the country, north and south, young and old, know his towering crimes and hope that our army will quickly launch the counter-offensive, overthrow Chiang Kai-shek and liberate all China.

We are the army of the Chinese people and in all things we take the will of the Chinese people as our will. The policies of our army represent the urgent demands of the Chinese people and chief among them are the following:

(1)   Unite workers, peasants, soldiers, intellectuals and business-men, all oppressed classes, all people's organizations, democratic parties, minority nationalities, overseas Chinese and other patriots; form a national united front; overthrow the dictatorial Chiang Kai-shek government; and establish a democratic coalition government.

(2)   Arrest, try and punish the civil war criminals headed by Chiang Kai-shek.

(3)   Abolish the Chiang Kai-shek dictatorship, carry out the sys-tem of people's democracy and guarantee freedom of speech, of the press, of assembly and of association for the people.

(4)   Abolish the rotten institutions of the Chiang Kai-shek regime, clear out all corrupt officials and establish clean government.

(5)   Confiscate the property of the four big families[9] of Chiang Kai-shek, T. V. Soong, H. H. Kung and the Chen Li-fu brothers, and the property of the other chief war criminals; confiscate bureaucrat-capital, develop the industry and commerce of the national bourgeoi-sie, improve the livelihood of workers and employees, and give relief to victims of natural calamities and to poverty-stricken people.

(6)   Abolish the system of feudal exploitation and put into effect the system of land to the tillers.

(7)   Recognize the right to equality and autonomy of the minority nationalities within the borders of China.

(8)   Repudiate the traitorous foreign policy of Chiang Kai-shek's dictatorial government, abrogate all the treasonable treaties and repu-diate all the foreign debts contracted by Chiang Kai-shek during the civil war period.   Demand that the U.S. government withdraw its troops stationed in China, which are a menace to China's indepen-dence, and oppose any foreign country's helping Chiang Kai-shek to carry on civil war or trying to revive the forces of Japanese aggression. Conclude treaties of trade and friendship with foreign countries on the basis of equality and reciprocity.   Unite in a common struggle with all nations which treat us as equals.

The above are the basic policies of our army.   They will be put into practice at once wherever our army goes.   These policies con-form with the demands of more than 90 per cent of the people in our country.

Our army does not reject all Chiang Kai-shek's personnel but adopts a policy of dealing with each case on its merits.   That is, the chief criminals shall be punished without fail, those who are accomplices under duress shall go unpunished and those who perform deeds of merit shall be rewarded.   As for Chiang Kai-shek, the archcriminal who started the civil war and who has committed most heinous crimes, and as for all his hardened accomplices who have trampled the people underfoot and are branded as war criminals by the broad masses, our army will hunt them down, even to the four corners of the earth, and will surely bring them to trial and punishment. Our army warns all officers and men in Chiang Kai-shek's army, all officials in his government and all members of his party whose hands are not yet stained with the blood of innocent people that they should strictly refrain from joining these criminals in their evil-doing.   Those who have been doing evil should immediately stop, repent and start anew and break with Chiang Kai-shek, and we will give them a chance to make amends for their crimes by good deeds.   Our army will not kill or humiliate any of Chiang Kai-shek's army officers and men who lay down their arms, but will accept them into our service if they are willing to remain with us or send them home if they wish to leave.   As for those troops of Chiang Kai-shek who rise in revolt and join our army and those who work for our army openly or in secret, they shall be rewarded.

In order to overthrow Chiang Kai-shek and form a democratic coalition government at an early date, we call on our fellow-countrymen in all walks of life to co-operate actively with us wherever our army goes in cleaning up the reactionary forces and setting up a democratic order.   In places we have not yet reached, they should take up arms on their own, resist pressganging and the grain levy, distribute the land, repudiate debts and take advantage of the enemy's gaps to develop guerrilla warfare.

In order to overthrow Chiang Kai-shek and form a democratic coalition government at an early date, we call on the people in the Liberated Areas to carry through the land reform, consolidate the foundations of democracy, develop production, practise economy, strengthen the people's armed forces, eliminate the remaining strongholds of the enemy and support the fighting at the front.

All comrade commanders and fighters of our army!   We are shouldering the most important, the most glorious task in the history of our country's revolution.   We should make great efforts to accomplish our task.   Our efforts will decide the day when our great motherland will emerge from darkness into light and our beloved fellow-countrymen will be able to live like human beings and to choose the government they wish. All officers and fighters of our army must improve their military art, march forward courageously towards sure victory in the war and resolutely, thoroughly, wholly and completely wipe out all enemies. They must all raise their level of political consciousness, learn the two skills of wiping out the enemy forces and arousing the masses, unite intimately with the masses and rapidly build the new Liberated Areas into stable areas. They must heighten their sense of discipline and resolutely carry out orders, carry out policy, carry out the Three Main Rules of Discipline and the Eight Points for Attention – with army and people united, army and government united, officers and soldiers united, and the whole army united – and permit no breach of discipline. All our officers and fighters must always bear in mind that we are the great People's Liberation Army, we are the troops led by the great Communist Party of China. Provided we constantly observe the directives of the Party, we are sure to win.

Down with Chiang Kai-shek!

Long live New China!

NOTES

[1] See "The Situation and Our Policy After the Victory in the War of Resistance Against Japan", Note 7, p. 23 of this volume.

[2] See "On a Statement by Chiang Kai-shek's Spokesman", Note 2, pp. 44-45 of this volume.

[3] The "four pledges" were made by Chiang Kai-shek at the opening session of the Political Consultative Conference in 1946. They were, to guarantee freedom of the people, to guarantee the legal status of political parties, to hold a general election and to release political prisoners.

[4] By miscellaneous troops are meant the Kuomintang's irregular troops which included the local peace preservation corps, communications police corps, gendarmes, the puppet troops taken over and reorganized by the Kuomintang, etc.

[5] The Japanese invaders carried out the policy of three atrocities – burn all, kill all, loot all – against the Liberated Areas in China.

[6] On July 4, 1947, the reactionary Kuomintang government adopted Chiang Kai-shek's "General Mobilization Bill" and immediately afterwards issued the "Order for General Mobilization to Suppress the Insurrection of the Communist Bandits". In fact, Chiang Kai-shek had carried out a general mobilization for his counter-revolutionary civil war much earlier. By that time the Chinese People's Liberation Army had begun to shift to a country-wide offensive. Chiang Kai-shek himself

admitted that his regime was in a "serious crisis". The "Order for General Mobilization" was merely his dying kick.

[7] This refers to the "Sino-U.S. Treaty of Friendship, Commerce and Navigation" concluded between the Chiang Kai-shek government and the U.S. government on November 4, 1946. The treaty sold out China's sovereign rights to the United States. See "Greet the New High Tide of the Chinese Revolution", Note 6, p. 126 of this volume.

[8] Yuan Shih-kai was the head of the Northern warlords in the last years of the Ching Dynasty. After the Ching Dynasty was overthrown by the Revolution of 1911, he usurped the presidency of the Republic and organized the first government of the Northern warlords, which represented the big landlord and big comprador classes; he did this by relying on a counter-revolutionary armed force and the support of the imperialists and by taking advantage of the compromising nature of the bourgeoisie then leading the revolution. In 1915 he wanted to make himself emperor and, to gain the support of the Japanese imperialists, he accepted Japan's Twenty-one Demands which were designed to obtain exclusive control of all China. In December of the same year an uprising against his assumption of the throne took place in Yunnan Province and promptly won country-wide response and support. Yuan Shih-kai died in June 1916.

[9] This refers to the four big monopoly capitalist groups of Chiang Kai-shek, T. V. Soong, H. H. Kung and Chen Li-fu. See "The Present Situation and Our Tasks", Section 6, pp. 167-69 of this volume.

ON THE REISSUE OF
THE THREE MAIN RULES OF DISCIPLINE AND
THE EIGHT POINTS FOR ATTENTION
—INSTRUCTION OF
THE GENERAL HEADQUARTERS OF
THE CHINESE PEOPLE'S LIBERATION ARMY

October 10, 1947

1. Our Army's Three Main Rules of Discipline and Eight Points for Attention[1] have been practised for many years, but their contents vary slightly in army units in different areas. They have now been unified and are hereby reissued. It is expected that you will take this version as the standard one for thorough education and strict enforcement. As to other matters needing attention, the high command of the armed forces in different areas may lay down additional points in accordance with specific conditions and order their enforcement.

2. The Three Main Rules of Discipline are as follows:
    (1) Obey orders in all your actions.
    (2) Don't take a single needle or piece of thread from the masses.
    (3) Turn in everything captured.

3. The Eight Points for Attention are as follows:
    (1) Speak politely.
    (2) Pay fairly for what you buy.
    (3) Return everything you borrow.
    (4) Pay for anything you damage.
    (5) Don't hit or swear at people.
    (6) Don't damage crops.
    (7) Don't take liberties with women.
    (8) Don't ill-treat captives.

NOTES

[1] The Three Main Rules of Discipline and the Eight Points for Attention were the rules of discipline laid down by Comrade Mao Tse-tung for the Chinese Workers' and Peasants' Red Army during the Second Revolutionary Civil War. They formed an important part of the political work of the Red Army and played a great role in building the people's armed forces, handling relations within the army correctly, forging unity with the masses of the people and laying down the correct policy of the people's army towards captives. From the earliest days of the Red Army, Comrade Mao Tse-tung required the soldiers to speak politely to the masses, pay fairly for all purchases and never impress people into forced labour or hit or swear at people. In the spring of 1928, when the Workers' and Peasants' Red Army was in the Chingkang Mountains, Comrade Mao Tse-tung set down Three Rules of Discipline: (1) Obey orders in your actions; (2) Don't take anything from the workers and peasants; and (3) Turn in all things taken from local bullies. In the summer of 1928 he set forth Six Points for Attention: (1) Put back the doors you have taken down for bed-boards; (2) Put back the straw you have used for bedding; (3) Speak politely; (4) Pay fairly for what you buy; (5) Return everything you borrow; and (6) Pay for anything you damage. After 1929 Comrade Mao Tse-tung made the following changes: Rule 2 became "Don't take a single needle or piece of thread from the masses", and Rule 3 was changed first to "Turn in all money raised" and then to "Turn in everything captured". To the Six Points for Attention he added two more: "Don't bathe within sight of women" and "Don't search the pockets of captives". This was the origin of the Three Main Rules of Discipline and the Eight Points for Attention.

THE PRESENT SITUATION AND OUR TASKS*

December 25, 1947

I

The Chinese people's revolutionary war has now reached a turning point. That is, the Chinese People's Liberation Army has beaten back the offensive of several million reactionary troops of Chiang Kai-shek, the running dog of the United States of America, and gone over to the offensive. Already in the first year of the present war, from July 1946 to June 1947, the People's Liberation Army beat back Chiang Kai-shek's offensive on several fronts and forced him onto the defensive. And beginning with the first quarter of the second year of the war, July-September 1947, the People's Liberation Army went over to the offensive on a national scale and wrecked Chiang Kai-shek's counter-revolutionary plan of continuing to carry the war into the Liberated Areas in order to destroy them completely. Now the war is no longer being fought chiefly in the Liberated Areas but in the Kuomintang areas; the main forces of the People's Liberation Army have carried the fight into the Kuomintang areas.[1] In this land of China, the People's Liberation Army has turned back the wheel of counter-revolution – of U.S. imperialism and its lackey, the Chiang Kai-shek bandit gang – and sent it down the road to destruction and has pushed the wheel of revolution forward along the road to victory. This is a turning point in history. It is the turning point from growth to extinction for Chiang Kai-shek's twenty-year counter-revolutionary rule. It is the turning point from growth to extinction for imperialist rule in China, now over a hundred years old. This is a momentous event. It is momentous because it is occurring in a country with a population of 475 million and, having occurred, it will certainly culminate in victory throughout the country. Furthermore, it is momentous because it is occurring in the East, where over 1,000 million people – half of

157

mankind – suffer under imperialist oppression. The turn of the Chinese People's War of Liberation from the defensive to the offensive cannot but gladden and inspire these oppressed nations. It is also of assistance to the oppressed people now struggling in many countries in Europe and the Americas.

II

From the day Chiang Kai-shek started his counter-revolutionary war we said that we not only must defeat him but can defeat him. We must defeat him because the war he started is a counter-revolutionary war directed by U.S. imperialism against the independence of the Chinese nation and the liberation of the Chinese people. After the conclusion of World War II and the overthrow of Japanese imperialism, the task of the Chinese people was to complete the new-democratic transformation politically, economically and culturally, to achieve national unification and independence and to change China from an agricultural into an industrial country. But at that time, after the victorious conclusion of the anti-fascist Second World War, U.S. imperialism and its lackeys in various countries stepped into the shoes of German and Japanese imperialism and their lackeys and formed a reactionary camp against the Soviet Union, against the People's Democracies in Europe, against the workers' movements in the capitalist

---

* This report was made by Comrade Mao Tse-tung to a meeting of the Central Committee of the Communist Party of China held on December 25-28, 1947, at Yangchiakou, Michih County, northern Shensi.   In addition to those members and alternate members of the Central Committee able to attend, responsible comrades of the Shensi-Kansu-Ningsia Border Region and the Shansi-Suiyuan Border Region were present.   The meeting discussed and adopted this report and also another document written by Comrade Mao Tse-tung, "Some Points in Appraisal of the Present International Situation" (see pp. 87-88 of this volume).   Concerning Comrade Mao Tse-tung's report, the decision adopted at the meeting stated, "This report is a programmatic document in the political, military and economic fields for the entire period of the overthrow of the reactionary Chiang Kai-shek ruling clique and of the founding of a new-democratic China.   The whole Party and the whole army should carry on intensive education around, and strictly apply in practice, this document and, in connection with it, the documents published on October 10, 1947 [namely, 'Manifesto of the Chinese People's Liberation Army', 'Slogans of the Chinese People's Liberation Army', 'Instruction on the Reissue of the Three Main Rules of Discipline and the Eight Points for Attention', 'Outline Land Law of China' and 'Resolution of the Central Committee of the Communist Party of China on the Promulgation of the

countries, against the national movements in the colonies and semi-colonies and against the liberation of the Chinese people. At such a time the Chinese reactionaries headed by Chiang Kai-shek acted as the running dog for U.S. imperialism, just as Wang Ching-wei had done for Japanese imperialism, sold out China to the United States and unleashed a war against the Chinese people to check the advance of their liberation. At such a time, if we had shown weakness or given ground and had not dared to rise resolutely to oppose counter-revolutionary war with revolutionary war, China would have become a world of darkness and the future of our nation would have been forfeited. The Communist Party of China has led the Chinese People's Liberation Army in firmly waging a patriotic, just and revolutionary war against Chiang Kai-shek's offensive. The Communist Party of China, having made a clear-headed appraisal of the international and domestic situation on the basis of the science of Marxism-Leninism, recognized that all attacks by the reactionaries at home and abroad not only had to be defeated but could be defeated. When dark clouds appeared in the sky, we pointed out that this was only temporary, that the darkness would soon pass and the sun break through. When the Chiang Kai-shek bandit gang launched the country-wide counter-revolutionary war in July 1946, they thought it would take them only three to six months to defeat the People's Liberation Army. They reckoned that they had a regular army of two million, more than a million irregulars and another million or more men in the military establishments and armed units in the rear, making a total military strength

---

Outline Land Law of China']. In carrying out policies in different places any departure from the principles laid down in the report should be rectified at once." Other important decisions taken at the meeting were:

(1) That every effort should be made to carry the Chinese people's revolutionary war forward uninterruptedly to complete victory, and that the enemy should not be allowed to use stalling tactics (peace negotiations) to gain time for rest and reorganization for a fresh attack on the people.

(2) That the time was not yet ripe for the formation of a revolutionary central government, which was to be considered only when our army had won greater victories, and that the promulgation of a constitution was even more a question for the future.

The meeting also discussed in detail current tendencies in the Party and certain specific policies in the land reform and the mass movements. The results of these discussions were subsequently set forth by Comrade Mao Tse-tung in the article "On Some Important Problems of the Party's Present Policy" (see pp. 181-89 of this volume). All the articles in this book starting with this report and ending with "A Circular on the Situation", dated March 20, 1948 (pp. 219-26), were written at Yangchiakou, Michih County, northern Shensi.

of more than four million; that they had taken time to complete their preparations for the offensive; that they had regained control of the big cities; that they had a population of more than 300 million; that they had taken over all the equipment of a million Japanese invading troops; and that they had received huge military and financial aid from the U.S. government. They also reckoned that the People's Liberation Army was tired after fighting for eight years in the War of Resistance Against Japan and was far inferior to the Kuomintang army in numbers and equipment; that the population of the Liberated Areas was only a little more than 100 million; and that in most of these areas the reactionary feudal forces had not yet been cleaned up and the land reform had not yet been universally and thoroughly carried out, namely, that the rear area of the People's Liberation Army had not yet been consolidated. Proceeding from this appraisal, the Chiang Kai-shek bandit gang ignored the Chinese people's desire for peace, finally tore up the truce agreement signed by the Kuomintang and the Communist Party in January 1946 as well as the resolutions adopted by the Political Consultative Conference of all parties and launched an adventurist war. We said then that Chiang Kai-shek's superiority in military forces was only transient, a factor which could play only a temporary role, that U.S. imperialist aid was likewise a factor which could play only a temporary role, while the anti-popular character of Chiang Kai-shek's war and the feelings of the people were factors that would play a constant role, and that in this respect the People's Liberation Army was in a superior position. Patriotic, just and revolutionary in character, the war waged by the People's Liberation Army was bound to win the support of the people of the whole country. That was the political foundation for victory over Chiang Kai-shek. The experience of eighteen months of war has fully confirmed our judgement.

III

In seventeen months of fighting (from July 1946 to November 1947; December figures are not yet available), we killed, wounded and captured 1,690,000 of Chiang Kai-shek's regular and irregular troops – 640,000 killed and wounded and 1,050,000 captured. Thus we were able to beat back Chiang Kai-shek's offensive, preserve the main territories of the Liberated Areas and go over to the offensive. Speaking from the military aspect, we were able to do this because we employed the correct strategy. Our principles of operation are:

1. Attack dispersed, isolated enemy forces first; attack concentrated, strong enemy forces later.

2. Take small and medium cities and extensive rural areas first; take big cities later.

3. Make wiping out the enemy's effective strength our main objective; do not make holding or seizing a city or place our main objective. Holding or seizing a city or place is the outcome of wiping out the enemy's effective strength, and often a city or place can be held or seized for good only after it has changed hands a number of times.

4. In every battle, concentrate an absolutely superior force (two, three, four and sometimes even five or six times the enemy's strength), encircle the enemy forces completely, strive to wipe them out thoroughly and do not let any escape from the net. In special circumstances, use the method of dealing crushing blows to the enemy, that is, concentrate all our strength to make a frontal attack and also to attack one or both of his flanks, with the aim of wiping out one part and routing another so that our army can swiftly move its troops to smash other enemy forces. Strive to avoid battles of attrition in which we lose more than we gain or only break even. In this way, although we are inferior as a whole (in terms of numbers), we are absolutely superior in every part and every specific campaign, and this ensures victory in the campaign. As time goes on, we shall become superior as a whole and eventually wipe out all the enemy.

5. Fight no battle unprepared, fight no battle you are not sure of winning; make every effort to be well prepared for each battle, make every effort to ensure victory in the given set of conditions as between the enemy and ourselves.

6. Give full play to our style of fighting – courage in battle, no fear of sacrifice, no fear of fatigue, and continuous fighting (that is, fighting successive battles in a short time without rest).

7. Strive to wipe out the enemy through mobile warfare. At the same time, pay attention to the tactics of positional attack and capture enemy fortified points and cities.

8. With regard to attacking cities, resolutely seize all enemy fortified points and cities which are weakly defended. Seize at opportune moments all enemy fortified points and cities defended

with moderate strength, provided circumstances permit. As for strongly defended enemy fortified points and cities, wait till conditions are ripe and then take them.

9. Replenish our strength with all the arms and most of the personnel captured from the enemy. Our army's main sources of manpower and matériel are at the front.

10. Make good use of the intervals between campaigns to rest, train and consolidate our troops. Periods of rest, training and consolidation should in general not be very long, and the enemy should so far as possible be permitted no breathing space.

These are the main methods the People's Liberation Army has employed in defeating Chiang Kai-shek. They are the result of the tempering of the People's Liberation Army in long years of fighting against domestic and foreign enemies and are completely suited to our present situation. The Chiang Kai-shek bandit gang and the U.S. imperialist military personnel in China are very well acquainted with these military methods of ours. Seeking ways to counter them, Chiang Kai-shek has often assembled his generals and field officers for training and distributed for their study our military literature and the documents captured in the war. The U.S. military personnel have recommended to Chiang Kai-shek one kind of strategy and tactics after another for destroying the People's Liberation Army; they have trained Chiang Kai-shek's troops and supplied them with military equipment. But none of these efforts can save the Chiang Kai-shek bandit gang from defeat. The reason is that our strategy and tactics are based on a people's war; no army opposed to the people can use our strategy and tactics. On the basis of a people's war and of the principles of unity between army and people, of unity between commanders and fighters and of disintegrating the enemy troops, the People's Liberation Army has developed its vigorous revolutionary political work, which is an important factor in winning victory over the enemy. When we abandoned many cities on our own initiative in order to evade fatal blows from superior enemy forces and shift our forces to destroy the enemy in mobile warfare, our enemies were jubilant. They took this to be their victory and our defeat. They became dizzy with this momentary "victory". On the afternoon of the day he seized Changchiakou, Chiang Kai-shek ordered the convening of his reactionary National Assembly, as though his reactionary regime had from that moment become as stable as Mount Taishan. The U.S. imperialists, too, danced with joy, as though their wild scheme for converting China into a U.S. colony could now be realized without obstruction. But with the lapse of time, Chiang Kai-shek and his U.S. masters began to change their tune. Now all our enemies, domestic and foreign, are gripped by pessimism. They heave great sighs, wail about a crisis and no longer show any sign of joy. In the past eighteen months, most of Chiang Kai-shek's high-ranking field commanders have been replaced for losing battles. Among them are Liu Chih (Chengchow), Hsueh Yueh (Hsuchow), Wu Chi-wei (northern Kiangsu), Tang En-po (southern Shantung), Wang Chung-lien (northern Honan), Tu Yu-ming and Hsiung Shih-hui (Shenyang) and Sun Lien-chung (Peiping). Chen Cheng, too, was relieved of his post as Chiang Kai-shek's chief of staff in over-all command of operations and demoted to command a single front in the Northeast.[2] However, it was in the very period when Chiang Kai-shek himself assumed over-all command in Chen Cheng's place that the situation changed and that his armies shifted from the offensive to the defensive, while the People's Liberation Army went over from the defensive to the offensive. By now the reactionary Chiang Kai-shek clique and its U.S. masters should have realized their mistake. They had regarded as signs of cowardice and weakness all the efforts for peace and against civil war which the Communist Party of China, representing the wishes of the Chinese people, had made over a long period after the surrender of Japan. They had overestimated their own strength, underestimated the strength of the revolution and rashly unleashed the war and so were caught in their own trap. Our enemy's strategic calculations failed completely.

IV

The rear areas of the People's Liberation Army are much more consolidated now than eighteen months ago. The reason is that our Party, standing resolutely on the side of the peasants, has carried out the land reform. During the War of Resistance Against Japan, our Party, on its own initiative and for the sake of forming an anti-Japanese united front with the Kuomintang and uniting with those who could still oppose Japanese imperialism, changed its pre-war policy of confiscating the land of the landlords and distributing it among the peasants to the policy of reducing rent and interest. This was entirely necessary. After the Japanese surrender, the peasants urgently demanded land, and we made a timely decision to change our land policy from reducing rent and interest to confiscating the land of the landlord class for distribution among the peasants. The directive issued by the Central Committee of our Party on May 4, 1946,[3] marked this change. In September 1947 our Party called the National Land Conference and drew up the Outline Land Law of China,[4] which was promptly carried out in all areas. This measure not only reaffirmed the policy set forth in last year's "May 4th Directive" but also explicitly corrected a certain lack of thoroughness in that directive. The Outline Land Law provides for equal distribution of land per head,[5] based on the principle of abolishing the land system of feudal and semi-feudal exploitation and putting into effect the system of land to the tillers. This is a method which most thoroughly abolishes the feudal system and fully meets the demands of the broad masses of China's peasants. To carry out the land reform resolutely and thoroughly, it is necessary to organize in the villages, as lawful bodies for carrying out the reform, not only peasant associations on the broadest mass basis, including farm labourers, poor peasants and middle peasants and their elected committees, but first of all poor peasant leagues composed of poor peasants and farm labourers and their elected committees; and these poor peasant leagues should be the backbone of leadership in all rural struggles. Our policy is to rely on the poor peasants and unite solidly with the middle peasants to abolish the feudal and semi-feudal system of exploitation by the landlord class and by the old-type rich peasants. Landlords or rich peasants must not be allotted more land and property than the peasant masses. But there should be no repetition of the wrong ultra-Left policy, which was carried out in 1931-34, of "allotting no land to the landlords and poor land to the rich peasants". Although the proportion of landlords and rich peasants in the rural population varies from place to place, it is generally only about 8 per cent (in terms of households), while their holdings usually amount to 70 to 80 per cent of all the land. Therefore the targets of our land reform are very few, while the people in the villages who can and should take part in the united front for land reform are many – more than 90 per cent (in terms of households). Here two fundamental principles must be observed. First, the demands of the poor peasants and farm labourers must be satisfied; this is the most fundamental task in the land reform. Second, there must be firm unity with the middle peasants, and their interests must not be damaged. As long as we grasp these two basic principles, we can certainly carry out our tasks in the land reform successfully. The reason why, under the principle of equal distribution, the surplus land and part of the property of the old-type rich peasants should be handed over for distribution is that the rich peasants in China generally and to a great degree have the character of feudal and semi-feudal exploiters; most of them also rent out land and practise usury and they hire labour on semi-feudal terms.[6] Furthermore, as the rich peasants have more and better land,[7] the demands of the poor peasants and farm labourers cannot be satisfied unless this land is distributed. However, in accordance with the Outline Land Law, rich peasants should generally be treated differently from landlords. In the land reform, the middle peasants show approval of equal distribution because it does no harm to their interests. Under equal distribution, the land of one section of the middle peasants remains unchanged and that of another is increased; only the section of well-to-do middle peasants has a little surplus land, and they are willing to hand it over for equal distribution because their burden of land tax will then be lightened. Nevertheless, in carrying out equal distribution of land in different places, it is necessary to listen to the opinions of the middle peasants and make concessions to them if they object. During the confiscation and distribution of the land and property of the feudal class, the needs of certain middle peasants should receive attention. In determining class status care must be taken to avoid the mistake of classifying middle peasants as rich peasants. The active middle peasants must be drawn into the work of the peasant association committees and the government. With respect to the burdens of the land tax and of supporting the war, the principle of being fair and reasonable must be observed. These are the specific policies our Party must follow in carrying out its strategic task of uniting solidly with the middle peasants. The whole Party must understand that thoroughgoing reform of the land system is a basic task of the Chinese revolution in its present stage. If we can solve the land problem universally and completely, we shall have obtained the most fundamental condition for the defeat of all our enemies.

V

To carry out the land reform resolutely and thoroughly and to consolidate the rear areas of the People's Liberation Army, it is necessary to educate and reorganize the ranks of our Party.   On the whole, the rectification movement[8] inside the Party during the War of Resistance Against Japan was successful.   Its main success was that our leading bodies and large numbers of cadres and Party members obtained a firmer grasp of our basic orientation, which is to unite the universal truth of Marxism-Leninism with the concrete practice of the Chinese revolution.   In this respect our Party has taken a big stride forward as compared with all the historical stages before the War of Resistance.   However, in the Party's local organizations, especially the organizations at the primary level in the countryside, the problem of impurities in the class composition of our ranks and in our style of work is still unsolved.   During the eleven years 1937-47 the membership of our Party has grown from several tens of thousands to 2,700,000, and this is a very big leap forward.   This has made our Party a more powerful party than any in Chinese history.   It has enabled us to defeat Japanese imperialism, beat back Chiang Kai-shek's offensives, lead the Liberated Areas with a population of more than 100 million and lead a People's Liberation Army two million strong.   But shortcomings have also cropped up.   Many landlords, rich peasants and riffraff have seized the opportunity to sneak into our Party.   In the rural areas they control a number of Party, government and people's organizations, tyrannically abuse their power, ride roughshod over the people, distort the Party's policies and thus alienate these organizations from the masses and prevent the land reform from being thorough.   This grave situation sets us the task of educating and reorganizing the ranks of our Party.   We cannot make headway in the countryside unless we perform this task.   The Party's National Land Conference discussed this problem thoroughly and laid down the proper measures and methods.   These are now being resolutely applied everywhere, together with the decision on the equal distribution of land.   First and foremost comes the unfolding of criticism and self-criticism within the Party and the thorough exposure of mistaken ideas and serious situations in the local organizations, which are departures from the Party line.   All Party members must realize that a decisive link in the solution of the land problem and for the support of the long-drawn-out war is the removal of impurities from Party organizations and the education and reorganization of the Party's ranks, so that the Party and the broadest masses of working people can all march in the same direction and the Party can lead the masses forward.

VI

Confiscate the land of the feudal class and turn it over to the peasants. Confiscate monopoly capital, headed by Chiang Kai-shek, T. V. Soong, H. H. Kung and Chen Li-fu, and turn it over to the new-democratic state. Protect the industry and commerce of the national bourgeoisie. These are the three major economic policies of the new-democratic revolution. During their twenty-year rule, the four big families, Chiang, Soong, Kung and Chen, have piled up enormous fortunes valued at ten to twenty thousand million U.S. dollars and monopolized the economic lifelines of the whole country. This monopoly capital, combined with state power, has become state-monopoly capitalism. This monopoly capitalism, closely tied up with foreign imperialism, the domestic landlord class and the old-type rich peasants, has become comprador, feudal, state-monopoly capitalism. Such is the economic base of Chiang Kai-shek's reactionary regime. This state-monopoly capitalism oppresses not only the workers and peasants but also the urban petty bourgeoisie, and it injures the middle bourgeoisie. This state-monopoly capitalism reached the peak of its development during the War of Resistance and after the Japanese surrender; it has prepared ample material conditions for the new-democratic revolution. This capital is popularly known in China as bureaucrat-capital. This capitalist class, known as the bureaucrat-capitalist class, is the big bourgeoisie of China. Besides doing away with the special privileges of imperialism in China, the task of the new-democratic revolution at home is to abolish exploitation and oppression by the landlord class and by the bureaucrat-capitalist class (the big bourgeoisie), change the comprador, feudal relations of production and unfetter the productive forces. The upper petty bourgeoisie and middle bourgeoisie, oppressed and injured by the landlords and big bourgeoisie and their state power, may take part in the new-democratic revolution or stay neutral, though they are themselves bourgeois. They have no ties, or comparatively few, with imperialism and are the genuine national bourgeoisie. Wherever the state power of New Democracy extends, it must firmly and unhesitatingly protect them. In Chiang Kai-shek's areas, there are a small number of people among the upper petty bourgeoisie and the middle bourgeoisie, the right wing of these classes, who have reactionary political tendencies, spread illusions about U.S. imperialism and the reactionary Chiang Kai-shek clique and oppose the people's democratic revolution. As

long as their reactionary tendencies can affect the masses, we should
unmask them before the people under their political influence, attack
this influence and liberate the masses from it. But political attack and
economic annihilation are two different matters, and we shall make
mistakes if we confuse the two. The new-democratic revolution aims
at wiping out only feudalism and monopoly capitalism, only the landlord class and the bureaucrat-capitalist class (the big bourgeoisie),
and not at wiping out capitalism in general, the upper petty bourgeoisie or the middle bourgeoisie. In view of China's economic
backwardness, even after the country-wide victory of the revolution,
it will still be necessary to permit the existence for a long time of a
capitalist sector of the economy represented by the extensive upper
petty bourgeoisie and middle bourgeoisie. In accordance with the
division of labour in the national economy, a certain development of
all parts of this capitalist sector which are beneficial to the national
economy will still be needed. This capitalist sector will still be an
indispensable part of the whole national economy. The upper petty
bourgeoisie referred to here are small industrialists and merchants
employing workers or assistants. In addition, there are also great
numbers of small independent craftsmen and traders who employ no
workers or assistants and, needless to say, they should be firmly protected. After the victory of the revolution all over the country, the new-
democratic state will possess huge state enterprises taken over from
the bureaucrat-capitalist class and controlling the economic lifelines
of the country, and there will be an agricultural economy liberated
from feudalism which, though it will remain basically scattered and
individual for a fairly long time, can later be led to develop, step by
step, in the direction of co-operatives. In these circumstances the
existence and development of these small and middle capitalist sectors
will present no danger. The same is true of the new rich peasant
economy which will inevitably emerge in the rural areas after the
land reform. It is absolutely impermissible to repeat such wrong
ultra-Left policies towards the upper petty bourgeois and middle
bourgeois sectors in the economy as our Party adopted during 1931-34
(unduly advanced labour conditions, excessive income tax rates, encroachment on the interests of industrialists and merchants during the
land reform, and the adoption as a goal of the so-called "workers'
welfare", which was a short-sighted and one-sided concept, instead of
the goal of developing production, promoting economic prosperity, giving consideration to both public and private interests and benefiting

both labour and capital). To repeat such mistakes would certainly damage the interests both of the working masses and of the new-democratic state. One of the provisions in the Outline Land Law of China reads, "The property and lawful business of industrialists and merchants shall be protected from encroachment." "Industrialists and merchants" refers to all small independent craftsmen and traders as well as all small and middle capitalist elements. To sum up, the economic structure of New China will consist of: (1) the state-owned economy, which is the leading sector; (2) the agricultural economy, developing step by step from individual to collective; and (3) the economy of small independent craftsmen and traders and the economy of small and middle private capital. These constitute the whole of the new-democratic national economy. The principles guiding the new-democratic national economy must closely conform to the general objective of developing production, promoting economic prosperity, giving consideration to both public and private interests and benefiting both labour and capital. Any principle, policy or measure that deviates from this general objective is wrong.

VII

The People's Liberation Army issued a manifesto in October 1947 which stated in part:

Unite workers, peasants, soldiers, intellectuals and businessmen, all oppressed classes, all people's organizations, democratic parties, minority nationalities, overseas Chinese and other patriots; form a national united front; overthrow the dictatorial Chiang Kai-shek government; and establish a democratic coalition government.

That is the fundamental political programme of the People's Liberation Army and of the Communist Party of China. On the surface, our revolutionary national united front appears to have narrowed in the present period as compared with the period of the War of Resistance. As a matter of fact, it has been precisely in the present period, after Chiang Kai-shek sold out the nation's interests to U.S. imperialism and launched the country-wide civil war against the people and after the crimes of U.S. imperialism and the reactionary Chiang Kai-shek clique were completely exposed before the Chinese people, that our national united front has really broadened.   During the War of Resistance, Chiang Kai-shek and the Kuomintang were not yet completely discredited among the Chinese people and were still able to deceive them in many ways.   Now it is different; all their deceptions have been shown up by their own deeds, they no longer have any mass following, they are completely isolated.   In contrast to the Kuomintang, the Communist Party of China not only has the confidence of the broadest masses of the people in the Liberated Areas but has also won the support of the broad masses in the areas and big cities under Kuomintang control.   If in 1946 a section of the upper petty bourgeois and middle bourgeois intellectuals under Chiang Kai-shek's rule still cherished the idea of a so-called third road,[9] this idea is now bankrupt. Because our Party adopted a thoroughgoing land policy, it has won whole-hearted support from much broader masses of peasants than during the War of Resistance.   As a result of U.S. imperialist aggression, Chiang Kai-shek's oppression and our Party's correct policy of firmly protecting the interests of the masses, our Party has won the sympathy of the broad masses of the working class, the peasantry and the urban petty and middle bourgeoisie in Chiang Kai-shek's areas. Driven by hunger, political oppression and Chiang Kai-shek's civil war against the people, which has made life impossible, the masses have been waging incessant struggles against U.S. imperialism and Chiang Kai-shek's reactionary government; their basic slogans are against hunger, against persecution, against civil war and against U.S. interference in China's internal affairs.   Never before has their awakening reached such a level, neither before nor during the War of Resistance, nor in the period immediately after the Japanese surrender.   That is why we say that our new-democratic revolutionary united front is now broader and more consolidated than ever.   This development is not only linked with our land and urban policies but is also closely linked with the whole political situation – with the victories of the People's Liberation Army, with Chiang Kai-shek's turn from the offensive to the defensive, with the People's Liberation Army's turn from the defensive to the offensive, with the period of a new high tide in the Chinese revolution.   Realizing that Chiang Kai-shek's regime is inevitably doomed, people now place their hopes on the Communist Party of China and the People's Liberation Army, and this is quite natural.   Without the broadest united front of the overwhelming majority of the population, it will be impossible to win victory in China's new-democratic revolution.   Moreover, this united front must be under the firm leadership of the Communist Party of China. Without the Party's firm leadership, no revolutionary united front can win victory. When the Northern Expedition reached its climax in 1927, the capitulationists in our Party's leading body voluntarily gave up the Party's leadership of the peasant masses, urban petty bourgeoisie and middle bourgeoisie, and in particular gave up the Party's leadership of the armed forces, thus causing the defeat of the revolution. During the War of Resistance, our Party combated ideas similar to those of the capitulationists, that is, such ideas as making concessions to the Kuomintang's anti-popular policies, having more confidence in the Kuomintang than in the masses, not daring to arouse and give full rein to mass struggles, not daring to expand the Liberated Areas and the people's armies in the Japanese-occupied areas, and handing over the leadership in the War of Resistance to the Kuomintang. Our Party waged a resolute struggle against such impotent and degenerate ideas, which run counter to the principles of Marxism-Leninism, resolutely carried out its political line of "developing the progressive forces, winning over the middle forces and isolating the die-hard forces" and resolutely expanded the Liberated Areas and the People's Liberation Army. This ensured not only that our Party was able to defeat Japanese imperialism in the period of its aggression, but also that, in the period after the Japanese surrender when Chiang Kai-shek launched his counter-revolutionary war, our Party was able to switch smoothly and without loss to the course of opposing Chiang Kai-shek's counter-revolutionary war with a people's revolutionary war and to win great victories in a short time. All Party comrades must keep these lessons of history firmly in mind.

VIII

When the reactionary Chiang Kai-shek clique launched the country-wide civil war against the people in 1946, the reason they dared take this risk was that they relied not merely on their own superior military strength but mainly on the U.S. imperialists with their atom bombs, whom they regarded as "exceptionally powerful" and "matchless in the world". On the one hand, they thought U.S. imperialism could meet their military and financial needs with a stream of supplies. On the other hand, they wildly speculated that "war between the United States and the Soviet Union is inevitable" and that "the outbreak of a third world war is inevitable". This dependence on U.S. imperialism is the common feature of the reactionary forces in all countries since World War II. It reflects the severity of the blows world capitalism received in World War II; it reflects the weakness of the reactionary forces in all countries, their panic and loss of confidence; and it reflects the might of the world revolutionary forces – all of which make reactionaries in all countries feel that there is no way out except to rely on U.S. imperialist support. But, in fact, is U.S. imperialism after World War II as powerful as Chiang Kai-shek and the reactionaries of other countries imagine? Can it really pour out a stream of supplies for them? No, that is not so. The economic power of U.S. imperialism, which grew during World War II, is confronted with unstable and daily shrinking domestic and foreign markets. The further shrinking of these markets will cause economic crises to break out. The war boom in the United States of America was only temporary. The strength of the United States of America is only superficial and transient. Irreconcilable domestic and international contradictions, like a volcano, menace U.S. imperialism every day. U.S. imperialism is sitting on this volcano. This situation has driven the U.S. imperialists to draw up a plan for enslaving the world, to run amuck like wild beasts in Europe, Asia and other parts of the world, to muster the reactionary forces in all countries, the human dregs cast off by their peoples, to form an imperialist and anti-democratic camp against all the democratic forces headed by the Soviet Union, and to prepare for war in the hope that in the future, at a distant time, some day, they can start a third world war to defeat the democratic forces. This is a preposterous plan. The democratic forces of the world must defeat this plan and certainly can defeat it. The strength of the world anti-imperialist camp has surpassed that of the imperialist camp. It is we, not the enemy, who are in the superior position. The anti-imperialist camp headed by the Soviet Union has already been formed. The socialist Soviet Union is free from crises, on the ascendant and cherished by the world's broad masses; its strength has already surpassed that of the imperialist United States, which is seriously menaced by crises, on the decline and opposed by the world's broad masses. The People's Democracies in Europe are consolidating themselves internally and are uniting with each other. In the European capitalist countries the people's anti-imperialist forces are developing, with those in France and Italy taking the lead. Within the United States, there are people's democratic forces which are getting stronger every day. The peoples of Latin America are not slaves obedient to U.S. imperialism. In the whole of Asia a great national liberation movement has arisen. All the forces of the anti-imperialist camp are uniting and forging ahead. The Communist and Workers' Parties of nine European countries have established their Information Bureau and issued a call to the people of the world to rise against the imperialist plan of enslavement.[10] This call to battle has inspired the oppressed people of the world, charted the course of their struggle and strengthened their confidence in victory. It has thrown world reaction into panic and confusion. All the anti-imperialist forces in the countries of the East, too, should unite together, oppose oppression by imperialism and by their domestic reactionaries and make the goal of their struggle the emancipation of the more than 1,000 million oppressed people of the East. We certainly should grasp our own destiny in our own hands. We should rid our ranks of all impotent thinking. All views that overestimate the strength of the enemy and underestimate the strength of the people are wrong. If everyone makes strenuous efforts, we, together with all the democratic forces of the world, can surely defeat the imperialist plan of enslavement, prevent the outbreak of a third world war, overthrow all reactionary regimes and win lasting peace for mankind. We are soberly aware that on our way forward there will still be all kinds of obstacles and difficulties and that we should be prepared to deal with the maximum resistance and desperate struggle by all our enemies, domestic and foreign. But so long as we can grasp the science of Marxism-Leninism, have confidence in the masses, stand closely together with the masses and lead them forward, we shall be fully able to surmount any obstacle and overcome any difficulty. Our strength will be invincible. This is the historic epoch in which world capitalism and imperialism are going down to their doom and world socialism and people's democracy are marching to victory. The dawn is ahead, we must exert ourselves.

NOTES

[1] For the circumstances of how the People's Liberation Army went over to the offensive on various fronts in succession and carried the war into the Kuomintang areas, see "On the Great Victory in the Northwest and on the New Type of Ideological Education Movement in the Liberation Army", Note 4, pp. 215-16 of this volume.

² Liu Chih, Director of the Kuomintang's Pacification Headquarters in Chengchow, Honan Province, was dismissed in November 1946 for his defeat in the battle of Tingtao, southwestern Shantung Province, in September. Hsueh Yueh, Director of the Kuomintang's Pacification Headquarters in Hsuchow, Kiangsu Province, was dismissed in March 1947 for a series of heavy defeats suffered by the Kuomintang troops under his command: in the campaign in the area north of Suchien, Kiangsu Province, in December 1946; in the campaign in southern Shantung in January 1947; and in the Laiwu campaign, central Shantung, in February 1947. Wu Chi-wei, Deputy Director of the Kuomintang's Pacification Headquarters in Hsuchow, was dismissed in March 1947 for his defeat in the campaign in the area north of Suchien in December 1946. Tang En-po, Commander of the Kuomintang's 1st Army, was dismissed in June 1947 because the Kuomintang's Reorganized 74th Division was wiped out in the battle of Mengliangku, southern Shantung, in May. Wang Chung-lien, Commander of the Kuomintang's 4th Army, was dismissed in August 1947 for his defeat in the Southwestern Shantung campaign in July. Tu Yu-ming, Commander of the Kuomintang's Peace Preservation Headquarters in the Northeast, and Hsiung Shih-hui, Director of the Kuomintang Generalissimo's Headquarters in the Northeast, were both dismissed for being severely defeated by the People's Liberation Army in its summer offensive in the Northeast in June 1947. Sun Lien-chung, Commander of the Kuomintang's 11th War Zone, was demoted to Director of the Pacification Headquarters in Paoting, Hopei Province, for his defeats in the Ching-Tsang campaign and the campaign in the Hsushui area north of Paoting in June 1947. Chen Cheng, Chiang Kai-shek's chief of general staff, was demoted to governor-general of the Northeast in August 1947 because of the successive defeats of the campaigns he directed in Shantung Province.

³ For the directive, see "A Three Months' Summary", Note 4, p. 118 of this volume.

⁴ The National Land Conference of the Communist Party of China was held in September 1947 in Hsipaipo Village, Pingshan County, Hopei Province. The Outline Land Law of China, adopted by the conference on September 13, was published by the Central Committee of the Communist Party of China on October 10, 1947. It stipulated the following:

Abolish the land system of feudal and semi-feudal exploitation and put into effect the system of land to the tillers.

All the land of the landlords and the public land in the villages is to be taken over by the local peasant associations and, together with all other land there, is to be equally distributed among the entire rural population, regardless of sex or age.

The peasant associations of the villages shall take over the draught animals, farm tools, houses, grain and other property of the landlords, requisition the surplus of such property of the rich peasants, distribute all this property among the peasants and other poor people who are in need of it and allot the same share to the landlords.

Thus the Outline Land Law not only confirmed the principle of "confiscation of the land of the landlords and its distribution among the peasants" laid down in the "May 4th Directive" of 1946 but also made up for the lack of thoroughness in that directive, which had shown too much consideration for certain landlords.

⁵ Subsequently in the implementation some changes were made in the method of equal distribution of land provided in the Outline Land Law of China. In February 1948 the Central Committee of the Communist Party of China specified in its "Directive on the Work of Land Reform and of Party Consolidation in the Old and

Semi-Old Areas" that in the old and semi-old Liberated Areas where the feudal system had already been overthrown, there would be no further equal distribution of land, but that the poor peasants and farm labourers who had not yet completely shaken off the feudal yoke should, if circumstances so required, be given a certain amount of land and other means of production through readjustment, by the method of taking from those who had a surplus and giving to those who had a shortage and taking from those who had better and giving to those who had worse, while the middle peasants would be allowed to keep more land than the average poor peasant. In areas where the feudal system still existed, equal distribution was confined mainly to the land and property of landlords and the surplus land and property of old-type rich peasants. In all areas, it was permissible to take the surplus land of middle peasants and new-type rich peasants for purposes of readjustment only if this was actually necessary and if the owners really consented. In the land reform in the new Liberated Areas, no land was to be taken from any middle peasant.

[6] The question of the rich peasants in China's land reform was a peculiar one arising from her specific historical and economic conditions. China's rich peasants differed from those in many capitalist countries in two respects: first, they generally and to a great degree had the character of feudal and semi-feudal exploiters and, second, this rich peasant economy did not occupy an important place in the country's agricultural economy. In the struggle against feudal exploitation by the landlord class in China, the broad masses of poor peasants and farm labourers also demanded the abolition of feudal and semi-feudal exploitation by the rich peasants. During the War of Liberation, the Communist Party of China adopted the policy of requisitioning the surplus land and property of rich peasants for distribution among the peasants, and thus satisfied the demands of the masses of poor peasants and farm labourers and ensured victory in the People's War of Liberation. As the war progressed towards victory, the Central Committee of the Communist Party of China in February 1948 laid down new policies for the land reform in the new Liberated Areas. The reform was to be divided into two stages: in the first stage, neutralize the rich peasants and concentrate the blows on the landlords, primarily the big landlords; in the second stage, while distributing the land of the landlords, also distribute the land rented out by rich peasants and their surplus land, but continue to treat the rich peasants differently from the landlords (see "Essential Points in Land Reform in the New Liberated Areas", pp. 201-02 of this volume). After the founding of the People's Republic of China, the Central People's Government in June 1950 promulgated the Land Reform Law, which provided that in the land reform only the land rented out by the rich peasants should partly or wholly be requisitioned, while the rest of their land and property was to be protected. In the subsequent stage of socialist revolution, the rich peasant economy disappeared as the movement for agricultural co-operation deepened and the rural economy developed.

[7] That is to say, a rich peasant household owned on the average more and better land than a poor peasant household. Taking the country as a whole, the quantity of the means of production owned by China's rich peasants and the volume of their farm produce were both very small. The rich peasant economy did not occupy an important place in China's rural economy.

[8] This refers to the movement for rectifying the style of work conducted by the Communist Party of China in 1942-43 throughout the Party; its content was the combating of subjectivism, sectarianism and stereotyped writing. Under the leadership of Comrade Mao Tse-tung, this rectification movement adopted the principles of "learning from past mistakes to avoid their repetition, curing the sickness to save the patient" and "clearing up wrong thinking while uniting with

comrades". Through the method of criticism and self-criticism, the movement corrected the "Left" and Right errors which had occurred on various occasions in the history of the Party by getting down to their ideological roots, greatly raised the ideological level of the broad ranks of Party cadres, helped immensely to unify thinking within the Party on the basis of Marxism-Leninism and thus brought about a high degree of unity in the whole Party.

[9] In the early stage of the People's War of Liberation some democratic personages fancied that they could find a so-called third road, apart from the Kuomintang dictatorship of big landlords and big bourgeoisie and apart from the people's democratic dictatorship led by the Communist Party of China. This third road was in fact the road of a dictatorship of the bourgeoisie on the British and U.S. pattern.

[10] The Information Bureau of the Communist and Workers' Parties was founded at a meeting held in Warsaw, Poland, in September 1947 by representatives of the Communist and Workers' Parties of Bulgaria, Rumania, Hungary, Poland, the Soviet Union, France, Czechoslovakia, Italy and Yugoslavia. Later, at a meeting in Rumania in June 1948, the Bureau announced the expulsion of the Yugoslav Communist Party because the latter persisted in its anti-Marxist-Leninist stand and adopted an attitude opposed to the Soviet Union and the socialist camp. The Information Bureau's call to the people of the world to rise against the imperialist plan of enslavement, mentioned here by Comrade Mao Tse-tung, was the "Declaration on the International Situation" adopted at the September 1947 meeting of the Information Bureau.

ON SETTING UP A SYSTEM OF REPORTS*

January 7, 1948

In order to provide the Central Committee with timely information so that it can help all areas, either before or after the event, to avoid mistakes or commit fewer mistakes and win even greater victories in the revolutionary war, the following system of reports is instituted, beginning with this year.

1. For each bureau or sub-bureau of the Central Committee, the secretary is responsible for submitting to the Central Committee and its chairman a comprehensive bi-monthly report (written by himself, not by his assistants). The report should cover military, political, land reform, Party consolidation, economic, propaganda and cultural activities, the problems and tendencies that have arisen in these activities and the methods of dealing with them. Each report should be limited to about a thousand words and, except in special cases, should not exceed two thousand words. When all questions cannot be covered in one report, write two. Or the first report may concentrate on certain questions and deal briefly with the rest, and the next report may concentrate on the latter and deal briefly with the former. The comprehensive report should be concise in content and succinct in wording and point out the problems or controversial issues. It should be written and telegraphed early in every odd month. This is to be the regular report and request for instructions which the secretary of each bureau or sub-bureau is personally responsible for submitting to the Central Committee and its chairman. When the secretary is at the front directing military operations, he should, in addition to submitting his own reports, authorize the acting secretary or deputy secretary to report on rear-area activities. The above does not include occasional reports and requests for instructions which the bureaus or sub-bureaus should continue to submit to the Central Committee.

We are instituting this system of regular comprehensive policy reports and requests for instructions because, after the Seventh

177

National Congress of our Party, some (not all) comrades in the bureaus or sub-bureaus still do not realize the necessity and importance of submitting reports to the Central Committee and asking for instructions before or after the event, or they send reports and requests for instructions only on technical points; and, as a result, the Central Committee is not clear or is not sufficiently clear about their major activities and policies (not those of secondary importance or of a technical nature), and therefore certain things have occurred that cannot be remedied or are hard to remedy, or can be remedied but have already caused losses. Those bureaus and sub-bureaus that have asked for prior instructions and submitted reports afterwards have avoided or reduced such losses. Beginning with this year, the Party's leading bodies at all levels must correct the bad habit of neither asking the higher level for prior instructions nor submitting reports afterwards. The bureaus and sub-bureaus, being organs appointed by the Central Committee to carry out on its behalf the tasks entrusted to them, must keep in the closest possible contact with the Central Committee. Also, the provincial or area Party committees must keep in close contact with the bureaus and sub-bureaus of the Central Committee. At a time when the revolution has entered a period of new high tide, it is imperative to strengthen these contacts.

2. Leaders of field armies and military areas, apart from their obligation to submit reports and requests for instructions on matters of strategy when necessary and their obligation to submit, as previously required, monthly reports on combat gains, on losses and munitions consumed and on the actual strength of their forces, must

---

* This inner-Party directive was drafted by Comrade Mao Tse-tung for the Central Committee of the Communist Party of China. The system of reports instituted in the directive was a development under new conditions in the long struggle of the Central Committee firmly to uphold democratic centralism and combat tendencies of indiscipline and anarchy. The problem was especially important at that time because there had been tremendous progress in the revolutionary situation. Many Liberated Areas had been linked together, many cities had been or were about to be liberated, the People's Liberation Army had become much more of a regular army, the People's War of Liberation had become much more of a regular war, and country-wide victory was in sight. This situation demanded that the Party should speedily overcome any conditions of indiscipline or anarchy existing in the Party and the army and should concentrate in the Central Committee all the powers that had to be and could be centralized. The setting up of a strict system of reports was an important step taken by the Party for this purpose. On this question, see also "The Work of Land Reform and of Party Consolidation in 1948", Section 6, p. 258 and "On the September Meeting – Circular of the Central Committee of the Communist Party of China", Point 4, pp. 273-74, of this volume.

also submit comprehensive policy reports and requests for instructions every two months, beginning this year. These should cover the discipline of the troops, their living conditions, the morale of commanders and fighters, any deviations that have arisen among commanders and fighters and the methods for overcoming them, the progress or retrogression in technique and tactics, the strong and weak points of the enemy forces and whether their morale is high or low, the political work of our army, its implementation of land policy, urban policy and policy concerning captives and the methods of overcoming deviations from these policies, the relations between the army and the people and the trends among different strata of the people. The length, method of writing and time of dispatch of these reports should be the same as those laid down for reports by the bureaus and sub-bureaus of the Central Committee. If intense fighting is going on when a report is due (that is, early in every odd month), its submission may be advanced or postponed a few days, but the reasons must be given. The section dealing with political work should be drafted by the director of the army's political department, examined and corrected by the commander and political commissar and then jointly signed by all three. These reports should be telegraphed to the Chairman of the Party's Military Commission. We require these comprehensive policy reports for the same reasons as we require such reports from the bureaus and sub-bureaus.

ON SOME IMPORTANT PROBLEMS OF
THE PARTY'S PRESENT POLICY*

January 18, 1948

I. THE PROBLEM OF COMBATING ERRONEOUS
TENDENCIES WITHIN THE PARTY

Oppose overestimation of the enemy's strength. For example: fear of U.S. imperialism; fear of carrying the battle into the Kuomintang areas; fear of wiping out the comprador-feudal system, of distributing the land of the landlords and of confiscating bureaucrat-capital; fear of a long-drawn-out war; and so on. All these are incorrect. Imperialism throughout the world and the rule of the reactionary Chiang Kai-shek clique in China are already rotten and have no future. We have reason to despise them and we are confident and certain that we shall defeat all the domestic and foreign enemies of the Chinese people. But with regard to each part, each specific struggle (military, political, economic or ideological), we must never take the enemy lightly; on the contrary, we should take the enemy seriously and concentrate all our strength for battle in order to win victory. While we correctly point out that, strategically, with regard to the whole, we should take the enemy lightly, we must never take the enemy lightly in any part, in any specific struggle. If, with regard to the whole, we overestimate the strength of our enemy and hence do not dare to overthrow him and do not dare to win victory, we shall be committing a Right opportunist error. If, with regard to each part, each specific problem, we are not prudent, do not carefully study and perfect the art of struggle, do not concentrate all our strength for battle and do not pay attention to winning over all the allies that should be won over (middle peasants, small independent craftsmen and traders, the middle bourgeoisie, students, teachers, professors and ordinary intellectuals, ordinary government employees, professionals

and enlightened gentry), we shall be committing a "Left" opportunist error.

In combating "Left" and Right deviations within the Party, we
must decide on our policy according to specific circumstances. For
example, the army must guard against "Left" deviations in times of
victory and guard against Right deviations in times of defeat or when
we are unable to win many battles. In land reform, Right deviations
must be combated where the masses have not yet been aroused in
earnest and the struggle has not yet unfolded, and "Left" deviations
must be guarded against where the masses have been aroused in
earnest and the struggle has already unfolded.

II. SOME CONCRETE PROBLEMS OF POLICY IN THE LAND REFORM AND MASS MOVEMENTS

1. The interests of the poor peasants and farm labourers and the
forward role of the poor peasant leagues must be our first concern.
Our Party must launch the land reform through the poor peasants and
farm labourers and must enable them to play the forward role in the
peasant associations and in the government organs of the rural districts.
This forward role consists in forging unity with the middle peasants
for common action and not in casting aside the middle peasants
and monopolizing the work. The position of the middle peasants is
especially important in the old Liberated Areas where the middle
peasants are the majority and the poor peasants and farm labourers a
minority. The slogan, "the poor peasants and farm labourers conquer
the country and should rule the country", is wrong. In the villages,
it is the farm labourers, poor peasants, middle peasants and other
working people, united together under the leadership of the Chinese
Communist Party, who conquer the country and should rule the country, and it is not the poor peasants and farm labourers alone who
conquer the country and should rule the country. In the country as
a whole, it is the workers, peasants (including the new rich peasants),
small independent craftsmen and traders, middle and small capitalists
oppressed and injured by the reactionary forces, the students, teachers,

---

* This inner-Party directive was drafted by Comrade Mao Tse-tung for the Central
Committee of the Communist Party of China. See the introductory note to "The
Present Situation and Our Tasks", pp. 158-59 of this volume.

professors and ordinary intellectuals, professionals, enlightened gentry, ordinary government employees, oppressed minority nationalities and overseas Chinese, all united together under the leadership of the working class (through the Communist Party), who conquer the country and should rule the country, and it is not merely some of the people who conquer the country and should rule the country.

2. We must avoid adopting any adventurist policies towards the middle peasants. In the cases of middle peasants and persons of other strata whose class status has been wrongly determined, correction should be made without fail, and any of their belongings that have been distributed should be returned, as far as that is possible. The tendency to exclude middle peasants from the ranks of the peasants' representatives and from the peasants' committees and the tendency to counterpose them to the poor peasants and farm labourers in the land reform struggle must be corrected. Peasants with an income from exploitation should be classified as middle peasants if such income is less than 25 per cent of their total income, and classified as rich peasants if it is more.[1] The land of well-to-do middle peasants must not be distributed without the owner's consent.

3. We must avoid adopting any adventurist policies towards middle and small industrialists and merchants. The policy, adopted in the past in the Liberated Areas, of protecting and encouraging the development of all private industry and commerce beneficial to the national economy was correct and should be continued in the future. The policy of encouraging landlords and rich peasants to switch to industry and commerce, adopted during the period of rent and interest reduction, was also correct; it is wrong to regard such switching as a "disguise" and therefore to oppose it and confiscate and distribute the property so switched. The industrial and commercial holdings of landlords and rich peasants should in general be protected; the only industrial and commercial holdings that may be confiscated are those of bureaucrat-capitalists and of real counter-revolutionary local tyrants. Among the industrial and commercial enterprises which should be confiscated, those beneficial to the national economy must continue to operate after they have been taken over by the state and the people and must not be allowed to break up or close down. The transactions tax on the industry and commerce which are beneficial to the national economy should be levied only to the extent that it does not hamper their development. In each public enterprise, the administration and the trade union must set up a joint management committee to strengthen

the work of management in order to reduce costs, increase output and see that both public and individual interests are benefited. Private capitalist enterprises should also try out this method in order to reduce costs, increase output and benefit both labour and capital. The workers' livelihood must be appropriately improved, but unduly high wages and benefits must be avoided.

4. We must avoid adopting any adventurist policies towards students, teachers, professors, scientific workers, art workers and ordinary intellectuals. The experience of China's student movements and revolutionary struggles has proved that the overwhelming majority of these people can take part in the revolution or remain neutral; the die-hard counter-revolutionaries are a tiny minority. Our Party should, therefore, adopt a careful attitude towards students, teachers, professors, scientific workers, art workers and ordinary intellectuals. We should unite with them, educate them and give them posts according to the merits of each case, and only a tiny number of die-hard counter-revolutionaries among them will have to be appropriately dealt with through the mass line.

5. On the question of the enlightened gentry. Our Party's co-operation with the enlightened gentry in government bodies (consultative councils and governments) in the Liberated Areas during the War of Resistance Against Japan was entirely necessary and also successful. Those enlightened gentry who went through hardships and tribulations together with our Party and actually made some contribution should be given consideration according to the merits of each case, provided that this does not interfere with land reform. Those who are fairly good politically and are competent should remain in the higher government bodies and be given appropriate work. Those who are fairly good politically but are not competent should have their livelihood assured. As for those who are of landlord or rich peasant origin but who have not incurred the people's deep resentment, their feudal landholdings and feudal property should be distributed according to the Land Law, but it should be seen to that they do not become targets of mass struggles. Those who have sneaked into our government bodies, who have in reality always been evil, who can be of no use to the people and who have incurred the extreme hatred of the broad masses, are to be handed over to the people's courts to be tried and punished like local tyrants.

6. We must distinguish between the new rich peasants and the old rich peasants.[2] The encouragement given to new rich peasants

and well-to-do middle peasants during the period of rent and interest reduction proved effective in reassuring the middle peasants and in developing agricultural production in the Liberated Areas. After the equal distribution of land, we must call on the peasants to develop production so that they will be well-fed and well-clothed, and advise them to set up organizations for mutual aid and co-operation in agriculture, such as labour-exchange teams, mutual-aid teams and work-exchange groups.[3] In the equal distribution of land the new rich peasants in the old Liberated Areas should be treated like well-to-do middle peasants, and their land should not be distributed without the owner's consent.

7. Among those landlords and rich peasants in the old Liberated Areas who changed their mode of living during the period of rent and interest reduction, the landlords who have engaged in physical labour for five years or more and the rich peasants whose condition has been reduced to that of middle or poor peasants for three years or more may now have their class status changed in accordance with their present condition, provided their behaviour has been good. Those who still possess a large amount of surplus property (not a small amount) should hand over the surplus in accordance with the peasants' demands.

8. The heart of land reform is the equal distribution of the land of the feudal classes and of their property in grain, animals and farm implements (rich peasants hand over only their surplus property); we should not overemphasize the struggle to unearth hidden wealth[4] and in particular should not spend too much time on this matter lest it should interfere with the main work.

9. In dealing with landlords and rich peasants we should distinguish between them in accordance with the Outline Land Law.

10. Within the framework of the principle of equal distribution of land, we should also distinguish among the big, middle and small landlords, as well as between those landlords and rich peasants who are local tyrants and those who are not.

11. After the people's courts have given the handful of arch-criminals who are really guilty of the most heinous crimes a serious trial and sentenced them and the sentences have been approved by appropriate government organizations (committees organized by local governments at county or sub-regional level), it is entirely necessary for the sake of revolutionary order to shoot them and announce their execution. That is one side of the matter. The other side is that we

must insist on killing less and must strictly forbid killing without discrimination. To advocate killing more or killing without discrimination is entirely wrong; this would only cause our Party to forfeit sympathy, become alienated from the masses and fall into isolation. Trial and sentence by the people's courts, a form of struggle provided in the Outline Land Law, must be carried out in earnest; it is a powerful weapon of the peasant masses for striking at the worst elements among the landlords and rich peasants; it also avoids the mistake of beating and killing without discrimination. At the proper time (after the land struggle has reached its height), we should teach the masses to understand their own long-term interests – to regard those landlords and rich peasants who do not persist in wrecking the war effort or the land reform and who number tens of millions in the country as a whole (as many as 36 million out of a rural population of about 360 million) as a labour force for the country and to save and remould them. Our task is to abolish the feudal system, to wipe out the landlords as a class, not as individuals. In accordance with the Land Law we must give them means of production and means of livelihood, but not more than to the peasants.

12. We must criticize and struggle with certain cadres and Party members who have committed serious mistakes and certain bad elements among the masses of workers and peasants. In such criticism and struggle we should persuade the masses to adopt correct methods and forms and to refrain from rough actions. This is one side of the matter. The other side is that these cadres, Party members and bad elements should be made to pledge that they will not retaliate against the masses. It should be announced that the masses not only have the right to criticize them freely but also have the right to dismiss them from their posts when necessary or to propose their dismissal, or to propose their expulsion from the Party and even to hand the worst elements over to the people's courts for trial and punishment.

III. ON THE PROBLEM OF STATE POWER

1. The new-democratic state power is the anti-imperialist and anti-feudal state power of the masses of the people led by the working class. Here, the masses of the people include the working class, the peasantry, the urban petty bourgeoisie and the national bourgeoisie

who are oppressed and injured by imperialism and by the reactionary Kuomintang regime and the classes it represents, namely, the bureaucrat-capitalist class (the big bourgeoisie) and the landlord class. The main body of the masses consists of the workers, peasants (soldiers being chiefly peasants in uniform) and other working people. The masses of the people form their own state (the People's Republic of China) and establish a government (the Central Government of the People's Republic of China) to represent this state. The working class through its vanguard, the Communist Party of China, exercises the leadership in this state belonging to the masses of the people and in its government. The enemies this People's Republic and its government oppose are foreign imperialism and the Kuomintang reactionaries at home and the classes they represent – the bureaucrat-capitalist class and landlord class.

2.   The organs of state power of the People's Republic of China are the people's congresses at different levels and the governments at different levels which these congresses elect.

3.   In the rural areas in the present period, we can and should, in accordance with the demands of the peasants, convene village peasant meetings to elect the village governments, and convene district peasant congresses to elect the district governments. Since the governments at or above county or municipal level represent not only the peasants in the countryside but also the people of all strata and occupations in the towns, county seats, provincial capitals and big industrial and commercial cities, we should convene people's congresses at county, municipal, provincial or border region levels to elect the governments at corresponding levels. In the future after the revolution triumphs throughout the whole country, the central government and the local governments at all levels should be elected by the people's congresses at corresponding levels.

IV.   THE PROBLEM OF THE RELATIONSHIP BETWEEN THOSE WHO LEAD AND THOSE WHO ARE LED IN THE REVOLUTIONARY UNITED FRONT

The leading class and the leading party must fulfil two conditions in order to exercise their leadership of the classes, strata, political parties and people's organizations which are being led:

(a)   Lead those who are led (allies) to wage resolute struggles against the common enemy and achieve victories;

(b)   Bring material benefits to those who are led or at least not damage their interests and at the same time give them political education.

Without both these conditions, or with only one, leadership cannot be realized.   As an example, the Communist Party, in order to lead the middle peasants, must lead them to struggle resolutely together with us against the feudal classes and achieve victories (destroying the landlords' armed force and dividing up their land).   If there is no resolute struggle or if there is struggle but no victory, the middle peasants will vacillate.   Furthermore, we must allot part of the land and other property of the landlords to those middle peasants who are relatively poor and must not damage the interests of the well-to-do middle peasants.   In the peasant associations and the village and district governments we must draw the activists among the middle peasants into the work and must provide suitable quotas for them (for instance, one-third of the committee members).   Do not make mistakes in determining the class status of middle peasants and be fair to them in regard to the land tax and civilian war service.   At the same time, give the middle peasants political education.   If we do not do all these things, we will lose the support of the middle peasants.   In the cities, the same holds true for the working class and the Communist Party in exercising their leadership of the middle bourgeoisie, democratic parties and people's organizations oppressed and injured by the reactionary forces.

NOTES

[1] For the criteria for class identification in the rural areas, see "How to Analyse the Classes in the Rural Areas", *Selected Works of Mao Tse-tung*, Vol. I, and "The Chinese Revolution and the Chinese Communist Party", Chapter 2, Section 4, *Selected Works of Mao Tse-tung*, Vol. II.

[2] The new rich peasants were those who had developed from middle peasants or poor peasants in the revolutionary base areas.   The old rich peasants were those who had already been rich peasants before the revolutionary base areas were established. The old rich peasants generally and to a great degree had the character of feudal and semi-feudal exploiters.   See "The Present Situation and Our Tasks", Note 6, p. 175 of this volume.

[3] Labour-exchange teams and work-exchange groups were organizations for mutual aid and co-operation in agriculture. "Labour-exchange" or "work-exchange" was a means by which the peasants adjusted labour-power among themselves and took such forms as the exchange of man-workdays for man-workdays, ox-workdays for ox-workdays and man-workdays for ox-workdays. Peasants who joined labour-exchange teams contributed their labour-power or animal-power to cultivate the land of each member-family in rotation or collectively. In settling accounts the workday was taken as the unit of exchange; those who contributed more man-workdays or animal-workdays were paid for the difference by those who contributed less.

[4] This refers to the valuables buried by the landlords.

THE DEMOCRATIC MOVEMENT IN THE ARMY*

January 30, 1948

The policy for political work in our army units is fully to arouse the masses of soldiers, the commanders and all working personnel in order to achieve, through a democratic movement under centralized leadership, three major objectives, namely, a high degree of political unity, an improvement in living conditions and a higher level of military technique and tactics. The Three Check-ups and Three Improvements[1] now being enthusiastically carried out in our army units are intended to attain the first two of these objectives through the methods of political and economic democracy.

With regard to economic democracy, the representatives elected by the soldiers must be ensured the right to assist (but not to bypass) the company leadership in managing the company's supplies and mess.

With regard to military democracy, in periods of training there must be mutual instruction as between officers and soldiers and among the soldiers themselves; and in periods of fighting the companies at the front must hold big and small meetings of various kinds. Under the direction of the company leadership, the masses of soldiers should be roused to discuss how to attack and capture enemy positions and how to fulfil other combat tasks. When the fighting lasts several days, several such meetings should be held. This kind of military democracy was practised with great success in the battle of Panlung[2] in northern Shensi and in the battle of Shihchiachuang[3] in the Shansi-Chahar-Hopei area. It has been proved that the practice can only do good and can do no harm whatsoever.

The masses of soldiers should have the right to expose the errors and misdeeds of bad elements among the cadres. We should be confident that the soldiers will cherish all the good and comparatively good cadres. Moreover, the soldiers should have the right, when necessary, to nominate those whom they trust from their own ranks for lower-level cadre posts, subject to appointment by the higher level. When there is an acute shortage of lower-level cadres, this kind of nomination is very useful. It is not to be the rule, however, but is to be done only when necessary.

NOTES

[1] The "Three Check-ups" and "Three Improvements" constituted an important movement for Party consolidation and for ideological education in the army which was carried out by our Party in conjunction with the land reform during the People's War of Liberation. In the localities, the "Three Check-ups" meant checking on class origin, ideology and style of work; in the armed units, the check-ups were on class origin, performance of duty and will to fight. The "Three Improvements" meant organizational consolidation, ideological education and rectification of style of work.

[2] Panlung, northeast of Yenan, was a town where the Northwest People's Liberation Army surrounded and wiped out over 6,700 Kuomintang troops under the command of Hu Tsung-nan in May 1947.

[3] Shihchiachuang was liberated by units of the People's Liberation Army of the Shansi-Chahar-Hopei Border Region on November 12, 1947. Its enemy garrison of more than 24,000 men was totally destroyed. It was the first important city liberated by the People's Liberation Army in northern China.

---

* This inner-Party directive was drafted by Comrade Mao Tse-tung for the Revolutionary Military Commission of the Central Committee of the Communist Party of China.

DIFFERENT TACTICS FOR CARRYING OUT THE LAND LAW IN DIFFERENT AREAS

February 3, 1948

In carrying out the Land Law, it is necessary to distinguish three kinds of areas and to adopt different tactics for each.

1. Old Liberated Areas established before the Japanese surrender. In general, land in these areas has long been distributed, and only a part of the distribution needs to be readjusted. Our work here should centre on educating and consolidating the ranks of the Party and solving the contradictions between the Party and the masses by combining the efforts of Party and non-Party people according to the experience gained in Pingshan County.[1] In these old Liberated Areas what should be done is not to distribute the land a second time under the Land Law, or artificially and arbitrarily to organize poor peasant leagues to lead the peasant associations, but to organize poor peasant groups within the peasant associations. Activists in these groups can hold leading posts in the peasant associations and in the organs of political power in the rural areas, but it should not be made the rule that such posts go to the poor peasants to the exclusion of the middle peasants. In these areas the leading posts in the peasant associations and the organs of political power should be assumed by those activists among the poor and middle peasants who are correct in their thinking and fair and just in running affairs. The great majority of former poor peasants in these areas have developed into middle peasants, and the middle peasants now form the bulk of the rural population; therefore we must draw in the activists among the middle peasants to participate in the leadership of these rural areas.

2. Areas liberated between the Japanese surrender and the time of the general counter-offensive, that is, in the two years between September 1945 and August 1947. These now form the largest part of the Liberated Areas and can be called the semi-old Liberated Areas.

193

In these areas, through the struggle to settle accounts during the last two years and through the carrying out of the "May 4th Directive",[2] the level of political consciousness and the degree of organization of the masses have been raised considerably, and there has been a preliminary solution of the land problem. But the political consciousness and the organization of the masses have not yet reached a high level, and the land problem is not yet thoroughly solved. In these areas the Land Law is entirely applicable, the distribution of land should be universal and thorough, and if it is not done well the first time, we should be prepared for a second distribution with one or two check-ups afterwards. In these areas the middle peasants are a minority and are taking a wait-and-see attitude. The poor peasants are the majority and are eagerly demanding land. Poor peasant leagues must therefore be organized and their leading position established in the peasant associations and the organs of political power in the rural areas.

3. Areas newly liberated since the general counter-offensive. In these areas the masses have not yet been aroused, the Kuomintang, the landlords and the rich peasants still have great influence, and all our work has not yet taken root. Therefore, we should not try to enforce the Land Law all at once but should do it in two stages. The first stage is to neutralize the rich peasants and strike blows exclusively at the landlords. This stage should be further sub-divided into several steps, namely, propaganda, preliminary organization, distribution of the movable property[3] of the big landlords, distribution of the land of the big and middle landlords with some consideration being given to the small landlords, and finally the distribution of the land of the landlord class. During this stage, poor peasant leagues should be organized as the backbone of leadership, and peasant associations may also be organized with the poor peasants as the main body. The second stage is to distribute the land rented out by the rich peasants, their surplus land[4] and part of their other property, and to distribute that portion of the land of the landlords which was not thoroughly distributed in the first stage. The first stage should take about two years and the second a year. Haste will certainly do no good. Land reform and Party consolidation in the old and semi-old Liberated Areas should also take three years (counting from this January); here haste will do no good either.

NOTES

[1] Pingshan County, situated in western Hopei Province, was then part of the Shansi-Chahar-Hopei Liberated Area.   The experience of Pingshan here referred to consisted in inviting non-Party people to attend Party meetings so as to help the consolidation of the Party's primary organizations in the rural areas during the land reform.

[2] This refers to the "Directive on the Land Question" issued by the Central Committee of the Communist Party of China on May 4, 1946.   See "A Three Months' Summary", Note 4, p. 118 of this volume.

[3] "Movable property" refers to grain, money, clothing, etc.

[4] See "The Present Situation and Our Tasks", Note 6, p. 175 of this volume.

CORRECT THE "LEFT" ERRORS IN LAND REFORM PROPAGANDA*

February 11, 1948

In the past few months our news agency and newspapers in many places have publicized without discrimination or analysis many unsound reports and articles containing "Left" deviationist errors. Here are some examples.

1. They did not propagate the line of relying on the poor peasants and farm labourers and firmly uniting with the middle peasants in order to abolish the feudal system, but one-sidedly propagated a poor peasant-farm labourer line. They did not propagate the view that the proletariat should unite with all working people and others who are oppressed, the national bourgeoisie, the intellectuals and other patriots (including the enlightened gentry who do not oppose land reform) in order to overthrow the rule of imperialism, feudalism and bureaucrat-capitalism and establish a People's Republic of China and a people's democratic government, but one-sidedly propagated the view that the poor peasants and farm labourers conquer the country and should rule the country, or that the democratic government should be a government of the peasants only, or that the democratic government should listen only to the workers, poor peasants and farm labourers, while no mention at all was made of the middle peasants, the independent craftsmen, the national bourgeoisie and the intellectuals. This is a serious error of principle. Yet reports of this kind have been circulated by our news agency, newspapers and radio stations. And the propaganda departments of the Party committees in various places have failed to report these errors to the higher levels. In the past few months such propaganda, though not widespread, has been fairly frequent and has created an atmosphere in which people have been misled into believing that it might represent the correct leading ideas. Because the Northern Shensi Radio Station broadcast some incorrect items, people even

197

mistakenly believed that these were views approved by the Central Committee.

2. On the question of Party consolidation, there has not been sufficiently vigorous propaganda in some areas either against taking no account of class origin or against taking account of class origin alone; and there has even been erroneous propaganda which advocates taking account of class origin alone.

3. On the question of land reform, in some areas propaganda against both hesitation and rashness has been taken well in hand; but in many areas rashness has been encouraged and articles praising it have even been published. On the question of the relationship between the leadership and the masses, attention has been given in some areas to conducting propaganda against both commandism and tailism, but in many areas there has been an erroneous emphasis on "doing everything as the masses want it done" and an accommodation to wrong views existing among the masses. Even wrong views held not by the masses but only by a few individuals have been uncritically accepted. This negates the leading role of the Party and encourages tailism.

4. With regard to policies concerning industry and commerce and the working-class movement, serious "Left" deviations existing in certain Liberated Areas have been either praised or ignored.

To sum up, in the past few months our propaganda work has correctly reflected and guided the great struggles – the war, the land reform, Party consolidation, production and support for the front – and contributed to their great achievements; this is the major aspect of our propaganda work, and it must be affirmed first of all. But some errors and shortcomings must also be noted. They are of an ultra-Left character. A few run completely counter to the principles and standpoint of Marxism-Leninism and depart completely from the line of the Central Committee. It is expected that the bureaus and sub-bureaus of the Central Committee, their propaganda departments, the central and regional head offices of the Hsinhua News Agency and the comrades working on all the newspapers will check up on the propaganda work of the last few months on the basis of Marxist-Leninist principles and the line of the Central Committee, extend their achievements, correct their errors and see to it that their work

---

* This inner-Party directive was drafted by Comrade Mao Tse-tung for the Central Committee of the Communist Party of China.

helps to ensure victory in these great struggles – the war, the land reform, Party consolidation, the working-class movement – and to ensure victory in the whole anti-imperialist and anti-feudal revolution. The propaganda departments of the Party committees in all areas and the central office of the Hsinhua News Agency should assume the main responsibility for this check-up and should submit, in their own names, policy reports on its results to the Propaganda Department of the Central Committee.

ESSENTIAL POINTS IN LAND REFORM
IN THE NEW LIBERATED AREAS*

February 15, 1948

1. Do not be impetuous. The speed of land reform should be determined according to the circumstances, the level of political consciousness of the masses and the strength of leading cadres. Do not attempt to complete the land reform in a few months, but prepare to complete it in each area in two or three years. This also applies to the old or semi-old Liberated Areas.

2. Land reform in a new Liberated Area should be divided into two stages. In the first stage strike blows at the landlords and neutralize the rich peasants. This stage is to be sub-divided into several steps; strike blows at the big landlords first, and then at the other landlords. Treatment must be different for those who are local tyrants and those who are not, and different also for big, middle and small landlords. The second stage is the equal distribution of land, including the land rented out by the rich peasants and their surplus land. However, the treatment of rich peasants should differ from that of landlords. The total scope of attack should generally not exceed 8 per cent of the households or 10 per cent of the population. In the semi-old Liberated Areas the differences in treatment and the total scope of attack should be the same. These questions do not arise in the old Liberated Areas, where in general only minor adjustments in the distribution of land[1] are needed.

3. Organize poor peasant leagues first and then, after a few months, peasant associations. Strictly prohibit landlords and rich peasants from sneaking into the peasant associations and poor peasant leagues. Activists in the poor peasant leagues should become the backbone of leadership in peasant associations, but a section of the activists among the middle peasants must also be drawn into the committees of peasant associations. In the land reform struggle, the

201

middle peasants must be drawn in to participate, and their interests should be given consideration.

4. Do not start the work in all places at the same time, but choose strong cadres to carry it out first in certain places to gain experience, then spread the experience step by step and expand the work in waves. This applies to a whole strategic area as well as to a single county. It also applies to the old and the semi-old Liberated Areas.

5. Distinguish between consolidated Liberated Areas and guerrilla zones. In the former, land reform can proceed step by step. In the latter, we should confine ourselves to propaganda, covert organizational work and the distribution of a certain amount of movable property. Mass organizations should not be openly set up and land reform should not be carried out, lest the enemy should persecute the masses.

6. The reactionary armed bands of the landlords and the reactionary secret police must be destroyed and must not be utilized.

7. Reactionaries must be suppressed, but killing without discrimination is strictly forbidden; the fewer killings, the better. Death sentences should be reviewed and approved by a committee formed at the county level. The power to try and to deal with the cases of political suspects is vested in committees at the district Party committee level. This applies in the old as well as the semi-old Liberated Areas.

8. Local revolutionary intellectuals and semi-intellectuals who come from landlord or rich peasant families but support land reform should be utilized and drawn into the work of building the base areas. But we must intensify our educational work among them and prevent them from entrenching themselves in power and hindering land reform. In general we should not let them work in their native districts or townships. Emphasis should be placed on employing intellectuals or semi-intellectuals from peasant families.

9. Pay strict attention to the protection of industry and commerce. Take a long-term view in the planning and management of economic and financial affairs. The armed forces and district and township governments should all guard against waste.

NOTES

[1] See "Greet the New High Tide of the Chinese Revolution", Note 14, p. 127 of this volume.

---

* This inner-Party directive was drafted by Comrade Mao Tse-tung for the Central Committee of the Communist Party of China.

ON THE POLICY CONCERNING
INDUSTRY AND COMMERCE*

February 27, 1948

1. Party organizations in certain places have violated the policy of the Central Committee of the Party concerning industry and commerce and seriously damaged both. These mistakes must be speedily corrected. In correcting them the Party committees in these places must make a careful check-up from the two aspects of guiding policies and methods of leadership.

2. Guiding policies. Precautions should be taken against the mistake of applying in the cities the measures used in rural areas for struggling against landlords and rich peasants and for destroying the feudal forces. A sharp distinction should be made between the feudal exploitation practised by landlords and rich peasants, which must be abolished, and the industrial and commercial enterprises run by landlords and rich peasants, which must be protected. A sharp distinction should also be made between the correct policy of developing production, promoting economic prosperity, giving consideration to both public and private interests and benefiting both labour and capital, and the one-sided and narrow-minded policy of "relief", which purports to uphold the workers' welfare but in fact damages industry and commerce and impairs the cause of the people's revolution. Education should be conducted among comrades in the trade unions and among the masses of workers to enable them to understand that they should not see merely the immediate and partial interests of the working class while forgetting its broad, long-range interests. Under the local government's leadership, workers and capitalists should be led to organize joint committees for the management of production and to do everything possible to reduce costs, increase output and stimulate sales so as to attain the objectives of giving consideration to both public and private interests, benefiting both labour and capital and

supporting the war. The mistakes committed in many places are due to the failure to grasp all, most or some of the above policies. The bureaus and sub-bureaus of the Central Committee should raise this question clearly, analyse, check up, formulate correct policies and issue inner-Party directives and government decrees.

3. Methods of leadership. After policies have been fixed and directives issued, a bureau or sub-bureau of the Central Committee should keep in close contact with its area and prefectural Party committees[1] or with its own working teams by telegraph or telephone, by couriers on vehicles or on horseback, or by personal interviews; it should use the newspaper as an important instrument of organization and leadership. It should constantly have a grip on the progress of the work, exchange experience and correct mistakes; it should not wait several months, half a year or a year before holding summing-up meetings for a general check-up and a general correction of mistakes. Waiting leads to great loss, while correcting mistakes as soon as they occur reduces loss. In ordinary circumstances a bureau of the Central Committee should strive to keep in close contact with its subordinate organizations, always take care to draw a sharp line between what should and what should not be done, and constantly remind its subordinate organizations of this so that they may make as few mistakes as possible. All these are questions of methods of leadership.

4. All comrades in the Party should understand that the enemy is now completely isolated. But his isolation is not tantamount to our victory. If we make mistakes in policy, we shall still be unable to win victory. To put it concretely, we shall fail if we make, and do not correct, mistakes of principle with regard to any of the five policies – on the war, Party consolidation, land reform, industry and commerce, and the suppression of counter-revolution. Policy is the starting-point of all the practical actions of a revolutionary party and manifests itself in the process and the end-result of that party's actions. A revolutionary party is carrying out a policy whenever it takes any action. If it is not carrying out a correct policy, it is carrying out a wrong policy; if it is not carrying out a given policy consciously, it is doing so blindly. What we call experience is the process and the end-result of carrying out a policy. Only through the practice of the people, that is, through experience, can we verify whether a policy is correct or wrong and determine to what extent it is correct or wrong. But

* This inner-Party directive was drafted by Comrade Mao Tse-tung for the Central Committee of the Communist Party of China.

people's practice, especially the practice of a revolutionary party and the revolutionary masses, cannot but be related to one policy or another. Therefore, before any action is taken, we must explain the policy, which we have formulated in the light of the given circumstances, to Party members and to the masses. Otherwise, Party members and the masses will depart from the guidance of our policy, act blindly and carry out a wrong policy.

NOTES

[1] The prefectural Party committee was a leading body lower than the provincial Party committee or Border Region Party committee but higher than the county Party committee.

ON THE QUESTION OF
THE NATIONAL BOURGEOISIE AND
THE ENLIGHTENED GENTRY*

March 1, 1948

The Chinese revolution at the present stage is in its character a revolution against imperialism, feudalism and bureaucrat-capitalism waged by the broad masses of the people under the leadership of the proletariat. By the broad masses of the people is meant all those who are oppressed, injured or fettered by imperialism, feudalism and bureaucrat-capitalism, namely, workers, peasants, soldiers, intellectuals, businessmen and other patriots, as clearly stated in the Manifesto of the Chinese People's Liberation Army of October 1947.[1] In the manifesto "intellectuals" means all intellectuals who are persecuted and fettered. "Businessmen" means all the national bourgeois who are persecuted and fettered, that is, the middle and petty bourgeois. "Other patriots" refers primarily to the enlightened gentry. The Chinese revolution at the present stage is a revolution in which all these people form a united front against imperialism, feudalism and bureaucrat-capitalism and in which the working people are the main body. By working people are meant all those engaged in manual labour (such as workers, peasants, handicraftsmen, etc.) as well as those engaged in mental labour who are close to those engaged in manual labour and are not exploiters but are exploited. The aim of the Chinese revolution at the present stage is to overthrow the rule of imperialism, feudalism and bureaucrat-capitalism and to establish a new-democratic republic of the broad masses of the people with the working people as the main force; its aim is not to abolish capitalism in general.

We should not abandon the enlightened gentry who co-operated with us in the past and continue to co-operate with us at present, who approve of the struggle against the United States and Chiang Kai-shek and who approve of the land reform. Take, for instance, people like Liu Shao-pai of the Shansi-Suiyuan Border Region and Li Ting-ming of the Shensi-Kansu-Ningsia Border Region.[2] Since they gave us considerable help in the hard times during and after the War of Resistance Against Japan and did not obstruct or oppose the land reform when we were carrying it out, we should continue the policy of uniting with them. But uniting with them does not mean treating them as a force that determines the character of the Chinese revolution. The forces that determine the character of a revolution are the chief enemies on the one side and the chief revolutionaries on the other. At present our chief enemies are imperialism, feudalism and bureaucrat-capitalism, while the main forces in our struggle against these enemies are the people engaged in manual and mental labour, who make up 90 per cent of the country's population. And this determines that our revolution at the present stage is a new-democratic, a people's democratic revolution in character and is different from a socialist revolution such as the October Revolution.

The few right-wingers among the national bourgeoisie who attach themselves to imperialism, feudalism and bureaucrat-capitalism and oppose the people's democratic revolution are also enemies of the revolution, while the left-wingers among the national bourgeoisie who attach themselves to the working people and oppose the reactionaries are also revolutionaries, as are the few enlightened gentry who have broken away from the feudal class. But the former are not the main body of the enemy any more than the latter are the main body among the revolutionaries; neither is a force that determines the character of the revolution. The national bourgeoisie is a class which is polit-ically very weak and vacillating. But the majority of its members may either join the people's democratic revolution or take a neutral stand, because they too are persecuted and fettered by imperialism, feudalism and bureaucrat-capitalism. They are part of the broad masses of the people but not the main body, nor are they a force that determines the character of the revolution. However, because they are important economically and may either join in the struggle against the United States and Chiang Kai-shek or remain neutral in that struggle, it is possible and necessary for us to unite with them. Before the birth of the Communist Party of China, the Kuomintang headed by Sun Yat-sen represented the national bourgeoisie and acted as the leader of the Chinese revolution of that time (a non-thorough demo-

---

* This inner-Party directive was drafted by Comrade Mao Tse-tung for the Central Committee of the Communist Party of China.

cratic revolution of the old type). But after the Communist Party of China was born and demonstrated its ability, the Kuomintang could no longer be the leader of the Chinese revolution (a new-democratic revolution). The national bourgeoisie joined the 1924-27 revolutionary movement[3] and during the years 1927-31 (before the September 18th Incident of 1931) quite a few of them sided with the reaction under Chiang Kai-shek. But one must not on this account think that we should not have tried during that period to win over the national bourgeoisie politically or to protect it economically, or that our ultra-Left policy towards the national bourgeoisie was not adventurist. On the contrary, in that period our policy should still have been to protect the national bourgeoisie and win it over so as to enable us to concentrate our efforts on fighting the chief enemies. In the period of the War of Resistance the national bourgeoisie was a participant in the war, wavering between the Kuomintang and the Communist Party. At the present stage the majority of the national bourgeoisie has a growing hatred of the United States and Chiang Kai-shek; its left-wingers attach themselves to the Communist Party and its right-wingers to the Kuomintang, while its middle elements take a hesitant, wait-and-see attitude between the two parties. These circumstances make it necessary and possible for us to win over the majority of the national bourgeoisie and isolate the minority. To achieve this aim, we should be prudent in dealing with the economic position of this class and in principle should adopt a blanket policy of protection. Otherwise we shall commit political errors.

The enlightened gentry are individual landlords and rich peasants with democratic leanings. Such people have contradictions with bureaucrat-capitalism and imperialism and to a certain extent also with the feudal landlords and rich peasants. We unite with them not because they are a political force to be reckoned with nor because they are of any economic importance (their feudal landholdings should be handed over with their consent to the peasants for distribution) but because they gave us considerable help politically during the War of Resistance and during the struggle against the United States and Chiang Kai-shek. During the period of land reform, it will help the land reform throughout the country if some of the enlightened gentry favour it. In particular, it will help win over the intellectuals (most of whom come from landlord or rich peasant families), the national bourgeoisie (most of whom have ties with the land) and the enlightened gentry throughout the country (who number several hundred thousand) and help isolate the chief enemy of the Chinese revolution, the Chiang Kai-shek reactionaries. It is precisely because they have this role that the enlightened gentry also constitute an element in the revolutionary united front against imperialism, feudalism and bureaucrat-capitalism; therefore, attention must also be paid to the question of uniting with them. During the period of the War of Resistance, what we required of the enlightened gentry was that they should favour resistance against Japan, favour democracy (not be anti-Communist) and favour reduction of rent and interest; at the present stage, what we require of them is that they favour the struggle against the United States and Chiang Kai-shek, favour democracy (not be anti-Communist) and favour the land reform. If they can meet these requirements, we should unite with them without exception and while uniting with them educate them.

NOTES

[1] See the first of the eight policies listed in "Manifesto of the Chinese People's Liberation Army", p. 150 of this volume.

[2] Liu Shao-pai, an enlightened landlord of the Shansi-Suiyuan Border Region, had been elected Vice-Chairman of the Provisional Council of the Shansi-Suiyuan Border Region. Li Ting-ming, an enlightened landlord of northern Shensi Province, had been elected Vice-Chairman of the Shensi-Kansu-Ningsia Border Region Government.

[3] See "The Situation and Our Policy After the Victory in the War of Resistance Against Japan", Note 10, p. 23 of this volume.

ON THE GREAT VICTORY IN THE NORTHWEST AND ON THE NEW TYPE OF IDEOLOGICAL EDUCATION MOVEMENT IN THE LIBERATION ARMY*

March 7, 1948

Commenting on the recent great victory of the Northwest People's Liberation Army, a spokesman for the General Headquarters of the People's Liberation Army said: This victory has changed the situation in the Northwest and will affect the situation in the Central Plains. It has proved that through the new type of ideological education movement in the army by the methods of "pouring out grievances" and of the "three check-ups" the People's Liberation Army will make itself invincible.

The spokesman said: On this occasion, the Northwest People's Liberation Army suddenly encircled an enemy brigade at Yichuan, and Hu Tsung-nan ordered Liu Kan, Commander of his 29th Corps, to rush 4 brigades of 2 reorganized divisions from the Lochuan-Yichun line to the relief of Yichuan. They were the 31st and 47th Brigades of the Reorganized 27th Division and the 53rd and 61st Brigades of the Reorganized 90th Division, totalling more than 24,000 men; they reached the area southwest of Yichuan on February 28. The Northwest People's Liberation Army started a battle of annihilation and in thirty hours of fighting on February 29 and March 1 completely wiped out these reinforcements, letting none escape from the net. More than 18,000 men were captured, and more than 5,000 were killed and wounded; Liu Kan himself, Yen Ming, Commander of the 90th Division, and other officers were killed. Then on March 3 we captured Yichuan and here again wiped out over 5,000 men of the 24th Brigade of the enemy's Reorganized 76th Division which was defending the city. In this campaign we wiped out, all told, 1 corps headquarters,

2 division headquarters and 5 brigades of the enemy, a total of 30,000 men. This is our first great victory in the Northwest theatre.

Analysing the situation in the Northwest theatre, the spokesman said: Of the 28 brigades of the so-called "Central Army" directly commanded by Hu Tsung-nan, 8 belonged to his 3 crack divisions, the Reorganized 1st, 36th and 90th Divisions. Of these divisions, the 1st Brigade of the Reorganized 1st Division had been wiped out[1] by us once before at Fushan, southern Shansi, in September 1946 and the main force of the same division's 167th Brigade had been wiped out once at Panlung town, northern Shensi, in May last year; the 123rd and 165th Brigades of the Reorganized 36th Division had been wiped out once at Shachiatien in Michih County, northern Shensi, in August last year; and this time the Reorganized 90th Division was also completely wiped out. Of the remainder of Hu Tsung-nan's main force, only the 78th Brigade of the Reorganized 1st Division and the 28th Brigade of the Reorganized 36th Division have not yet been wiped out. Hu Tsung-nan's whole army can therefore be said to have practically no more crack units. As a result of the Yichuan battle of annihilation, of the 28 regular brigades formerly under Hu Tsung-nan's direct command, only 23 are left. These 23 brigades are distributed in the following areas: 1 brigade at Linfen in southern Shansi is immobilized and doomed, 9 brigades are on the Shensi-Honan border and along the Loyang-Tungkuan line to cope with our field army under Chen

---

* This commentary was drafted by Comrade Mao Tse-tung for the spokesman of the General Headquarters of the Chinese People's Liberation Army. At that time the enemy offensive in the Northwest theatre of war had been smashed, and our army had gone over to its own offensive. This commentary analysed the situation in the Northwest theatre and also outlined conditions in the other theatres of war. More important, it stressed the great significance of the new type of ideological education movement in the army, carried out by the methods of "pouring out grievances" and of the "three check-ups". This new type of movement was an important development of the political work and the democratic movement in the People's Liberation Army. It was the reflection in the army of the movements for land reform and Party consolidation then vigorously proceeding in all the Liberated Areas. This movement greatly enhanced the political consciousness, discipline and combat effectiveness of all officers and soldiers. At the same time it most effectively speeded the process of reforming large numbers of captured Kuomintang soldiers into Liberation Army fighters. Thus it played an important role in consolidating and expanding the People's Liberation Army and in ensuring victories in the field. For the significance of this movement, see also "The Democratic Movement in the Army", pp. 191-92, "Speech at a Conference of Cadres in the Shansi-Suiyuan Liberated Area", pp. 227-39, and "On the September Meeting – Circular of the Central Committee of the Communist Party of China", pp. 269-77, of this volume.

Keng and Hsieh Fu-chih, and another brigade in southern Shensi is guarding the Hanchung area. The remaining 12 brigades are distributed along the T-shaped communication lines from Tungkuan to Paoki and from Hsienyang to Yenan. Of these, 3 are "reserve brigades" composed entirely of recruits, 2 have been completely wiped out by our army and replenished recently, another 2 have received crushing blows from us and 5 have received relatively few blows. It can be seen that not only are these forces very weak but also they are mostly on garrison duty. In addition to Hu Tsung-nan's army, there are 2 brigades under Teng Pao-shan defending Yulin, while 9 brigades under Ma Hung-kuei of Ningsia Province and Ma Pu-fang of Chinghai Province are distributed in the Sanpien and Lungtung areas.[2] All the regular troops under Hu Tsung-nan, Teng Pao-shan and the two Mas now total 34 brigades, including the units replenished after having been wiped out once or twice.

That is how things stand with the enemy in the Northwest. To return to the T-shaped communication lines, of those 5 brigades which have received relatively few blows, 2 are hemmed in at Yenan and 3 are in the Greater Kuanchung Area.[3] As for the other brigades there, most of them have been recently replenished, and a few have received crushing blows. In other words, the enemy's forces in the whole Greater Kuanchung Area and especially in Kansu Province are very sparse and weak and cannot possibly stop the offensive of the People's Liberation Army. This situation is bound to affect some of the dispositions of Chiang Kai-shek's forces on the southern front and, first of all, his dispositions vis-à-vis our field army under Chen Keng and Hsieh Fu-chih on the Honan-Shensi border. In its present southward drive the Northwest People's Liberation Army has won victory as soon as its banner was displayed, gained resounding fame and changed the relation of forces between the enemy and ourselves in the Northwest; from now on it will be able to fight even more effectively in co-ordination with the forces of the People's Liberation Army on the southern fronts.

The spokesman said: Since last summer and autumn our three field armies, commanded respectively by Liu Po-cheng and Teng Hsiao-ping, Chen Yi and Su Yu, and Chen Keng and Hsieh Fu-chih, have advanced south across the Yellow River, swept through the length and breadth of the territory enclosed by the Yangtse, Huai, Yellow and Han Rivers, wiped out large numbers of enemy troops, manipulated and drawn towards themselves some 90 out of the 160 odd brigades which

Chiang Kai-shek has on the southern front, forced his armies into a passive position, played a decisive strategic role and won the acclaim of the people all over the country.[4] In its winter offensive our Northeast Field Army braved bitter cold of 30 degrees below zero, annihilated most of the enemy troops, captured one well-known city after another and won resounding fame throughout the country.[5] After wiping out large numbers of enemy troops in heroic battles last year,[6] our field armies in the Shansi-Chahar-Hopei area, Shantung, northern Kiangsu and the Shansi-Hopei-Shantung-Honan area completed their training and consolidation last winter, and they will soon unfold their spring offensive.[7] A review of the whole situation proves one truth. Provided we firmly oppose conservatism, fear of the enemy and fear of difficulties, and provided we follow the general strategy of the Central Committee of the Party and its directive on the ten major principles of operation,[8] we can unfold our offensives, wipe out vast numbers of enemy troops and strike such blows at the forces of the Chiang Kai-shek bandit gang that they can only parry them for a time without being able to hit back, or that they cannot even parry our blows and will be completely wiped out, one after another.

The spokesman emphatically pointed out: The combat effectiveness of our Northwest Field Army is far higher than at any time last year.[9] In last year's fighting the Northwest Field Army could destroy at most two enemy brigades at a time; now in the Yichuan campaign it has been able to wipe out five enemy brigades at one time. The reasons for this outstanding victory were many, among which we should point out the firm yet flexible command of the leading comrades at the front, the energetic support given by the leading comrades and the broad masses in the rear, the relative isolation of the enemy troops and a terrain favourable to us. What is most noteworthy, however, is the new type of ideological education movement in the army, which was carried out for more than two months last winter by the methods of pouring out grievances and the three check-ups. The correct unfolding of the movement for pouring out grievances (the wrongs done to the labouring people by the old society and by the reactionaries) and the three check-ups (on class origin, performance of duty and will to fight) greatly heightened the political consciousness of commanders and fighters throughout the army in the fight for the emancipation of the exploited working masses, for nation-wide land reform and for the destruction of the common enemy of the people, the Chiang Kai-shek bandit gang. It also greatly strengthened the firm unity of all commanders and fighters under the leadership of the Communist Party. On this basis, the army achieved greater purity in its ranks, strengthened discipline, unfolded a mass movement for training and further developed its political, economic and military democracy in a completely well-led and orderly way. Thus the army has become united as one man, with everybody contributing his ideas and his strength, fearless of sacrifice and capable of overcoming material difficulties, an army which displays mass heroism and daring in destroying the enemy. Such an army will be invincible.

The spokesman said: It is not only in the Northwest that this new type of ideological education movement in the army has been carried out; it has been, or is being, carried on in the People's Liberation Army throughout the country. Conducted between battles, the movement does not interfere with fighting. Taking in conjunction with the movement for Party consolidation and the land reform movement now being correctly carried out by our Party, taking in co-ordination with our Party's correct policy of narrowing the scope of attack by opposing only imperialism, feudalism and bureaucrat-capitalism, by strictly forbidding beating and killing without discrimination (the fewer killings, the better) and by firmly uniting the masses of the people who make up over 90 per cent of the country's population, and taking in co-ordination with the application of our Party's correct urban policy and its policy of firmly protecting and developing the industry and commerce of the national bourgeoisie, this ideological education movement is bound to make the People's Liberation Army invincible. However desperate the exertions of the Chiang Kai-shek bandit gang and its master, U.S. imperialism, against the great struggle of the Chinese people's democratic revolution, victory will certainly be ours.

NOTES

[1] See "Concentrate a Superior Force to Destroy the Enemy Forces One by One", Note 1, p. 106 of this volume.

[2] Sanpien is an area in northwestern Shensi Province. Lungtung is the eastern part of Kansu Province. Both Sanpien and Lungtung were then prefectures in the Shensi-Kansu-Ningsia Liberated Area.

[3] This refers to central Shensi and northwestern Kansu taken together.

[4] Starting from June 30, 1947, 7 columns of the Shansi-Hopei-Shantung-Honan Field Army led by Liu Po-cheng, Teng Hsiao-ping and other comrades forced the

Yellow River and pushed towards the Tapieh Mountains, thus ushering in the strategic offensive of the People's Liberation Army. By the end of March 1948, more than 100,000 enemy troops had been wiped out, and new base areas had been built on the Hupeh-Honan border, in western Anhwei, in the Tungpai mountain area on the Hupeh-Honan border, the plains between the Yangtse and Han Rivers and other places. Eight columns of the Eastern China Field Army led by Chen Yi, Su Yu and other comrades, having smashed the enemy's concentrated attacks on Shantung Province in August 1947, swept into southwestern Shantung and the Honan-Anhwei-Kiangsu Border Region, wiped out over 100,000 enemy troops, built the Honan-Anhwei-Kiangsu Liberated Area and isolated the enemy's strategic centres of Kaifeng and Chengchow. Two columns and one corps of the Taiyueh Army of the Shansi-Hopei-Shantung-Honan area, commanded by Chen Keng, Hsieh Fu-chih and other comrades, forced the Yellow River in southern Shansi in August 1947, advanced into western Honan, wiped out more than 40,000 enemy troops and built base areas on the Honan-Shensi-Hupeh border and in southern Shensi, completely isolating Loyang, the enemy's strategic centre in western Honan Province, and threatening Tungkuan.

[5] Fighting continuously for ninety days from December 15, 1947 to March 15, 1948, 10 columns and 12 independent divisions of the Northeast Field Army led by Lin Piao, Lo Jung-huan and other comrades waged a winter offensive on an unprecedented scale along the Szepingkai-Tashihchiao section of the Chinese Changchun Railway and the Shanhaikuan-Shenyang section of the Peiping-Liaoning Railway; they wiped out more than 156,000 enemy troops and captured the enemy's heavily-fortified strategic centre of Szepingkai and eighteen other cities. One enemy division garrisoning Yingkow revolted and came over to our side. The enemy force defending the city of Kirin fled towards Changchun. After this, the area under enemy control in the Northeast shrank to only 1 per cent of the whole, and the enemy lairs in the cities along the Changchun-Shenyang-Chinchow line were isolated.

[6] From early September to mid-November 1947, 5 columns of the Shansi-Chahar-Hopei Field Army led by Nieh Jung-chen and other comrades fought successive battles in the area north of the Taching River and in the Chingfengtien area and the battle for the liberation of Shihchiachuang, wiping out a total of nearly 50,000 enemy troops and linking up the Shansi-Chahar-Hopei and Shansi-Hopei-Shantung-Honan Liberated Areas into one contiguous territory. From September to December 1947, 3 columns of the Shantung Army belonging to the Eastern China Field Army and regional armed forces fought the Eastern Shantung campaign under the command of Hsu Shih-yu, Tan Chen-lin and other comrades, wiping out more than 63,000 of the enemy and recovering more than ten county towns; this changed the whole situation in Shantung Province. From August to December 1947, units of the Eastern China Field Army in northern Kiangsu, in successive battles at Yencheng, Lipao and other points, annihilated more than 24,000 enemy troops and recovered a wide area in northern Kiangsu. In December 1947, units of the Shansi-Hopei-Shantung-Honan Field Army led by Hsu Hsiang-chien and other comrades fought in co-ordination with units of the Northwest Field Army and captured Yuncheng, destroying more than 13,000 enemy troops; they wiped out all the enemy forces in southwestern Shansi and isolated the enemy at Linfen.

[7] In the spring of 1948, following a period of training and consolidation in the previous winter, the field armies of the People's Liberation Army launched successive offensives. Between March and May, the Shansi-Chahar-Hopei Field Army and units of the Shansi-Hopei-Shantung-Honan and Shansi-Suiyuan Field Armies campaigned in southern Chahar, eastern Suiyuan and the Linfen area of Shansi, wiping out more

than 43,000 enemy troops and recovering much territory. Between March 7 and May 29, units of the Central Plains and Eastern China Field Armies fought successive battles at Loyang and Sungho and in the sectors west and east of Nanyang, wiped out more than 56,000 enemy troops and thus crushed the enemy's defence system on the Central Plains and expanded and consolidated the Liberated Area there. Between March 11 and May 8, the Shantung Army of the Eastern China Field Army fought battles first on the western section of the Tsingtao-Tsinan Railway and then at Weihsien, wiping out more than 84,000 enemy troops. Thus, except for a few strong-points, such as Tsinan, Tsingtao, Linyi and Yenchow, which were held by the Kuomintang, Shantung Province was liberated. In March the Northern Kiangsu Army fought a successful battle at Yilin.

   [8] For the ten major principles of operation, see "The Present Situation and Our Tasks", Section 3, pp. 160-63 of this volume.

   [9] The Northwest Field Army led by Peng Teh-huai, Ho Lung, Hsi Chung-hsun and other comrades employed a main force of 2 columns and 2 brigades, totalling more than 25,000 men, in the fighting in northern Shensi in the summer of 1947. By the spring of 1948 the main force had increased to 5 columns, totalling more than 75,000 men. After having been steeled by a year's fighting and by the new type of ideological education movement in the army in the winter of 1947, the political consciousness of the broad masses of officers and soldiers and the combat effectiveness of the military units rose to unprecedented heights. This created the necessary conditions for the Northwest Field Army to turn to fighting on exterior lines in March 1948. On April 12, following its major victory at Yichuan, the Northwest Field Army launched a campaign in Hsifu (the area west of Sian and between the Chingshui and Weishui Rivers) and eastern Kansu, pushed forward into the broad area between the Chingshui and Weishui Rivers, cut the Sian-Lanchow highway, and on April 22 recovered Yenan.

A CIRCULAR ON THE SITUATION*

March 20, 1948

1. In recent months the Central Committee has concentrated on solving, in the new conditions, problems concerning specific policies and tactics for land reform, industry and commerce, the united front, Party consolidation and the work in the new Liberated Areas; it has also combated Right and "Left" deviations within the Party, mainly "Left" deviations. The history of our Party shows that Right deviations are likely to occur in periods when our Party has formed a united front with the Kuomintang and that "Left" deviations are likely to occur in periods when our Party has broken with the Kuomintang. At present the "Left" deviations consist chiefly in encroaching on the interests of the middle peasants and the national bourgeoisie; laying one-sided stress in the labour movement on the immediate interests of the workers; making no distinctions in the treatment of landlords and rich peasants; making no distinctions in the treatment of big, middle and small landlords, or of landlords who are local tyrants and those who are not; not leaving the landlords the necessary means of livelihood as required by the principle of equal distribution; overstepping certain demarcation lines of policy in the struggle to suppress counter-revolution; not wanting political parties which represent the national bourgeoisie; not wanting the enlightened gentry; neglecting the tactical importance of narrowing the scope of attack in the new Liberated Areas (that is, neglecting to neutralize the rich peasants and small landlords); and lacking the patience to work step by step. During the past two years or so, these "Left" deviations have occurred to a greater or lesser extent in all the Liberated Areas and in some cases have developed into serious adventurist tendencies. Fortunately, they are not very difficult to correct; in the main they have been corrected in the past few months, or are being corrected now. But leaders at all levels must make

strenuous efforts before deviations of this kind can be thoroughly corrected. The Right deviations consist chiefly in overestimating the strength of the enemy, being afraid of large-scale U.S. aid to Chiang Kai-shek, being somewhat weary of the long war, having certain doubts about the strength of the world democratic forces, not daring to arouse the masses fully in order to abolish feudalism, and being indifferent to impurities in the Party's class composition and style of work. Such Right deviations, however, are not the main ones at present; they too are not difficult to correct. In recent months our Party has made achievements in the war, in land reform, in Party consolidation, in ideological education in the army, in building new Liberated Areas and in winning over the democratic parties; and it has emphatically corrected, or is correcting, deviations that occurred in these fields of work. This will enable the entire revolutionary movement in China to advance along the path of sound development. Only when all the policies and tactics of the Party are on the correct path will it be possible for the Chinese revolution to win victory. Policy and tactics are the life of the Party; leading comrades at all levels must give them full attention and must never on any account be negligent.

2. Certain democratic personages, who had believed that a so-called "third road"[1] was still possible and had placed themselves midway between the Kuomintang and the Communist Party because of certain illusions about the United States and Chiang Kai-shek and because of their scepticism as to whether our Party and the people had the strength to defeat all enemies at home and abroad, found themselves in a passive position in the face of the sudden Kuomintang offensive; eventually, in January 1948, they accepted our Party's slogans and declared themselves against Chiang Kai-shek and the United States and for unity with the Communist Party and the Soviet Union.[2] We should pursue a policy of uniting with these persons, while suitably criticizing their erroneous views. In the future, when the Central People's Government is formed, it will be necessary and beneficial to invite some of them to take part in the work of the government. It is characteristic of these persons that they have always been unwilling

---

* This inner-Party circular was written by Comrade Mao Tse-tung for the Central Committee of the Communist Party of China. Subsequently, the Central Committee moved from the Shensi-Kansu-Ningsia Border Region to the Shansi-Chahar-Hopei Liberated Area by way of the Shansi-Suiyuan Liberated Area and in May 1948 reached Hsipaipo Village, Pingshan County, in western Hopei Province.

to have contact with the working people, are accustomed to life in the big cities and hesitate to come to the Liberated Areas. Even so, the social base they represent, the national bourgeoisie, has its importance and should not be ignored. Therefore it is necessary to win them over. Our estimate is that, after we achieve bigger victories and capture a number of cities like Shenyang, Peiping and Tientsin and after it becomes perfectly obvious that the Communist Party will win and that the Kuomintang will lose, these persons may be willing to come to the Liberated Areas to work with us if they are invited to take part in the Central People's Government.

3. We do not contemplate setting up the Central People's Government this year, because the time is not yet ripe. After the bogus National Assembly elects Chiang Kai-shek president[3] later in the year and he is even more thoroughly discredited, after we score bigger victories and expand our territories, preferably after the capture of one or two of the country's largest cities, and after northeastern China, northern China, Shantung, northern Kiangsu, Honan, Hupeh and Anhwei are all linked together in one contiguous area, it will be entirely necessary to establish the Central People's Government. The time will probably be in 1949. At present, we are merging the Shansi-Chahar-Hopei area, the Shansi-Hopei-Shantung-Honan area and the Pohai area in Shantung under the direction of a single Party committee (the Northern China Bureau), a single government and a single military command[4] (the inclusion of the Pohai area may be delayed for a while). These three areas comprise the broad expanse north of the Lunghai Railway, west of the Tientsin-Pukow Railway and the Pohai Gulf, east of the Tatung-Puchow Railway and south of the Peiping-Suiyuan Railway. They are already linked together in one contiguous area with a total population of fifty million, and their merger will probably be completed soon. This will enable us to give strong support to the war on the southern front and transfer large numbers of cadres to the new Liberated Areas. The leading centre of the merged area will be at Shihchiachuang.[5] The Central Committee is also preparing to move to northern China, and its Working Committee will merge with it.

4. Our troops on the southern front have all had rest and consolidation from December to February; these troops comprise the 9 brigades of the Shantung Army, 7 brigades of the Northern Kiangsu Army, 21 brigades of the army in the area between the Yellow and Huai Rivers, 10 brigades of the army in the Honan-Hupeh-Shensi area, 19 brigades of the army in the area between the Yangtse, Huai

and Han Rivers, 12 brigades of the army in northwestern China and
12 brigades of the army in southern Shansi and northern Honan.
The only exception was the main force of the army under Liu Po-cheng
and Teng Hsiao-ping in the area between the Yangtse, Huai and Han
Rivers, which had had no rest and consolidation because Pai Chung-
hsi concentrated his troops to attack the Tapieh Mountains;[6] it was
not until the end of February that this force was able to send some
of its units north of the Huai River for rest and consolidation. That
was our first period of rest and consolidation on a large scale in
the past twenty months of fighting. During that period the methods
we adopted were: pouring out grievances by the masses (the wrongs
done to the labouring people by the old society and by the reactionaries), the three check-ups (on class origin, performance of duty and
will to fight) and mass training (officers teaching soldiers, soldiers
teaching officers and soldiers teaching each other). By these methods
we developed high revolutionary enthusiasm among the commanders
and fighters of the whole army; reformed or weeded out the landlords, rich peasants and bad elements found in some army units;
heightened discipline; clearly explained various policies in the land
reform and the policies concerning industry and commerce and the
intellectuals; developed the democratic style of work in the army;
and raised the level of our military technique and tactics. As a result,
our army has greatly enhanced its combat effectiveness. Except for
that part of the army under Liu Po-cheng and Teng Hsiao-ping, which
is still having rest and consolidation, all our armies in succession have
started new military operations since late February or early March and
in two weeks have wiped out 9 enemy brigades. Of our troops on the
northern front, comprising the 46 brigades of the army in the Northeast, 18 brigades of the army in the Shansi-Chahar-Hopei area and 2
brigades of the army in the Shansi-Suiyuan area, the greater part fought
through the winter, while a part was having rest and consolidation.
Taking advantage of the freezing of the Liaoho River, our army in
the Northeast fought for three months, wiped out 8 brigades and won
over 1 brigade, occupied Changwu, Faku, Hsinlitun, Liaoyang, Anshan,
Yingkow and Szepingkai, and recaptured Kirin. This army has now
begun its rest and consolidation. Afterwards, it is to attack either
Changchun or the enemy along the Peiping-Liaoning Railway. The
army in the Shansi-Chahar-Hopei area has had more than a month of
rest and consolidation and is moving towards the Peiping-Suiyuan
Railway. The army in the Shansi-Suiyuan area is comparatively small,

and its main task is to tie down Yen Hsi-shan's troops. To sum up, we now have two fronts, the northern and the southern, with 10 armies, large and small, comprising 50 columns of regular troops (each equivalent to a Kuomintang reorganized division), or 156 brigades (each equivalent to a Kuomintang reorganized brigade), each brigade (3 regiments) averaging about 8,000 men – making a total of more than 1,322,000 men. In addition, there are more than 1,168,000 irregulars (of whom 800,000 are combat troops), including regional formations, regional troops, guerrilla detachments, rear-area military organizations and military academies. Our entire army thus totals more than 2,491,000 men. But before July 1946 we had only 28 columns of regular troops, or 118 brigades, each brigade (3 regiments) averaging less than 5,000 men – a total of 612,000; with the addition of more than 665,000 irregulars, the grand total was 1,278,000. It can be seen that our army has grown. The number of brigades has not increased much, but the number of men in each brigade has increased very much. After twenty months of war, our combat effectiveness has also increased greatly.

5. From July 1946 to the summer of 1947, the regular army of the Kuomintang was composed of 93 divisions with 248 brigades; now it has designations for 104 divisions with 279 brigades. Its dispositions are as follows. On the northern front there are 29 divisions with 93 brigades, totalling about 550,000 men (13 divisions with 45 brigades under Wei Li-huang in Shenyang, 11 divisions with 33 brigades under Fu Tso-yi in Peiping, 5 divisions with 15 brigades under Yen Hsi-shan in Taiyuan). On the southern front there are 66 divisions with 158 brigades, totalling about 1,060,000 men (38 divisions with 86 brigades under Ku Chu-tung in Chengchow, 14 divisions with 33 brigades under Pai Chung-hsi in Kiukiang, and 14 divisions with 39 brigades under Hu Tsung-nan in Sian). On the second line there are 9 divisions with 28 brigades, totalling about 196,000 men (4 divisions with 8 brigades in the northwestern area, i.e., the region west of Lanchow; 4 divisions with 10 brigades in the southwestern area, i.e., Szechuan, Sikang, Yunnan and Kweichow Provinces; 8 brigades in the southeastern area, i.e., the provinces south of the Yangtse River; and 1 division with 2 brigades in Taiwan). The reason the number of unit designations of the Kuomintang regular army has increased is that after large numbers of its troops had been wiped out by our army and after they had turned from the strategic offensive to the strategic defensive, the Kuomintang felt its shortage of troops acutely and therefore upgraded or reorganized many local armed units and puppet troops into its regular

army. Thus, on the northern front, 3 divisions with 14 brigades were added to Wei Li-huang's command and 2 divisions with 6 brigades to Fu Tso-yi's command; on the southern front, 6 divisions with 9 brigades were added to Ku Chu-tung's command and 2 brigades to Hu Tsung-nan's. The total increase was 11 divisions, or 31 brigades. As a result, the Kuomintang army now has 104 divisions instead of 93, and 279 brigades instead of 248. But, in the first place, the 6 divisions with 29 brigades which we wiped out in recent months (up to March 20) now exist only in name; there has been no time to rebuild or replenish them, and probably some can never be rebuilt or replenished. So, in fact, the Kuomintang army now has only 98 divisions with 250 brigades, an increase of only 5 divisional designations and 2 actual brigades since last summer. In the second place, of the 250 brigades which actually exist, only 118 have not received crushing blows from our army. All the remaining 132 brigades have been wiped out by our army once, twice or even thrice and then been replenished; or they have received one, two or even three crushing blows from our army (in the case of a brigade, to wipe it out means to destroy it completely or destroy the greater part, while to deal it a crushing blow means to destroy one or more of its regiments but not its main strength); and their morale and combat effectiveness are very low. Of the 118 brigades which have not yet received crushing blows, some are composed of recruits being trained at the second line and some are local armed units and puppet troops which have been upgraded or reorganized; their combat effectiveness is very low. In the third place, the Kuomintang armed forces have declined in numbers also. Before July 1946 they had 2,000,000 regulars, 738,000 irregulars, 367,000 men in the special arms, 190,000 men in the navy and air force and 1,010,000 men in rear-service establishments and military academies – a total of 4,305,000. In February 1948 they had 1,810,000 regulars, 560,000 irregulars, 280,000 men in the special arms, 190,000 men in the navy and air force and 810,000 men in rear-service establishments and military academies – a total of 3,650,000. That means a decrease of 655,000 men. In the nineteen months from July 1946 to January 1948, our army wiped out altogether 1,977,000 Kuomintang troops (the statistics for February and the first half of March have not been compiled, but the number is roughly 180,000). In other words, the Kuomintang has lost not only the more than 1,000,000 men it recruited in the course of the war but also a large number of its original troops. Under these circumstances, the Kuomintang has adopted a policy opposite to ours, a policy not of bringing its brigades to full strength but of cutting down the number of men in each brigade and increasing the number of brigade designations. While in 1946 the average strength of a Kuomintang brigade was approximately 8,000 men, at present it is only about 6,500. From now on, the area taken by our army will daily expand, and the Kuomintang's sources of troops and food supplies will daily contract; we estimate that by next spring, after another full year's fighting, our army and the Kuomintang army will be roughly equal in numbers. Our policy is to go ahead steadily and strike sure blows, not to seek quick results; all we are trying to do is to wipe out, on the average, about 8 brigades of the Kuomintang regular army each month, or about 100 brigades a year. Actually, since last autumn this number has been exceeded, and from now on it can be still further exceeded. It should be possible to wipe out the entire Kuomintang army in about five years (counting from July 1946).[7]

6. At present, there are two sectors on the southern and northern fronts where the enemy still has a fairly large striking force and can wage offensive campaigns, temporarily placing our troops there in a difficult position. The first sector is in the Tapieh Mountains, where the enemy has approximately 14 brigades which can be used as a striking force. The second is north of the Huai River, where the enemy has about 12 such brigades. In these two sectors the Kuomintang troops still hold the initiative (they hold the initiative in the sector north of the Huai River because we have moved 9 of our crack brigades to the north of the Yellow River for rest and consolidation, in preparation for use on other sectors). The enemy troops in all other theatres of war are in a passive position and are taking a beating. The theatres of war where the situation is particularly favourable to us are the Northeast, Shantung, the Northwest, northern Kiangsu, the Shansi-Chahar-Hopei area, the Shansi-Hopei-Shantung-Honan area and the vast area west of the Chengchow-Hankow Railway, north of the Yangtse and south of the Yellow River.

NOTES

[1] See "The Present Situation and Our Tasks", Note 9, p. 176 of this volume.

[2] In October 1947 the reactionary Kuomintang government ordered the dissolution of the Democratic League. Under pressure from the Kuomintang reactionaries, some wavering members of the Democratic League dissolved it and ceased activities.

Other democratic parties, also being persecuted by the Kuomintang reactionaries, were then unable to function openly in the Kuomintang areas. In January 1948 Shen Chun-ju and other leaders of the Democratic League at a meeting in Hongkong decided to re-establish the League's leading body and resume the League's activities. In the same month Li Chi-shen and other members of the democratic wing of the Kuomintang established the Revolutionary Committee of the Kuomintang in Hongkong. Both these bodies agreed with the position of the Communist Party of China about the current situation and issued declarations calling for unity with the Communist Party and other democratic parties, the overthrow of the Chiang Kai-shek dictatorship and opposition to U.S. armed intervention in China's internal affairs. The wavering members of the Democratic League also accepted these slogans at that time.

[3] The Kuomintang reactionaries held a bogus "National Assembly" in Nanking from March 29 to May 1, 1948, at which Chiang Kai-shek and Li Tsung-jen were "elected" "president" and "vice-president".

[4] In May 1948 the Shansi-Chahar-Hopei Liberated Area and the Shansi-Hopei-Shantung-Honan Liberated Area were merged, and the Northern China Joint Administrative Council and the Northern China Military Area were established. In August of the same year the Northern China Joint Administrative Council was renamed the Northern China People's Government.

[5] Shihchiachuang in western Hopei Province was the first major city in northern China liberated by the People's Liberation Army.

[6] In December 1947 Pai Chung-hsi began attacking the Tapieh mountain area with 33 brigades.

[7] At that time the estimate was that the entire Kuomintang army would be wiped out in about five years. The estimated time was later reduced to about three and a half years. See "The Momentous Change in China's Military Situation", pp. 287-88 of this volume.

SPEECH AT A CONFERENCE OF CADRES IN
THE SHANSI-SUIYUAN LIBERATED AREA

April 1, 1948

Comrades! Today I wish to speak chiefly on some problems relating to our work in the Shansi-Suiyuan Liberated Area and also on some problems relating to our work in the country as a whole.

I

In my opinion, the work of land reform and of Party consolidation carried out during the past year in the area led by the Shansi-Suiyuan Sub-Bureau of the Central Committee of the Communist Party of China has been successful.

This can be viewed from two aspects. On the one hand, the Shansi-Suiyuan Party organization has combated Right deviations, initiated mass struggles and has completed, or is completing, the land reform and the Party consolidation among two million several hundred thousand people out of the area's total population of over three million. On the other hand, it has also corrected several "Left" deviations which occurred in these campaigns and has thereby put its entire work on the path of sound development. It is from these two aspects that I consider the work of land reform and of Party consolidation in the Shansi-Suiyuan Liberated Area to have been successful.

"From now on," the people of the Shansi-Suiyuan Liberated Area are saying, "no one will ever again dare to be feudalist, to bully others or indulge in corruption." That is their conclusion about our work of land reform and Party consolidation. When they say, "No one will ever again dare to be feudalist," they mean that we have led them in initiating struggles through which the system of feudal exploitation in

227

the new Liberated Areas and its remnants in the old and semi-old Liberated Areas have been or are being destroyed. When they say, "No one will ever again dare to bully others or indulge in corruption," they refer to the serious phenomenon of a certain degree of impurity in the class composition and style of work in our Party and government organizations that existed in the past. A number of bad elements had sneaked into the Party and government organizations; a number of individuals had developed a bureaucratic style of work, abused their power and bullied the people, employed methods of coercion and commandism to get things done, thereby arousing discontent among the masses, or had indulged in corruption or encroached upon the interests of the masses. However, after a year's work of land reform and Party consolidation, these conditions have been fundamentally changed.

One of the comrades present told me, "We have rid ourselves of what would have proved fatal to us. We have acquired things we never had before." By "fatal" he meant the serious phenomenon of impurity in the class composition and style of work in Party and government organizations and the resultant discontent among the masses. This phenomenon has now been fundamentally eliminated. By "things we never had before but have now acquired" he meant the poor peasant leagues, the new peasant associations, the district and village people's representative conferences and the new atmosphere that prevails in the countryside as a result of the work of land reform and Party consolidation.

These comments, I think, give a true picture of how matters stand.

Such is the great success of the work of land reform and Party consolidation in the Shansi-Suiyuan Liberated Area. This is the first aspect of the success. It was on this basis that during the past year the Shansi-Suiyuan Party organization was able to perform war services on an immense scale in support of the great People's War of Liberation. Without our successful work in land reform and Party consolidation, it would have been difficult to fulfil such immense military tasks.

On the other hand, the Shansi-Suiyuan Party organization has corrected several "Left" deviations which occurred in the course of its work. There were three main deviations of this kind. First, in a number of places, in the process of identifying class status a number of working people were wrongly classified as landlords or rich peasants, although they engaged in no feudal exploitation or in only a little exploitation; the scope of attack was thus mistakenly broadened; and a most important strategic principle was forgotten, namely, that in the land reform we can and must unite about 92 per cent of the households or about 90 per cent of the population in the villages, in other words, unite all the rural working people to establish a united front against the feudal system. Now this deviation has been corrected. Consequently, people are very much reassured and the revolutionary united front has been consolidated. Secondly, in the land reform work, the industrial and commercial enterprises of landlords and rich peasants were encroached upon; in the struggle to uncover counter-revolution in the economic field, the prescribed scope of investigation was overstepped; and in tax policy, industry and commerce were harmed. These were the "Left" deviations in dealing with industry and commerce. Now they, too, have been corrected, and so industry and commerce can recover and develop. Thirdly, in the fierce struggles in the land reform of the past year, the Shansi-Suiyuan Party organization failed to adhere unequivocally to the Party's policy of strictly forbidding beating and killing without discrimination. As a result, in certain places some landlords and rich peasants were needlessly put to death, and the bad elements in the rural areas were able to exploit the situation to take revenge and foully murdered a number of working people. We consider it absolutely necessary and proper to sentence to death, through the people's courts and the democratic governments, those major criminals who have actively and desperately opposed the people's democratic revolution and sabotaged the land reform, that is, the most heinous counter-revolutionaries and local tyrants. If this were not done, democratic order could not be established. We must, however, forbid the killing without discrimination of ordinary personnel on the Kuomintang side, the common run of landlords and rich peasants and lesser offenders. Moreover, in trying criminals, a people's court or democratic government must not use physical violence. Deviations of this kind which occurred in the past year in the Shansi-Suiyuan area have likewise been corrected.

Now that all these deviations have been corrected in earnest, we can say on good evidence that the entire work under the leadership of the Shansi-Suiyuan Sub-Bureau of the Central Committee is on the path of sound development.

The most fundamental method of work which all Communists must firmly bear in mind is to determine our working policies according to actual conditions. When we study the causes of the mistakes we have made, we find that they all arose because we departed from the actual situation at a given time and place and were subjective in our working policies. This should be a lesson for all comrades.

As for the consolidation of Party organizations at the primary level, you have drawn upon the experience of Pingshan County in the Shansi-Chahar-Hopei Liberated Area in accordance with the Central Committee's directive on the work of land reform and Party consolidation in the old and semi-old Liberated Areas;[1] that is, you have invited activists from the non-Party masses to participate in Party branch meetings, unfolded criticism and self-criticism in order to remove the impurities in the class composition and style of work in Party organizations and enabled the Party to forge closer ties with the masses. This will enable you to accomplish the whole job of consolidating Party organizations in a sound way.

Those Party members and cadres who have made mistakes but can still be educated and are different from the incorrigibles should all be educated and not abandoned, whatever their class origin. It is likewise correct that you have carried out, or are carrying out, this policy.

In the struggle against the feudal system, the experience of setting up people's representative conferences at district and village (or township) levels on the basis of the poor peasant leagues and peasant associations is extremely valuable. The only true people's representative conference is one based on the will of really broad masses of the people. It is now possible for such people's representative conferences to emerge in all the Liberated Areas. Such a conference, once set up, should become the local organ of people's power, and all due authority must be vested in it and in the government council it elects. The poor peasant league and the peasant association will then become its helping hands. At one time we thought of setting up people's representative conferences in the rural districts only after the land reform had been completed in the main. Now that your own experience and that of other Liberated Areas have proved that it is possible and necessary to set up these people's representative conferences and their elected government councils at the district and village levels in the midst of the struggle for the land reform, that is the way you should continue to do it. All the Liberated Areas should do likewise. After the conferences have been generally set up at district and village levels, they can be established at the county level. When people's representative conferences are established up to the county level, it will be easy to set them up at higher levels. In people's representative conferences at various levels we must, wherever possible, include representatives of all democratic strata – workers, peasants, independent craftsmen, professionals, intellectuals, national bourgeois industrialists and merchants and enlightened gentry. Of course, it should not be done mechanically; we should distinguish between rural areas with towns and rural areas without towns, among towns of different sizes and between cities and rural areas, so as to fulfil naturally, and not mechanically, the task of uniting all democratic strata.

The great mass struggles for land reform and Party consolidation have taught and brought to the fore tens of thousands of activists and cadres. They are linked with the masses and will be a most precious asset of the People's Republic of China. Henceforth, we should strengthen their education so that they will make constant progress in their work. Meanwhile they should be warned not to let success and commendation make them conceited and self-satisfied.

In view of all this, in view of the successes in these various respects, we can say that the Shansi-Suiyuan Liberated Area is now more consolidated than ever before. Other Liberated Areas which have worked along the same lines have likewise become consolidated.

II

As far as leadership is concerned, the successes of the Shansi-Suiyuan Liberated Area are due mainly to the following causes:

1. Helped by the work done by Comrade Kang Sheng in the administrative village of Hochiapo in Linhsien County last spring and summer, the Shansi-Suiyuan Sub-Bureau held a conference of secretaries of prefectural Party committees last June. The conference criticized Right deviations which had existed in past work, thoroughly exposed the serious phenomenon of various departures from the Party line and decided on the policy of starting the land reform and Party consolidation in earnest. In the main, the conference was a success. Without it, land reform and Party consolidation on such a scale could not have been successful. The

shortcomings of the conference were that it failed to decide on working policies varying with the different conditions in the old, semi-old and new Liberated Areas; that on the question of identifying class status it adopted an ultra-Left policy; that on the question of how to destroy the feudal system it laid too much stress on unearthing the landlords' hidden property; and that on the question of dealing with the demands of the masses it failed to make a sober analysis and raised the sweeping slogan, "Do everything as the masses want it done". With respect to the latter point, which is a question of the Party's relationship with the masses, the Party must lead the masses to carry out all their correct ideas in the light of the circumstances and educate them to correct any wrong ideas they may entertain. The conference only emphasized that the Party should carry out the ideas of the masses but neglected to point out that the Party should also educate and lead the masses, and thus eventually exerted a wrong influence on the comrades in some districts and aggravated their mistakes of tailism.

2. In January this year the Shansi-Suiyuan Sub-Bureau took proper measures to correct the "Left" deviations. These measures were carried out after the comrades of the Sub-Bureau returned from the December meeting of the Central Committee.[2] For this purpose the Sub-Bureau issued a five-point directive.[3] These corrective measures were so well adapted to the wishes of the masses and were carried out with such speed and thoroughness that almost all the "Left" deviations were rectified within a short time.

                                         III

The line of leadership of the Shansi-Suiyuan Party organization during the War of Resistance Against Japan was basically correct. This was shown in the reduction of rent and interest; in the substantial restoration and development of agricultural production, home spinning and weaving, war industries and some light industries; in the laying of the foundation of Party organizations; and in the establishment of a democratic government and of people's armed forces numbering nearly a hundred thousand men. All this work formed the basis on which we victoriously fought the War of Resistance and repelled the attacks of

Yen Hsi-shan and other reactionaries. Of course, the Party and the government during that period had their shortcomings; as is now entirely clear to us all, these consisted in a certain degree of impurity in class composition and style of work, which had undesirable effects on our work. But, taken as a whole, the work during the War of Resistance was fruitful. We were thus provided with favourable conditions for defeating Chiang Kai-shek's counter-revolutionary attacks after the Japanese surrender. The shortcomings or mistakes of the leadership of the Shansi-Suiyuan Party organization during the War of Resistance consisted mainly in the failure to rely on the broadest masses to overcome a certain degree of impurity in class composition and style of work in Party and government organizations and the undesirable effect it had on the work. That task is left for you to fulfil now. One reason for that situation was that certain leading comrades in Shansi and Suiyuan then lacked understanding of a number of the actual conditions concerning the Party and the masses. This should also be a lesson to the comrades.

IV

The task before the Shansi-Suiyuan Party organization is to make the greatest effort to complete the land reform and Party consolidation, to continue and support the People's War of Liberation, to refrain from any further increase in the people's burden but appropriately to lighten it, and to restore and develop production. You are now holding a conference on production. For the next few years the aim of restoring and developing production will be to improve the people's livelihood on the one hand and to support the People's War of Liberation on the other. You have a widespread agriculture and handicraft industry as well as some light and heavy industries using machinery. I hope you will do a good job in leading these productive enterprises, otherwise you cannot be called good Marxists. In agriculture, those labour-exchange teams and co-operatives,[4] which were in the grip of bureaucrats and which harmed the people instead of benefiting them, have all collapsed. This is entirely understandable and should occasion no regret. Your task is carefully to preserve and develop those labour-exchange teams, co-operatives and other necessary economic organizations that have won mass support and to spread them everywhere.

V

The national situation is a matter of concern for our comrades. Following the Party's National Land Conference last year, which resolved to adopt a new policy and unfold land reform and Party consolidation, large conferences of cadres were held in practically all the Liberated Areas on Party consolidation and land reform. At these conferences, Rightist ideas existing in the Party were criticized, and the serious phenomenon of a certain degree of impurity in the Party's class composition and style of work was exposed. Afterwards, appropriate measures were taken in many areas, and the "Left" deviations have been or are being corrected. Thus, confronted with the new political situation and new political tasks, our Party has been able to set its work in the whole country on the path of sound development. In the last few months almost all the People's Liberation Army has made use of the intervals between battles for large-scale training and consolidation. This has been carried out in a fully guided, orderly and democratic way. It has therefore aroused the revolutionary fervour of the great masses of commanders and fighters, enabled them clearly to comprehend the aim of the war, eliminated certain incorrect ideological tendencies and undesirable manifestations in the army, educated the cadres and fighters and greatly enhanced the combat effectiveness of the army. From now on, we must continue to carry on this new type of ideological education movement in the army, a movement which has a democratic and mass character. You can see clearly that neither the Party consolidation, nor the ideological education in the army, nor the land reform, all of which we have accomplished and all of which have great historic significance, could be undertaken by our enemy, the Kuomintang. On our part, we have been very earnest in correcting our own shortcomings; we have united the Party and army virtually as one man and forged close ties between them and the masses of the people; we are effectively carrying out all the policies and tactics formulated by the Central Committee of our Party and are successfully waging the People's War of Liberation. With our enemy, everything is just the opposite. They are so corrupt, so torn by ever-increasing and irreconcilable internal quarrels, so spurned by the people and utterly isolated and so frequently defeated in battle that their doom is inevitable. This is the whole situation of revolution versus counter-revolution in China.

In this situation, all comrades must firmly grasp the general line of the Party, that is, the line of the new-democratic revolution. The new-democratic revolution is not any other revolution, but can only be and must be a revolution against imperialism, feudalism and bureaucrat-capitalism waged by the broad masses of the people under the leadership of the proletariat. This means that leadership in this revolution can and must be assumed by no class and party other than the proletariat and the Communist Party of China. This means that the united front of those joining this revolution is very broad, embracing the workers, peasants, independent craftsmen, professionals, intellectuals, the national bourgeoisie and the section of the enlightened gentry which has broken away from the landlord class. All these are what we refer to as the broad masses of the people. The state and the government to be founded by the broad masses of the people will be the People's Republic of China and the democratic coalition government of the alliance of all democratic classes under the leadership of the proletariat. The enemies to be overthrown in this revolution can only be and must be imperialism, feudalism and bureaucrat-capitalism. The concentrated expression of all these enemies is the reactionary regime of Chiang Kai-shek's Kuomintang.

Feudalism is the ally of imperialism and bureaucrat-capitalism and the foundation of their rule. Therefore, the reform of the land system is the main content of China's new-democratic revolution. The general line in the land reform is to rely on the poor peasants, unite with the middle peasants, abolish the system of feudal exploitation step by step and in a discriminating way, and develop agricultural production. The basic force to be relied upon in the land reform can only be and must be the poor peasants. Together with the farm labourers, they make up about 70 per cent of China's rural population. The main and immediate task of the land reform is to satisfy the demands of the masses of poor peasants and farm labourers. In the land reform it is necessary to unite with the middle peasants; the poor peasants and the farm labourers must form a solid united front with the middle peasants, who account for about 20 per cent of the rural population. Otherwise, the poor peasants and farm labourers will find themselves isolated and the land reform will fail. One of the tasks in the land reform is to satisfy the demands of certain middle peasants. A section of the middle peasants must be allowed to keep some land over and above the average obtained by the poor peasants. We support the peasants' demand for equal distribution of land in

order to help arouse the broad masses of peasants speedily to abolish
the system of landownership by the feudal landlord class, but we do
not advocate absolute equalitarianism. Whoever advocates absolute
equalitarianism is wrong. There is a kind of thinking now current in
the countryside which undermines industry and commerce and advocates absolute equalitarianism in land distribution. Such thinking is
reactionary, backward and retrogressive in nature. We must criticize
it. The target of the land reform is only and must be the system of
feudal exploitation by the landlord class and by the old-type rich peasants, and there should be no encroachment either upon the national
bourgeoisie or upon the industrial and commercial enterprises run by
the landlords and rich peasants. In particular, care must be taken
not to encroach upon the interests of the middle peasants, independent
craftsmen, professionals and new rich peasants, all of whom engage
in little or no exploitation. The aim of the land reform is to abolish
the system of feudal exploitation, that is, to eliminate the feudal landlords as a class, not as individuals. Therefore a landlord must receive
the same allotment of land and property as does a peasant and must
be made to learn productive labour and join the ranks of the nation's
economic life. Except for the most heinous counter-revolutionaries
and local tyrants, who have incurred the bitter hatred of the broad
masses, who have been proved guilty and who therefore may and
ought to be punished, a policy of leniency must be applied to all, and
any beating or killing without discrimination must be forbidden. The
system of feudal exploitation should be abolished step by step, that is,
in a tactical way. In launching the struggle we must determine our
tactics according to the circumstances and the degree to which the
peasant masses are awakened and organized. We must not attempt
to wipe out overnight the whole system of feudal exploitation. In
accordance with the actual conditions of the system of feudal exploitation in China's villages, the total scope of attack in the land reform
should generally not exceed about 8 per cent of the rural households
or about 10 per cent of the rural population. In the old and semi-old
Liberated Areas the percentage should be even smaller. It is dangerous to depart from actual conditions and mistakenly enlarge the
scope of attack. In the new Liberated Areas, moreover, it is necessary to distinguish between different places and different stages. By
distinguishing between places we mean that in those places which we
can hold securely we should concentrate our efforts on carrying out
appropriate land reform work that accords with the wishes of the

local masses, while in those places which for the time being are difficult to hold securely, until there is a change in the situation we should not be in a hurry to start the land reform but should confine ourselves to activities which are feasible and beneficial to the masses in the present circumstances. By distinguishing between stages we mean that in places recently occupied by the People's Liberation Army we should put forward and carry out the tactics of neutralizing the rich peasants, of neutralizing the middle and small landlords, and thus narrow the scope of the attack so as to destroy only the reactionary Kuomintang armed forces and deal blows at the bad gentry and local tyrants. We should concentrate all our efforts on accomplishing this task as the first stage of work in the new Liberated Areas. We should then advance step by step to the stage of total abolition of the feudal system, in accordance with the rising level of political consciousness and organization of the masses. In the new Liberated Areas we should distribute movable property and land only when conditions are relatively secure and the overwhelming majority of the masses have been fully roused to action; to act otherwise would be adventurist and undependable and would do harm rather than good. In the new Liberated Areas the experience gained during the War of Resistance must be fully utilized. By abolishing feudalism in a discriminating way we mean that we should distinguish between landlords and rich peasants, among big, middle and small landlords and between those landlords and rich peasants who are local tyrants and those who are not, and that, subject to the major premise of the equal distribution of land and the abolition of the feudal system, we should not decide on and give the same treatment to them all, but should differentiate and vary the treatment according to varying conditions. When we do this, people will see that our work is completely reasonable. The development of agricultural production is the immediate aim of the land reform. Only by abolishing the feudal system can the conditions for such development be created. In every area, as soon as feudalism is wiped out and the land reform is completed, the Party and the democratic government must put forward the task of restoring and developing agricultural production, transfer all available forces in the countryside to this task, organize co-operation and mutual aid, improve agricultural technique, promote seed selection and build irrigation works – all to ensure increased production. Party organizations in the rural areas must devote the greatest energy to restoring and developing agricultural production and also industrial production in small towns. In order to speed up this restoration and development, we must do our utmost, in the course of our struggle for the abolition of the feudal system, to preserve all useful means of production and of livelihood, take resolute measures against anyone's destroying or wasting them, oppose extravagant eating and drinking and pay attention to thrift and economy. In order to develop agricultural production, we must advise the peasants to organize, voluntarily and step by step, the various types of producers' and consumers' co-operatives based on private ownership, which are permissible under present economic conditions. The abolition of the feudal system and the development of agricultural production will lay the foundation for the development of industrial production and the transformation of an agricultural country into an industrial one. This is the ultimate goal of the new-democratic revolution.

You comrades know that our Party has laid down the general line and general policy of the Chinese revolution as well as various specific lines for work and specific policies. However, while many comrades remember our Party's specific lines for work and specific policies, they often forget its general line and general policy. If we actually forget the Party's general line and general policy, then we shall be blind, half-baked, muddle-headed revolutionaries, and when we carry out a specific line for work and a specific policy, we shall lose our bearings and vacillate now to the left and now to the right, and the work will suffer.

Let me repeat:

The revolution against imperialism, feudalism and bureaucrat-capitalism waged by the broad masses of the people under the leadership of the proletariat – this is China's new-democratic revolution, and this is the general line and general policy of the Communist Party of China at the present stage of history.

To rely on the poor peasants, unite with the middle peasants, abolish the system of feudal exploitation step by step and in a discriminating way, and develop agricultural production – this is the general line and general policy of the Communist Party of China in the work of land reform during the period of the new-democratic revolution.

NOTES

[1] Issued on February 22, 1948, this directive of the Central Committee of the Communist Party of China summed up the experience of work in the land reform and Party consolidation in various Liberated Areas, laid down a series of policies and methods for the land reform and Party consolidation and stressed the correction of "Left" deviations which had occurred during the execution of these two tasks in certain areas.

[2] See the introductory note to "The Present Situation and Our Tasks", pp. 158-59 of this volume.

[3] This refers to the "Directive on Correcting Mistakes in the Determination of Class Status and on Uniting with the Middle Peasants" issued by the Shansi-Suiyuan Sub-Bureau of the Central Committee of the Communist Party of China on January 13, 1948. The directive is divided into five sections. The following are its main points:

(1) Because the criteria for class identification had not been well-defined, quite a few persons were wrongly classified as bankrupt landlords or rich peasants on the spontaneous demands of the peasants, and in particular, well-to-do middle peasants were wrongly classified as rich peasants. This had an adverse effect on the effort to unite with the middle peasants and was wrong.

(2) Proper measures were to be taken resolutely to persuade the peasants to correct these mistakes. Suitable restitution was to be made of property that had been taken.

(3) It was to be explained to the peasants and the cadres that the only criterion in class identification should be the relationship of exploitation. Mistakes in determining class status were to be corrected.

(4) The principle of relying on poor peasants and farm labourers and uniting with middle peasants had to be grasped. The middle peasants were to be enabled to have one-third of the members of the peasant representative conferences and of the leading bodies of the peasant associations, and consideration was to be given to their interests in taxation and in the land reform.

(5) Responsible cadres were to make a serious study of the Party's class policy for the rural areas. Mistakes that departed from the Party's policies concerning the middle peasants had to be corrected; they had to be corrected through the masses.

Simultaneously with the issuance of this five-point directive, the Shansi-Suiyuan Sub-Bureau issued the "Directive on the Protection of Industry and Commerce" to correct the deviations of encroaching on industry and commerce during the land reform.

[4] This refers to the supply and marketing co-operatives.

A TALK TO THE EDITORIAL STAFF OF THE *SHANSI-SUIYUAN DAILY*

April 2, 1948

Our policy must be made known not only to the leaders and to the cadres but also to the broad masses. Questions concerning policy should as a rule be given publicity in the Party papers or periodicals. We are now carrying out the reform of the land system. The policies on land reform should be published in the papers and broadcast on the radio so that the broad masses all know them. Once the masses know the truth and have a common aim, they will work together with one heart. This is like fighting a battle; to win a battle the fighters as well as the officers must be of one heart. After the troops in northern Shensi went through training and consolidation and poured out their grievances against the old social order, the fighters heightened their political consciousness and became clear on why they were fighting and how they should fight; every one of them rolled up his sleeves for battle, their morale was very high and as soon as they went into action they won a victory. When the masses are of one heart, everything becomes easy. A basic principle of Marxism-Leninism is to enable the masses to know their own interests and unite to fight for their own interests. The role and power of the newspapers consists in their ability to bring the Party programme, the Party line, the Party's general and specific policies, its tasks and methods of work before the masses in the quickest and most extensive way.

There are people in our leading organs in some places who think that it is enough for the leaders alone to know the Party's policies and that there is no need to let the masses know them. This is one of the basic reasons why some of our work cannot be done well. For over twenty years our Party has carried on mass work every day, and for the past dozen years it has talked about the mass line every day. We have always maintained that the revolution must rely on the masses of the people, on everybody's taking a hand, and have opposed relying merely on a few persons issuing orders.   The mass line, however, is still not being thoroughly carried out in the work of some comrades; they still rely solely on a handful of people working coolly and quietly by themselves.   One reason is that, whatever they do, they are always reluctant to explain it to the people they lead and that they do not understand why or how to give play to the initiative and creative energy of those they lead.   Subjectively, they too want everyone to take a hand in the work, but they do not let other people know what is to be done or how to do it.   That being the case, how can everyone be expected to get moving and how can anything be done well?   To solve this problem the basic thing is, of course, to carry out ideological education on the mass line, but at the same time we must teach these comrades many concrete methods of work. One such method is to make full use of the newspapers.   To run a newspaper well, to make it interesting and absorbing, to give correct publicity in the newspapers to the Party's general and specific policies and to strengthen the Party's ties with the masses through the newspapers – this is an important question of principle in our Party's work which is not to be taken lightly.

You comrades are newspapermen.   Your job is to educate the masses, to enable the masses to know their own interests, their own tasks and the Party's general and specific policies.   Running a newspaper is like all other work, it must be done conscientiously if it is to be done well, if it is to be lively.   With our newspapers, too, we must rely on everybody, on the masses of the people, on the whole Party to run them, not merely on a few persons working behind closed doors. Our papers talk about the mass line every day, yet frequently the mass line is not carried out in the work of the newspaper office itself. For instance, misprints often crop up in the papers simply because their elimination has not been tackled as a serious job.   If we apply the method of the mass line, then when misprints appear, we should assemble the entire staff of the paper to discuss nothing but this matter, tell them clearly what the mistakes are, explain why they occur and how they can be got rid of and ask everyone to give the matter serious attention.   After this has been done three times, or five times, such mistakes can certainly be overcome.   This is true of small matters, and of big matters, too.

To be good at translating the Party's policy into action of the masses, to be good at getting not only the leading cadres but also the broad masses to understand and master every movement and every struggle we launch – this is an art of Marxist-Leninist leadership. It is also the dividing line that determines whether or not we make mistakes in our work. If we tried to go on the offensive when the masses are not yet awakened, that would be adventurism. If we insisted on leading the masses to do anything against their will, we would certainly fail. If we did not advance when the masses demand advance, that would be Right opportunism. Chen Tu-hsiu's opportunist error consisted precisely in lagging behind the awakening of the masses, being unable to lead the masses forward and even opposing their forward march. There are many comrades who still don't understand these questions. Our papers should propagate these ideas well so that everyone can understand them.

To teach the masses, newspaper workers should first of all learn from the masses. You comrades are all intellectuals. Intellectuals are often ignorant and often have little or no experience in practical matters. You can't quite understand the pamphlet "How to Analyse the Classes in the Rural Areas"[1] issued in 1933; on this point, the peasants are more than a match for you, for they understand it fully as soon as they are told about it. Over 180 peasants in two districts of Kuohsien County met for five days and settled many problems concerning the distribution of land. If your editorial department were to discuss those problems, I am afraid you would discuss them for two weeks without settling them. The reason is quite simple; you do not understand those problems. To change from lack of understanding to understanding, one must do things and see things; that is learning. Comrades working on the newspapers should go out by turns to take part in mass work, in land reform work for a time; that is very necessary. When not going out to participate in mass work, you should hear a great deal and read a great deal about the mass movements and devote time and effort to the study of such material. Our slogan in training troops is, "Officers teach soldiers, soldiers teach officers and soldiers teach each other". The fighters have a lot of practical combat experience. The officers should learn from the fighters, and when they have made other people's experience their own, they will become more capable. Comrades working on the newspapers, too, should constantly study the material coming from below, gradually enrich their practical knowledge and become experienced. Only thus will you be able to do your work well, will you be able to shoulder your task of educating the masses.

The *Shansi-Suiyuan Daily* made very great progress following the conference of secretaries of prefectural Party committees last June. Then the paper was rich in content, sharp, pungent and vigorous; it reflected the great mass struggles, it spoke for the masses. I liked reading it very much. But since January this year, when we began to correct "Left" deviations, your paper seems to have lost some of its spirit; it is not clear-cut enough, not pungent enough, has become less informative and does not have much appeal for the reader. Now you are examining your work and summing up your experience; this is very good. When you have summed up your experience in combating Right and "Left" deviations and become more clear-headed, your work will improve.

The struggle against Right deviations waged by the *Shansi-Suiyuan Daily* from last June on was completely correct. In that struggle you did a very conscientious job and fully reflected the actual situation in the mass movement. You made comments, in the form of editorial notes, on the viewpoints and materials which you regarded as wrong. There were shortcomings too in some of your later comments, but the conscientious spirit was good. Your shortcomings lay chiefly in drawing the bow-string much too tight. If a bow-string is too taut, it will snap. The ancients said, "The principle of Kings Wen and Wu was to alternate tension with relaxation."[2] Now "relax" a bit and the comrades will become more clear-headed. You achieved successes in your work, but there were also shortcomings, mainly "Left" deviations. Now you are making an over-all summing-up and, after correcting the "Left" deviations, you will achieve greater successes.

When we are correcting deviations, some people look on the work of the past as utterly fruitless and all wrong. That is not right. These people fail to see that the Party has led a huge number of peasants to obtain land, overthrown feudalism, consolidated the Party organizations and improved the cadres' style of work, and that now it has also corrected the "Left" deviations and educated the cadres and masses. Are all these not great achievements? We should be analytical with regard to our work and the undertakings of the masses, and should not negate everything. In the past "Left" deviations arose because people had no experience. Without experience it is hard to avoid mistakes. From inexperience to experience, one must go through a process. Through the struggles against the Right and "Left" deviations in the short period since June last year, people have come to understand what struggle against Right deviations means and what struggle against "Left" deviations means. Without this process, people would not understand.

After you have examined your work and summed up your experience, I am sure that your paper will be run even better. You must retain the former merits of your paper – it should be sharp, pungent and clear-cut, and it should be run conscientiously. We must firmly uphold the truth, and truth requires a clear-cut stand. We Communists have always disdained to conceal our views. Newspapers run by our Party and all the propaganda work of our Party should be vivid, clear-cut and sharp and should never mutter and mumble. That is the militant style proper to us, the revolutionary proletariat. Since we want to teach the people to know the truth and arouse them to fight for their own emancipation, we need this militant style. A blunt knife draws no blood.

NOTES

[1] See "How to Analyse the Classes in the Rural Areas", *Selected Works of Mao Tse-tung*, Vol. I.

[2] From the *Book of Rites*, "Miscellaneous Records", Part II. "Kings Wen and Wu could not keep a bow in permanent tension without relaxation. Nor would they leave it in a permanent state of relaxation without tension. The principle of Kings Wen and Wu was to alternate tension with relaxation." Wen and Wu were the first two kings of the Chou Dynasty (12th-3rd century B.C.).

TELEGRAM TO THE HEADQUARTERS OF THE LOYANG FRONT AFTER THE RECAPTURE OF THE CITY*

April 8, 1948

Loyang is now recaptured[1] and can probably be securely held. In our urban policy, pay attention to the following points:

1. Be very prudent in the liquidation of the organs of Kuomintang rule, arrest only the chief reactionaries and do not involve too many persons.

2. Set a clear line of demarcation in defining bureaucrat-capital; do not designate as bureaucrat-capital and do not confiscate all the industrial and commercial enterprises run by Kuomintang members. The principle should be laid down that the democratic government should take over and operate all industrial and commercial enterprises which are definitely verified as having been run by the Kuomintang's central, provincial, county or municipal governments, that is, enterprises operated wholly by official bodies. But if, for the time being, the democratic government is not yet ready to take them over or is unable to do so, the individuals previously in charge should be temporarily entrusted with the responsibility of management so that these enterprises can function as usual until the democratic government appoints people to take over. The workers and technicians in these industrial and commercial enterprises should be organized to participate in management, and their competence should be trusted. If the Kuomintang personnel have fled and the enterprise has suspended operations, a management committee of representatives elected by the workers and technicians should be set up, pending the appointment by the democratic government of managers and directors who will manage it together with the workers. Enterprises run by notorious big bureaucrats of the Kuomintang should be dealt with in conformity with the principles and measures stated above. Industrial

247

and commercial enterprises run by small bureaucrats or by landlords, however, are not subject to confiscation. Encroachment on any enterprise run by the national bourgeoisie is strictly prohibited.

3. Forbid peasant organizations to enter the city to seize landlords and settle scores with them. Landlords whose land is in the villages but who live in the city should be dealt with by the democratic municipal government according to law. Upon the request of the village peasant organizations those who have committed the most heinous crimes may be sent back to the villages to be dealt with.

4. On entering the city, do not lightly advance slogans of raising wages and reducing working hours. In war time it is good enough if production can continue and existing working hours and original wage levels can be maintained. Whether or not suitable reductions in working hours and increases in wages are to be made later will depend on economic conditions, that is, on whether the enterprises thrive.

5. Do not be in a hurry to organize the people of the city to struggle for democratic reforms and improvements in livelihood. These matters can be properly handled in the light of local conditions only when the municipal administration is in good working order, public feeling has become calm, careful surveys have been made, a clear idea of the situation has been gained and appropriate measures have been worked out.

6. In the big cities, food and fuel are now the central problems; they must be handled in a planned way. Once a city comes under our administration, the problem of the livelihood of the city poor must be solved step by step and in a planned way. Do not raise the slogan, "Open the granaries to relieve the poor". Do not foster among them the psychology of depending on the government for relief.

7. Members of the Kuomintang and its Three People's Principles Youth League must be properly screened and registered.

8. Plan everything on a long-term basis. It is strictly forbidden to destroy any means of production, whether publicly or privately owned, and to waste consumer goods. Extravagant eating and drinking are forbidden, and attention should be paid to thrift and economy.

9. Appoint as secretaries of the Party's municipal committee and

---

* This telegram was drafted by Comrade Mao Tse-tung for the Central Committee of the Communist Party of China. Since its contents were applicable not only to Loyang but, in the main, to all newly liberated cities, it was sent concurrently to the leading comrades on other fronts and in other areas.

as mayor and deputy mayors only persons who have a grasp of policy and are capable.   They should train all their personnel and explain urban policies and tactics to them.   Now that the city belongs to the people, everything should proceed in the spirit that the people themselves are responsible for managing the city.   It would be entirely wrong to apply our policies and tactics for cities under Kuomintang administration to a city under the people's own administration.

NOTES

[1] Loyang was an important stronghold of the Kuomintang troops in the western part of Honan Province.   The People's Liberation Army first took Loyang on March 14, 1948, subsequently evacuated the city on its own initiative to facilitate the wiping out of the enemy's effective strength and recaptured Loyang on April 5, 1948.

TACTICAL PROBLEMS OF RURAL WORK
IN THE NEW LIBERATED AREAS

May 24, 1948

It is necessary to give over-all consideration to the tactical problems of rural work in the new Liberated Areas. In these areas we must make full use of the experience gained in the period of the War of Resistance Against Japan; for a considerable period after their liberation we should apply the social policy of reducing rent and interest and properly adjusting the supplies of seed and food grains and the financial policy of reasonable distribution of burdens; we should aim our main blows only at the important counter-revolutionaries who side politically with the Kuomintang and stubbornly oppose our Party and our army, just as we only arrested the traitors and confiscated their property during the period of the War of Resistance, and we should not immediately apply the social reform policy of distributing movable property and land. The reason is that only a few bolder elements would welcome the premature distribution of movable property and that the basic masses would not get anything and would therefore be dissatisfied. Moreover, hasty dispersal of social wealth is to the disadvantage of the army. Premature distribution of land would prematurely place the entire burden of military requirements on the peasants instead of on the landlords and rich peasants. In the sphere of social reform, it is better not to distribute movable property and land but instead to reduce rent and interest universally so that the peasants will receive tangible benefits, and in financial policy we should effect a reasonable distribution of burdens so that the landlords and rich peasants will pay more. In this way, social wealth will not be dispersed and public order will be comparatively stable, and this will help us concentrate all our forces on destroying the Kuomintang reactionaries. After one, two or even three years, when the Kuomintang reactionaries have been wiped out in extensive base areas,

251

when conditions have become stable, when the masses have awakened and organized themselves and when the war has moved far away, we can enter the stage of land reform – the distribution of movable property and land as in northern China.   The stage of rent and interest reduction cannot be skipped in any new Liberated Area, and we shall make mistakes if we skip it.   The above tactics must also be carried out in those parts of the large Liberated Areas in northern, northeastern and northwestern China which border on enemy territory.

THE WORK OF LAND REFORM
AND OF PARTY CONSOLIDATION IN 1948*

May 25, 1948

I

It is necessary to pay attention to the seasons. In areas designated by the bureaus or sub-bureaus of the Central Committee, the whole of next autumn and winter, that is, the seven months from this September to next March, must be devoted to carrying out the following tasks in the proper order:

1. Make an investigation of rural conditions.

2. Carry out the initial work for Party consolidation in accordance with correct policy. A working corps or working team sent by a higher organ to a rural district must first of all unite with all the activists and better members in the local Party branch and together with them lead the work of land reform.

3. Organize or reorganize or strengthen the poor peasant leagues and the peasant associations and launch the land reform struggle.

4. Identify class status according to correct criteria.

5. Distribute feudal land and property in accordance with correct policy. The final result of the distribution must be such that it is considered fair and reasonable by all the main strata and that the landlords too feel that there is a way for them to make a living and that this is assured.

6. Form people's representative conferences and elect government councils at the township (or village), district and county levels.

7. Issue land certificates fixing the ownership of land.

8. Adjust or revise the rates of the agricultural tax (*i.e.*, public grain). These rates must conform to the principle of giving

consideration to both public and private interests; in other words, they must on the one hand help support the war and on the other get the peasants interested in restoring and developing production, which will help improve their livelihood.

9. Complete the work of the organizational consolidation of the Party branches in accordance with correct policy.

10. Shift our work from land reform to rallying all the rural working people and to organizing the labour power of the landlords and rich peasants in a general struggle to restore and develop agricultural production. Start organizing small-scale work-exchange groups and other co-operative units according to the principles of voluntary participation and exchange of equal values; prepare seed, fertilizer and fuel; work out production plans; issue agricultural credits (chiefly loans for means of production, to be definitely repaid and to be strictly distinguished from relief grants) when necessary and possible; draw up plans, where possible, for building water conservancy works.

This is the whole process of work from land reform to production, a process which all comrades directly engaged in land reform must be brought to understand so that they can avoid one-sidedness in their work and, without missing the seasons, accomplish all the above tasks in the coming autumn and winter.

II

To achieve these aims, it is necessary to get the following work done in the next three months – from June through August:

1. Designate the areas for land reform. Each such area must meet the following three conditions:

   a. All the enemy armed forces must have been wiped out and conditions must have become stable; it must not be an unstable guerrilla zone.

   b. The overwhelming majority of the basic masses (the farm labourers, poor peasants and middle peasants), not

---

* This inner-Party directive was drafted by Comrade Mao Tse-tung for the Central Committee of the Communist Party of China.

just a minority, must already be demanding the distribution of land.

c. Party cadres must be adequate both in numbers and in quality to grasp the work of land reform and must not leave it to the spontaneous activity of the masses.

An area where any one of these three conditions is lacking should not be designated for land reform in 1948. For instance, since they do not meet the first condition, we should not include in this year's plan for land reform those parts of the Liberated Areas in northern and eastern China, the Northeast and the Northwest, which border on enemy territory, nor most of the area enclosed by the Yangtse, Huai, Yellow and Han Rivers, which is under the jurisdiction of the Central Plains Bureau of the Central Committee. Whether they are to be included in next year's plan will depend on circumstances. In these areas we should make full use of the experience acquired during the period of the War of Resistance Against Japan and put into effect the social policy of reducing rent and interest and of properly adjusting supplies of seed and food grains, as well as the financial policy of reasonable distribution of burdens, so as to unite with or neutralize all social forces that can be united with or can be neutralized, help the People's Liberation Army to wipe out all the Kuomintang armed forces and strike blows at the local tyrants who are politically the most reactionary. Neither land nor movable property should be distributed in these areas, because they are newly liberated and border on enemy territory, and distribution there would not be of advantage to uniting with or neutralizing all social forces that can be united with or neutralized for the accomplishment of the basic task of wiping out the Kuomintang forces of reaction.

2. Make cadres' conferences a success. At cadres' conferences concerned with the work of land reform and Party consolidation, all the correct policies relating to these two tasks must be fully explained and a clear line must be drawn between what is and what is not permitted. All cadres working on land reform and Party consolidation are required to study seriously and understand fully the important documents issued by the Central Committee; cadres must be enjoined to adhere to them all and must not make any unauthorized change. In case parts of the documents do not suit local conditions, cadres may and should propose amendments,

but they must secure the approval of the Central Committee before
actually making any change. The higher leading organs of the
various areas must make adequate and proper preparations beforehand for the cadres' conferences which are to be held at different
levels this year. That is to say, before a conference is convened,
there should be discussions among a few persons (with one of them
taking the main responsibility), in the course of which questions
are raised and analysed and an outline is written; this outline must
be carefully worked out in content and wording (be sure to make
it clear and concise and avoid long-windedness). Then a report
should be made at the conference, discussion should be unfolded,
the outline should be supplemented, revised and finalized in the
light of the views expressed in the discussion, and the final document should be circulated in the whole Party and published, as far
as possible, in the newspapers. It is necessary to oppose holding
meetings in an empiricist way, that is, with no advance preparations, no problems raised or analysed and no report, carefully
prepared and well-weighed in content and wording, submitted to
the cadres' conference, but with the participants allowed to indulge
in pointless, random talk so that the sessions drag on without
reaching any clear, well-considered conclusion. Pay attention to
eliminating this harmful empiricist way if it is found in the leadership work of any bureau or sub-bureau of the Central Committee,
or in any area, provincial or prefectural Party committee. Conferences to discuss policy should not be attended by too many people
and can be shortened if there is enough preparation. Generally
it is proper for a dozen or so people, or twenty to thirty, or forty
to fifty – the number varying according to circumstances – to meet
for about a week. Meetings for transmitting policy may have a
larger attendance but must not last too long either. The only
conferences which may have a larger attendance and may last
longer are those for Party consolidation among senior and middle-
rank cadres.

3. By the first half or at the latest the second half of September, all cadres who are to take a direct part in the land reform must
arrive in the villages and start work. Otherwise, it will be impossible to utilize the whole of the coming autumn and winter to
complete the land reform, the Party consolidation and the formation of organs of political power and to prepare for spring ploughing.

III

At cadres' conferences as well as in their work, cadres must be taught how to analyse concrete situations and how, proceeding from the concrete situations in different areas with different historical conditions, to decide on their tasks and methods of work in a given place and time. Distinctions must be drawn between the cities and the rural areas and among the old Liberated Areas, semi-old Liberated Areas, areas bordering on enemy territory and new Liberated Areas; otherwise mistakes will be made.

IV

The land problem should be considered solved and the question of land reform should not be raised again in areas where the feudal system has been fundamentally abolished, where the poor peasants and farm labourers have all acquired roughly the average amount of land and where there is still a difference (which is permissible) between their holdings and those of the middle peasants, but where the difference is not great. In these areas the central tasks are to restore and develop production, to complete the Party consolidation and the formation of organs of political power and to support the front. If, in certain villages in these areas, some land is still to be distributed or readjusted, the class status of some individuals still needs to be revised and some land certificates still have to be issued, these tasks should of course be completed in accordance with the actual circumstances.

V

In all the Liberated Areas, whether or not the land reform has been completed, we must direct the peasants to cultivate the wheat fields and to plough part of the land this autumn. In the winter, the peasants should be called upon to collect fertilizer. All this is vitally important to agricultural production and the 1949 harvests in the

Liberated Areas and must be accomplished through administrative measures co-ordinated with mass work.

VI

It is necessary resolutely to overcome certain manifestations of indiscipline or anarchy existing in many places. There are people who, without authorization, modify the policies and tactics adopted by the Central Committee or other higher Party committees and apply extremely harmful policies and tactics, which go against the united will and discipline but which they opinionatedly believe to be correct. There are also people who, on the pretext of pressure of work, adopt the wrong attitude of neither asking for instructions before an action is taken nor submitting a report afterwards and who regard the area they administer as an independent realm. All this is extremely harmful to the interests of the revolution. Party committees at every level must discuss this matter again and again and work earnestly to overcome such indiscipline and anarchy so that all the powers that can and must be centralized will be concentrated in the hands of the Central Committee and its agencies.[1]

VII

The Central Committee, its bureaus (or sub-bureaus), the area (or provincial) Party committees and the prefectural, county and district Party committees down to the level of Party branches must establish close contact with each other in order to have a good grasp of trends in the various movements, constantly exchange information and experience, and promptly correct mistakes and spread successes. For these purposes, they should make full use of such means of communication as the radio, telegraph, telephone, posts and couriers; of such methods of consultation as small meetings (of four or five persons), joint local conferences (of a few counties) and personal talks; of such inspection tours as may be made by small groups (of three to five persons) or by individual committee members with prestige; and of the news agency and newspapers. There should be no waiting for several months, half a year or even longer before a lower organization submits its summary report to the one above, or before a higher organization issues general directives to those below.   For such reports and directives often become out of date, losing all or part of their usefulness. And mistakes are made and cannot be corrected in time, causing serious damage.   What the whole Party urgently needs is reports and directives that are timely, lively and concrete.

VIII

In exercising their leadership, the bureaus and sub-bureaus of the Central Committee and the area, provincial, prefectural and municipal Party committees must give proper attention to both urban and rural work, to the tasks of both industrial and agricultural production. That is to say, they should not, on account of directing the land reform and agricultural production, neglect to give leadership to urban work and industrial production or slacken their efforts in this regard.   Since we now have many big, medium and small cities and a vast network of industries, mines and communications, we shall make mistakes if any of the leading organizations concerned becomes negligent or slackens its efforts in this respect.

NOTES

[1] The agencies of the Central Committee, as referred to here, were its bureaus and sub-bureaus.

THE CONCEPT OF OPERATIONS
FOR THE LIAOHSI-SHENYANG CAMPAIGN[1]*

September and October 1948

I. THE TELEGRAM OF SEPTEMBER 7

We are prepared to bring about the fundamental overthrow of the Kuomintang in about five years, counting from July 1946.[2] This is possible. Our objective can be attained provided we destroy about 100 brigades of Kuomintang regular troops every year, or some 500 brigades over the five years. In the past two years our army has annihilated a total of 191 brigades of enemy regulars, an average of $95^1/_2$ brigades a year, or nearly 8 brigades a month. In the next three years it is required that our army should wipe out 300 or more brigades of enemy regulars. Between July this year and June next year we expect to destroy some 115 brigades of enemy regulars. This total is apportioned among our various field armies and armies.[3] The Eastern China Field Army is required to wipe out about 40 brigades (including the 7 already wiped out in July) and capture Tsinan and a number of large, medium and small cities in northern Kiangsu, eastern Honan and northern Anhwei. The Central Plains Field Army is required to wipe out about 14 brigades (including the 2 brigades wiped out in July) and capture a number of cities in the provinces of Hupeh, Honan and Anhwei. The Northwest Field Army is required to wipe out about 12 brigades (including the $1^1/_2$ brigades wiped out in August). The army in northern China commanded by Hsu Hsiang-chien and Chou Shih-ti is required to wipe out about 14 brigades under Yen Hsi-shan (including the 8 brigades annihilated in July) and capture Taiyuan. You are required, in co-ordination with the 2 armies commanded by Lo Jui-ching and Yang Cheng-wu, to wipe out about 35 brigades of the 2 army groups under Wei Li-huang and Fu Tso-yi (including 1 brigade wiped out by Yang Cheng-wu in July) and capture all the cities along the Peiping-Liaoning, Peiping-Suiyuan, Peiping-Chengteh and Peiping-Paoting Railways, except Peiping, Tientsin and Shenyang. The decisive factors for the achievement of this objective are the proper disposition and command of troops in campaigns and a proper balance between fighting and rest. If in the two months of September and October, or a little longer, you can wipe out the enemy along the line from Chinchow to Tangshan and take Chinchow, Shanhaikuan and Tangshan, you will have achieved the task of wiping out some 18 enemy brigades. In order to wipe them out, you must now prepare to employ your main force on this line, leaving the enemy forces at Changchun and Shenyang alone. When you are attacking Chinchow, be prepared also to wipe out the enemy forces that may come to its rescue from Changchun and Shenyang. Because the enemy forces in and near Chinchow, Shanhaikuan and Tangshan are isolated from each other, success in attacking and wiping them out is pretty certain, and there is also a fair hope of success in capturing Chinchow and in attacking enemy reinforcements. If, however, you were to dispose your main force at Hsinmin and its northern environs in preparation for attacking the enemy forces which might come out from Changchun and Shenyang, then the enemy might not dare come out at all because you would be too great a menace. On the one hand, the enemy at Changchun and Shenyang might not come out. And, on the other hand, because the forces you dispatch towards Chinchow, Shanhai-kuan and Tangshan would be too small, the enemy in and near these three cities (comprising 18 brigades) would probably fall back on

---

* These telegrams addressed to Lin Piao, Lo Jung-huan and other comrades were drawn up by Comrade Mao Tse-tung for the Revolutionary Military Commission of the Central Committee of the Communist Party of China. The concept of operations he set forth here for the Liaohsi-Shenyang campaign was fully carried out later. The results of the campaign were as follows:

(1) The destruction of 470,000 enemy troops, plus the victories in other theatres during that period, made the qualitatively superior People's Liberation Army superior to the Kuomintang army in numbers as well.

(2) The entire territory of northeastern China was liberated, and the conditions were created for the liberation of Peiping, Tientsin and all northern China.

(3) Our army gained experience in fighting large-scale campaigns of annihilation.

(4) As a result of the liberation of northeastern China, a strategically secure rear area with a fair industrial base was won for the War of Liberation, and the Party and the people obtained favourable conditions for gradually turning to economic rehabilitation.

Chinchow and Tangshan, and you would find it rather difficult and yet necessary to attack them, wasting time and energy and thus perhaps landing yourselves in a passive position. For these reasons, it will be better to leave the enemy at Changchun and Shenyang alone and focus your attention on the enemy at Chinchow, Shanhaikuan and Tangshan. Another point: you must prepare to fight three big campaigns in the ten months from September to next June and to spend about two months on each campaign, making a total of about six months and leaving four months for rest. During the Chinchow-Shanhaikuan-Tangshan campaign (the first big campaign), if the enemy at Changchun and Shenyang sallies forth in full strength to rescue Chinchow (because your main force will be disposed not at Hsinmin but around Chinchow, Wei Li-huang will be emboldened to come to the rescue), then, without leaving the Chinchow-Shanhaikuan-Tangshan line, you can follow up immediately with large-scale annihilating attacks on the enemy reinforcements and strive to wipe out all Wei Li-huang's troops on the spot. This would be the ideal situation. Hence, you should pay attention to the following:

(1) Be firmly determined to attack and capture Chinchow, Shanhaikuan and Tangshan and to take control of the entire line.

(2) Be firmly determined to fight a battle of annihilation on a scale larger than you have ever fought before, that is, dare to fight all Wei Li-huang's army when it comes to the rescue.

(3) In keeping with these two resolves, reconsider your plan of operations, make arrangements to meet the military requirements

---

The Liaohsi-Shenyang campaign was the first of the three greatest campaigns of decisive significance in the Chinese People's War of Liberation. The other two were the Huai-Hai and the Peiping-Tientsin campaigns. In these three great campaigns, which lasted four months and nineteen days, 144 divisions (brigades) of the enemy's regular troops and 29 divisions of its irregular troops, or more than 1,540,000 men in all, were wiped out. During this period the People's Liberation Army also launched offensives on other fronts, destroying large numbers of the enemy. In the first two years of the war, the People's Liberation Army had wiped out an average of about 8 enemy brigades per month. Now the number of enemy troops destroyed by the People's Liberation Army no longer averaged 8 brigades per month but 38 brigades. These three major campaigns virtually annihilated the crack troops on which the Kuomintang relied for waging the counter-revolutionary civil war and greatly speeded victory in the War of Liberation all over the country. For the Huai-Hai and Peiping-Tientsin campaigns, see "The Concept of Operations for the Huai-Hai Campaign", pp. 279-82 and "The Concept of Operations for the Peiping-Tientsin Campaign", pp. 289-93, of this volume.

of your whole force (food, ammunition, recruits, and so on) and to handle captives.

Please consider the above and telegraph your reply.

II. THE TELEGRAM OF OCTOBER 10

1. From the day you start attacking Chinchow, there will be a period when the tactical situation will be very tense. We hope that you will inform us by radio every two or three days of the enemy's situation (the strength of the resistance by his forces defending Chinchow, the progress of his reinforcements from Hulutao and Chinhsi and from Shenyang and the probable course of action of his troops in Changchun) and of our own situation (the progress of our attack on the city and the casualties sustained in attacking the city and holding off enemy reinforcements).

2. It is highly possible that, as you have said, the tactical situation during this period will develop most favourably, that is, that you will be able to wipe out not only the enemy's forces defending Chinchow but also a part of his reinforcements from Hulutao and Chinhsi and some or most of his forces fleeing from Changchun. If the enemy's reinforcements from Shenyang advance to the area north of the Taling River just after you have taken Chinchow and when you are thus able to shift your forces to encircle them, then it will be possible to wipe out these reinforcements as well. The key to all this lies in striving to capture Chinchow in about a week.

3. Decide on the disposition of your troops for checking the enemy reinforcements according to your progress in attacking Chinchow and their progress in advancing both from the east and from the west. In case the enemy reinforcements from Shenyang advance rather slowly (as may happen if, during your attack on Chinchow, the enemy besieged in Changchun breaks out but is caught and crushed by our 12th Column and other forces, in which case the enemy reinforcements from Shenyang may be so bewildered as to advance rather slowly or halt or turn back to rescue the Changchun forces) while the enemy reinforcements from Hulutao and Chinhsi advance rather quickly, you should be ready to throw in your general reserves to help the 4th and 11th Columns wipe out part of the latter reinforcements and, first of all, to check their advance. If the enemy reinforcements from Hulu-

tao and Chinhsi are being tied down and checked by our 4th and 11th Columns and other forces and therefore advance rather slowly or halt, if the enemy forces in Changchun do not break out, if the enemy reinforcements from Shenyang advance rather quickly, and if most of the Chinchow enemy forces have been wiped out and the capture of the city is imminent, then you should let the enemy forces from Shenyang advance deep into the area north of the Taling River, so that you can make a timely shift of your forces to encircle them and wipe them out at your convenience.

4. You must centre your attention on the operations in Chinchow and strive to capture this city as quickly as possible. Even if none of the other objectives is attained and Chinchow alone is captured, you will have won the initiative, which in itself will be a great victory. It is hoped that you will give due attention to all the above points. Especially during the first few days of the battle for Chinchow, the enemy reinforcements from both the east and the west will not make any major moves, and you should concentrate all your energies on the operations on the Chinchow front.

NOTES

[1] The Liaohsi-Shenyang campaign was a gigantic campaign fought by the Northeast People's Liberation Army in the western part of Liaoning Province and in the Shenyang-Changchun area between September 12 and November 2, 1948. On the eve of the campaign, the total strength of the Kuomintang forces in northeastern China consisted of 4 armies, made up of 14 corps, or 44 divisions. These forces had shortened their lines and dug themselves in at three sectors isolated from each other, Changchun, Shenyang and Chinchow. With the aim of completely wiping out the enemy troops in the Northeast and quickly liberating the whole of the Northeast, the People's Liberation Army in this region, supported by the broad masses of the local people, began the Liaohsi-Shenyang campaign in September 1948 with a main force of 12 columns, 1 artillery column and regional armed forces, altogether totalling 53 divisions or over 700,000 men. Chinchow, on the Peiping-Liaoning Railway, was the strategic link between northeastern and northern China. The enemy forces garrisoning the Chinchow sector consisted of 8 divisions, with more than 100,000 men under Fan Han-chieh, Deputy Commander-in-Chief of the Kuomintang's Northeast "Bandit Suppression" Headquarters. The capture of Chinchow was the key to the success of the Liaohsi-Shenyang campaign. Acting on the directives of Comrade Mao Tse-tung, the Northeast People's Liberation Army used 1 column and 7 independent divisions to continue the siege operations against Changchun; 6 columns, 1 artillery column and 1 tank battalion to surround and attack Chinchow; and 2 columns, placed in the Tashan-Kaochiao sector southwest of Chinchow, along with 3 columns in the Heishan-Tahushan-Changwu sector

to intercept any reinforcements the enemy might send from Chinhsi and Hulutao and from Shenyang to relieve Chinchow. The fighting in the Chinchow area started on September 12. Just as our army was mopping up the enemy in the outskirts of Chinchow after taking Ihsien, Chiang Kai-shek hurriedly flew to the Northeast to take personal charge of the operations and urgently summoned 5 enemy divisions from the Northern China "Bandit Suppression" Headquarters on the Peiping-Liaoning Railway and 2 divisions from Shantung Province to join the 4 divisions in Chinhsi; all these 11 divisions began a furious attack on our positions at Tashan on October 10 but could not break through. Meanwhile, the Kuomintang 9th Army under Liao Yao-hsiang, with 11 divisions and 3 cavalry brigades, which had sallied out from Shenyang to rescue Chinchow, was intercepted by our army northeast of Heishan and Tahushan. Our army began the assault on Chinchow on October 14 and, after thirty-one hours of fierce fighting, completely wiped out the defending enemy forces, capturing Fan Han-chieh, Deputy Commander-in-Chief of the Northeast "Bandit Suppression" Headquarters, Lu Chun-chuan, Commander of the 6th Army, and more than 100,000 men under their command. The liberation of Chinchow impelled part of the enemy forces at Changchun to revolt against the Kuomintang and the rest to surrender. The complete collapse of the Kuomintang troops in the Northeast then became a foregone conclusion. But Chiang Kai-shek, still dreaming of recapturing Chinchow and of reopening the line of communications between northeastern and northern China, gave strict orders to the army under Liao Yao-hsiang to continue its advance towards Chinchow. After taking Chinchow, the People's Liberation Army immediately swung back to the northeast and closed in on Liao's army from the north and south of Heishan and Tahushan. On October 26 the People's Liberation Army succeeded in surrounding the enemy in the Heishan-Tahushan-Hsinmin sector and, after stiff fighting lasting two days and one night, completely wiped them out, capturing army commander Liao Yao-hsiang, corps commanders Li Tao, Pai Feng-wu and Cheng Ting-chi, and more than 100,000 men. Our army vigorously followed up this victory and liberated Shenyang and Yingkow on November 2, wiping out over 149,000 enemy troops. The whole of the Northeast was thus liberated. A total of more than 470,000 enemy troops were wiped out in the campaign.

  2 See "A Circular on the Situation", Note 7, p. 226 of this volume.

  3 On November 1, 1948, the Revolutionary Military Commission of the Central Committee of the Communist Party of China classified all troops in the big strategic areas into field, regional and guerrilla forces in accordance with decisions made at the September meeting of the Political Bureau of the Central Committee. The field forces were organized into field armies. A field army was composed of armies, an army of corps (originally called columns), a corps of divisions, and a division of regiments. In accordance with their locations, the field armies were designated the Northwest Field Army, Central Plains Field Army, Eastern China Field Army, Northeast Field Army and Northern China Field Army of the Chinese People's Liberation Army. The number of armies, corps and divisions in each field army differed according to the concrete conditions in each big strategic area. Later, the Northwest Field Army was renamed the First Field Army, comprising 2 armies; the Central Plains Field Army was renamed the Second Field Army, comprising 3 armies; the Eastern China Field Army was renamed the Third Field Army, comprising 4 armies; and the Northeast Field Army was renamed the Fourth Field Army, comprising 4 armies. The 3 armies making up the Northern China Field Army were placed under the direct command of the General Headquarters of the Chinese People's Liberation Army.

ON STRENGTHENING
THE PARTY COMMITTEE SYSTEM*

September 20, 1948

The Party committee system is an important Party institution for ensuring collective leadership and preventing any individual from monopolizing the conduct of affairs. It has recently been found that in some (of course not all) leading bodies it is the habitual practice for one individual to monopolize the conduct of affairs and decide important problems. Solutions to important problems are decided not by Party committee meetings but by one individual, and membership in the Party committee has become nominal. Differences of opinion among committee members cannot be resolved and are left unresolved for a long time. Members of the Party committee maintain only formal, not real, unity among themselves. This situation must be changed. From now on, a sound system of Party committee meetings must be instituted in all leading bodies, from the bureaus of the Central Committee to the prefectural Party committees; from the Party committees of the fronts to the Party committees of brigades and military areas (sub-commissions of the Revolutionary Military Commission or leading groups); and the leading Party members' groups in government bodies, people's organizations, the news agency and the newspaper offices. All important problems (of course, not the unimportant, trivial problems, or problems whose solutions have already been decided after discussion at meetings and need only be carried out) must be submitted to the committee for discussion, and the committee members present should express their views fully and reach definite decisions which should then be carried out by the members concerned. The same procedure should be followed by Party committees below the prefectural and brigade levels. In the higher leading bodies there should also be meetings of the leading cadres in the departments (for example, the propaganda department and the organizational department), commissions (for example, the labour, women's and youth commissions), schools (for example, Party schools) and offices (for example, the research offices). Of course, we must see to it that the meetings are not too long or too frequent and they must not get bogged down in discussion of petty matters lest the work be hindered. On important problems which are complicated and on which opinions differ, there must, in addition, be personal consultations before the meeting to enable the members to think things over, lest decisions by the meeting become a mere formality or no decision can be reached. Party committee meetings must be divided into two categories, standing committee meetings and plenary sessions, and the two should not be confused. Furthermore, we must take care that neither collective leadership nor personal responsibility is overemphasized to the neglect of the other. In the army, the person in command has the right to make emergency decisions during battle and when circumstances require.

---

*This decision was drafted by Comrade Mao Tse-tung for the Central Committee of the Communist Party of China.

ON THE SEPTEMBER MEETING
—CIRCULAR OF THE CENTRAL COMMITTEE
OF THE COMMUNIST PARTY OF CHINA*

October 10, 1948

1. In September 1948 the Central Committee convened a meeting of the Political Bureau, attended by seven members of the Political Bureau, fourteen members and alternate members of the Central Committee and ten important functionaries, including principal leading comrades in the Party and army in northern China, eastern China, the Central Plains and northwestern China. This meeting convened by the Central Committee had the largest attendance of any since the Japanese surrender. The meeting examined the work of the past period and set the tasks for the period ahead.

2. Since the Party's Seventh National Congress in April 1945, the Central Committee and the leading cadres of the whole Party have displayed even greater unity than during the War of Resistance Against Japan. This unity has enabled our Party to cope with many important events at home and abroad in the three years since the Japanese surrender; and in the course of these events our Party has pushed the Chinese revolution a big step forward, shattered the political influence of U.S. imperialism among the broad masses of the Chinese people, combated the new betrayal by the Kuomintang,[1] repulsed its military attacks and enabled the People's Liberation Army to shift from the defensive to the offensive.

In the last two years of fighting, from July 1946 to June 1948, the People's Liberation Army has wiped out 2,640,000 enemy troops, including 1,630,000 captured. The main war booty of the two years amounts to nearly 900,000 rifles, over 64,000 heavy and light machine-guns, 8,000 pieces of light artillery, 5,000 pieces of infantry artillery and 1,100 heavy mountain and field guns. In these two years the People's Liberation Army has grown from 1,200,000 men to 2,800,000. Our

269

regular troops have increased from 118 brigades to 176, that is, from 610,000 men to 1,490,000. The Liberated Areas now cover 2,350,000 square kilometres, or 24.5 per cent of China's total area of 9,597,000 square kilometres; their population is 168 million, or 35.3 per cent of China's total of 475 million; and they have 586 large, medium and small cities, from county towns up, or 29 per cent of China's total of 2,009 such cities.

Because our Party has firmly led the peasants in carrying out the reform of the land system, the land problem has been thoroughly solved in areas having about 100 million people, and the land of the landlord class and of the old-type rich peasants has been more or less equally distributed among the rural population and, first of all, among the poor peasants and farm labourers.

Our Party membership has increased from 1,210,000 in May 1945 to 3,000,000 at present. (In 1927, before the Kuomintang betrayal of the revolution, it was 50,000; after the Kuomintang betrayal of that year, it dropped to about 10,000; in 1934, as a result of the successful development of the agrarian revolution, it rose to 300,000; in 1937, owing to the defeat of the revolution in the south,[2] it dropped again to about 40,000; in 1945, because of the successful development of the War of Resistance Against Japan, it rose to 1,210,000; and now, because of the successful development of the anti-Chiang Kai-shek war and the agrarian revolution, it has reached 3,000,000.) On the one hand, the Party has in the past year basically overcome, and is continuing to overcome, some unhealthy phenomena which existed to a certain degree in its ranks; these were impurities in class composition (landlord and rich peasant elements), impurities in ideology (landlord and rich peasant ideology) and impurities in style of work (bureaucracy and commandism). On the other hand, the Party has in the past year overcome, and is continuing to overcome, some "Left" mistakes which accompanied the large-scale mobilization of the peasant masses in the struggles to solve the land problem; these were the partial but fairly numerous encroachments on the interests of the middle peasants, the

---

* This inner-Party circular was drafted by Comrade Mao Tse-tung for the Central Committee of the Communist Party of China. The September 1948 meeting was held in Hsipaipo Village, Pingshan County, Hopei Province. This meeting convened by the Central Committee had the largest attendance of any since the Japanese surrender. Previously it had not been possible to hold such large meetings, because the great majority of Central Committee members were in various Liberated Areas directing the tense War of Liberation and communications were extremely difficult.

damage done to some private industrial and commercial enterprises and the overstepping in some places of certain lines of demarcation in the policy for suppressing counter-revolutionaries. Through the great, fierce revolutionary struggles of the past three years, and especially of the past year, and the conscientious correction of our own mistakes, the whole Party has made a big step forward in political maturity.

The Party's work in the Kuomintang areas has been crowned with tremendous success. This can be seen from the fact that in the big cities we have won over to the side of our Party the broad masses of workers, students, teachers, professors, cultural workers, ordinary residents and national capitalists as well as all the democratic parties and people's organizations, and have thus resisted Kuomintang oppression and completely isolated the Kuomintang. In several large areas in the south (the Fukien-Kwangtung-Kiangsi, the Hunan-Kwangtung-Kiangsi, the Kwangtung-Kwangsi and the Kwangsi-Yunnan border areas, southern Yunnan, the Anhwei-Chekiang-Kiangsi border area and eastern and southern Chekiang), bases for guerrilla warfare have been established, and their guerrilla forces have grown to more than 30,000.

During the past two years and especially last year, we have carried out an orderly, well-led democratic movement in the People's Liberation Army, with all fighters and commanders taking part. In this movement we have unfolded self-criticism, have overcome and are continuing to overcome bureaucracy in the army and have restored the Party committee system at various levels of the army and the soldiers' committee system in the companies, both of which produced good results from 1927 to 1932 but were later abolished. All this has greatly heightened the political enthusiasm and consciousness of commanders and fighters, strengthened their combat effectiveness and discipline and helped us to absorb some 800,000 captured Kuomintang soldiers and change them into liberated fighters[3] who have turned their guns against the Kuomintang. During the past two years, in the Liberated Areas, we have mobilized some 1,600,000 of the peasants who obtained land to join the People's Liberation Army.

We already have quite a number of railways, mines and industries, and our Party is learning on a large scale how to manage industry and carry on trade. In the past two years our war industries have grown considerably. But they are not yet adequate to meet the needs of the war. We lack some important raw materials and machines and, generally speaking, still cannot make steel.

In areas in northern China with a population of 44 million we have set up a unified people's government in which our Party cooperates with non-Party democrats. In order to facilitate support to the front, we have decided to entrust this government with the task of unifying the work of leading and administering the economy, finance, trade, banking, communications and war industries in three regions, northern China, eastern China (with a population of 43 million) and the Northwest (with a population of 7 million), and we are prepared in the near future to extend the unification of this work to two additional regions, the Northeast and the Central Plains.

3. In the light of our successes in the past two years' fighting and of the general situation as between the enemy and ourselves, the meeting convened by the Central Committee considered it fully possible to build a People's Liberation Army of five million in a period of about five years (beginning from July 1946), to wipe out a total of some 500 brigades (divisions) of the enemy's regular forces (an average of about 100 brigades a year), to wipe out a total of some 7,500,000 men of his regular and irregular forces and of the special arms (an average of about 1,500,000 men a year) and to overthrow the reactionary rule of the Kuomintang completely.

The military strength of the Kuomintang was 4,300,000 men in July 1946. In the past two years, 3,090,000 of its men have either been wiped out or have deserted, and 2,440,000 have been recruited. Its present strength is 3,650,000 men. It is estimated that in the coming three years the Kuomintang may still be able to recruit 3,000,000 men and that some 4,500,000 will probably be wiped out or desert. Thus, as a result of five years' fighting, the remaining military strength of the Kuomintang will probably be only some 2,000,000. Our army now has 2,800,000 men. In the coming three years we plan to admit into our forces 1,700,000 captured soldiers (estimated at 60 per cent of the total we shall capture) and to mobilize 2,000,000 peasants to join the army. Allowing for depletion, our army, as a result of five years' fighting, will probably approach 5,000,000 men. If five years' fighting brings these results, then it may be said that we have overthrown the reactionary rule of the Kuomintang completely.

To fulfil this task, we must wipe out each year about 100 brigades (divisions) of the enemy's regular forces, making a total of about 500 brigades (divisions) in five years. This is the key to the solution of all problems. In view of the fact that the enemy's regular forces we wiped out amounted to 97 brigades (divisions) in the first year and to 94 brigades (divisions) in the second year, our targets can be fulfilled and even overfulfilled.   Of the Kuomintang's existing military strength totalling 3,650,000 men, 70 per cent are at the fronts (north of the line of the Yangtse River and the Pashan Mountains, east of the line of Lanchow and the Holan Mountains and south of the Chengteh-Changchun line); only about 30 per cent are in the rear (including those south of the line of the Yangtse River and the Pashan Mountains and those west of the line of Lanchow and the Holan Mountains). Of all the existing Kuomintang regular forces, which consist of 285 brigades or 1,980,000 men, 249 brigades or 1,742,000 men are at the fronts (99 brigades or 694,000 men on the northern front, and 150 brigades or 1,048,000 men on the southern front).   Only 36 brigades or 238,000 men are in the rear, and most of them are newly formed troops of low combat effectiveness.   Therefore, the Central Committee has decided that during the third year the whole of the People's Liberation Army will continue to operate north of the Yangtse River and in northern China and the Northeast.   To accomplish the task of wiping out the enemy, it is necessary to utilize large numbers of captured soldiers in addition to mobilizing people in the Liberated Areas, in a planned and prudent way, to join the army.

4.   Because our Party and our army were long in a position in which we were cut apart by the enemy, were waging guerrilla warfare and were in the rural areas, we allowed very considerable autonomy to the leading organs of the Party and army in the different areas. This enabled the Party organizations and armed forces to bring their initiative and enthusiasm into play and to come through long periods of grave difficulties, but at the same time it gave rise to certain phenomena of indiscipline and anarchy, localism and guerrilla-ism, which were harmful to the cause of the revolution.   The present situation demands that our Party should do its utmost to overcome these phenomena of indiscipline and anarchy, localism and guerrilla-ism and centralize all the powers that can and must be concentrated in the hands of the Central Committee and its agencies, so as to bring about the transition in the form of the war from guerrilla to regular warfare. In the past two years both the army and its operations have become more regular in character, but this is not enough and in the third year another big step forward must be made.   For this purpose, we must do everything possible to repair and operate modern means of communications, such as railways, highway transport and steamships, to strengthen the administration of cities and industry and to shift the

centre of gravity of our Party work step by step from the rural areas
to the cities.

5. The task of seizing political power throughout the country
demands that our Party should quickly and systematically train large
numbers of cadres to administer military, political, economic, Party,
cultural and educational affairs. In the third year of the war, we must
prepare thirty to forty thousand cadres of lower, middle and higher
ranks, so that in the fourth year when the army advances they can
march with it and bring orderly administration to newly liberated
areas with a population of some 50 to 100 million. China's territory
is very large, her population is very numerous, and the revolutionary
war is developing very rapidly; but our supply of cadres is very
inadequate – this is a very great difficulty. In preparing cadres during the third year, while we should rely on the old Liberated Areas
to supply the greater part, we must also pay attention to enrolling
cadres from the big cities controlled by the Kuomintang. In the big
cities in Kuomintang areas there are many workers and intellectuals
who can take part in our work and who have, generally speaking, a
higher cultural level than the workers and peasants in the old Liberated
Areas. We should make use of large numbers of working personnel
from the Kuomintang's economic, financial, cultural and educational
institutions, excluding the reactionary elements. School education in
the Liberated Areas must be restored and developed.

6. The slogan of convening a political consultative conference[4] has
rallied around our Party all democratic parties and people's organizations and all democrats without party affiliation in the Kuomintang
areas. We are arranging for representatives of these parties and
organizations to come to the Liberated Areas and are preparing to
convene a conference in 1949 of the representatives of all China's
democratic parties, people's organizations and democrats without party
affiliation, in order to establish the provisional central government of
the People's Republic of China.

7. The restoration and development of industrial and agricultural
production in the Liberated Areas is an important link in supporting
the war and in defeating the Kuomintang reactionaries. The meeting
convened by the Central Committee held that, on the one hand, the
People's Liberation Army must develop its victorious offensive into
the Kuomintang areas and obtain from the Kuomintang forces and
areas the large supply of manpower and material resources needed
for the war; and that, on the other hand, in the old Liberated Areas

every effort must be made to restore and develop industrial and agricultural production so as to raise their level to some extent. Only if these two tasks are fulfilled will it be possible to ensure the overthrow of the reactionary rule of the Kuomintang; otherwise, that will not be possible.

We will have many difficulties in carrying out these two tasks. When our armies enter the Kuomintang areas in force to make war with no rear area or with no adequate rear area, they will have to get all or most of their military supplies themselves on the spot. The restoration and development of industrial and agricultural production requires good organizational work, good leadership of markets in the Liberated Areas, control of trade with outside areas, the overcoming of shortages of certain machinery and raw materials and, first of all, the solution of the problems of communications, transport and the repair of railways, highways and waterways. At present there are great difficulties in the economic and financial situation in the Liberated Areas. Although our difficulties are much smaller than those of the Kuomintang, they do exist. The main ones are that our material resources and manpower are inadequate for the needs of the war and that inflation has developed to a considerable degree. And one cause of these difficulties is the inadequacy of our organizational work, especially in the financial and economic sphere. We believe these difficulties can be overcome and must be overcome. In the struggle to do so, we must fight waste and practise economy. At the front we must see to it that everything captured is handed in, must cherish our effective strength, take good care of weapons, use ammunition sparingly and protect captured soldiers. In the rear we must reduce government expenses, reduce the mobilization of manpower and draught animals not urgently needed, reduce time taken by meetings, observe agricultural seasons so that farm work is done on time, reduce costs in industrial production, raise labour productivity, mobilize the whole Party to learn to manage industrial and agricultural production and carry on trade, make the greatest possible efforts to organize the economies of the Liberated Areas properly, overcome disorder in the markets and wage the necessary struggles against all speculators and manipulators. By getting down to all these jobs, we can certainly overcome the difficulties facing us.

8. Raising the cadres' theoretical level and broadening inner-Party democracy are important links in the fulfilment of the above tasks. The meeting convened by the Central Committee adopted a

special decision on broadening inner-Party democracy.[5] It also discussed the problem of raising the cadres' theoretical level and drew the attention of all comrades present to the problem.

9. The Sixth National Labour Congress has been successfully held and the All-China Federation of Trade Unions[6] has been founded. In the first half of next year a National Women's Congress will be convened to form the All-China Federation of Democratic Women,[7] a National Youth Congress will be convened to form the All-China Youth Federation,[8] and the New Democratic Youth League will be established.[9]

NOTES

[1] The first betrayal by the Kuomintang was in 1927. The betrayal here mentioned is the all-out counter-revolutionary civil war launched by the Kuomintang after the conclusion of the War of Resistance Against Japan.

[2] The defeat of the revolution in the south was the defeat of the Chinese Red Army's fifth campaign against the Kuomintang's "encirclement and suppression" and the withdrawal of our main force from the southern revolutionary bases in 1934; this was the consequence of the third "Left" deviationist line represented in the Party by Wang Ming.

[3] This refers to Kuomintang soldiers who were liberated through capture by the People's Liberation Army and joined its ranks after having been educated.

[4] The slogan of convening a political consultative conference was put forward by Comrade Mao Tse-tung. At his suggestion, one of the "May Day Slogans" for 1948 issued by the Central Committee of the Communist Party of China stated, "All democratic parties, people's organizations and public personages should quickly call a political consultative conference to discuss and carry out the convening of a people's congress and the formation of a democratic coalition government." This slogan won an immediate warm response from the democratic parties, people's organizations and democrats without party affiliation in the Kuomintang areas. The political consultative conference was later renamed the New Political Consultative Conference and finally the Chinese People's Political Consultative Conference. See "Address to the Preparatory Meeting of the New Political Consultative Conference", Note 1, pp. 408-09 of this volume.

[5] This refers to "The Resolution of the Central Committee of the Communist Party of China on the Convening of Congresses and Conferences of the Party at Various Levels". The resolution made the following provisions for the broadening and building of regular democratic life within the Party: Party committees at various levels should regularly convene Party congresses and conferences at their respective levels, as required by the Party Constitution. These congresses and conferences should be vested with all the powers stipulated in the Party Constitution, and there must be no infringement. Adequate preparations should be made before meetings. Inner-Party controversies should be reported promptly and truthfully to the higher levels and important controversies must be reported to the Central Committee.

The resolution also provided for strengthening the Party committee system and required that the rule that important questions must be decided collectively after discussion by the Party committee should be enforced by Party committees at all levels, that no decisions on important matters should be made by an individual and that neither collective leadership nor individual responsibility should be overemphasized to the neglect of the other.

[6] The Sixth National Labour Congress was held in Harbin in August 1948. The All-China Federation of Trade Unions, the unified national organization of the Chinese working class, was re-established at the congress. The previous five National Labour Congresses were held in 1922, 1925, 1926, 1927 and 1929 respectively.

[7] The First National Women's Congress was held in March 1949 in Peiping. The All-China Federation of Democratic Women, the leading body for the organizations of the masses of women throughout the country, was founded at this congress. It was later renamed the National Women's Federation of the People's Republic of China.

[8] The first session of the National Youth Congress was held in May 1949 in Peiping. The All-China Federation of Democratic Youth was founded at this session. It was later renamed the All-China Youth Federation.

[9] The New Democratic Youth League was founded in January 1949 in accordance with a decision by the Central Committee of the Communist Party of China. Its First National Congress was held in Peiping in April 1949. It was renamed the Communist Youth League at its Third National Congress in May 1957.

THE CONCEPT OF OPERATIONS FOR
THE HUAI-HAI CAMPAIGN*

October 11, 1948

Here are a few points for your consideration concerning the dispositions for the Huai-Hai campaign.[1]

1. In the first stage of this campaign, the central task is to concentrate forces to wipe out Huang Po-tao's army, effect a breakthrough in the centre and capture Hsinanchen, the Grand Canal Railway Station, Tsaopachi, Yihsien, Tsaochuang, Lincheng, Hanchuang, Shuyang, Pihsien, Tancheng, Taierhchuang and Linyi. To achieve these objectives, you should use two columns to wipe out each enemy division, that is to say, use six or seven columns to cut up and wipe out the enemy's 25th, 63rd and 64th Divisions. Use five or six columns to hold off and attack enemy reinforcements. Use one or two columns to annihilate the one brigade under Li Mi at Lincheng and Hanchuang and strive to capture those two towns in order to menace Hsuchow from the north so that the two armies under Chiu Ching-chuan and Li Mi will not dare move east in full strength as reinforcements. Use one column plus regional formation in southwestern Shantung to make a flank attack on the Hsuchow-Shangchiu section of the railway in order to tie down a portion of Chiu Ching-chuan's army (as three enemy divisions under Sun Yuan-liang are about to move east, it is hoped that Liu Po-cheng, Chen Yi and Teng Hsiao-ping will dispose their troops at once to attack the Chengchow-Hsuchow line and so tie down Sun Yuan-liang's army). Use one or two columns to operate in the Suchien-Suining-Lingpi area to hold down Li Mi's army. These dispositions mean that before the objective of annihilating the three divisions of Huang Po-tao's army can be achieved, more than half our total force has to be employed against the two armies under Chiu Ching-chuan and Li Mi to tie down, check and destroy part of them. The dispositions should, by and large, be similar to those of last

September for capturing Tsinan and attacking the enemy's reinforcements;[2] otherwise it will be impossible to achieve the objective of
annihilating the three divisions of Huang Po-tao's army. You must
strive to conclude the first stage two to three weeks after the start of
the campaign.

2.   In the second stage, use about five columns to attack and wipe
out the enemy in Haichow, Hsinpu, Lienyunkang and Kuanyun and
capture these towns. It is calculated that by then the enemy's 54th
and 32nd Divisions will very likely have been transported by sea
from Tsingtao to the Haichow-Hsinpu-Lienyunkang area.[3] Altogether
three enemy divisions will be in that area, including the one division
already there; therefore we must use five columns to attack them and
employ the remaining forces (our main strength) to tie down the two
armies under Chiu Ching-chuan and Li Mi, again on the principle
underlying the dispositions made in September for capturing Tsinan
and attacking the enemy's reinforcements. You must strive to conclude this stage also in two to three weeks.

3.   In the third stage, it may be assumed that the battle will be
fought around Huaiyin and Huai-an. By that time the enemy will
have increased his strength by about one division (the Reorganized 8th
Division in Yentai is being shipped south); therefore we must be
prepared again to use about five columns as the attacking force, while
using the rest of our main force to strike at and hold down the enemy's
reinforcements. This stage will also take about two to three weeks.

These three stages will take about a month and a half to two
months.

---

    * This telegram, addressed to the Eastern China and Central Plains Field
Armies and the Bureaus of the Central Committee of the Communist Party of China
in those two areas, was drafted by Comrade Mao Tse-tung for the Revolutionary
Military Commission of the Party's Central Committee. The Huai-Hai campaign
was one of the three greatest campaigns of decisive significance in the Chinese
People's War of Liberation. The campaign was fought jointly by the Eastern China
and Central Plains Field Armies and the regional troops of the eastern China and
Central Plains areas. In this campaign over 555,000 Kuomintang troops were
wiped out. The concept of operations set forth by Comrade Mao Tse-tung in this
telegram led to complete success; in fact, the campaign proceeded more smoothly
than expected, and the victory was therefore quicker and greater. After this campaign, Nanking, the capital of the reactionary Kuomintang government, became subject
to direct threat by the People's Liberation Army. The Huai-Hai campaign was
concluded on January 10, 1949, and on January 21 Chiang Kai-shek announced his
"retirement"; after that, the reactionary Kuomintang ruling clique in Nanking
fell apart.

4. You are to complete the Huai-Hai campaign in two months, November and December. Rest and consolidate your forces next January. From March to July you will be fighting in co-ordination with Liu Po-cheng and Teng Hsiao-ping to drive the enemy to points along the Yangtse River, where he will dig in. By autumn your main force will probably be fighting to cross the Yangtse.

NOTES

[1] The Huai-Hai campaign was a campaign of decisive importance fought by the People's Liberation Army over a large territory in Kiangsu, Shantung, Anhwei and Honan Provinces, centring on Hsuchow, and extending as far as Haichow in the east, Shangchiu in the west, Lincheng (now renamed Hsuehcheng) in the north and the Huai River in the south. The Kuomintang forces massed in this theatre of war consisted of 5 armies and the troops of three Pacification Zones – the 4 armies and the troops of three Pacification Zones under Liu Chih and Tu Yu-ming (respectively Commander and Deputy Commander of the Kuomintang's "Bandit Suppression" Headquarters at Hsuchow) and the army under Huang Wei, which was later dispatched there from central China as reinforcements. On the side of the People's Liberation Army, a force more than 600,000 strong took part in the campaign – it included 16 columns from the Eastern China Field Army, 7 columns from the Central Plains Field Army and regional armed forces from the Eastern China Military Area, the Central Plains Military Area and the Hopei-Shantung-Honan Military Area (then a part of the Northern China Military Area). The campaign lasted sixty-five days, from November 6, 1948 to January 10, 1949; 22 corps, or 56 divisions, of the Kuomintang's crack forces, comprising 555,000 men, were completely wiped out (including 4½ divisions which revolted and came over), and 2 armies under Liu Ju-ming and Li Yen-nien (reinforcements from Nanking) were repulsed. As a result of the campaign, those parts of the eastern China and Central Plains areas north of the Yangtse River were almost entirely liberated. The campaign took place in three stages. During the first stage, November 6-22, the Eastern China Field Army, in co-ordination with the Central Plains Field Army, surrounded and wiped out the army under Huang Po-tao in the Hsinanchen-Nienchuang sector east of Hsuchow, killing Huang Po-tao and liberating large territories on both sides of the Lunghai Railway east of Nienchuang, on both sides of the Hsuchow-Pengpu section of the Tientsin-Pukow Railway, and to the west and north of Hsuchow. In the Taierhchuang-Tsaochuang sector, 3½ divisions of the Kuomintang 3rd Pacification Zone, totalling over 23,000 men, revolted and came over to us. During the second stage, from November 23 to December 15, the Central Plains Field Army, in co-ordination with the main force of the Eastern China Field Army, surrounded and wiped out the army under Huang Wei at and around Shuangtuichi, southwest of Suhsien, capturing Huang Wei and Wu Shao-chou, the commander and deputy commander of the army; 1 division of this army revolted and came over to us. At the same time, our forces wiped out the army under Sun Yuan-liang which was fleeing west from Hsuchow. Only Sun Yuan-liang managed to escape. During the third stage, from January 6 to 10, 1949, the Eastern China Field Army,

in co-ordination with the Central Plains Field Army, surrounded and annihilated in the Chinglungchi-Chenkuanchuang sector, northeast of Yungcheng, 2 Kuomintang armies which were fleeing westward from Hsuchow and were commanded respectively by Chiu Ching-chuan and Li Mi, under the personal command of Tu Yu-ming. Tu Yu-ming was captured, Chiu Ching-chuan was killed and Li Mi barely escaped. This marked the successful end of the great Huai-Hai campaign.

[2] "Capturing Tsinan and attacking the enemy's reinforcements" refers to the tactics employed by the People's Liberation Army during the Tsinan campaign in the middle of September 1948. Tsinan, a strategic position of the Kuomintang in Shantung Province, was garrisoned by over 110,000 men of the Kuomintang 2nd Pacification Zone. In addition, 23 brigades of the Kuomintang's main forces, with some 170,000 men, which were disposed in the Hsuchow area, were ready to move north to relieve Tsinan. Our Eastern China Field Army formed a group of 7 columns to assault the city and another group of 8 columns to strike at the enemy's reinforcements. The onslaught against Tsinan started on the evening of September 16, 1948. On September 24, after eight days and nights of continuous fighting, the enemy garrison was completely wiped out (1 corps revolted and came over to us), and Wang Yao-wu, Commander of the Kuomintang 2nd Pacification Zone, was captured. Our forces took Tsinan so rapidly that the enemy at Hsuchow did not dare to go north to its rescue.

[3] In fact, these 2 enemy divisions did not dare to come.

REVOLUTIONARY FORCES OF THE WORLD UNITE, FIGHT AGAINST IMPERIALIST AGGRESSION!*

November 1948

At this time, when the awakened working class and all genuine revolutionaries of the world are jubilantly celebrating the thirty-first anniversary of the Great October Socialist Revolution of the Soviet Union, I recall a well-known article by Stalin, written in 1918 on the first anniversary of that revolution. In that article Stalin said:

> The great world-wide significance of the October Revolution chiefly consists in the fact that:
>
> 1) It has widened the scope of the national question and converted it from the particular question of combating national oppression in Europe into the general question of emancipating the oppressed peoples, colonies and semi-colonies from imperialism;
>
> 2) It has opened up wide possibilities for their emancipation and the right paths towards it, has thereby greatly facilitated the cause of the emancipation of the oppressed peoples of the West and the East, and has drawn them into the common current of the victorious struggle against imperialism;
>
> 3) *It has thereby erected a bridge between the socialist West and the enslaved East*, having created a new front of revolutions *against* world imperialism, extending from the proletarians of the West, through the Russian revolution, to the oppressed peoples of the East.[1]

History has developed in the direction pointed out by Stalin. The October Revolution has opened up wide possibilities for the emancipation of the peoples of the world and opened up the realistic paths towards it; it has created a new front of revolutions against world imperialism, extending from the proletarians of the West, through the Russian revolution, to the oppressed peoples of the East. This front of revolutions has been created and developed under the brilliant guidance of Lenin and, after Lenin's death, of Stalin.

If there is to be revolution, there must be a revolutionary party. Without a revolutionary party, without a party built on the Marxist-Leninist revolutionary theory and in the Marxist-Leninist revolutionary style, it is impossible to lead the working class and the broad masses of the people to defeat imperialism and its running dogs. In the more than one hundred years since the birth of Marxism, it was only through the example of the Russian Bolsheviks in leading the October Revolution, in leading socialist construction and in defeating fascist aggression that revolutionary parties of a new type were formed and developed in the world. With the birth of revolutionary parties of this type, the face of the world revolution has changed. The change has been so great that transformations utterly inconceivable to people of the older generation have come into being amid fire and thunder. The Communist Party of China is a party built and developed on the model of the Communist Party of the Soviet Union. With the birth of the Communist Party of China, the face of the Chinese revolution took on an altogether new aspect. Is this fact not clear enough?

The world revolutionary united front, with the Soviet Union at its head, defeated fascist Germany, Italy and Japan. This was a result of the October Revolution. If there had been no October Revolution, if there had been no Communist Party of the Soviet Union, no Soviet Union and no anti-imperialist revolutionary united front in the West and in the East led by the Soviet Union, could one conceive of victory over fascist Germany, Italy, Japan and their running dogs? If the October Revolution opened up wide possibilities for the emancipation of the working class and the oppressed peoples of the world and opened up realistic paths towards it, then the victory of the anti-fascist Second World War has opened up still wider possibilities for the emancipation of the working class and the oppressed peoples of the world and has opened up still more realistic paths towards it. It will be a very great mistake to underestimate the significance of the victory of World War II.

Since the victory of World War II, U.S. imperialism and its running dogs in various countries have taken the place of fascist Germany,

---

* This article was written by Comrade Mao Tse-tung in commemoration of the thirty-first anniversary of the October Revolution for the organ of the Information Bureau of the Communist and Workers' Parties of Europe, *For A Lasting Peace, For A People's Democracy*. It appeared in the 21st issue of the publication in 1948.

Italy and Japan and are frantically preparing a new world war and menacing the whole world; this reflects the utter decay of the capitalist world and its fear of imminent doom. This enemy still has strength; therefore, all the revolutionary forces of each country must unite, and the revolutionary forces of all countries must likewise unite, must form an anti-imperialist united front headed by the Soviet Union and follow correct policies; otherwise, victory will be impossible. This enemy has a weak and fragile foundation, he is disintegrating internally, he is alienated from the people, he is confronted with inextricable economic crises; therefore, he can be defeated. It will be a very great mistake to overestimate the enemy's strength and underestimate the strength of the revolutionary forces.

Under the leadership of the Communist Party of China, tremendous victories have now been won in the great Chinese people's democratic revolution directed against the frenzied aggression of U.S. imperialism in China and against the traitorous, dictatorial and reactionary Kuomintang government that has been slaughtering the Chinese people by civil war. During the two years from July 1946 to June 1948, the People's Liberation Army led by the Communist Party of China beat back the attacks of 4,300,000 troops of the reactionary Kuomintang government and went over from the defensive to the offensive. During those two years of fighting (not including developments since July 1948), the People's Liberation Army captured and wiped out 2,640,000 Kuomintang troops. China's Liberated Areas now cover 2,350,000 square kilometres, or 24.5 per cent of the country's 9,597,000 square kilometres; they have a population of 168 million, or 35.3 per cent of the country's 475 million; and they contain 586 cities and towns, or 29 per cent of the 2,009 in the whole country. Because our Party has resolutely led the peasants to carry out the reform of the land system, the land problem has been thoroughly solved in areas with a population of about 100 million, and the land of the landlords and old-type rich peasants has been more or less equally distributed among the peasants, primarily among the poor peasants and farm labourers. The membership of the Communist Party of China has grown from 1,210,000 in 1945 to 3,000,000 today. The task of the Communist Party of China is to unite the revolutionary forces of the whole country to drive out the aggressive forces of U.S. imperialism, overthrow the reactionary rule of the Kuomintang and establish a united, democratic people's republic. We know that there are still many difficulties ahead. But we are not afraid of them. We believe that difficulties must be and can be overcome.

The radiance of the October Revolution shines upon us.   The long-suffering Chinese people must win their liberation, and they firmly believe they can.   Always isolated in the past, China's revolutionary struggle no longer feels isolated since the victory of the October Revolution.   We enjoy the support of the Communist Parties and the working class of the world.   This point was understood by Dr. Sun Yat-sen, forerunner of the Chinese revolution, who established the policy of alliance with the Soviet Union against imperialism.   On his death-bed he wrote a letter to the Soviet Union as part of his testament. It is the Chiang Kai-shek bandit gang of the Kuomintang that is betraying Sun Yat-sen's policy, standing on the side of the imperialist counter-revolutionary front and opposing the people of their own country.   But before long, people will witness the complete destruction of the whole reactionary regime of the Kuomintang by the Chinese people.   The Chinese people are brave, so is the Communist Party of China, and they are determined to liberate all China.

NOTES

[1] From "The October Revolution and the National Question", Section III, "The World-wide Significance of the October Revolution", J. V. Stalin, *Works*, Eng. ed., Moscow, 1953, Vol. IV, pp. 169-70.

THE MOMENTOUS CHANGE IN CHINA'S MILITARY SITUATION*

November 14, 1948

The military situation in China has reached a new turning point and the balance of forces between the two sides in the war has undergone a fundamental change. The People's Liberation Army, long superior in quality, has now become superior in numbers as well. This is a sign that the victory of the Chinese revolution and the realization of peace in China are at hand.

At the end of the second year of the war, that is, at the end of June this year, the Kuomintang army still had a total of some 3,650,000 men. This was 650,000 less than the 4,300,000 men the Kuomintang had in July 1946 when it started the country-wide civil war. The Kuomintang recruited about 2,440,000 men during the two years of war, which is the reason why the decrease was only 650,000, although in that period approximately 3,090,000 were wiped out or captured, or deserted (2,640,000 were wiped out or captured). Recently a sudden change took place. In the first four months of the third year of the war, from July 1 to November 2 when Shenyang was liberated, the Kuomintang army lost 1,000,000 men. Its replacements during these four months have not yet been ascertained; supposing it was able to recruit 300,000 men, then the net decrease would be 700,000. Thus the whole of the Kuomintang's armed forces – army, navy and air force, regulars and irregulars, combat troops and men in the rear-service establishments – are now only some 2,900,000. On the other hand, the People's Liberation Army, which had 1,200,000 men in June 1946, grew to 2,800,000 in June 1948 and has now increased to more than 3,000,000. Thus, the numerical superiority long enjoyed by the Kuomintang army has rapidly turned into inferiority. This is the result of heroic fighting by the People's Liberation Army during the past four months in all the war theatres of the country; it is especially the result of the Sui-Ki and Tsinan campaigns[1] on the southern front and of the Chinchow, Changchun, Liaohsi and Shenyang

287

campaigns[2] on the northern front.   Up to the end of June this year, the Kuomintang still had designations for 285 divisions because it had frantically incorporated its irregulars into its regular forces.   In these four months, the battalions and larger units wiped out by the People's Liberation Army totalled 83 divisions, including 63 whole divisions.

Accordingly, the war will be much shorter than we originally estimated.   The original estimate was that the reactionary Kuomintang government could be completely overthrown in about five years, beginning from July 1946.   As we now see it, only another year or so may be needed to overthrow it completely.   A longer time will be needed, however, to eliminate the reactionary forces in all parts of the country and complete the liberation of the people.

The enemy is collapsing rapidly, but the Communists, the People's Liberation Army and people of all walks of life throughout the country must continue to unite as one man and redouble their efforts; only thus can we finally and completely wipe out the reactionary forces and build a united, democratic people's republic in the whole country.

NOTES

[1] The Sui-Ki campaign, also known as the Eastern Honan campaign, was fought by the People's Liberation Army in the sector comprising Kaifeng, Suihsien and Kihsien. The campaign started on June 17, 1948. On June 22 our army captured Kaifeng. To save his critical military situation, Chiang Kai-shek went to the front, took personal command and mustered 3 armies under Chiu Ching-chuan, Ou Shou-nien and Huang Po-tao to start an attack on Kaifeng from several directions. Six columns of our Eastern China Field Army, 2 columns of our Central Plains Field Army and our Kwangtung-Kwangsi Column surrounded the armies under Ou Shou-nien and Huang Po-tao in the Suihsien-Kihsien sector and, after nine days and nights of fierce fighting (June 27-July 6), they wiped out 2 divisions, or 6 brigades, of Ou Shou-nien's army and a part of Huang Po-tao's army, a total of over 90,000 men. Ou Shou-nien, army commander, and Shen Cheng-nien, Commander of the Reorganized 75th Division, were captured. For the Tsinan campaign, see "The Concept of Operations for the Huai-Hai Campaign", Note 2, p. 282 of this volume.

[2] The Chinchow, Changchun, Liaohsi and Shenyang campaigns in northeastern China, taken together, were called the Liaohsi-Shenyang campaign. See "The Concept of Operations for the Liaohsi-Shenyang Campaign", Note 1, pp. 265-66 of this volume.

* This commentary was written by Comrade Mao Tse-tung for the Hsinhua News Agency. Here Comrade Mao Tse-tung, basing himself on the new situation, that is, the change in the relation of forces between the enemy and ourselves after the Liaohsi-Shenyang campaign, made a new estimate of the time needed to win victory in the People's War of Liberation and pointed out that the reactionary rule of the Kuomintang could be overthrown in no more than a year from November 1948. Subsequent developments in China's military situation fully confirmed his prediction.

THE CONCEPT OF OPERATIONS
FOR THE PEIPING-TIENTSIN CAMPAIGN[1]*

December 11, 1948

1. The enemy forces in Changchiakou, Hsinpao-an and Huailai and in the entire area of Peiping, Tientsin, Tangku and Tangshan – except a few units, such as certain divisions of the 35th, 62nd and 94th Corps, which still have a fairly high combat effectiveness for the defence of fortified positions – have little offensive spirit; they are like birds startled by the mere twang of a bow-string. This is especially the case since you advanced south of the Great Wall. You should on no account overrate the enemy's combat effectiveness. Some of our comrades have suffered through overrating the enemy's combat effectiveness, but they have arrived at a correct understanding after being criticized. The enemy at both Changchiakou and Hsinpao-an is definitely encircled and will in all probability find it extremely difficult to break through and escape. About half the 16th Corps has been speedily wiped out. The enemy's 104th Corps at Huailai has hurriedly fled south and will probably be wiped out today or tomorrow. After that is done, you will be ready to dispatch the 4th Column from the southwest[2] to the northeast to cut the link between Nankow and Peiping. We think this may not be easy to accomplish; for, either the remnants of the 94th and 16th Corps will quickly withdraw to Peiping, or the 94th, 16th and 92nd Corps will concentrate in the Nankow-Changping-Shahochen region for joint defence. But this move by our 4th Column will directly menace the northwestern and northern suburbs of Peiping and tie down those enemy forces so that they dare not move. If they should dare to move further west to reinforce the 35th Corps, we could either directly cut off their retreat or launch a direct attack on Peiping; therefore they will probably not dare to move further west. The army in northern China commanded by Yang Teh-chih, Lo Jui-ching and Keng Piao is employing 9 divisions

to encircle 3 divisions of the enemy's 35th Corps; this is absolute superiority.   They have proposed to wipe out these enemy divisions at an
early date, but we intend to ask them not to attack for the time being
so as to lure the enemy at Peiping and Tientsin and make it difficult
for him to come to a decision to flee by sea.   They have employed 2
columns to encircle the 35th Corps and 1 column to check the 104th
Corps and have beaten back both these enemy forces.

2.   We now agree to your sending the 5th Column immediately
to the vicinity of Nankow to menace the enemy at Peiping, Nankow
and Huaijou from the northeast.   This column will remain there so
that later (in about ten or fifteen days, that is, when the army in
northern China commanded by Yang Teh-chih, Lo Jui-ching and Keng
Piao has annihilated the 35th Corps) your 4th Column can be released
for service in the east.   Therefore, please order the 5th Column to
continue its march west today.

3.   The 3rd Column should on no account go to Nankow but, in
accordance with our telegram of the 9th, should move to the region
east of Peiping and south of Tunghsien to threaten Peiping from the
east and, together with the 4th, 11th and 5th Columns, form an encirclement around Peiping.

4.   But our real aim is not to encircle Peiping first but rather to
encircle Tientsin, Tangku, Lutai and Tangshan first.

5.   We estimate that your 10th, 9th, 6th and 8th Columns, your
Artillery Column and your 7th Column will have assembled in the
region around Yutien by about December 15.   We propose that, in the
few days between December 20 and 25, you move with lightning speed
and employ the 6 columns – the 3rd (which is to march east from the
eastern suburbs of Peiping), the 6th, 7th, 8th, 9th and 10th – to encircle
the enemy at Tientsin, Tangku, Lutai and Tangshan, provided that the
enemy's situation at those points remains roughly the same as now.
The method is to place 2 columns around Wuching – at Langfang,
Hohsiwu and Yangtsun – and to use 5 columns as wedges to be driven

---

* This was a telegram drafted by Comrade Mao Tse-tung for the Revolutionary
Military Commission of the Central Committee of the Communist Party of China
and addressed to Lin Piao, Lo Jung-huan and other comrades.   The Peiping-Tientsin
campaign was the last of the three greatest campaigns of decisive significance in
the Chinese People's War of Liberation.   In this campaign, we wiped out or reorganized over 520,000 Kuomintang troops, liberated the important cities of Peiping,
Tientsin and Changchiakou and concluded, in the main, the fighting for the liberation
of northern China.   The concept of operations for the campaign, set forth here by
Comrade Mao Tse-tung, was fully realized in practice.

between enemy positions at Tientsin, Tangku, Lutai, Tangshan and Kuyeh and so cut off contacts between the enemy forces. All these columns should build two-way blocking positions to ensure that the enemy cannot escape. Then they should rest and consolidate their troops and, after recovering from fatigue, attack and wipe out some small enemy groups. In the meantime the 4th Column should move from northwest to east of Peiping. Before the 4th Column starts to move, the army in northern China commanded by Yang Teh-chih, Lo Jui-ching and Keng Piao should wipe out the enemy in Hsinpao-an. In the east, according to circumstances, every effort should be made to wipe out the enemy in Tangku first and control that seaport. If these two points, Tangku (the most important) and Hsinpao-an, are captured, you will have the initiative on the whole chessboard. The above dispositions constitute, in reality, the wholesale encirclement of the enemy in Changchiakou, Hsinpao-an, Nankow, Peiping, Huaijou, Shunyi, Tunghsien, Wanping (Chohsien and Lianghsiang have been captured), Fengtai, Tientsin, Tangku, Lutai, Tangshan and Kaiping.

6. This method is generally the same as that you used in the fighting along the line through Ihsien, Chinchow, Chinhsi, Hsingcheng, Suichung, Shanhaikuan and Luanhsien.[3]

7. In the two weeks beginning from today (December 11-25), the basic principle is to encircle without attacking (in the case of Changchiakou and Hsinpao-an) and, in some cases, to cut off without encircling (in the case of Peiping, Tientsin and Tungchow, to make only a strategic encirclement and cut the links between the enemy forces, but not to make a tactical encirclement) in order to wait for the completion of our dispositions and then wipe out the enemy forces one by one. In particular, you must not wipe out all the enemy forces at Changchiakou, Hsinpao-an and Nankow because that would compel the enemy east of Nankow to make a quick decision to bolt. Please make sure you understand this point.

8. In order not to prompt Chiang Kai-shek quickly to decide to ship his troops in the Peiping-Tientsin area south by sea, we are going to order Liu Po-cheng, Teng Hsiao-ping, Chen Yi and Su Yu, after they have wiped out Huang Wei's army, to spare the remainder of Tu Yu-ming's armies under Chiu Ching-chuan, Li Mi and Sun Yuan-liang (about half of which have already been destroyed) and for two weeks to make no dispositions for their final annihilation.

9. To prevent the enemy from fleeing towards Tsingtao, we are going to order our troops in Shantung to mass certain forces to control

a section of the Yellow River near Tsinan and to make preparations along the Tsingtao-Tsinan Railway.

10.   There is little or no possibility that the enemy will flee towards Hsuchow, Chengchow, Sian or Suiyuan.

11.   The main or the only concern is that the enemy might flee by sea.   Therefore, in the coming two weeks the general method should be to encircle without attacking or to cut off without encircling.

12.   This plan is beyond the enemy's range of expectation, and it will be very difficult for him to discern it before you complete your final dispositions.   At present, the enemy is probably calculating that you will attack Peiping.

13.   The enemy always underrates the energy of our army and overrates his own strength, though at the same time he is like a bird startled by the mere twang of a bow-string.   The enemy at Peiping and Tientsin will never expect you to be able to complete the above dispositions by December 25.

14.   In order to complete these dispositions by December 25, you should inspire your troops in the next two weeks to ignore fatigue, to have no fear of depletion of numbers and have no fear of cold and hunger; after these dispositions have been made, they can rest and consolidate and take their time in attacking.

15.   The sequence of attacks will be roughly the following: first, the Tangku-Lutai sector; second, Hsinpao-an; third, the Tangshan sector; fourth, the Tientsin and Changchiakou sectors; and, lastly, the Peiping sector.

16.   What are your views on this plan?   What are its shortcomings?   Are there any difficulties in its execution?   Please consider all this and reply by telegraph.

NOTES

[1] The Peiping-Tientsin campaign, fought by the Northeast Field Army and two armies of the Northern China People's Liberation Army under the command of Lin Piao, Lo Jung-huan, Nieh Jung-chen and other comrades, began early in December 1948, immediately after the victorious conclusion of the Liaohsi-Shenyang campaign in the Northeast.   Acting upon Comrade Mao Tse-tung's instructions, the Northeast Field Army, immediately after it had victoriously fulfilled its task of liberating the whole Northeast, swept south of the Great Wall and joined the armies of the People's Liberation Army in northern China in co-ordinated actions to

encircle and wipe out the Kuomintang troops in northern China. Greatly alarmed by the victory of the People's Liberation Army in the Northeast, more than 600,000 Kuomintang troops under Fu Tso-yi, Commander-in-Chief of the Kuomintang's Northern China "Bandit Suppression" Headquarters, hurriedly shortened their lines of defence with the intention of fleeing south by sea or west to Suiyuan Province. Our army, moving with lightning speed, cut apart the enemy forces and surrounded them separately at five strong-points – Peiping, Tientsin, Changchiakou, Hsinpao-an and Tangku – thus blocking their escape routes to the south and west. On December 22, the enemy's main force at Hsinpao-an (the headquarters of his 35th Corps and 2 divisions) was surrounded and wiped out. On the 24th, Changchiakou was taken and a corps headquarters and 7 divisions of the enemy's 11th Army, over 54,000 men in all, were wiped out. On January 14, 1949, our troops surrounding Tientsin launched a general offensive against the city after Chen Chang-chieh, commander of the enemy garrison, refused to surrender. The city was liberated after twenty-nine hours' fierce fighting, the enemy garrison of over 130,000 men was wiped out and Chen Chang-chieh was captured. As a result, more than 200,000 enemy troops garrisoning Peiping were tightly surrounded by our troops and their fate was sealed. Owing to the efforts we made to win it over, the enemy's Peiping garrison, commanded by General Fu Tso-yi, accepted peaceful reorganization. On January 31, our troops entered Peiping, the city was proclaimed peacefully liberated and the Peiping-Tientsin campaign came to a victorious close. During this campaign, with the exception of the enemy garrison of over 50,000 men in Tangku, which fled by sea, over 520,000 Kuomintang troops were put out of action and reorganized by our army. In September 1949 the Kuomintang troops in Suiyuan Province declared by telegram that they had revolted and come over to the people and that they would accept reorganization.

2 This means the area southwest of Nankow.

3 In September 1948, to prevent the enemy forces in Ihsien, Chinchow, Chinhsi, Hsingcheng, Suichung, Shanhaikuan, Luanhsien and Changli, all points along the Peiping-Liaoning Railway, from shortening their lines and concentrating, the Northeast Field Army, then operating along that railway, adopted the method of first using part of its troops to encircle and cut apart the enemy units at these points and then wiping them out one by one.

MESSAGE URGING TU YU-MING AND OTHERS
TO SURRENDER*

December 17, 1948

General Tu Yu-ming, General Chiu Ching-chuan, General Li Mi and all corps, division and regiment commanders of the two armies under Generals Chiu Ching-chuan and Li Mi:

You are now at the end of your rope. Huang Wei's army was completely wiped out on the night of the 15th, Li Yen-nien's army has taken to its heels and fled south, and it is hopeless for you to think of joining them. Are you hoping to break through? How can you break through when the People's Liberation Army is all around? During the last few days you have tried to break through, but what came of it? Your planes and tanks, too, are useless. We have more planes and tanks than you, that is, artillery and explosives which people call our home-made planes and tanks. Aren't they ten times more formidable than your foreign-made planes and tanks? Your army under Sun Yuan-liang is finished, and more than half the men in your two remaining armies have been wounded or captured. You have brought many miscellaneous and idle personnel of various organizations and many young students from Hsuchow and forced them into your army, but how can these people fight? For more than ten days, you have been surrounded ring upon ring and received blow upon blow, and your position has shrunk greatly. You have such a tiny place, only a little more than ten *li* square, and so many people are crowded together that a single shell from us can kill a lot of you. Your wounded soldiers and the families who have followed the army are complaining to high heaven. Your soldiers and many of your officers have no stomach for any more fighting. You, as deputy commander-in-chief, as commanders of armies, corps, divisions and regiments, should understand and sympathize with the feelings of your subordinates and families, hold their lives dear, find a way out for them as early as possible and stop sending them to a senseless death.

Now that Huang Wei's army has been completely wiped out and Li Yen-nien's army has fled towards Pengpu, we are able to concentrate an attacking force several times your strength. This time we have fought for only forty days, and you have already lost 10 divisions under Huang Po-tao, 11 under Huang Wei, 4 under Sun Yuan-liang, 4 under Feng Chih-an, 2 under Sun Liang-cheng, 1 under Liu Ju-ming, 1 division in Suhsien and another in Lingpi – altogether you have lost 34 whole divisions. Of these, $27\frac{1}{2}$ divisions were completely wiped out by our army; the only exceptions were the $3\frac{1}{2}$ divisions led by Ho Chi-feng and Chang Ke-hsia and 1 division led by Liao Yun-chou, which revolted and came over to our side, and 1 division led by Sun Liang-cheng and the 2 half-divisions led by Chao Pi-kuang and Huang Tse-hua, which surrendered.[1] You have seen with your own eyes the fate of the 3 armies under Huang Po-tao, Huang Wei and Sun Yuan-liang. You should learn from the example of General Cheng Tung-kuo in Changchun[2] and from the current example of corps commander Sun Liang-cheng and division commanders Chao Pi-kuang and Huang Tse-hua and immediately order all your troops to lay down their arms and cease resistance. Our army will guarantee life and safety to you, high-ranking officers, and to all officers and men. This is your only way out. Think it over! If you feel this is right, then do it. If you still want to fight another round, you can have it, but you will be finished off anyway.[3]

Headquarters of the Central Plains
People's Liberation Army

Headquarters of the Eastern China
People's Liberation Army

---

* This broadcast message was written by Comrade Mao Tse-tung for the Headquarters of the Central Plains and the Eastern China People's Liberation Armies.

NOTES

[1] Ho Chi-feng and Chang Ke-hsia, Deputy Commanders of the Kuomintang's 3rd Pacification Zone, revolted against the Kuomintang in the Chiawang sector, northeast of Hsuchow, on November 8, 1948, during the first stage of the Huai-Hai campaign, and came over to the People's Liberation Army with 1 corps headquarters, 3 divisions and 1 regiment, totalling more than 20,000 men. Liao Yun-chou, Commander of the 110th Division of the Kuomintang's 85th Corps, revolted against the Kuomintang at Lochi, southwest of Suhsien, Anhwei Province, on November 27, 1948, during the second stage of the Huai-Hai campaign, and came over to the People's Liberation Army with his division headquarters and 2 full regiments, totalling 5,500 men. Sun Liang-cheng, Deputy Commander of the Kuomintang's 1st Pacification Zone and Commander of the 107th Corps, came over to the People's Liberation Army with his corps headquarters and 1 division, totalling 5,800 men, northwest of Suining, Kiangsu Province, on November 13, 1948, during the first stage of the Huai-Hai campaign. Chao Pi-kuang, Commander of the 150th Division of the Kuomintang's 44th Corps, came over to the People's Liberation Army with over 2,000 of his remaining troops in the Nienchuang sector, east of Hsuchow, Kiangsu Province, on November 18, 1948, during the first stage of the Huai-Hai campaign. Huang Tse-hua, Commander of the 23rd Division of the Kuomintang's 85th Corps, came over to the People's Liberation Army with his division headquarters and the remnants of 2 regiments at Shuangtuichi, northeast of Mengcheng, Anhwei Province, in December 1948, during the second stage of the Huai-Hai campaign.

[2] Changchun had been besieged by the Northeast People's Liberation Army since the winter of 1947. After the capture of Chinchow by our army, when all the enemy troops in the Northeast were in a shaky position, Cheng Tung-kuo, Kuomintang commander in Changchun and Deputy Commander-in-Chief of the Kuomintang's Northeast "Bandit Suppression" Headquarters, led the army troops of the 1st Army and the officers and men of the New 7th Corps to surrender on October 19, 1948.

[3] After receiving this message, Tu Yu-ming, Deputy Commander-in-Chief of the Kuomintang's Hsuchow "Bandit Suppression" Headquarters, Chiu Ching-chuan, Commander of the Kuomintang's 2nd Army, and Li Mi, Commander of the Kuomintang's 13th Army, continued to resist desperately with the result that all their troops were wiped out by our army's powerful offensive. Tu Yu-ming was captured, Chiu Ching-chuan was killed and only Li Mi managed to escape.

CARRY THE REVOLUTION THROUGH
TO THE END*

December 30, 1948

The Chinese people will win final victory in the great War of Liberation. Even our enemy no longer doubts the outcome.

The war has followed a tortuous course. When the reactionary Kuomintang government started the counter-revolutionary war, it had approximately three and a half times as many troops as the People's Liberation Army; the equipment, manpower and material resources of its army were far superior to those of the People's Liberation Army; it had modern industries and modern means of communication, which the People's Liberation Army lacked; it had received large-scale military and economic aid from U.S. imperialism and had made long preparations. Therefore, during the first year of the war (July 1946-June 1947) the Kuomintang was on the offensive and the People's Liberation Army on the defensive. In 1946 in the Northeast, the Kuomintang occupied Shenyang, Szepingkai, Changchun, Kirin, Antung and other cities and most of Liaoning, Liaopei and Antung Provinces;[1] south of the Yellow River, it occupied the cities of Huaiyin and Hotse and most of the Hupeh-Honan-Anhwei, Kiangsu-Anhwei, Honan-Anhwei-Kiangsu and Southwestern Shantung Liberated Areas; and north of the Great Wall, it occupied the cities of Chengteh, Chining and Changchiakou and most of Jehol, Suiyuan and Chahar Provinces. The Kuomintang blustered and swaggered like a conquering hero. The People's Liberation Army adopted the correct strategy, which had as its main objective to wipe out the Kuomintang's effective strength rather than to hold territory, and in each month destroyed an average of some eight brigades of the Kuomintang regular troops (the equivalent of eight present-day divisions). As a result, the Kuomintang was finally compelled to abandon its plan for the over-all offensive and by the first half of 1947 it had to limit the major targets of its attack to the two wings of the southern front, *i.e.*, Shantung and northern Shensi. In the second year (July 1947-June 1948) a fundamental change took place in the war. Having wiped out large numbers of Kuomintang regulars, the People's Liberation Army went over from the defensive to the offensive on the southern and northern fronts, while the Kuomintang had to turn from the offensive to the defensive. The People's Liberation Army not only recovered most of the territories lost in northeastern China, Shantung and northern Shensi but also extended the battle front into the Kuomintang areas north of the Yangtse and Weishui Rivers. Moreover, in the course of attacking and capturing Shihchiachuang, Yuncheng, Szepingkai, Loyang, Yichuan, Paoki, Weihsien, Linfen and Kaifeng, our army mastered the tactics of storming heavily fortified points.[2] The People's Liberation Army formed its own artillery and engineer corps. Don't forget that the People's Liberation Army had neither aircraft nor tanks, but once it had formed an artillery and an engineer corps superior to those of the Kuomintang army, the defensive system of the Kuomintang, with all its aircraft and tanks, appeared negligible by contrast. The People's Liberation Army was already able to conduct not only mobile warfare but positional warfare as well. In the first half of the third year of the war (July-December 1948), another fundamental change has occurred. The People's Liberation Army, so long outnumbered, has gained numerical superiority. It has been able not only to capture the Kuomintang's heavily fortified cities but also to surround and destroy strong formations of Kuomintang crack troops, a hundred thousand or several hundred thousand at a time. The rate at which the People's Liberation Army is wiping out Kuomintang troops has become much faster. Look at the statistics on the number of Kuomintang regular units of battalion level and above which we have destroyed (including enemy troops who have revolted and come over to our side). In the first year, 97 brigades, including 46 brigades entirely wiped out; in the second year, 94 brigades, including 50 brigades entirely wiped out; and in the first half of the third year, according to incomplete figures, 147 divisions, including 111 divisions entirely wiped out.[3] In these six months, the number of enemy divisions entirely wiped out was 15 more than the grand total for the previous two years. The enemy front as a whole

---

* This New Year message for 1949 was written by Comrade Mao Tse-tung for the Hsinhua News Agency.

has completely crumbled. The enemy troops in the Northeast have been entirely wiped out; those in northern China will soon be entirely wiped out, and in eastern China and the Central Plains only a few enemy forces are left. The annihilation of the Kuomintang's main forces north of the Yangtse River greatly facilitates the forthcoming crossing of the Yangtse by the People's Liberation Army and its southward drive to liberate all China. Simultaneously with victory on the military front, the Chinese people have scored tremendous victories on the political and economic fronts. For this reason public opinion the world over, including the entire imperialist press, no longer disputes the certainty of the country-wide victory of the Chinese People's War of Liberation.

The enemy will not perish of himself. Neither the Chinese reactionaries nor the aggressive forces of U.S. imperialism in China will step down from the stage of history of their own accord. Precisely because they realize that the country-wide victory of the Chinese People's War of Liberation can no longer be prevented by purely military struggle, they are placing more and more importance each day on political struggle. On the one hand, the Chinese reactionaries and the U.S. aggressors are using the existing Kuomintang government for their "peace" plot; on the other hand, they are scheming to use certain persons who have connections both with them and with the revolutionary camp, inciting and instigating these persons to work artfully, strive to infiltrate the revolutionary camp and form a so-called opposition faction within it. The purpose is to preserve the reactionary forces and undermine the revolutionary forces. According to reliable information, the U.S. government has decided on this scheme and begun to carry it out in China. The U.S. government has changed its policy of simply backing the Kuomintang's counter-revolutionary war to a policy embracing two forms of struggle:

1. Organizing the remnants of the Kuomintang's armed forces and the so-called local forces to continue to resist the People's Liberation Army south of the Yangtse River and in the remote border provinces, and

2. Organizing an opposition faction within the revolutionary camp to strive with might and main to halt the revolution where it is or, if it must advance, to moderate it and prevent it from encroaching too far on the interests of the imperialists and their running dogs.

The British and French imperialists support this U.S. policy. Many people do not yet see this situation clearly, but it probably will not be long before they do.

The question now facing the Chinese people, all democratic parties and all people's organizations is whether to carry the revolution through to the end or to abandon it half-way. If the revolution is to be carried through to the end, we must use the revolutionary method to wipe out all the forces of reaction resolutely, thoroughly, wholly and completely; we must unswervingly persist in overthrowing imperialism, feudalism and bureaucrat-capitalism; and we must overthrow the reactionary rule of the Kuomintang on a country-wide scale and set up a republic that is a people's democratic dictatorship under the leadership of the proletariat and with the worker-peasant alliance as its main body. In this way, the Chinese nation will completely throw off the oppressor; the country will be transformed from a semi-colony into a genuinely independent state; the Chinese people will be fully emancipated, overthrowing once and for all both feudal oppression and oppression by bureaucrat-capital (Chinese monopoly capital) and will thus achieve unity, democracy and peace, create the prerequisites for transforming China from an agricultural into an industrial country and make it possible for her to develop from a society with exploitation of man by man into a socialist society. If the revolution is abandoned half-way, it will mean going against the will of the people, bowing to the will of the foreign aggressors and Chinese reactionaries and giving the Kuomintang a chance to heal its wounds, so that one day it may pounce suddenly to strangle the revolution and again plunge the whole country into darkness. That is how clearly and sharply the question is now posed. Which of these two roads to choose? Every democratic party, every people's organization in China must consider this question, must choose its road and clarify its stand. Whether China's democratic parties and people's organizations can sincerely co-operate without parting company half-way depends on whether they are agreed on this question and take unanimous action to overthrow the common enemy of the Chinese people. What is needed here is unanimity and co-operation, not the setting up of any "opposition faction" or the pursuit of any "middle road".[4]

In the long period of more than twenty years from the counter-revolutionary coup d'état of April 12, 1927 [5] to this day, have the Chinese reactionaries headed by Chiang Kai-shek and his ilk not given proof enough that they are a gang of blood-stained executioners, who slaughter people without blinking?   Have they not given proof enough that they are a band of professional traitors and the running dogs of imperialism?   Think it over, everybody!   How magnanimous the Chinese people have been towards this gang of bandits in the hope of achieving internal peace with them, since the Sian Incident of December 1936, since the Chungking negotiations of October 1945 and since the Political Consultative Conference of January 1946!   But has all this goodwill changed their class nature by one jot or tittle?   In their history not a single one of these bandits can be separated from U.S. imperialism.   Relying on U.S. imperialism, they have plunged 475 million of our compatriots into a huge civil war of unprecedented brutality and slaughtered millions upon millions of men and women, young and old, with bombers, fighter planes, guns, tanks, rocket-launchers, automatic rifles, gasoline bombs, gas projectiles and other weapons, all supplied by U.S. imperialism.   And relying on these criminals, U.S. imperialism on its part has seized China's sovereign rights over her own territory, waters and air space, seized inland navigation rights and special commercial privileges, seized special privileges in China's domestic and foreign affairs and even seized the privilege of killing people, beating them up, driving cars over them and raping women, all with impunity.   Can it be said that the Chinese people, who have been compelled to fight such a long and bloody war, should still show affection and tenderness towards these most vicious enemies and should not completely destroy or expel them?   Only by completely destroying the Chinese reactionaries and expelling the aggressive forces of U.S. imperialism can China gain independence, democracy and peace.   Isn't this truth clear enough by now?

What deserves attention is that all of a sudden the enemies of the Chinese people are doing their best to assume a harmless and even a pitiable look (readers, please remember that in the future they will try to look pitiable again).   Didn't Sun Fo, who has now become president of the Kuomintang's Executive Yuan, state in June last year that a "settlement will finally come, provided militarily we fight to the end"?   But this time, the moment he took office he talked glibly about an "honourable peace" and said that "the Government has been striving for peace and only resorted to fighting because peace could not be realized, but the ultimate objective of fighting is still to restore peace".   Immediately afterwards, on December 21, a United Press dispatch from Shanghai predicted that Sun Fo's statement would meet with widespread approval in U.S. official quarters and among the

Kuomintang liberals.   At present, U.S. officials have not only become
deeply interested in "peace" in China but also repeatedly assert that
ever since the Moscow Conference of Foreign Ministers of the Soviet
Union, the United States and Britain in December 1945, the United
States has adhered to a "policy of non-interference in China's internal
affairs".   How are we to deal with these worthies from the "Land of
Gentlemen"?   Here, it is fitting to quote an ancient Greek fable.
One winter's day, a farmhand found a snake frozen by the cold.
Moved by compassion, he picked it up and put it in his bosom.   The
snake was revived by the warmth, its natural instincts returned, and
it gave its benefactor a fatal bite.   The dying farmhand said, "I've
got what I deserve for taking pity on an evil creature."[6]   Venomous
snakes, foreign and Chinese, hope that the Chinese people will die
like the farmhand, that like him the Chinese Communist Party and all
Chinese revolutionary democrats will be kind-hearted to them.   But
the Chinese people, the Chinese Communist Party and the genuine
revolutionary democrats of China have heard the labourer's dying
words and will well remember them.   Moreover, the serpents infest-
ing most of China, big or small, black or white, baring their poisonous
fangs or assuming the guise of beautiful girls, are not yet frozen by
the cold, although they already sense the threat of winter.

The Chinese people will never take pity on snake-like scoundrels,
and they honestly believe that no one is their true friend who guile-
fully says that pity should be shown these scoundrels and says that
anything else would be out of keeping with China's traditions, fall
short of greatness, etc.   Why should one take pity on snake-like
scoundrels?   What worker, what peasant, what soldier, says that such
scoundrels should be pitied?   True, there are "Kuomintang liberals"
or non-Kuomintang "liberals" who advise the Chinese people to accept the "peace" offered by the United States and the Kuomintang,
that is, to enshrine and worship the remnants of imperialism, feudalism
and bureaucrat-capitalism so that these treasures shall not become
extinct on earth.   But they are decidedly not workers, peasants or
soldiers, nor are they the friends of workers, peasants and soldiers.

We hold that the Chinese people's revolutionary camp must be
expanded and must embrace all who are willing to join the revolutionary cause at the present stage.   The Chinese people's revolution needs
a main force and also needs allies, for an army without allies cannot
defeat the enemy.   The Chinese people, now at the high tide of
revolution, need friends and they should remember their friends and

not forget them.   In China there are undoubtedly many friends faithful to the people's revolutionary cause, who try to protect the people's interests and are opposed to protecting the enemy's interests, and undoubtedly none of these friends should be forgotten or cold-shouldered.   Also, we hold that we must consolidate the Chinese people's revolutionary camp and not allow bad elements to sneak in or wrong views to prevail.   Besides keeping their friends in mind, the Chinese people, now at the high tide of revolution, should also keep their enemies and the friends of their enemies firmly in mind. As we said above, since the enemy is cunningly using the method of "peace" and the method of sneaking into the revolutionary camp to preserve and strengthen his position, whereas the fundamental interests of the people demand that all reactionary forces be destroyed thoroughly and that the aggressive forces of U.S. imperialism be driven out of China, those who advise the people to take pity on the enemy and preserve the forces of reaction are not friends of the people, but friends of the enemy.

The raging tide of China's revolution is forcing all social strata to decide their attitude.   A new change is taking place in the balance of class forces in China.   Multitudes of people are breaking away from Kuomintang influence and control and coming over to the revolutionary camp; and the Chinese reactionaries have fallen into hopeless straits, isolated and abandoned.   As the People's War of Liberation draws closer and closer to final victory, all the revolutionary people and all friends of the people will unite more solidly and, led by the Communist Party of China, resolutely demand the complete destruction of the reactionary forces and the thoroughgoing development of the revolutionary forces until a people's democratic republic on a country-wide scale is founded and a peace based on unity and democracy is achieved.   The U.S. imperialists, the Chinese reactionaries and their friends, on the contrary, are incapable of uniting solidly and will indulge in endless squabbles, mutual abuse, recrimination and betrayal. On one point, however, they will co-operate – in striving by every means to undermine the revolutionary forces and preserve the reactionary forces.   They will use every means, open and secret, direct and indirect.   But it can definitely be stated that their political intrigues will meet with the same defeats as their military attacks. Having had plenty of experience, the Chinese people and their general staff, the Communist Party of China, are certain to smash the enemy's political intrigues, just as they have shattered his military attacks, and to carry the great People's War of Liberation through to the end.

In 1949, the Chinese People's Liberation Army will advance south of the Yangtse River and will win even greater victories than in 1948.

In 1949, on the economic front we shall achieve even greater successes than in 1948. Our agricultural and industrial production will rise to a higher level than before, and rail and highway traffic will be completely restored. In their operations the main formations of the People's Liberation Army will discard certain survivals of guerrilla habits and reach a higher level of regularization.

In 1949, the Political Consultative Conference, with no reactionaries participating and having as its aim the fulfilment of the tasks of the people's revolution, will be convened, the People's Republic of China will be proclaimed, and the Central Government of the Republic will be established. This government will be a democratic coalition government under the leadership of the Communist Party of China, with the participation of appropriate persons representing the democratic parties and people's organizations.

These are the main concrete tasks which the Chinese people, the Communist Party of China and all the democratic parties and people's organizations in China should strive to fulfil in 1949. We shall brave all difficulties and unite as one to fulfil these tasks.

In our struggle we shall overthrow once and for all the feudal oppression of thousands of years and the imperialist oppression of a hundred years. The year 1949 will be a year of tremendous importance. We should redouble our efforts.

NOTES

[1] Following the Japanese surrender in 1945, the Kuomintang government divided the three northeastern provinces of Liaoning, Kirin and Heilungkiang into nine provinces, Liaoning, Liaopei, Antung, Kirin, Hokiang, Sungkiang, Heilungkiang, Nunkiang and Hsingan. In 1949 our Northeast Administrative Commission redivided the area into five provinces, Liaotung, Liaohsi, Kirin, Heilungkiang and Sungkiang. Together with Jehol, these provinces were then referred to as the six northeastern provinces. In 1954 the Central People's Government Council merged the two provinces of Liaotung and Liaohsi into the one province of Liaoning and the two provinces of Sungkiang and Heilungkiang into the one province of Heilungkiang, while Kirin remained unchanged. In 1955 Jehol Province was abolished and the area previously under its jurisdiction was divided and incorporated into the provinces of Hopei and Liaoning and the Inner Mongolian Autonomous Region.

² The dates of the taking of these key points were: Shihchiachuang, November 12, 1947; Yuncheng, December 28, 1947; Szepingkai, March 13, 1948; Loyang, first on March 14, 1948, and again on April 5, 1948; Yichuan, March 3, 1948; Paoki, April 26, 1948; Weihsien, April 27, 1948; Linfen, May 17, 1948; and Kaifeng, June 22, 1948. All these cities were fortified with many groups of blockhouses, and some had high, thick city walls; also, they all had auxiliary defence works, including multiple lines of trenches, barbed-wire entanglements and abatis. Our army at the time had neither planes nor tanks, and little or no artillery. In attacking and taking these cities, our army learned a complete set of tactics for taking strong fortifications. These tactics were:

(1) successive demolition – using explosives to demolish the enemy's different defence installations in succession;

(2) tunnel operations – secretly digging tunnels to and under the enemy's blockhouses or city walls, then blowing them up with explosives and following up with fierce attacks;

(3) approach trench operations – digging trenches towards the enemy's fortifications, then approaching under cover to make sudden attacks;

(4) explosive package projectors – shooting packages of explosives from missile-projectors or mortars to destroy the enemy's defences;

(5) "sharp knife" tactics – concentrating manpower and firepower to effect a breakthrough and to cut up the enemy forces.

³ The brigades mentioned here were those designated as brigades after the reorganization of the Kuomintang army, while the divisions were pre-reorganization divisions (which were practically the same as the reorganized brigades).

⁴ The "middle road" was also called the "third road". See "The Present Situation and Our Tasks", Note 9, p. 176 of this volume.

⁵ See "The Situation and Our Policy After the Victory in the War of Resistance Against Japan", Note 8, p. 23 of this volume.

⁶ "Evil for Good" in *Aesop's Fables.*

ON THE WAR CRIMINAL'S SUING FOR PEACE*

January 5, 1949

In order to preserve the forces of Chinese reaction and U.S. aggression in China, Chiang Kai-shek, China's No. 1 war criminal and chieftain of the Kuomintang bandit gang, issued a statement on New Year's Day suing for peace. The war criminal Chiang Kai-shek says:

> I have no desire of my own other than that the peace negotiations should not impair the country's independence and integrity but instead should help the rehabilitation of the people; that the sacred constitution should not be violated by my action and that democratic constitutionalism should not be thereby undermined; that the form of government of the Republic of China should be guaranteed and the legally constituted authority of the Republic of China should not be interrupted; that the armed forces should be definitely preserved and that the people should be allowed to continue their free way of life and maintain their present minimum standard of living.
>
> ... If only peace can be realized, I certainly do not care whether I remain in office or retire, but will abide by the common will of the people.

People should not think that there is something ridiculous about a war criminal suing for peace, nor should they think that such a bid for peace is really disgusting. It should be understood that for the No. 1 war criminal and chieftain of the Kuomintang bandit gang to sue personally for peace and issue such a statement is obviously of some benefit to the Chinese people, because it enables them to see through the plots of the Kuomintang bandit gang and the U.S. imperialists. For the Chinese people can tell from this that the "peace" about which there has lately been so much clamour is exactly what this Chiang Kai-shek gang of murderers and their U.S. master urgently need.

Chiang Kai-shek has confessed the gang's whole plot. The main points of this plot are as follows:

"The peace negotiations should not impair the country's independence and integrity" – this is first in importance. "Peace" is all right, but "peace" is a million times wrong if it impairs the "independence and integrity" of the state of the four big families and the comprador and landlord classes. "Peace" is absolutely all wrong if it impairs such treaties as the Sino-U.S. Treaty of Friendship, Commerce and Navigation, the Sino-U.S. Air Transport Agreement[1] and the Sino-U.S. bilateral agreement,[2] or if it impairs such prerogatives enjoyed by the United States in China as the stationing of ground, naval and air forces, the building of military bases, the exploitation of mines and the monopoly of trade, or if it interferes with China's becoming a U.S. colony – in short, if it impairs any such measures as protect the "independence and integrity" of Chiang Kai-shek's reactionary state.

"Help the rehabilitation of the people" – that is, "peace" must help the rehabilitation of the Chinese reactionaries, who have been defeated but not yet wiped out, so that, once rehabilitated, they can stage a comeback and extinguish the revolution. This is exactly what "peace" is for. The war has been going on for two and a half years, "the running dog can no longer run" and the Americans are angry; a rest-cure, however brief, is better than none.

"The sacred constitution should not be violated by my action and democratic constitutionalism should not be thereby undermined; the form of government of the Republic of China should be guaranteed and the legally constituted authority of the Republic of China should not be interrupted" – all this means guaranteeing the ruling position of China's reactionary classes and reactionary government and guaranteeing that the "legally constituted authority" of these classes and their government will not be "interrupted". This "legally constituted authority" certainly must not be "interrupted", for to "interrupt" it would be very dangerous – it would mean the finish of the whole of the comprador and landlord classes, the end of the Kuomintang

---

* This commentary was the first of a series written by Comrade Mao Tse-tung for the Hsinhua News Agency to expose the Kuomintang's use of peace negotiations in order to preserve the counter-revolutionary forces. Other commentaries in the series included "Why Do the Badly Split Reactionaries Still Idly Clamour for 'Total Peace'?", "The Kuomintang Reactionaries Turn from an 'Appeal for Peace' to an Appeal for War", "On the Kuomintang's Different Answers to the Question of Responsibility for the War" and "Whither the Nanking Government?"

gang of bandits and the arrest and punishment of all the war criminals, big, medium and small.

"The armed forces should be definitely preserved" – they are the lifeline of the comprador and landlord classes, and although several millions have been wiped out by the detested People's Liberation Army, there still remain one million several hundred thousand troops which must be "preserved", and "definitely" so. If they were "preserved", but not "definitely", the comprador and landlord classes would lose their capital, their "legally constituted authority" would still be "interrupted", the Kuomintang bandit gang would still be finished, all the war criminals, big, medium and small, would still be arrested and punished. Just as the life of Chia Pao-yu of the Grand View Garden depended upon a piece of jade in his necklace,[3] the life of the Kuomintang depends upon its army, so how can one say that its army should not be "preserved", or should only be "preserved" but not "definitely" so?

"The people should be allowed to continue their free way of life and maintain their present minimum standard of living" – this means the Chinese comprador and landlord classes must preserve their freedom to oppress and exploit the people of the whole country and their freedom to maintain their present standard of lordly, luxurious, loose and idle living, while the Chinese working people must preserve their freedom to be oppressed and exploited and maintain their present standard of living, a life of cold and hunger. That is the ultimate aim of the war criminals in suing for peace. What is the use of peace, if the war criminals and the classes to which they belong cannot preserve their freedom to oppress and exploit and cannot maintain their standard of lordly, luxurious, loose and idle living? To preserve all this, it is of course necessary for the workers, peasants, intellectuals, government employees and teachers to maintain their present "free way of life and minimum standard of living", a life of cold and hunger. Once our beloved President Chiang puts forward this condition, the tens of millions of workers, handicraftsmen and professionals, the hundreds of millions of peasants, and the millions of intellectuals, government employees and teachers can only clap their hands in unison, prostrate themselves and shout, "Long live the President!" If the Communist Party still refuses peace, so that this wonderful way of life and standard of living cannot be maintained, then it will be guilty of a crime for which it deserves to die ten thousand deaths, and "the Communist Party will be held responsible for all the consequences".

In saying all this, however, we have not exhausted the whole treasury of wonderful ideas in the war criminal's statement of January 1 suing for peace.   Here is another gem – what Chiang Kai-shek in his New Year message calls "a decisive battle in the Nanking-Shanghai sector".   Where is the strength for such a "decisive battle"? Chiang Kai-shek says, "It must be understood that today the strength of the government in the military, political, economic or any other field is several times or even tens of times greater than that of the Communist Party."   Oh!   Ho!   How can people not be scared to death by such immense strength?   Leaving political and economic strength aside and taking only military strength, one sees that the People's Liberation Army now has over three million men, that two times "greater" than this number is over six million and that ten times "greater" is over thirty million.   And how many will "tens of times" be?   All right, let's take twenty times, which gives over sixty million men; no wonder President Chiang says he has "full confidence in winning the decisive battle".   Why then should he beg for peace?   Certainly not because he can no longer fight.   For if he were to bring the pressure of over sixty million troops to bear, could there be any chance of survival for the Communist Party or any other party in the world? All of course would be crushed to powder.   It is clear then that when he begs for peace, it is certainly for no other reason than "to plead for the life of the people".

But is everything going well, without any hitch?   There is a hitch, it is said.   What is the hitch?   President Chiang says:

> It is regrettable that there are people in our government who have come under the influence of malicious Communist propaganda and are consequently in a wavering state of mind, having almost lost their self-confidence.   Spiritually menaced by the Communists, they see only the enemy's strength but not our own huge strength, which is tens of times greater than the enemy's.

Well, every year brings its crop of news, but this year's is something very special.   Isn't it an extra-special piece of news that members of the Kuomintang, with their sixty million odd officers and men, see only the People's Liberation Army of three million odd men but not their own army of over sixty million?

One may ask, "Is there a market for such news?" and "Is it worth even a glance?"   According to information received from inside the city of Peiping, "On New Year's Day prices dropped slightly in the morning but recovered in the afternoon." And a foreign news agency reports, "Shanghai's response to Chiang Kai-shek's New Year message is cold." This answers the question as to whether the war criminal Chiang Kai-shek has any market. As we said long ago, Chiang Kai-shek has lost his soul, is merely a corpse, and no one believes him any more.

NOTES

[1] The "Sino-U.S. Air Transport Agreement" between the Chiang Kai-shek government and U.S. imperialism was signed on December 20, 1946. In this agreement, Chiang Kai-shek completely sold out China's sovereignty over her air space. According to its provisions, U.S. aircraft were allowed to fly, load and unload or trans-ship anywhere within China, and the United States gained complete control of the country's air transport. U.S. aircraft were also accorded the right of "non-traffic stop", that is, of military landings on Chinese territory.

[2] The "Sino-U.S. bilateral agreement" was the so-called Sino-U.S. Economic Aid Agreement signed at Nanking on July 3, 1948 between the representatives of the Chiang Kai-shek government and U.S. imperialism. It stipulated that U.S. imperialism was to have supreme authority to supervise and decide the financial and economic affairs of the Chiang Kai-shek government, that U.S. personnel exercising direct control in China were to enjoy "extraterritorial rights", and that U.S. imperialism could obtain from China any strategic materials it needed and was to be kept informed regularly by the Chiang Kai-shek government about their availability. In this agreement the Chiang Kai-shek government also guaranteed that U.S. goods could be dumped in China.

[3] Chia Pao-yu was a character in *The Dream of the Red Chamber*, an 18th century Chinese novel, and the Grand View Garden was his family garden. It was said that Chia Pao-yu was born with a piece of jade in his mouth. This jade was "the root of his life" and had to be worn constantly around his neck. He was not to part with it. If he lost it, he would lose his wits.

STATEMENT ON THE PRESENT SITUATION
BY MAO TSE-TUNG, CHAIRMAN OF
THE CENTRAL COMMITTEE OF
THE COMMUNIST PARTY OF CHINA

January 14, 1949

Two and a half years have gone by since July 1946, when the reactionary Nanking Kuomintang government, with the aid of the U.S. imperialists, violated the will of the people, tore up the truce agreement and the resolutions of the Political Consultative Conference and launched the country-wide counter-revolutionary civil war. In these two and a half years of war, the reactionary Nanking Kuomintang government has, in violation of the will of the people, convened a bogus National Assembly, promulgated a bogus constitution, elected a bogus president and issued a bogus decree on the so-called "mobilization for putting down the rebellion"; sold out the national interest wholesale to the U.S. government and received loans amounting to thousands of millions of U.S. dollars; invited the U.S. navy and air force to occupy China's territory and territorial sea and air; signed a large batch of treasonable treaties with the U.S. government and accepted the U.S. Military Advisory Group's participation in China's civil war; and obtained from the U.S. government huge quantities of aircraft, tanks, light and heavy artillery, machine-guns, rifles, shells, bullets and other war matériel for slaughtering the Chinese people. And it was on the basis of these reactionary and traitorous basic policies, domestic and foreign, that the reactionary Nanking Kuomintang government ordered millions of troops to launch ruthless attacks on the Chinese People's Liberated Areas and the Chinese People's Liberation Army. All the People's Liberated Areas in eastern China, the Central Plains, northern China, the Northwest and the Northeast were, without exception, trampled upon by the Kuomintang troops. The leading cities in the Liberated Areas, such as Yenan, Changchiakou, Huaiyin,

Hotse, Taming, Linyi, Yentai, Chengteh, Szepingkai, Changchun, Kirin and Antung, were all occupied by these bandit troops at one time or another. Wherever they went, they massacred and raped, burned and looted, and stopped at nothing. In the areas under its rule, the reactionary Nanking Kuomintang government sucks the life-blood of the broad masses of the people – the workers, peasants, soldiers, intellectuals and businessmen – by exacting grain levies, taxes and forced labour for "putting down the rebellion and suppressing the bandits". The reactionary Nanking Kuomintang government deprives the people of all their freedoms and rights; it oppresses all the democratic parties and the people's organizations, denying them their legal status; it suppresses the righteous movement of the students against civil war, hunger and persecution and against U.S. interference in China's internal affairs and U.S. fostering of the forces of aggression in Japan; it floods the country with the bogus national currency and the bogus gold yuan notes, thus ruining the economic life of the people and reducing the broad masses to bankruptcy; and by various means of expropriation it concentrates the greatest part of the nation's wealth in the hands of the bureaucrat-capitalists headed by the four big families of Chiang, Soong, Kung and Chen. In short, the reactionary Nanking Kuomintang government has plunged the whole nation into dire suffering by waging a civil war based on its reactionary and traitorous basic policies, domestic and foreign; it absolutely cannot escape full responsibility. In contrast to the Kuomintang, the Communist Party of China did all it could after Japan's surrender to press the Kuomintang government to prevent and stop the civil war and realize domestic peace. Basing itself on this policy, the Communist Party of China struggled steadfastly and, with the support of the people of the whole country, first secured the signing of the Summary of Conversations between the Kuomintang and the Communist Party in October 1945. In January 1946 the Party again signed a truce agreement with the Kuomintang and, in co-operation with the democratic parties, forced the Kuomintang to accept the joint resolutions of the Political Consultative Conference. From then on the Communist Party of China, together with the democratic parties and people's organizations, strove to uphold the agreement and the resolutions. But it is regrettable that the reactionary Kuomintang government showed no respect for any of the actions we took in defence of internal peace and the democratic rights of the people. On the contrary, they were taken as signs of weakness and as beneath notice.

The reactionary Kuomintang government thought that the people could be bullied, that the truce agreement and the resolutions of the Political Consultative Conference could be torn up at will, that the People's Liberation Army could not withstand even a single blow while its own troops several million strong could overrun the country, and that aid from the U.S. government was inexhaustible. Therefore, the reactionary Kuomintang government had the audacity to violate the will of the people of the whole country and unleash the counter-revolutionary war. In these circumstances, the Communist Party of China had no choice but to rise resolutely against the Kuomintang government's reactionary policies and fight to safeguard the country's independence and the people's democratic rights. Since July 1946, the Communist Party of China has led the heroic People's Liberation Army to repulse the attacks of 4,300,000 troops of the reactionary Kuomintang government and then to go over to the counter-offensive, recover all the lost territories of the Liberated Areas and liberate many large cities, such as Shihchiachuang, Loyang, Tsinan, Chengchow, Kaifeng, Shenyang, Hsuchow and Tangshan. The People's Liberation Army has overcome unparalleled difficulties, grown in strength and equipped itself with huge quantities of arms given to the Kuomintang government by the U.S. government. In two and a half years, it has wiped out the main military forces of the reactionary Kuomintang government and all its crack divisions. Today the People's Liberation Army is superior to the remnant military forces of the reactionary Kuomintang government in numbers, morale and equipment. It is only now that the Chinese people can begin to breathe freely. The present situation is quite clear – the whole structure of the reactionary Kuomintang regime will crumble and perish if the People's Liberation Army launches a few more powerful attacks against its remnant forces. Having pursued a policy of civil war, the reactionary Kuomintang government is now reaping what it has sown, the masses are in rebellion, its close followers are deserting, and it can no longer maintain itself. In these circumstances, in order to preserve the remnant forces of the Kuomintang government and in order to gain a breathing space before making new onslaughts to destroy the revolutionary forces, Chiang Kai-shek, China's No. 1 war criminal, chieftain of the Kuomintang bandit gang and bogus president of the Nanking government, advanced the proposal on January 1 of this year that he was willing to hold peace negotiations with the Communist Party of China. The Communist Party of China considers this proposal hypocritical. The reason is that Chiang Kai-shek has proposed as the basis for the peace negotiations such terms as preserving the bogus constitution, preserving the bogus "constituted authority" and preserving the armed forces of reaction, terms which the people throughout the country cannot accept. These are terms for continuing the war, not for peace. In the last ten days the people throughout the country have made their will clear. They eagerly hope for an early peace, but they do not approve the so-called peace of the war criminals, do not approve their reactionary terms. Basing itself on the will of the people, the Communist Party of China declares that although the People's Liberation Army has ample strength and abundant reason to wipe out completely the remnant armed forces of the reactionary Kuomintang government in not too long a period and has full confidence that it can do so, nevertheless, in order to hasten the end of the war, bring about genuine peace and alleviate the people's sufferings, the Communist Party of China is willing to hold peace negotiations with the reactionary Nanking Kuomintang government or with any local governments or military groups of the Kuomintang on the basis of the following terms:

(1)   Punish the war criminals;
(2)   Abolish the bogus constitution;
(3)   Abolish the bogus "constituted authority";
(4)   Reorganize all reactionary troops on democratic principles;
(5)   Confiscate bureaucrat-capital;
(6)   Reform the land system;
(7)   Abrogate treasonable treaties;
(8)   Convene a political consultative conference without the participation of reactionary elements, and form a democratic coalition government to take over all the powers of the reactionary Nanking Kuomintang government and of its subordinate governments at all levels.[1]

The Communist Party of China holds that the above terms express the common will of the people throughout the country and that only a peace based on these terms can be called a genuine democratic peace. If the persons in the reactionary Nanking Kuomintang government wish to achieve a genuine democratic peace, and not a false reactionary peace, they should give up their reactionary terms and accept the eight terms put forth by the Communist Party of China as the basis for peace negotiations. Otherwise their so-called peace will prove to be nothing but a fraud. We hope that the people throughout the country and all democratic parties and people's organizations will rise to fight for a genuine democratic peace and against a false reactionary peace. The patriots in the Nanking Kuomintang governmental system should also support this peace proposal. Comrade commanders and fighters of the People's Liberation Army, attention! You should not slacken your fighting efforts in the slightest until the reactionary Nanking Kuomintang government has accepted a genuine democratic peace and carried it out. Any reactionaries who dare to resist must be resolutely, thoroughly, wholly and completely annihilated.

NOTES

[1] The eight terms for peace put forward by Comrade Mao Tse-tung in this statement became the basis for the peace negotiations held in April 1949 between the delegation of the Chinese Communist Party and the Kuomintang government delegation headed by Chang Chih-chung. The Agreement on Internal Peace, drafted in the course of these negotiations, set forth concrete provisions for the eight peace terms. For details, see "Order to the Army for the Country-wide Advance", Note 1, pp. 390-96 of this volume.

COMMENT BY THE SPOKESMAN
FOR THE COMMUNIST PARTY OF CHINA
ON THE RESOLUTION OF
THE NANKING EXECUTIVE YUAN

January 21, 1949

The Central News Agency, the official news agency of the reactionary Nanking Kuomintang government, said in a dispatch of January 19 that the Executive Yuan, at a meeting at 9 a.m. on the same day, had extensively discussed the current situation and passed the following resolution:

> In deference to the desire of the people of the whole country to realize an early peace, the Government hereby expresses its considered wish, first, together with the Communist Party of China, to effect an immediate and unconditional cessation of hostilities, and then, to appoint delegates to enter into peace negotiations.

The spokesman for the Communist Party of China states: This resolution of the Nanking Executive Yuan makes no mention of the statement proposing peace negotiations issued on January 1 by Chiang Kai-shek, the bogus Nanking president, or of the statement proposing peace negotiations issued on January 14 by Chairman Mao Tse-tung of the Communist Party of China; nor does it indicate which of the two statements it supports and which it opposes, but instead puts forward a proposal of its own, as if neither the Kuomintang nor the Communist Party had made any proposals on January 1 and January 14; all this is utterly incomprehensible. As a matter of fact, the Nanking Executive Yuan has not only completely ignored the Chinese Communist Party's proposal of January 14 but has also flatly repudiated the proposal made on January 1 by the bogus President Chiang Kai-shek. He said in his January 1 proposal:

321

As soon as the Communist Party has a sincere desire for peace and can give definite indications of this, the Government will certainly meet it in all sincerity and be willing to discuss concrete measures for ending hostilities and restoring peace.

Now, nineteen days later, an organ of this selfsame government, that is, the "Executive Yuan" of the Nanking government, repudiates the statement made by the "president" of that government and, instead of saying that the government "will certainly meet" the Communist Party "in all sincerity and be willing to discuss concrete measures for ending hostilities and restoring peace", it says, "first, effect an immediate and unconditional cessation of hostilities, and then, appoint delegates to enter into peace negotiations." We should like to ask the gentlemen of the "Executive Yuan" at Nanking: after all, which proposal stands, yours or that of your "president"? Your "president" regarded "ending hostilities and restoring peace" as one and the same thing and professed sincerity and willingness to discuss concrete measures for doing so with the Communist Party of China, whereas you divorce war from peace as two separate things and are reluctant to appoint delegates to discuss with us concrete measures for ending hostilities and, instead, indulge in the wildest fantasy, proposing "first, to effect an immediate and unconditional cessation of hostilities" and then to appoint delegates to "enter into peace negotiations". Which proposal is right, yours or that of your "president"? We hold that the bogus Executive Yuan at Nanking has acted beyond its authority; it has no right to cast aside the proposal of its bogus president and arbitrarily make a new proposal of its own. We regard this new proposal as unreasonable; having fought such a large-scale, protracted and cruel war, both sides should as a matter of course appoint delegates to discuss basic peace terms and work out a mutually acceptable truce agreement; only thus can the war be stopped. Not only do the people desire this, even on the Kuomintang side many persons have expressed this desire. If the absolutely groundless "resolution" of the Nanking Executive Yuan is followed and the Kuomintang is unwilling to carry on peace negotiations unless there is first a cessation of hostilities, then where is its sincere desire for peace? The "resolution" of the Nanking Executive Yuan has been adopted, there can be no peace negotiations unless there is first a cessation of hostilities, and from now on the door to peace is shut tight; if there are to be negotiations, the only thing to do is to annul this absolutely groundless "resolution". It must be one or the other. If the Nanking Executive Yuan is unwilling to annul its own "resolution", this will only show that the reactionary Nanking Kuomintang government has no sincere desire to hold peace negotiations with the opposing side. People will ask, if Nanking is sincere, why is it unwilling to discuss concrete peace terms? Hasn't the conclusion been confirmed that Nanking's peace proposal is hypocritical? The spokesman for the Communist Party says: Nanking has now fallen into a state of anarchy, the bogus president has one proposal and the bogus Executive Yuan has another. With whom is one to deal?

ON ORDERING THE REACTIONARY KUOMINTANG GOVERNMENT TO RE-ARREST YASUJI OKAMURA, FORMER COMMANDER-IN-CHIEF OF THE JAPANESE FORCES OF AGGRESSION IN CHINA, AND TO ARREST THE KUOMINTANG CIVIL WAR CRIMINALS — STATEMENT BY THE SPOKESMAN FOR THE COMMUNIST PARTY OF CHINA

January 28, 1949

The Central News Agency of the reactionary Nanking Kuomintang government reported in a dispatch dated January 26:

A Government spokesman made the following statement.   In the past month the Government has taken various measures and steps for an early conclusion of the war in order to alleviate the sufferings of the people.   Furthermore, on the 22nd of this month, the Government formally appointed a delegation[1] to the peace negotiations.   During the last few days, the Government has only been waiting for the Communist Party of China to appoint its delegation and agree on a meeting place so that the negotiations may proceed.   But in the statement broadcast from northern Shensi by the Hsinhua News Agency on the 25th,[2] a spokesman for the Communist Party of China, while indicating willingness to negotiate a peaceful settlement with the Government, resorted to unbridled insults and vilification and used absurd and offensive language.   He also said that the place for the negotiations could not be fixed until Peiping was completely liberated.   We should like to ask, if the Communist Party of China, on the pretext of

325

awaiting the so-called complete liberation of Peiping, does not immediately appoint its delegation and agree on a meeting place and
furthermore does not stop military operations, is it not stalling
for time and prolonging the disaster of war?   One should know
that the hope of the people of the whole country to put an end to
the disaster of war brooks no delay.   To demonstrate its profound
sincerity, the Government once again expresses the wish that the
Communist Party of China will clearly realize that the salvation
of the people should be the primary consideration today and that
it will therefore appoint a delegation to the negotiations as soon as
possible, so that peace can be realized at an early date.

In another dispatch dated January 26, Nanking's Central News Agency
reported from Shanghai:

> Following a review of his case on the 26th by the National
> Defence Ministry's Military Court for the Trial of War Criminals,
> the Japanese war criminal General Yasuji Okamura, former
> Commander-in-Chief of the Japanese Expeditionary Forces in
> China, was declared not guilty at 4 o'clock this afternoon by Shih
> Mei-yu, the president of the court.   The atmosphere in the court-
> room was tense.   Okamura, standing at attention, smiled a little
> on hearing the verdict.

In view of the above, the spokesman for the Communist Party of
China makes the following statement:

1.   The Communist Party of China and the General Headquarters
of the Chinese People's Liberation Army declare that it is impermissible for the Military Court for the Trial of War Criminals set
up by the reactionary Nanking Kuomintang government to return a
verdict of "not guilty" on the Japanese war criminal General Yasuji
Okamura, former Commander-in-Chief of the Japanese Expeditionary
Forces in China and the arch-criminal among all war criminals in
the Japanese Expeditionary Forces of aggression against China.[3]   The
Chinese people, after untold human and material sacrifices during the
eight years of the War of Resistance Against Japan, finally won victory and captured this war criminal, and they will never allow the
reactionary Nanking Kuomintang government arbitrarily to declare
him not guilty.   The people of the whole country, all the democratic
parties and people's organizations and also the patriots in the reactionary Nanking Kuomintang governmental system must rise at once

to oppose the criminal act of that government in betraying the national interests and collaborating with the Japanese fascist militarists. We hereby give a serious warning to the gentlemen of the reactionary Nanking government. You must re-arrest Yasuji Okamura immediately and return him to prison without fail. This matter is closely related to your request for negotiations with us. We hold that all your present actions are an attempt to use fake peace negotiations to cover up your new preparations for war, which include your conspiracy to induce Japanese reactionaries to come to China and join you in massacring the Chinese people; it is exactly for this purpose that you have set Yasuji Okamura free. Therefore, we absolutely will not permit you to do it. We have the right to order you to re-arrest Yasuji Okamura and be responsible for turning him over to the People's Liberation Army at a time and place to be specified by us. As to the other Japanese war criminals, they are to be in your temporary custody, pending further instructions, and you must not take it upon yourselves to release any of them or let any escape; those of you who disobey will be severely punished.

2. We have learned from the January 26 statement of the spokesman for the reactionary Nanking Kuomintang government that you gentlemen of Nanking are all so very tense, eager, solicitous and anxious about peace negotiations, all, it is said, for the sake of "shortening the duration of the war", "alleviating the sufferings of the people" and "treating the salvation of the people as the primary consideration"; we have also learned that you feel that the Communist Party of China is so very untense, uneager, unsolicitous and unanxious in its response to your wish and "furthermore does not stop military operations" and is in reality "stalling for time and prolonging the disaster of war". We tell you gentlemen of Nanking frankly: you are war criminals, you will be brought to trial. We have no faith in your mouthings about "peace" or "the will of the people". You relied on the power of the United States, violated the will of the people, tore up the truce agreement and the resolutions of the Political Consultative Conference and launched this most ruthless, anti-popular, anti-democratic, counter-revolutionary civil war. You were then so tense, eager, solicitous and anxious that you would not listen to advice from anybody. And when you convened a bogus National Assembly, drew up a bogus constitution, elected a bogus president and promulgated a bogus decree of "mobilization for putting down the rebellion", you were again so tense, eager, solicitous and anxious about it all that

again you would not listen to advice from anybody. At that time in Shanghai, Nanking and other major cities, the so-called consultative councils, chambers of commerce, trade unions, peasant associations, women's organizations and cultural organizations, all of which are either run by your government or serve as your tools, kicked up such a fuss about "supporting the mobilization for putting down the rebellion" and "annihilating the Communist bandits" and once again were so tense, eager, solicitous and anxious about it all that they would not listen to advice from anybody. Two and a half years have now passed, and during this period the number of people slaughtered by you has run into many millions, and the villages burned down, the women raped and the wealth plundered by you, as well as the lives and property destroyed by your air force, are beyond count; you have committed heinous crimes, and we must settle accounts with you. We hear that you are quite opposed to the struggle for settling accounts. But this time there is good cause for the struggle to settle accounts, there must be an accounting, there must be a settlement, there must be a fight, there must be a struggle. You are defeated. You have enraged the people. And the people have all risen against you in a life-and-death struggle. The people do not like you, the people condemn you, the people have risen, and you are isolated; that is why you have been defeated. You proposed five terms[4] for peace negotiations and we proposed eight;[5] the people at once gave their support to our eight terms, not to your five. You don't dare to rebut our eight terms or insist upon your five. You declare that you are willing to take our eight terms as the basis for the negotiations. Isn't that fine? Then why not hurry up and negotiate? So it seems that you are very tense, eager, solicitous and anxious and that you are very much for "unconditional cessation of hostilities", for "shortening the duration of the war", for "alleviating the sufferings of the people" and for "treating the salvation of the people as the primary consideration". And we? We, obviously, are not tense, not eager, not solicitous nor anxious and we are "stalling for time and prolonging the disaster of war". But wait a moment, gentlemen of Nanking. We are going to be tense, eager, solicitous and anxious; the duration of the war will surely be shortened; and the sufferings of the people will surely be alleviated. Since you have already agreed to our eight terms as the basis for the negotiations, you and we are both going to be busy. The carrying out of these eight terms will keep you, us, all the democratic parties, people's organizations and people in all walks of life throughout the country busy for several months, half a year, a whole year, or several years – perhaps even then we shall not have finished the job! Listen, gentlemen of Nanking! The eight terms are not abstract items, they must have concrete content; during the present short period it is important for everybody to do some thinking, and the people will forgive us a little delay. To speak frankly, the opinion of the people is that we should prepare well for these negotiations. There will certainly be negotiations, and it absolutely will not be permitted that anyone break them off in the middle and refuse to negotiate. Therefore your delegates must get ready to come. But we still need some time to complete our preparations and we will not allow war criminals to set the date of the negotiations for us. We and the people of Peiping are now doing an important job; we are working out a peaceful settlement of the Peiping question on the basis of the eight terms. Your men in Peiping, such as General Fu Tso-yi, are also participating in this work, which you admitted to be proper in the communiqué of your news agency.[6] This will not only provide a place for the peace negotiations, but will set an example of peaceful settlement for Nanking, Shanghai, Wuhan, Sian, Taiyuan, Kueisui, Lanchow, Tihua, Chengtu, Kunming, Changsha, Nanchang, Hangchow, Foochow, Canton, Taiwan, Hainan Island, etc. This work is therefore praiseworthy, and you gentlemen of Nanking should not adopt a casual attitude towards it. We are now discussing with the democratic parties, people's organizations and the democrats without party affiliation in both our areas and yours the problem of drawing up a list of war criminals and working out the concrete details of the first of our eight terms. It will probably not be long before this list is officially issued. Gentlemen of Nanking, as you know, we have not yet had time to discuss such a list with the democratic parties and people's organizations and officially publish it. For this we beg your pardon. The reason for the delay is that your request for peace negotiations came a little late. Had it come earlier, our preparations might have been completed by now. But this does not mean you have nothing to do. Besides arresting the Japanese war criminal Yasuji Okamura, you must at once set about arresting a batch of civil war criminals and, first of all, those in Nanking, Shanghai, Fenghua and Taiwan who were among the forty-three war criminals listed in the statement by an authoritative person in the Communist Party of China on December 25, 1948. The most important among them are Chiang Kai-shek, T. V. Soong, Chen Cheng, Ho Ying-chin, Ku Chu-tung, Chen Li-fu, Chen Kuo-fu, Chu Chia-hua,

Wang Shih-chieh, Wu Kuo-chen, Tai Chuan-hsien, Tang En-po, Chou Chih-jou, Wang Shu-ming and Kuei Yung-ching.[7] Of particular importance is Chiang Kai-shek, who has now fled to Fenghua[8] and will very likely flee abroad and seek the protection of U.S. or British imperialism; therefore, you must quickly arrest this criminal and not let him escape. You shall assume full responsibility for this matter. Should there be any escapes, you shall be punished for the crime of setting bandits free, and no leniency whatsoever shall be shown. Let no one say he has not been warned. We hold that only by arresting these war criminals will one do a serious job in shortening the duration of the war and alleviating the people's sufferings. As long as the war criminals are at large, the duration of the war will be lengthened and the sufferings of the people will be aggravated.

3. We demand that the reactionary Nanking government reply to the above two points.

4. Nanking will be notified at another time concerning the preparations both sides should make in connection with the remainder of the eight terms.

NOTES

[1] The delegation appointed by the reactionary Kuomintang government for the peace negotiations consisted of Shao Li-tse, Chang Chih-chung, Huang Shao-hung, Peng Chao-hsien and Chung Tien-hsin.

[2] On January 25, 1949, a spokesman for the Chinese Communist Party pointed out in his statement concerning the peace negotiations: "We have permitted the reactionary Nanking government to send a delegation for peace negotiations with us not because we recognize that government as still qualified to represent the Chinese people, but because it still has some remnants of the reactionary armed forces. If that government feels that it has completely forfeited the people's confidence and that the remnants of its reactionary armed forces are unable to resist the powerful People's Liberation Army and if that government is willing to accept the eight terms for peace proposed by the Chinese Communist Party, then it is of course preferable and beneficial to the cause of the liberation of the people to settle the matter by negotiations, so as to lessen the people's sufferings." As to the meeting place, the statement said, "It can be decided only after the complete liberation of Peiping and will probably be Peiping." As to the Nanking delegates, it stated, "Peng Chao-hsien is one of the key figures of the Kuomintang CC clique, which has been most vehemently clamouring for war, and people consider him a war criminal; the Chinese Communist Party cannot receive such a delegate."

[3] Yasuji Okamura was one of the Japanese war criminals with the longest and blackest record of crimes of aggression against China. From 1925 to 1927, he was military adviser to Sun Chuan-fang, one of the Northern warlords. In 1928, as

commanding officer of a Japanese infantry regiment, he took part in the war in which Japan attacked and seized Tsinan and was the butcher in the Tsinan Massacre. In 1932 he served as deputy chief of staff of the Japanese Expeditionary Forces which attacked and occupied Shanghai. In 1933 he represented the Japanese government at the signing of the "Tangku Agreement" with the traitorous Kuomintang government. From 1937 to 1945, he was successively the Commander of Japan's 11th Corps, Northern China Front Army and 6th Front Army and the Commander-in-Chief of the Japanese Expeditionary Forces in China. He enforced the extremely brutal policy of "burn all, kill all, loot all" in China. He was among the chief Japanese war criminals on the list published at Yenan in August 1945. During the People's War of Liberation he was Chiang Kai-shek's secret military adviser and planned Chiang's attacks on the Liberated Areas. In January 1949 he was declared not guilty and set free by the reactionary Kuomintang government and returned to Japan. In 1950 he accepted Chiang Kai-shek's offer of the post of senior training officer in the so-called Research Institute of Revolutionary Practice. Since 1955 he has organized ex-servicemen of the Japanese army and navy into the "League of Comrades in Arms" (later called the League of Retired Comrades in Arms) and has played a vigorous role in the reactionary activities to revive Japanese militarism.

[4] The "five terms" proposed by the reactionary Kuomintang government for the peace negotiations were put forward in Chiang Kai-shek's statement on New Year's Day, 1949. They were: 1. The peace negotiations "should not impair the country's independence and integrity". 2. The peace negotiations "should help the rehabilitation of the people". 3. "The sacred constitution should not be violated by my action and democratic constitutionalism should not be thereby undermined; the form of government of the Republic of China should be guaranteed and the legally constituted authority of the Republic of China should not be interrupted". 4. "The armed forces should be definitely preserved". 5. "The people should be allowed to continue their free way of life and maintain their present minimum standard of living". Comrade Mao Tse-tung promptly and sternly refuted these five terms. See "On the War Criminal's Suing for Peace", pp. 309-13 of this volume.

[5] The "eight terms" proposed by the Communist Party of China for the peace negotiations were put forward in Comrade Mao Tse-tung's statement of January 14, 1949, on the current situation. See "Statement on the Present Situation by Mao Tse-tung, Chairman of the Central Committee of the Communist Party of China", pp. 315-19 of this volume.

[6] According to a Kuomintang Central News Agency dispatch dated January 27, 1949, the Ministry of National Defence of the Nanking government stated: "In northern China, in order to shorten the war, secure peace and thereby preserve the foundations of the ancient capital, Peiping, and its cultural objects and historic monuments, Commander-in-Chief Fu Tso-yi issued a proclamation on January 22 to the effect that hostilities were to cease as from 10 o'clock that day. On orders from General Headquarters, the bulk of our troops in Peiping have withdrawn from the city limits to certain designated areas." It further stated, "Cessation of hostilities will be effected also in Suiyuan and Tatung."

[7] T. V. Soong, a plutocrat of the Kuomintang regime, had served as minister of finance, president of the Executive Yuan, minister of foreign affairs and special emissary of the Kuomintang government in the United States. Chen Cheng, formerly chief of the general staff, was then the Kuomintang governor of Taiwan Province. Ho Ying-chin had been the Kuomintang's chief of the general staff and minister of national defence. Ku Chu-tung was then chief of the general staff of the

Kuomintang army.   Chen Li-fu, Chen Kuo-fu and Chu Chia-hua were all chieftains of the Kuomintang CC clique.   Wang Shih-chieh had been Kuomintang minister of foreign affairs.   Wu Kuo-chen was the Kuomintang mayor of Shanghai.   Tai Chuan-hsien, also known as Tai Chi-tao, had long been a member of Chiang Kai-shek's "brain trust" and was then a member of the Standing Committee of the Kuomintang Central Executive Committee.   Tang En-po was commander-in-chief of the Kuomintang garrison forces in the Nanking-Shanghai-Hangchow area.   Chou Chih-jou was commander-in-chief of the Kuomintang's air force.   Wang Shu-ming was deputy commander-in-chief and chief of staff of the air force.   Kuei Yung-ching was commander-in-chief of the Kuomintang navy.

[8] A county in Chekiang Province, the birthplace of Chiang Kai-shek.

PEACE TERMS MUST INCLUDE THE PUNISHMENT OF JAPANESE WAR CRIMINALS AND KUOMINTANG WAR CRIMINALS — STATEMENT BY THE SPOKESMAN FOR THE COMMUNIST PARTY OF CHINA

February 5, 1949

The statement on the question of peace negotiations made on January 28 by the spokesman for the Communist Party of China was answered on January 31 by a spokesman of the reactionary traitorous Kuomintang government. In his reply, the spokesman of the reactionary traitorous Kuomintang government quibbled about the points raised by the spokesman for the Communist Party of China. Concerning the demand of the Communist Party of China that the reactionary traitorous Kuomintang government should be responsible for re-arresting Yasuji Okamura, the chief criminal in Japan's invasion of China, turning him over to the People's Liberation Army, keeping the other Japanese war criminals in custody and preventing their escape, the Kuomintang spokesman said, "This is a judicial question. It has nothing whatsoever to do with peace negotiations, much less can it be made a precondition for peace negotiations." Concerning the demand of the Communist Party of China that the reactionary traitorous Kuomintang government should be responsible for arresting Chiang Kai-shek and other war criminals, the Kuomintang spokesman said, "For genuine peace, no preconditions should be imposed." The statement of the spokesman for the Communist Party of China, he added, "does not seem to be serious enough in its attitude" and, moreover, "causes complications". On this, the spokesman for the Communist Party of China states: As recently as January 28, our attitude was indeed not serious enough insofar as we still spoke of the reactionary traitorous Kuomintang government as a government.

Does this so-called "government" still really exist? Does it exist in Nanking? There is no longer any administrative organ in Nanking. Does it exist in Canton? There is no administrative head in Canton. Does it exist in Shanghai? There is neither an administrative organ nor an administrative head in Shanghai. Does it exist in Fenghua? In Fenghua there is only a bogus president, who has already announced his "retirement"; there is nothing else. Therefore, speaking seriously, we should not have regarded it as a government; it is, at most, a hypothetical or token government. But let us go on supposing that there is such a token "government" and that there is a spokesman who can speak for that "government". Then its spokesman should realize that this hypothetical, token, reactionary, traitorous Kuomintang government has not only contributed nothing towards peace negotiations, but has in fact caused endless complications. Didn't you cause complication, for instance, by suddenly declaring Yasuji Okamura not guilty at a time when you were so anxious for negotiations? Didn't you cause further complication by sending him to Japan, along with 260 other Japanese war criminals, after the Communist Party of China had demanded his re-arrest? Who rules Japan today? Can it be said that the Japanese people rule Japan, and not the imperialists? Japan is a place you love so much that you believe the Japanese war criminals will enjoy greater security and comfort and receive more appropriate treatment there than in the areas you rule. Is that a judicial question? And why has this judicial question arisen? Can it be that you have forgotten that the Japanese aggressors fought against us for eight whole years? Does this question have nothing whatsoever to do with peace negotiations? When the Communist Party of China put forward the eight terms for peace negotiations on January 14, the release of Yasuji Okamura had not yet occurred. That occurred on January 26, and so it should be raised; it is certainly relevant to the peace negotiations. On January 31 you obeyed MacArthur's orders and sent 260 Japanese war criminals to Japan, together with Yasuji Okamura; the matter thus became even more relevant to the peace negotiations. Why do you sue for peace? Because you have been defeated in war. And why have you been defeated? Because you launched a civil war against the people. And when did you launch this civil war? After the Japanese surrender. And against whom did you launch this war? Against the People's Liberation Army and the People's Liberated Areas, which had rendered extraordinary service in the War of Resistance Against Japan. And by what means have you waged the civil war? In addition to U.S. aid, by means of the men you have snatched and the wealth you have plundered from the people in the areas under your rule. No sooner had the Chinese people's great decisive fight with the Japanese aggressors ended, no sooner had the external war ended, than you launched this civil war. You were defeated and you asked for negotiations, but suddenly you declared the chief Japanese war criminal Yasuji Okamura not guilty. And no sooner had we lodged a protest, demanding that you put him back in prison and be ready to hand him over to the People's Liberation Army, than you hurriedly sent him to Japan with 260 other Japanese war criminals. Gentlemen of the reactionary traitorous Kuomintang government, this action of yours is too unreasonable and is too gross a violation of the people's will. We have now deliberately added the word "traitorous" to your title, and you ought to accept it. Your government has long been traitorous, and it was only for the sake of brevity that we sometimes omitted the word; now we can omit it no longer. In addition to all the crimes of treason you committed in the past, you have now committed another, and a very serious one, which must be discussed at the meeting for peace negotiations. Whether or not you call it causing complication, the matter must be discussed; and since it happened after January 14 and was not included in the eight terms we originally presented, we therefore deem it necessary to add to the first term a new item, the punishment of Japanese war criminals. So the first term now contains two items, (a) the punishment of Japanese war criminals and (b) the punishment of civil war criminals. We are justified in adding this new item; it reflects the will of the people of the whole country. The people of the whole country demand that the Japanese war criminals be punished. Even within the Kuomintang, many think that the punishment of Yasuji Okamura and other Japanese war criminals and the punishment of Chiang Kai-shek and other civil war criminals are both natural and right. Whether you say we are sincere about peace or not, the question of these two types of war criminal must be negotiated, and both types must be punished. As to our demand that you arrest a batch of civil war criminals before the negotiations begin and prevent their escape, you hold that "no preconditions should be imposed". Gentlemen of the reactionary traitorous Kuomintang government, this is not a precondition but a demand which follows naturally from your acceptance of the term concerning the punishment of war criminals as a basis for negotiations.

We instructed you to arrest them for fear that they would escape. At this time, when we have not yet completed preparations for the negotiations, you are pathetically anxious to negotiate and you are restless because you have too much leisure; therefore we have assigned you a reasonable job. These war criminals have to be arrested; even if they flee to the remotest corners of the globe, they must be arrested. Since you are all infinitely compassionate and merciful saviours of afflicted mankind, since you desire to "shorten the duration of the war", "alleviate the sufferings of the people" and "treat the salvation of the people as the primary consideration", and since you are great-hearted people, you should not cherish those who are responsible for the slaughter of millions of our fellow-countrymen. Judging by your willingness to accept the punishment of war criminals as part of the basis for negotiations, it seems you do not cherish these creatures very much. But, since you state that you find it rather difficult to arrest them immediately – all right, then, prevent them from escaping; under no circumstances must you let these creatures run away. Just imagine, gentlemen, after you have taken all the trouble to send a delegation to discuss with us the question of punishing these war criminals, what would we talk about if it should turn out that they have escaped? What a loss of face for the gentlemen of your delegation! How then would you show your great "sincerity for peace"? How then could you gentlemen prove that you really wish to "shorten the duration of the war", "alleviate the sufferings of the people" and "treat the salvation of the people as the primary consideration", and that you are not at all hypocritical? The Kuomintang spokesman also talked a great deal of other nonsense; such nonsense can fool nobody, and we consider it unnecessary to reply. Gentlemen of the hypothetical, token, reactionary, traitorous Kuomintang "government" (mind you, the word government is in inverted commas) at Nanking or Canton or Fenghua or Shanghai! If you think that our attitude in this statement is again not serious enough, please excuse us, for it is the only attitude we can take towards you.

TURN THE ARMY INTO A WORKING FORCE*

February 8, 1949

Your telegram of the 4th has been received. It is very good that you are speeding training and consolidation and preparing to start moving one month ahead of schedule.[1] Please proceed along these lines and do not slacken. Actually, however, training and consolidation must continue in March; the study of policy must be stressed and preparations must be made to take over and administer the large cities. From now on, the formula followed in the past twenty years, "first the rural areas, then the cities", will be reversed and changed to the formula, "first the cities, then the rural areas". The army is not only a fighting force, it is mainly a working force. All army cadres should learn how to take over and administer cities. In urban work they should learn how to be good at dealing with the imperialists and Kuomintang reactionaries, good at dealing with the bourgeoisie, good at leading the workers and organizing trade unions, good at mobilizing and organizing the youth, good at uniting with and training cadres in the new Liberated Areas, good at managing industry and commerce, good at running schools, newspapers, news agencies and broadcasting stations, good at handling foreign affairs, good at handling problems relating to the democratic parties and people's organizations, good at adjusting the relations between the cities and the rural areas and solving the problems of food, coal and other daily necessities and good at handling monetary and financial problems. In short, all urban problems, with which in the past our army cadres and fighters were unfamiliar, should from now on be shouldered by them. You are to advance and occupy four or five provinces, and in addition to the cities you will have to attend to vast rural areas. Since in the south all the rural areas will be newly liberated, the work will be fundamentally different from that in the old Liberated Areas of the north. In the first year, the policy of reducing rent and interest cannot be applied, and rent and interest

337

will have to be paid in roughly the same way as before. Our rural
work will have to proceed under these conditions. Therefore, rural
work must also be learned afresh. However, as compared with urban
work, rural work is easy to learn. Urban work is more difficult and
is the main subject you are studying. If our cadres cannot quickly
master the administration of cities, we shall encounter extreme difficulties. Consequently you must settle all other problems in February
and use the whole month of March to learn how to work in the cities
and in the new Liberated Areas. The Kuomintang has only one
million several hundred thousand troops, scattered over a huge territory. Of course, there are still many battles to fight, but there is
little possibility of such large-scale fighting as in the Huai-Hai campaign, and it may even be said that there is no such possibility and that
the period of severe fighting is over. The army is still a fighting force,
and in this respect there must be absolutely no relaxing; to relax would
be a mistake. Nevertheless, the time has come for us to set ourselves
the task of turning the army into a working force. If we do not now
set ourselves this task and resolve to perform it, we shall be making
an extremely big mistake. We are preparing to send 53,000 cadres
south with the army, but this is a very small number. The occupation
of eight or nine provinces and scores of big cities will require a huge
number of working cadres, and to solve this problem the army must
rely chiefly on itself. The army is a school. Our field armies of
2,100,000 are equivalent to several thousand universities and secondary
schools. We have to rely chiefly on the army to supply our working
cadres. You must understand this point clearly. Since severe fighting is basically over, replenishment of the army's manpower and
equipment should be kept within suitable limits, and too much must

---

* This telegram was written by Comrade Mao Tse-tung for the Revolutionary
Military Commission of the Central Committee of the Communist Party of China
in reply to one from the Second and Third Field Armies. It was sent also to the
other field armies concerned and to the bureaus of the Central Committee concerned.
Considering that the period of severe fighting had ended after the three great campaigns of Liaohsi-Shenyang, Huai-Hai and Peiping-Tientsin, Comrade Mao Tse-tung
in this telegram pointed out in good time that the People's Liberation Army was not
only a fighting force but at the same time had to be a working force and that under
certain conditions it should function mainly as a working force. This policy played
a very important role in solving the cadre problem of that period in the new Liberated
Areas and in ensuring the smooth development of the people's revolutionary cause.
On the nature of the People's Liberation Army as both a fighting and a working
force, see also "Report to the Second Plenary Session of the Seventh Central Committee of the Communist Party of China", Section 2, pp. 362-63 of this volume.

not be demanded as regards quantity, quality and completeness, lest this should cause financial crisis. That is another point you should seriously consider. The above policies apply fully to the Fourth Field Army, and Comrades Lin Piao and Lo Jung-huan are likewise asked to pay attention to them. We have talked at length with Comrade Kang Sheng and asked him to hurry to your place by the 12th to confer with you. After conferring, please inform us promptly by telegram of your views and what you propose to do. The Eastern China Bureau and the Eastern China Military Area Headquarters should move at once to Hsuchow to work jointly with the General Front Committee[2] and with the Front Committee of the Third Field Army in a concentrated effort to plan the march to the south. Turn all your rear-area work over to the Shantung Sub-Bureau.

NOTES

[1] The Second and Third Field Armies had planned to advance the date of crossing the Yangtse River from April to March 1949. The crossing was postponed to late April because of the peace negotiations with the reactionary Kuomintang government.

[2] In order to meet the needs of the Huai-Hai campaign, the Revolutionary Military Commission of the Central Committee of the Communist Party of China decided on November 16, 1948 to form a General Front Committee consisting of Comrades Liu Po-cheng, Chen Yi, Teng Hsiao-ping, Su Yu and Tan Chen-lin, with Comrade Teng Hsiao-ping as secretary, to assume unified leadership of the Central Plains Field Army and the Eastern China Field Army and to exercise command over military affairs and operations on the Huai-Hai front.

WHY DO THE BADLY SPLIT REACTIONARIES STILL IDLY CLAMOUR FOR "TOTAL PEACE"?

February 15, 1949

The reactionary Kuomintang rule is collapsing more rapidly than was expected. It is only a little over four months since the People's Liberation Army captured Tsinan and only a little over three months since it captured Shenyang, but all the remnant forces of the Kuomintang in the military, political, economic, cultural and propaganda fields are already hopelessly split and disintegrated. The general collapse of Kuomintang rule began with the Liaohsi-Shenyang and Peiping-Tientsin campaigns on the northern front and the Huai-Hai campaign on the southern front. In less than four months, from early October last year to the end of January this year, these three campaigns cost the Kuomintang a total of more than 1,540,000 men, including 144 entire divisions of its regular army. The general collapse of Kuomintang rule is the inevitable outcome of the great victories of the Chinese People's War of Liberation and of the revolutionary movement of the Chinese people, but the clamour for "peace" by the Kuomintang and its U.S. masters has played a considerable part in hastening this collapse. On January 1 of this year, the Kuomintang reactionaries began to lift a rock called the "peace offensive"; they intended to hurl it at the Chinese people, but now it has dropped on their own feet. To be more exact, the rock has smashed the Kuomintang to pieces. Besides General Fu Tso-yi, who has helped the People's Liberation Army to achieve a peaceful settlement of the Peiping question, there are plenty of people everywhere who hope for a peaceful settlement. The Americans are looking on in impotent fury because their brats have failed them. In fact, this magic weapon, the peace offensive, was made in U.S. factories and was delivered to the Kuomintang more than half a year ago. It was Leighton Stuart himself who let out the

341

secret.   After Chiang Kai-shek issued his so-called New Year's Day
message, Stuart told a correspondent of the Central News Agency that
this was "what I myself have consistently worked for".   According to
U.S. news agencies, that correspondent lost his rice bowl for publishing this "off the record" remark.   The reason the Chiang Kai-shek
clique did not dare to obey this American order for quite a long time
was clearly explained in a directive issued by the Propaganda
Department of the Kuomintang Central Executive Committee on
December 27, 1948:

> If we cannot fight, we cannot make peace.   If we can fight,
> then to talk about peace will only demoralize the troops and the
> people.   Hence, whether we can fight or not, we have everything
> to lose and nothing to gain by talking about peace.

The Kuomintang issued this directive at that time because some Kuomintang factions other than Chiang's were already advocating peace
talks.   Last December 25, Pai Chung-hsi and the Hupeh Provincial
Council under his direction raised the question of a "peaceful settlement"[1] with Chiang Kai-shek, who was compelled to issue a statement
on January 1 about holding peace negotiations on the basis of his five
terms.   He hoped to snatch the patent for inventing the peace offensive from Pai Chung-hsi and to continue his old rule under a new
trade mark.   On January 8 he sent Chang Chun to Hankow to enlist
the support of Pai Chung-hsi and on the same day he asked the governments of the United States, Britain, France and the Soviet Union
to intervene in China's civil war.[2]   But all these moves failed
completely.   The statement by Chairman Mao Tse-tung of the Communist Party of China on January 14 dealt a fatal blow to Chiang
Kai-shek's plot for a sham peace and compelled him to "retire" backstage a week later.   Although Chiang Kai-shek and Li Tsung-jen
and the Americans had made all kinds of arrangements for this plot
and hoped to put on a fairly good puppet show, the result was contrary
to their expectations; not only did the audience dwindle, but even the
actors themselves vanished from the stage one after another.   In
Fenghua, Chiang Kai-shek continues to direct his remnant forces in
his "status of retirement", but he has lost his legal status and those
people who believe in him are getting fewer and fewer.   On its own
initiative, Sun Fo's "Executive Yuan" has proclaimed "the moving
of the Government to Canton"; it has broken away not only from the
"president" and "acting president" of the government but also from

the "Legislative Yuan" and "Control Yuan". Sun Fo's "Executive Yuan" calls for war,[3] but the "Ministry of National Defence", which is charged with conducting the war, is neither in Canton nor in Nanking, and the only thing that is known of it is that its spokesman is in Shanghai. Thus, all that is left for Li Tsung-jen to see from the ramparts of the "Stone City" is,

> *The sky brooding low over the land of Wu and Chu,*
> *With nothing between to meet the eye.*[4]

None of the orders issued by Li Tsung-jen since he assumed office on January 21 has been carried out. Although the Kuomintang no longer has any "total" "government" and although activities for local peace are going on in many places, the Kuomintang die-hards oppose local peace and demand a so-called "total peace", and they actually aim at rejecting peace in the vain hope of carrying on the war; they are terribly afraid that these local peace activities will spread and get out of hand. The farce of the badly split and disintegrating Kuomintang's demand for a "total peace" reached its climax in the statement issued on February 9 in Shanghai by the war criminal Teng Wen-yi, head of the Bureau for Political Work of the bogus Ministry of National Defence. Like Sun Fo, Teng Wen-yi repudiated Li Tsung-jen's January 22 statement, which accepted the eight terms of the Communist Party of China as the basis for peace negotiations; instead he demanded a so-called "peace on an equal footing, a total peace", failing which, he said, "we will stop at no sacrifices in order to fight the Communists to the bitter end". But Teng Wen-yi failed to mention with whom we, his opponents, should now negotiate for a "peace on an equal footing, a total peace". It seems that to approach Teng Wen-yi will get us nowhere and that not to approach Teng Wen-yi or anyone else will also get us nowhere. How very trying this is! According to a Central News Agency dispatch from Shanghai on February 9:

> Teng Wen-yi was asked by a reporter, "Has Acting President Li approved the four points in your public statement?"[5] Teng Wen-yi answered, "I am speaking from the stand of the Ministry of National Defence, and the four points made today were not submitted beforehand to Acting President Li."

Here, Teng Wen-yi is not only inventing a partial stand of the bogus Ministry of National Defence, as distinct from the total stand of the bogus Kuomintang government, but is in fact inventing a smaller partial stand of the Bureau for Political Work of the bogus Ministry of National Defence, as distinct from the larger partial stand of the bogus Ministry of National Defence. For Teng Wen-yi openly opposes and maligns the peaceful settlement in Peiping, while the bogus Ministry of National Defence hailed it on January 27 as an act "to shorten the war, secure peace and thereby preserve the foundations of the ancient capital, Peiping, and its cultural objects and historic monuments" and declared that "cessation of hostilities will be effected" in the same way in places like Tatung and Suiyuan.[6] From this it can be seen that those reactionaries who are the most energetic in their clamour for "total peace" are the very reactionaries with the least total stand. A Bureau for Political Work of the Ministry of National Defence can contradict the Ministry of National Defence as well as the acting president. These reactionaries are the greatest obstacle to the realization of peace in China today. They dream of agitating for a total war under the slogan of a "total peace"; in their own words, "if there is to be war, let it be a total war; if there is to be peace, let it be a total peace." But as a matter of fact they have neither the power to bring about a total peace nor the power to wage a total war. Total power is in the hands of the Chinese people, the Chinese People's Liberation Army, the Communist Party of China and the other democratic parties, not in the hands of the badly split and disintegrating Kuomintang. One side wields total power, while the other is hopelessly split and disintegrated, and this is the result of the prolonged struggle of the Chinese people and the prolonged evil-doing of the Kuomintang. No serious person can ignore this basic fact of the political situation in China today.

NOTES

[1] Taking advantage of the extremely unfavourable situation then facing Chiang Kai-shek, Pai Chung-hsi, Commander-in-Chief of the Central China "Bandit Suppression" Headquarters of the Kuomintang, proposed a "peaceful settlement" of the civil war to Chiang, with the purpose of forcing him to step down and of raising the position of the Kwangsi clique to which Pai belonged. Under Pai Chung-hsi's direction the bogus Hupeh Provincial Council sent a telegram to Chiang Kai-shek, warning him that "if the disaster of war continues to spread and no attempt is made to change the course immediately, both the state and the people will be ruined", and advising him to "follow the normal course of political settlement and seek ways to resume peace negotiations".

[2] The request for intervention was rejected by the governments of the United States, Britain, France and the Soviet Union. In its *aide-mémoire* to the Kuomintang government on January 12, the U.S. government explained that the United States had rejected the request of the Kuomintang government because "it is not believed that any useful purpose would be served". This meant that the U.S. government was already aware that it could no longer avert the doom of the reactionary Chiang Kai-shek regime it had fostered.

[3] On February 6 and 7, 1949, Sun Fo, president of the bogus Executive Yuan of the Kuomintang government, made two statements at Canton opposing Li Tsung-jen's statement about accepting the eight terms for peace put forward by the Communist Party of China as the basis for negotiations. He said that "the Government has begun functioning in Canton where it has moved, and we should make a critical review of our past". He also said that "the term on the punishment of war criminals proposed by the Communists is absolutely unacceptable".

[4] Lines from an ode by the 14th century Chinese poet, Sadul, of the Yuan Dynasty. The first half of the ode reads:

From the ramparts of the Stone City
One sees the sky brooding low over the land of Wu and Chu,
With nothing between to meet the eye.
Pointing to strategic points famous in the Six Dynasties,
Only the green hills stand like walls.
Where army flags blotted the sun
And masts of war vessels touched the clouds
Snow-white skeletons lie scattered.
North and south of the River
How many warriors died!

The "Stone City" was an ancient name for Nanking.

[5] In his written statement on the "Development of Peace and War", Teng Wen-yi set forth the following "four points": (1) "The Government wants peace"; (2) "The Chinese Communist Party wants war"; (3) "The local peace at Peiping has become a hoax"; (4) "We will stop at no sacrifices in order to fight the Communists to the bitter end".

[6] After the liberation of Tientsin and Peiping, only a few isolated strong-points in northern China remained in the hands of the Kuomintang forces. They included Taiyuan, Tatung, Hsinhsiang, Anyang and Kueisui. The enemy at Taiyuan was completely wiped out on April 24, 1949. The enemy at Tatung submitted to peaceful reorganization on May 1. The enemy at Hsinhsiang surrendered on May 5. The enemy at Anyang was wiped out on May 6. Kueisui was peacefully liberated on September 19.

THE KUOMINTANG REACTIONARIES
TURN FROM AN "APPEAL FOR PEACE"
TO AN APPEAL FOR WAR

February 16, 1949

From the time the bandit Chiang Kai-shek launched his peace offensive on January 1, the heroes of the reactionary Kuomintang clique kept on repeating at great length their willingness to "shorten the duration of the war", "alleviate the sufferings of the people" and "treat the salvation of the people as the primary consideration". But early in February they suddenly began to play down their peace tune and strike up the old tune of "fighting the Communists to the bitter end". This has been especially so in the last few days. On February 13 the Propaganda Department of the Kuomintang Central Executive Committee issued a "Special Directive for Propaganda" to "all party headquarters and party papers" which stated:

Yeh Chien-ying has been spreading propaganda over our rear areas about the Chinese Communist Party's good faith in seeking peace, while condemning the Government's military moves as showing a lack of good faith in seeking peace. All our papers must emphatically refute this, directly and indirectly, in accordance with the following points.

The "Special Directive" gives quite a number of reasons why this "refutation" should be made:

Rather than surrender unconditionally, the Government should fight to the bitter end.

The eight terms Mao Tse-tung put forward in his January 14 statement would ruin the nation, and the Government should not have accepted them.

The Communist Party of China should bear the responsibility for wrecking peace. Instead, it has now drawn up a list of

so-called war criminals which includes all the Government leaders
and has even demanded that the Government first arrest them;
this clearly shows how truculent and unreasonable the Communist Party is.   Unless the Communist Party of China changes
this behaviour, it will indeed be difficult to find a way to peace
negotiations.

There is no more of the pathetic anxiety for peace negotiations of
two weeks ago.   There is no further mention of those famous phrases,
"shorten the duration of the war", "alleviate the sufferings of the
people" and "treat the salvation of the people as the primary consideration", phrases which gladdened the heart and spread everywhere.
If the Communist Party of China is unwilling to change its "behaviour"
and insists on the punishment of the war criminals, then peace talks
will be impossible.   Which, then, is the primary consideration –
the salvation of the people or the salvation of the war criminals?   According to the "Special Directive for Propaganda" issued by these
heroes of the Kuomintang, they prefer the latter.   The Communist
Party of China is still consulting the democratic parties and people's
organizations about the list of war criminals, and opinions have now
been received from several quarters.   Judging by the opinions so far
received, they all disapprove of the list put forward on December 25
last year by an authoritative person in the Communist Party of China.
They consider that a list containing the names of only forty-three war
criminals is too short; they consider that those to be held responsible
for launching the counter-revolutionary war and butchering several
million people should certainly not be limited to forty-three, but should
be well over a hundred.   For the time being, let us suppose that the
number of war criminals will be set at well over a hundred.   Then we
should like to ask the heroes of the Kuomintang, why do you oppose
the punishment of war criminals?   Aren't you willing to "shorten the
duration of the war" and "alleviate the sufferings of the people"?   If
the war continues because of this opposition of yours, won't that be
stalling for time and prolonging the disaster of war?   "Stalling for time
and prolonging the disaster of war" was the very accusation you made
against the Communist Party of China in the statement issued in the
name of the Nanking government spokesman on January 26, 1949;
can it be that now you want to take it back, write it on a placard
and hang it on yourselves as a badge of honour?   You are men of
infinite compassion and mercy, who profess to "treat the salvation of

the people as the primary consideration". Then why do you suddenly change and treat the salvation of the war criminals as the primary consideration? According to the statistics of your government's Ministry of the Interior, the number of the Chinese people is not 450 million, but 475 million; compare that with 100 odd war criminals – which number is bigger? You heroes have studied arithmetic; please do a careful sum in accordance with your arithmetic textbook and then draw your conclusion. If, without doing this sum, you hastily change your original formula of "treating the salvation of the people as the primary consideration" – a good formula with which we agree and the people of the whole country agree – into the formula of "treating the salvation of more than a hundred war criminals as the primary consideration", then be careful, for you certainly will not be able to maintain your ground. After having "appealed for peace" over several weeks, those individuals who have repeatedly mouthed the phrase, "treat the salvation of the people as the primary consideration", are no longer "appealing for peace" but are appealing for war. The reason the Kuomintang die-hards are in trouble is this: they have stubbornly opposed the people, ridden roughshod over them and thus have isolated themselves on the pinnacle of a pagoda; moreover, they will not repent, even unto death. All you broad masses of the people of the Yangtse valley and the south – workers, peasants, intellectuals, urban petty bourgeoisie, national bourgeoisie, enlightened gentry and Kuomintang members with a conscience – your attention, please! The days of the Kuomintang die-hards who have been riding roughshod over you are numbered. You and we are on the same side. The handful of die-hards will soon topple from their pinnacle, and a people's China will soon emerge.

ON THE KUOMINTANG'S DIFFERENT ANSWERS TO THE QUESTION OF RESPONSIBILITY FOR THE WAR

February 18, 1949

"After the conclusion of the War of Resistance, the Government, following a policy of peace and national reconstruction, endeavoured to solve peacefully the problem of the Communist Party of China. For a period of a year and a half the Communist Party of China broke every agreement and therefore it should bear the responsibility for wrecking peace. Instead, it has now drawn up a list of so-called war criminals which includes all the Government leaders and has even demanded that the Government first arrest them; this clearly shows how truculent and unreasonable the Communist Party is. Unless the Communist Party of China changes this behaviour, it will indeed be difficult to find a way to peace negotiations."

The above is the entire argument on the question of the responsibility for the war which the Propaganda Department of the Central Executive Committee of the Kuomintang advanced in a "Special Directive for Propaganda", issued on February 13, 1949.

It is the argument of none other than War Criminal No. 1, Chiang Kai-shek. In his New Year's Day statement he said:

As a devoted adherent of the Three People's Principles and the teachings of the Father of the Republic, I was reluctant to follow the conclusion of the war against Japan with the armed suppression of the bandits and thereby to aggravate the sufferings of the people. Therefore, as soon as the War of Resistance came to an end, our Government proclaimed its policy of peace and national reconstruction and moreover sought to solve the Communist problem by means of political consultation and military

351

mediation. But contrary to our expectations, the Communist Party for a period of a year and a half wilfully obstructed all agreements and proposals and made it impossible to carry them out by the measures which were originally intended. Finally, it even started an all-out armed rebellion which threatened the very existence of the state. This Government was thus driven to the painful necessity of mobilization to put down the rebellion.

On December 25, 1948, seven days before Chiang Kai-shek made this statement, an authoritative person in the Communist Party of China put forward a list of forty-three war criminals and illustrious at the head of the list was none other than this same Chiang Kai-shek. The war criminals, who want both to sue for peace and to shirk their responsibility, have no alternative but to shift the blame onto the Communist Party. But the two are irreconcilable. Since the Communist Party should bear the responsibility for launching the war, then the Communist Party should be punished. Since the Communists are "bandits", then the "bandits" should be "suppressed". Since they "started an all-out armed rebellion", then the "rebellion" should be "put down". "Bandit suppression" and "the putting down of rebellion" are a hundred per cent right, so why should they be abandoned? Why has the term "Communist bandits" been changed into "Communist Party" in all Kuomintang public documents issued since January 1, 1949?

Sun Fo, feeling that something was amiss, put forward a different argument about the responsibility for the war in a speech broadcast on the evening of the same day Chiang Kai-shek issued his New Year's Day statement. Sun Fo said:

We remember that in the early period following the victory of the War of Resistance, three years ago, because the people needed rehabilitation, the country needed active reconstruction and there was still common understanding of these needs among the various parties, we called together representatives from various quarters and public personages for a Political Consultative Conference. After three weeks' effort and thanks especially to the kind mediation of Mr. Marshall, President Truman's special envoy, we agreed upon a programme for peace and national reconstruction and upon specific measures for settling various disputes. If we had then carried out all these measures in good time, just think how prosperous China would be today, and how happy her people would be! Unfortunately, at the time none of the various parties concerned would entirely forgo its selfish interests, the people throughout the country did not exert themselves to the utmost to promote the success of the peace movement, and so the disaster of war again occurred, plunging the people into misery and suffering.

Sun Fo is a little bit more "fair" than Chiang Kai-shek. You see, unlike Chiang Kai-shek, he does not shift the responsibility for the war entirely onto the Communist Party, but divides the blame equally among "the various parties concerned" by the method of "equalization of landownership".[1] Those involved are the Kuomintang, also the Communist Party, also the Democratic League and also the public personages. That isn't all; "the people throughout the country" are also involved; not one of our 475 million fellow-countrymen can escape responsibility. While Chiang Kai-shek caned the Communist Party alone, Sun Fo canes all the parties, all the people without party affiliation, every one of his fellow-countrymen; even Chiang Kai-shek, and perhaps even Sun Fo himself, will get a caning. Here you see two Kuomintangites at loggerheads, Sun Fo and Chiang Kai-shek.

A third Kuomintangite has come forward, saying, "No, in my opinion, the responsibility should be borne entirely by the Kuomintang." His name is Li Tsung-jen. On January 22, 1949, Li Tsung-jen issued a statement in his capacity as "acting president". Regarding the responsibility for the war, he said:

> The three years' civil war that followed the eight years' War of Resistance has not only completely destroyed the country's last hope of recovery after the victory in the War of Resistance but has also spread ruin everywhere north and south of the Yellow River, devastating innumerable farmsteads and houses, killing and wounding thousands upon thousands of innocent people, breaking up countless families and causing people everywhere to lament in hunger and cold. Such a terrible holocaust is really without parallel in the history of civil wars in our country.

Here Li Tsung-jen makes a statement but names no names; he fixes the responsibility neither on the Kuomintang, nor on the Communist Party, nor on any other quarter; yet he has stated one fact, that this "terrible holocaust" has occurred in no other place than "north and south of the Yellow River". Wherefore, let us examine who caused this "terrible holocaust" in the area from the Yellow River

south to the Yangtse River and north to the Sungari River.   Could
it have been caused by the people and the people's army there, fighting
among themselves?   Since Li Tsung-jen was once Chief of Chiang
Kai-shek's Peiping Headquarters and since the troops of his Kwangsi
clique together with Chiang's troops once fought into the Yi-Meng
mountain area in Shantung Province,[2] he has reliable information
about where and how this "holocaust" took place. If there is nothing
else good about Li Tsung-jen, at least it is good that he has made this
one honest statement.   What is more, instead of speaking about "putting down the rebellion" or "suppressing the bandits", he calls the
war a "civil war", and this, for the Kuomintang, may be said to be
quite novel.

Following his own logic, Li Tsung-jen declared in the same statement that "the Government is willing to start negotiations immediately
on the basis of the eight terms proposed by the Communist Party of
China".   Li Tsung-jen knows that the first of the eight terms is the
punishment of war criminals and that his own honourable name is
among them.   That the war criminals should be punished is a logical
conclusion from the "holocaust".   For this reason the Kuomintang
die-hards are even now muttering complaints against Li Tsung-jen,
saying that "the eight terms Mao Tse-tung put forward in his January
14 statement would ruin the nation, and the Government should not
have accepted them".

There are reasons why the die-hards can only mutter and dare
not speak out openly.   Before Chiang Kai-shek "retired", the die-
hards had thought of rejecting our eight terms, but then Chiang
Kai-shek on second thoughts decided not to do so, probably because
he considered that to reject them would leave no way out; this was
the state of affairs on January 19.   On that morning, Chang Chun-mai[3]
upon his return to Shanghai from Nanking said that "the Government may issue another statement soon in reply to the eight terms
put forward by the Communist Party of China", whereupon the Central News Agency sent a service message the same evening, saying:

Add the following note to the Shanghai dispatch on Chang
Chun-mai's statement that has just come through.   As regards
his assertion that the Government will soon issue another statement, a Central News Agency correspondent has just learned from
the quarters concerned that the Government has no intention of
making another statement.

In the January 21 statement on his "retirement", Chiang Kai-shek said not a single word in criticism of the eight terms and even revoked his own five terms, changing them into "attaining peace on the principle that the integrity of territory and sovereignty is maintained, that the historic culture and social order are not destroyed and that the people's livelihood and right to freedom are safeguarded". He no longer dared raise such matters as the constitution, the legally constituted authority or the army. That is why on January 22 Li Tsung-jen dared to accept the eight terms of the Communist Party of China as the basis for negotiations and why the Kuomintang die-hards dared not openly reject them, but could only mutter that "the Government should not have accepted them".

Did Sun Fo consistently maintain his policy of "equalization of landownership"? No. After he "moved the Government to Canton" on February 5, 1949, he made a speech on February 7 about the question of war responsibility, saying:

> In the last six months the spread of the disaster of war has brought about serious changes in the situation and inflicted untold suffering on the people. All this has its origin in past mistakes, failures and unreasonableness, and today's grave situation is the consequence. We are all convinced that China needs the Three People's Principles. So long as the Three People's Principles are not put into effect, China's problems can never be solved. It may be recalled that twenty years ago the *Tsungli* of our party personally entrusted the Three People's Principles to our party as his legacy in the hope that they would be put into effect step by step. If they had been put into effect, the situation would never have developed into such a hopeless mess.

People will please note that here the president of the Executive Yuan of the Kuomintang government is not apportioning responsibility for the war equally among the various parties and all his fellow-countrymen but is putting it on the Kuomintang itself. It makes people feel exceedingly good to see Sun Fo applying the cane to the backside of the Kuomintang alone. What about the Communist Party? President Sun says:

> We can see that the Communist Party of China has been able to lure and dupe the people merely by appealing for the equalization of landownership, which is one part of the Three People's Principles, the Principle of the People's Livelihood. We ought to

feel deeply ashamed, sharpen our vigilance and examine afresh our past mistakes.

Thank you, dear President! Although the Communist Party is still charged with the crime of "luring and duping the people", at least it is innocent of other horrible crimes and hence escapes a caning and is let off with its head and its backside unscathed.

Nor is President Sun lovable for this reason alone. In the same speech, he says:

> The spread of Communist influence today is a result of our failure to put into effect the principles we believe in. Our party's greatest mistake in the past was that certain members worshipped force too much and scrambled for power among themselves, thus giving the enemy opportunities to sow dissension in our ranks. The conclusion of the eight years' War of Resistance should have been the occasion for realizing the country's peaceful unification, an opportunity of a thousand years, and originally the Government had a plan of settling domestic disputes by political means, but unfortunately it was not carried out. After years of war and chaos the people urgently needed rehabilitation. The renewal of armed conflict made life impossible for the people, and the suffering was great; it also lowered the morale of the troops and caused repeated military setbacks. In deference to the feelings of the people and because he realized that military means had failed to solve the problem, President Chiang issued a New Year's Day message calling for peace.

Good! Here this war criminal Sun Fo has made a voluntary confession, and a frank and truthful one too, although he has not been arrested or caned. Who was it who worshipped force, launched the war and sued for peace only after military means had failed to solve the problem? None other than the Kuomintang, none other than Chiang Kai-shek himself. President Sun is very precise in his choice of words when he says that "certain members" of his party worshipped force too much. This conforms with the demand of the Communist Party of China that only a certain number of Kuomintang members be punished and branded as war criminals, but no more than this number, and of course not its entire membership.

So we have no dispute with Sun Fo over the number. We differ with him as to the conclusion to be drawn. We hold that "certain members" of the Kuomintang must be punished as war criminals because they "worshipped force" and caused the "renewal of armed conflict", which "made life impossible for the people". But Sun Fo does not agree. He says:

> In delaying the appointment of its delegation and constantly stalling for time, the Communist Party has shown that it also worships force, believes it has now become full-fledged and can conquer the whole country by force; it therefore refuses to cease hostilities as a first step. Its motive is all too clear. I hereby propose in all seriousness that in order to obtain lasting peace negotiations should be conducted by the two parties on an equal footing and that the terms should be fair and reasonable and acceptable to the people of the whole country.

From this you can see that President Sun is not quite so lovable. He seems to think that the punishment of war criminals is not a fair and reasonable term. On the question of war criminals, his words reveal an attitude similar to that of the "Special Directive for Propaganda" issued by the Kuomintang Propaganda Department on February 13, and similarly he only mutters and dares not openly object. He differs sharply from Li Tsung-jen who dares to accept the punishment of war criminals as one of the basic terms for negotiations.

But there is still something lovable about President Sun, for he says that although the Communist Party "also worships force", as shown by two points, "delaying the appointment of its delegation" and "refusing to cease hostilities as a first step", yet it is not like the Kuomintang, which worshipped force as early as 1946 and unleashed a most cruel war. Well, the Communist Party has "delayed the appointment of its delegation" because making a list of war criminals is an important matter, it must be "acceptable to the people of the whole country" and a list that is too long or too short would be unrealistic and unacceptable to "the people of the whole country" (whose ranks do not include the war criminals and their accomplices). This requires consultation with the democratic parties and people's organizations; it has therefore caused some "stalling", and we were not able to appoint our delegates quickly, thus arousing the displeasure of Sun Fo and his like. But from this, one cannot jump to the conclusion that the Communist Party "also worships force". It is probable that before long the list of war criminals will be published, our delegates named and the negotiations started; and then President Sun will not be able to say that we "worship force".

As for "refusing to cease hostilities as a first step", this is a correct attitude adopted in obedience to President Chiang's New Year's Day message. In that message President Chiang said:

> As soon as the Communist Party has a sincere desire for peace and can give definite indications of this, the Government will certainly meet it in all sincerity and be willing to discuss concrete measures for ending hostilities and restoring peace.

On January 19 Sun Fo's Executive Yuan passed a resolution in violation of Chiang Kai-shek's message, saying "first, effect an immediate and unconditional cessation of hostilities, and then, appoint delegates to enter into peace negotiations". On January 21 a Chinese Communist Party spokesman sternly criticized this absurd resolution.[4] Curiously enough, the president of the Executive Yuan turned a deaf ear to the criticism and on February 7 again nonsensically said that the Communist Party's "refusal to cease hostilities as a first step" was proof that it "also worships force". Even such a war criminal as Chiang Kai-shek knows that without negotiations it is impossible to cease hostilities and restore peace; on this point Sun Fo is far behind Chiang Kai-shek.

As is generally known, Sun Fo is listed as a war criminal because he has all along supported Chiang Kai-shek in launching and continuing the war. As late as June 22, 1947, he was still saying that a "settlement will finally come, provided militarily we fight to the end" and that "at present peace negotiations are out of the question, and the Government must crush the Communist Party of China or be overthrown by it".[5] Sun Fo himself is one of those "certain members" of the Kuomintang who worshipped force. But now he is making irresponsible and carping comments from the side-lines, as if he himself had never worshipped force and bore no responsibility for the failure to carry out the Three People's Principles. This is dishonest. Whether tried according to the law of the state or judged according to the party discipline of the Kuomintang, Sun Fo cannot escape the caning he deserves.

NOTES

[1] A famous slogan of Sun Yat-sen. (See "On New Democracy", Section 6, *Selected Works of Mao Tse-tung*, Vol. II.) Here it is used as a pun in ridicule of Sun Fo.

[2] This refers to the region of the Yi and Meng Mountains in Shantung Province. It was the 46th Army of the Kwangsi clique which attacked this region jointly with Chiang Kai-shek's troops. This army had been brought from Hainan Island by sea and landed at Tsingtao in October 1946. It was completely wiped out in February 1947 in the Laiwu region of Shantung Province.

[3] A reactionary politician, the head of the small reactionary Democratic Socialist Party. See "Greet the New High Tide of the Chinese Revolution", Note 8, p. 126 of this volume and "On New Democracy", Note 9, *Selected Works of Mao Tse-tung*, Vol. II.

[4] See "Comment by the Spokesman for the Communist Party of China on the Resolution of the Nanking Executive Yuan", pp. 321-23 of this volume.

[5] This refers to the remarks made in Nanking on June 22, 1947 by Sun Fo, then vice-president of the Kuomintang government, when he received reporters of the Associated Press, the Kuomintang *Central Daily News* and the *Hsin Min Pao*.

REPORT TO THE SECOND PLENARY SESSION OF THE SEVENTH CENTRAL COMMITTEE OF THE COMMUNIST PARTY OF CHINA*

March 5, 1949

I

With the conclusion of the Liaohsi-Shenyang, Huai-Hai and Peiping-Tientsin campaigns, the main force of the Kuomintang army has been destroyed. Only a million odd of its combat troops are left, dispersed over vast areas from Sinkiang to Taiwan and over extremely long fronts. From now on there can be only three patterns for disposing of these Kuomintang troops – the Tientsin pattern, the Peiping pattern or the Suiyuan pattern.[1] To dispose of the enemy forces by fighting, as we did in Tientsin, must still be the primary object of our attention and preparations. The commanders and fighters of the entire Chinese People's Liberation Army absolutely must not relax in the least their will to fight; any thinking that relaxes the will to fight and belittles the enemy is wrong. The possibility has increased for solutions on the Peiping pattern, that is, to compel enemy troops to reorganize peacefully, quickly and thoroughly into the People's Liberation Army in conformity with the latter's system. For the purpose of rapidly eliminating the vestiges of counter-revolution and liquidating its political influence, this solution is not quite as effective as the solution by fighting. However, it is bound to occur and is unavoidable after the main force of the enemy has been destroyed; furthermore, it is advantageous to our army and the people because casualties and destruction can be avoided. Therefore, the leading comrades of the various field armies should all pay attention to this form of struggle and learn how to use it. This is one form of struggle, a form of struggle without bloodshed; it does not mean that problems can be solved

361

without struggle. The Suiyuan pattern is deliberately to keep part of the Kuomintang troops wholly or nearly intact, that is, to make temporary concessions to these troops in order to help win them over to our side or neutralize them politically. Thereby, we can concentrate our forces to finish off the main part of the remnant Kuomintang forces first and then, after a certain period (say, a few months, half a year or a year later), proceed to reorganize these troops into the People's Liberation Army in conformity with its system. That is another form of struggle. It will preserve more of the vestiges and political influence of counter-revolution than the Peiping form and for a longer period. But there is not the slightest doubt that they will eventually be eliminated. It must never be assumed that, once they yield to us, the counter-revolutionaries turn into revolutionaries, that their counter-revolutionary ideas and designs cease to exist. Definitely not. Many of the counter-revolutionaries will be remoulded, some will be sifted out, and certain die-hard counter-revolutionaries will be suppressed.

II

The People's Liberation Army is always a fighting force. Even after country-wide victory, our army will remain a fighting force during the historical period in which classes have not been abolished in our country and the imperialist system still exists in the world. On this point there should be no misunderstanding or wavering. The People's Liberation Army is also a working force; this will be the case especially when the Peiping or the Suiyuan pattern of solution is used in the

---

* The Seventh Central Committee of the Communist Party of China held its Second Plenary Session in Hsipaipo Village, Pingshan County, Hopei Province, from March 5 to 13, 1949. Thirty-four members and nineteen alternate members of the Central Committee were present. This session, which was convened on the eve of the country-wide victory of the Chinese people's revolution, was extremely important. In his report at the session, Comrade Mao Tse-tung set forth policies to promote the speedy achievement of the country-wide victory of the revolution and to organize this victory. He explained that with this victory the centre of gravity of the Party's work should be shifted from the village to the city, defined the basic political, economic and foreign policies the Party should adopt after victory and set the general tasks and main course for transforming China from an agricultural into an industrial country, from a new-democratic into a socialist society. In particular, he analysed the current conditions in the different sectors of China's economy and the correct policies the Party had to adopt, pointed out the necessary ways to realize the socialist transforma-

south.   With the gradual decrease in hostilities, its function as a working force will increase.   There is a possibility that before very long the entire People's Liberation Army will be turned into a working force, and we must take this possibility into account.   The 53,000 cadres now ready to leave with the army for the south are very inadequate for the vast new areas we shall soon hold, and we must prepare to turn all the field armies, 2,100,000 strong, into a working force. In that event, there will be enough cadres and the work can develop over large areas.   We must look upon the field armies with their 2,100,000 men as a gigantic school for cadres.

III

From 1927 to the present the centre of gravity of our work has been in the villages – gathering strength in the villages, using the villages in order to surround the cities and then taking the cities. The period for this method of work has now ended.   The period of "from the city to the village" and of the city leading the village has now begun.   The centre of gravity of the Party's work has shifted from the village to the city.   In the south the People's Liberation Army will occupy first the cities and then the villages.   Attention must be given to both city and village and it is necessary to link closely urban and rural work, workers and peasants, industry and agriculture. Under no circumstances should the village be ignored and only the city given attention; such thinking is entirely wrong.   Nevertheless, the centre of gravity of the work of the Party and the army must be

tion in China, criticized various "Left" and Right deviations on this question and expressed the firm conviction that China's economy would develop at a comparatively high speed.   Comrade Mao Tse-tung appraised the new situation in the class struggle both at home and abroad following the victory of the Chinese people's democratic revolution and gave timely warning that the "sugar-coated bullets" of the bourgeoisie would become the main danger to the proletariat.   All this gives the document great significance for a long historical period.   This report and his article *On the People's Democratic Dictatorship*, written in June of the same year, formed the basis for the policies embodied in the Common Programme adopted by the First Plenary Session of the Chinese People's Political Consultative Conference, which served as a provisional constitution after the founding of New China.   The Second Plenary Session of the Seventh Central Committee of the Party adopted a resolution based on Comrade Mao Tse-tung's report.   After the session, the Central Committee of the Communist Party of China moved from Hsipaipo, Pingshan County, Hopei Province to Peiping.

in the cities; we must do our utmost to learn how to administer and
build the cities.   In the cities we must learn how to wage political,
economic and cultural struggles against the imperialists, the Kuomintang and the bourgeoisie and also how to wage diplomatic struggles
against the imperialists.   We must learn how to carry on overt struggles against them, we must also learn how to carry on covert struggles
against them.   If we do not pay attention to these problems, if we do
not learn how to wage these struggles against them and win victory
in the struggles, we shall be unable to maintain our political power,
we shall be unable to stand on our feet, we shall fail.   After the
enemies with guns have been wiped out, there will still be enemies
without guns; they are bound to struggle desperately against us; we
must never regard these enemies lightly.   If we do not now raise and
understand the problem in this way, we shall commit very grave
mistakes.

IV

On whom shall we rely in our struggles in the cities?   Some
muddle-headed comrades think we should rely not on the working
class but on the masses of the poor.   Some comrades who are even more
muddle-headed think we should rely on the bourgeoisie.   As for the
direction of industrial development, some muddle-headed comrades
maintain that we should chiefly help the development of private enterprise and not state enterprise, whereas others hold the opposite view
that it suffices to pay attention to state enterprise and that private
enterprise is of little importance.   We must criticize these muddled
views.   We must whole-heartedly rely on the working class, unite
with the rest of the labouring masses, win over the intellectuals and
win over to our side as many as possible of the national bourgeois
elements and their representatives who can co-operate with us – or
neutralize them – so that we can wage a determined struggle against
the imperialists, the Kuomintang and the bureaucrat-capitalist class
and defeat these enemies step by step.   Meanwhile we shall set about
our task of construction and learn, step by step, how to administer cities
and restore and develop their production.   Regarding the problem
of restoring and developing production we must be clear about the
following: first comes the production of state industry, second the

production of private industry and third handicraft production. From the very first day we take over a city, we should direct our attention to restoring and developing its production. We must not go about our work blindly and haphazardly and forget our central task, lest several months after taking over a city its production and construction should still not be on the right track and many industries should be at a standstill, with the result that the workers are unemployed, their livelihood deteriorates and they become dissatisfied with the Communist Party. Such a state of affairs is entirely impermissible. Therefore, our comrades must do their utmost to learn the techniques of production and the methods of managing production as well as other closely related work such as commerce and banking. Only when production in the cities is restored and developed, when consumer-cities are transformed into producer-cities, can the people's political power be consolidated. Other work in the cities, for example, in Party organization, in organs of political power, in trade unions and other people's organizations, in culture and education, in the suppression of counter-revolutionaries, in news agencies, newspapers and broadcasting stations – all this work revolves around and serves the central task, production and construction. If we know nothing about production and do not master it quickly, if we cannot restore and develop production as speedily as possible and achieve solid successes so that the livelihood of the workers, first of all, and that of the people in general is improved, we shall be unable to maintain our political power, we shall be unable to stand on our feet, we shall fail.

V

Conditions in the south are different from those in the north, and the Party's tasks must also be different. The south is still under Kuomintang rule. There, the tasks of the Party and the People's Liberation Army are to wipe out the Kuomintang's reactionary armed forces in city and countryside, set up Party organizations, set up organs of political power, arouse the masses, establish trade unions, peasant associations and other people's organizations, build the people's armed forces, mop up the remnant Kuomintang forces and restore and develop production. In the countryside, our first tasks are to wage struggles step by step, to clean out the bandits and to oppose the local tyrants (the section of the landlord class in power) in order to complete preparations for the reduction of rent and interest; this reduction can then be accomplished within a year or two after the arrival of the People's Liberation Army, and the precondition for the distribution of land will thus be created. At the same time care must be taken to maintain the present level of agricultural production as far as possible and to prevent it from declining. In the north, except for the few new Liberated Areas, conditions are completely different. Here the Kuomintang rule has been overthrown, the people's rule has been established and the land problem has been fundamentally solved. Here the central task of the Party is to mobilize all forces to restore and develop production; this should be the centre of gravity in all work. It is also necessary to restore and develop cultural and educational work, wipe out the remnants of the reactionary forces, consolidate the entire north and support the People's Liberation Army.

VI

We have already carried out extensive economic construction, and the Party's economic policy has been implemented in practice and has achieved marked success. However, there are still many muddled views within the Party on the question of why we should adopt this kind of economic policy and not another, i.e., on a question of theory and principle. How should this question be answered? In our opinion, the answer should be as follows. Before the War of Resistance Against Japan, the proportions of industry and agriculture in the entire national economy of China were, modern industry about 10 per cent, and agriculture and handicrafts about 90 per cent. This was the result of imperialist and feudal oppression; this was the economic expression of the semi-colonial and semi-feudal character of the society of old China; and this is our basic point of departure for all questions during the period of the Chinese revolution and for a fairly long period after victory. This gives rise to a series of problems regarding our Party's strategy, tactics and policy. An important task for our Party at present is to reach a clearer understanding of these problems and their solution. That is to say:

1. China already has a modern industry constituting about 10 per cent of her economy; this is progressive, this is different from

ancient times. As a result, China has new classes and new political parties – the proletariat and the bourgeoisie, proletarian and bourgeois parties. The proletariat and its party, because they have been oppressed by manifold enemies, have become steeled and are qualified to lead the Chinese people's revolution. Whoever overlooks or belittles this point will commit Right opportunist mistakes.

2.   China still has scattered and individual agriculture and handicrafts, constituting about 90 per cent of her entire economy; this is backward, this is not very different from ancient times – about 90 per cent of our economic life remains the same as in ancient times. We have abolished, or will soon abolish, the age-old feudal ownership of land. In this respect, we have become, or will soon become, different from what we were in ancient times, and have or will soon have the possibility of modernizing our agriculture and handicrafts step by step. In their basic form, however, our agriculture and handicrafts today are still scattered and individual, somewhat as they were in ancient times, and they will remain so for a fairly long time to come. Whoever overlooks or belittles this point will commit "Left" opportunist mistakes.

3.   China's modern industry, though the value of its output amounts to only about 10 per cent of the total value of output of the national economy, is extremely concentrated; the largest and most important part of the capital is concentrated in the hands of the imperialists and their lackeys, the Chinese bureaucrat-capitalists. The confiscation of this capital and its transfer to the people's republic led by the proletariat will enable the people's republic to control the economic lifelines of the country and will enable the state-owned economy to become the leading sector of the entire national economy. This sector of the economy is socialist, not capitalist, in character. Whoever overlooks or belittles this point will commit Right opportunist mistakes.

4.   China's private capitalist industry, which occupies second place in her modern industry, is a force which must not be ignored. Because they have been oppressed or hemmed in by imperialism, feudalism and bureaucrat-capitalism, the national bourgeoisie of China and its representatives have often taken part in the people's democratic revolutionary struggles or maintained a neutral stand. For this reason and because China's economy is still backward, there will be need, for a fairly long period after the victory of the revolution, to make use of the positive qualities of urban and rural private capitalism as far as possible, in the interest of developing the national economy.

In this period, all capitalist elements in the cities and countryside which are not harmful but beneficial to the national economy should be allowed to exist and expand. This is not only unavoidable but also economically necessary. But the existence and expansion of capitalism in China will not be unrestricted and uncurbed as in the capitalist countries. It will be restricted from several directions – in the scope of its operation and by tax policy, market prices and labour conditions. We shall adopt well-measured and flexible policies for restricting capitalism from several directions according to the specific conditions in each place, each industry and each period. It is necessary and useful for us to apply Sun Yat-sen's slogan of "regulation of capital".[2] However, in the interest of the whole national economy and in the present and future interest of the working class and all the labouring people, we must not restrict the private capitalist economy too much or too rigidly, but must leave room for it to exist and develop within the framework of the economic policy and planning of the people's republic. The policy of restricting private capitalism is bound to meet with resistance in varying degrees and forms from the bourgeoisie, especially from the big owners of private enterprises, that is, from the big capitalists. Restriction versus opposition to restriction will be the main form of class struggle in the new-democratic state. It is entirely wrong to think that at present we need not restrict capitalism and can discard the slogan of "regulation of capital"; that is a Right opportunist view. But the opposite view, which advocates too much or too rigid restriction of private capital or holds that we can simply eliminate private capital very quickly, is also entirely wrong; this is a "Left" opportunist or adventurist view.

5. Scattered, individual agriculture and handicrafts, which make up 90 per cent of the total value of output of the national economy, can and must be led prudently, step by step and yet actively to develop towards modernization and collectivization; the view that they may be left to take their own course is wrong. It is necessary to organize producers', consumers' and credit co-operatives and leading organs of the co-operatives at national, provincial, municipal, county and district levels. Such co-operatives are collective economic organizations of the labouring masses, based on private ownership and under the direction of the state power led by the proletariat. The fact that the Chinese people are culturally backward and have no tradition of organizing co-operatives may confront us with difficulties, but co-operatives can and must be organized and must be promoted and

developed. If there were only a state-owned economy and no co-operative economy, it would be impossible for us to lead the individual economy of the labouring people step by step towards collectivization, impossible to develop from the new-democratic society to the future socialist society and impossible to consolidate the leadership of the proletariat in the state power. Whoever overlooks or belittles this point will also commit extremely serious mistakes. The state-owned economy is socialist in character and the co-operative economy is semi-socialist; these plus private capitalism, plus the individual economy, plus the state-capitalist economy in which the state and private capitalists work jointly, will be the chief sectors of the economy of the people's republic and will constitute the new-democratic economic structure.

6. The restoration and development of the national economy of the people's republic would be impossible without a policy of controlling foreign trade. When imperialism, feudalism, bureaucrat-capitalism and the concentrated expression of all three, the Kuomintang regime, have been eliminated in China, the problem of establishing an independent and integrated industrial system will remain unsolved and it will be finally solved only when our country has greatly developed economically and changed from a backward agricultural into an advanced industrial country. It will be impossible to achieve this aim without controlling foreign trade. After the country-wide victory of the Chinese revolution and the solution of the land problem, two basic contradictions will still exist in China. The first is internal, that is, the contradiction between the working class and the bourgeoisie. The second is external, that is, the contradiction between China and the imperialist countries. Consequently, after the victory of the people's democratic revolution, the state power of the people's republic under the leadership of the working class must not be weakened but must be strengthened. The two basic policies of the state in the economic struggle will be regulation of capital at home and control of foreign trade. Whoever overlooks or belittles this point will commit extremely serious mistakes.

7. China has inherited a backward economy. But the Chinese people are brave and industrious. With the victory of the Chinese people's revolution and the founding of the people's republic, and with the leadership of the Communist Party of China, plus the support of the working class of the countries of the world and chiefly the support of the Soviet Union, the speed of China's economic construction will

not be very slow, but may be fairly fast. The day is not far off when China will attain prosperity. There is absolutely no ground for pessimism about China's economic resurgence.

VII

Old China was a semi-colonial country under imperialist domination. Thoroughly anti-imperialist in character, the Chinese people's democratic revolution has incurred the bitter hatred of the imperialists who have done their utmost to help the Kuomintang. This has aroused the Chinese people to even deeper indignation against the imperialists and deprived them of their last shred of prestige among the Chinese people. At the same time the whole imperialist system is very much weakened after World War II, while the strength of the world anti-imperialist front headed by the Soviet Union is greater than ever before. In these circumstances, we can and should adopt a policy of systematically and completely destroying imperialist domination in China. This imperialist domination manifests itself in the political, economic and cultural fields. In each city or place where the Kuomintang troops are wiped out and the Kuomintang government is overthrown, imperialist political domination is overthrown with it, and so is imperialist economic and cultural domination. But the economic and cultural establishments run directly by the imperialists are still there, and so are the diplomatic personnel and the journalists recognized by the Kuomintang. We must deal with all these properly in their order of urgency. Refuse to recognize the legal status of any foreign diplomatic establishments and personnel of the Kuomintang period, refuse to recognize all the treasonable treaties of the Kuomintang period, abolish all imperialist propaganda agencies in China, take immediate control of foreign trade and reform the customs system — these are the first steps we must take upon entering the big cities. When they have acted thus, the Chinese people will have stood up in the face of imperialism. As for the remaining imperialist economic and cultural establishments, they can be allowed to exist for the time being, subject to our supervision and control, to be dealt with by us after country-wide victory. As for ordinary foreign nationals, their legitimate interests will be protected and not encroached upon. As for the question of the recognition of our country by the imperialist countries, we should not be in a hurry to solve it now and need not be in a hurry to solve it even for a fairly long period after country-wide victory. We are willing to establish diplomatic relations with all countries on the principle of equality, but the imperialists, who have always been hostile to the Chinese people, will definitely not be in a hurry to treat us as equals. As long as the imperialist coun-tries do not change their hostile attitude, we shall not grant them legal status in China. As for doing business with foreigners, there is no question; wherever there is business to do, we shall do it and we have already started; the businessmen of several capitalist coun-tries are competing for such business. So far as possible, we must first of all trade with the socialist and people's democratic countries; at the same time we will also trade with capitalist countries.

VIII

All the conditions are ripe for convening the Political Consultative Conference and forming a democratic coalition government. All the democratic parties, people's organizations and democrats without party affiliation are on our side. The bourgeoisie in Shanghai and in the Yangtse valley are trying to establish contacts with us. Navigation and postal communications between north and south have been resumed. The disintegrating Kuomintang has alienated itself from all the masses. We are preparing to have negotiations with the reaction-ary Nanking government.[3] Its moving forces for negotiating with us are the warlords of the Kwangsi clique, those factions of the Kuomin-tang favouring peace and the Shanghai bourgeoisie. Their aims are to obtain a share in the coalition government, retain as many troops as possible, preserve the interests of the bourgeoisie in Shanghai and the south and do their best to moderate the revolution. These groups recognize our eight terms as the basis for negotiations, but they want to bargain so that their losses will not be too great. Those trying to wreck the negotiations are Chiang Kai-shek and his sworn followers. Chiang Kai-shek still has sixty divisions south of the Yangtse and they are preparing to fight. Our policy is not to refuse negotiations, but to demand that the other side accept the eight terms in their entirety and to allow no bargaining. In return, we would refrain from fighting the Kwangsi clique and the other Kuomintang factions which favour peace, postpone the reorganization of their troops for about a year, allow some individuals in the Nanking government to take part in the Political Consultative Conference and the coalition government and agree to protect certain interests of the bourgeoisie in Shanghai and in the south.   The negotiations are to be on an over-all basis and, if successful, they will reduce many obstacles to our advance into the south and to the take-over of the big cities there, which will have great advantages.   If they are not successful, then separate negotiations on a local basis will be held after our army advances.   The negotiations on an over-all basis are tentatively fixed for late March.   We hope to occupy Nanking by April or May, then convene the Political Con-sultative Conference in Peiping, form a coalition government and make Peiping the capital.   Since we have agreed to hold negotiations, we should be prepared for the many troubles which will arise after the success of the negotiations, and we should be ready with clear heads to deal with the tactics the other side will adopt, the tactics of the Monkey who gets into the stomach of the Princess of the Iron Fan to play the devil.[4]   As long as we are fully prepared mentally, we can beat any devilish Monkey.   Whether the peace negotiations are over-all or local, we should be prepared for such an eventuality.   We should not refuse to enter into negotiations because we are afraid of trouble and want to avoid complications, nor should we enter into negotiations with our minds in a haze.   We should be firm in prin-ciple; we should also have all the flexibility permissible and necessary for carrying out our principles.

IX

The people's democratic dictatorship, led by the proletariat and based on the worker-peasant alliance, requires that our Party con-scientiously unite the entire working class, the entire peasantry and the broad masses of revolutionary intellectuals; these are the leading and basic forces of the dictatorship.   Without this unity, the dictator-ship cannot be consolidated.   It is also required that our Party unite with as many as possible of the representatives of the urban petty bourgeoisie and national bourgeoisie who can co-operate with us and with their intellectuals and political groups, so that, during the rev-olutionary period, we can isolate the counter-revolutionary forces and completely overthrow both the counter-revolutionary and imperialist forces in China and so that, after the victory of the revolution, we can speedily restore and develop production, cope with foreign imperialism, steadily transform China from an agricultural into an industrial country and build China into a great socialist state.   There- fore, our Party's policy of long-term co-operation with non-Party democrats should be clearly established in the thinking and work of the whole Party.   We must regard the majority of non-Party democrats as we do our own cadres, consult with them sincerely and frankly to solve those problems that call for consultation and solution, give them work, entrust them with the responsibility and authority that should go with their posts and help them do their work well.   Proceed- ing from the desire to unite with them, we should carry out serious and appropriate criticism or struggle against their errors and shortcomings in order to attain the objective of unity.   It would be wrong to adopt an accommodating attitude towards their errors or shortcomings.   It would also be wrong to adopt a closed-door or perfunctory attitude towards them.   In each big or medium city, each strategic region and each province, we should develop a group of non-Party democrats who have prestige and can co-operate with us.   The incorrect attitude towards non-Party democrats, fostered by the closed-door style in our Party during the War of Agrarian Revolution, was not entirely overcome during the War of Resistance Against Japan, and it re- appeared in 1947 during the high tide of the land reform in the base areas.   This attitude would serve only to isolate our Party, prevent the consolidation of the people's democratic dictatorship and enable the enemy to obtain allies.   Now that China's first Political Consultative Conference under the leadership of our Party will soon be convened, that a democratic coalition government will soon be formed and that the revolution will soon be victorious throughout the country, the whole Party must make a serious and self-critical examination of this problem and understand it correctly; it must oppose the two deviations, the Right deviation of accommodation and the closed-door and perfunc- tory "Left" deviation, and adopt an entirely correct attitude.

X

Very soon we shall be victorious throughout the country.   This victory will breach the eastern front of imperialism and will have great international significance.   To win this victory will not require

much more time and effort, but to consolidate it will.   The bourgeoisie
doubts our ability to construct.   The imperialists reckon that eventually we will beg alms from them in order to live.   With victory,
certain moods may grow within the Party – arrogance, the airs of a
self-styled hero, inertia and unwillingness to make progress, love of
pleasure and distaste for continued hard living.   With victory, the
people will be grateful to us and the bourgeoisie will come forward to
flatter us.   It has been proved that the enemy cannot conquer us by
force of arms.   However, the flattery of the bourgeoisie may conquer
the weak-willed in our ranks.   There may be some Communists, who
were not conquered by enemies with guns and were worthy of the
name of heroes for standing up to these enemies, but who cannot withstand sugar-coated bullets; they will be defeated by sugar-coated
bullets.   We must guard against such a situation.   To win country-
wide victory is only the first step in a long march of ten thousand *li*.
Even if this step is worthy of pride, it is comparatively tiny; what
will be more worthy of pride is yet to come.   After several decades,
the victory of the Chinese people's democratic revolution, viewed in
retrospect, will seem like only a brief prologue to a long drama.   A
drama begins with a prologue, but the prologue is not the climax.
The Chinese revolution is great, but the road after the revolution will
be longer, the work greater and more arduous.   This must be made
clear now in the Party.   The comrades must be taught to remain
modest, prudent and free from arrogance and rashness in their style
of work.   The comrades must be taught to preserve the style of plain
living and hard struggle.   We have the Marxist-Leninist weapon of
criticism and self-criticism.   We can get rid of a bad style and keep
the good.   We can learn what we did not know.   We are not only
good at destroying the old world, we are also good at building the
new.   Not only can the Chinese people live without begging alms
from the imperialists, they will live a better life than that in the
imperialist countries.

NOTES

[1] On September 19, 1949, Tung Chi-wu, Kuomintang governor of Suiyuan
Province, and Sun Lan-feng, Kuomintang army commander, revolted and came over
with more than forty thousand men.   The regrouping of these units began on
February 21, 1950, under the leadership of the Suiyuan Military Command of the
People's Liberation Army.   They were reorganized into the People's Liberation Army
on April 10.

[2] "Regulation of capital" was one of Sun Yat-sen's well-known slogans. The Manifesto of the Kuomintang's First National Congress, in which the Kuomintang and the Communist Party co-operated, was published on January 23, 1924 and gave the following interpretation to this slogan: "Private industries, whether of Chinese or of foreign nationals, which are either of a monopolistic nature or are beyond the capacity of private individuals to develop, such as banking, railways, and navigation, shall be undertaken by the state, so that privately owned capital shall not control the economic life of the people."

[3] Concerning peace negotiations with the reactionary Nanking Kuomintang government, the Central Committee of the Communist Party of China made the following decisions on March 26, 1949:

(1)   Time for the negotiations to begin, April 1;

(2)   Place for the negotiations, Peiping;

(3)   Chou En-lai, Lin Po-chu, Lin Piao, Yeh Chien-ying and Li Wei-han are appointed as delegates (on April 1, the Central Committee decided to add Nieh Jung-chen to the list of delegates), with Chou En-lai as chief delegate, to negotiate with the Nanking delegation on the basis of Chairman Mao Tse-tung's Statement on the Present Situation made on January 14 and the eight terms set forth therein;

(4)   The reactionary Nanking Kuomintang government is to be immediately notified of the aforesaid by radio broadcast and told to send its delegation to the specified place, at the specified time and, in order to facilitate the negotiations, to bring all necessary material relating to the eight terms.

[4] For the story of how Sun Wu-kung, the Monkey, changed himself into a tiny insect, found his way into the stomach of the Princess of the Iron Fan and thus defeated her, see the Chinese novel, *Pilgrimage to the West*, Chapter 59.

METHODS OF WORK OF PARTY COMMITTEES*

March 13, 1949

1. The secretary of a Party committee must be good at being a "squad leader". A Party committee has ten to twenty members; it is like a squad in the army, and the secretary is like the "squad leader". It is indeed not easy to lead this squad well. Each bureau or sub-bureau of the Central Committee now leads a vast area and shoulders very heavy responsibilities. To lead means not only to decide general and specific policies but also to devise correct methods of work. Even with correct general and specific policies, troubles may still arise if methods of work are neglected. To fulfil its task of exercising leadership, a Party committee must rely on its "squad members" and enable them to play their parts to the full. To be a good "squad leader", the secretary should study hard and investigate thoroughly. A secretary or deputy secretary will find it difficult to direct his "squad" well if he does not take care to do propaganda and organizational work among his own "squad members", is not good at handling his relations with committee members or does not study how to run meetings successfully. If the "squad members" do not march in step, they can never expect to lead tens of millions of people in fighting and construction. Of course, the relation between the secretary and the committee members is one in which the minority must obey the majority, so it is different from the relation between a squad leader and his men. Here we speak only by way of analogy.

2. Place problems on the table. This should be done not only by the "squad leader" but by the committee members too. Do not talk behind people's backs. Whenever problems arise, call a meeting, place the problems on the table for discussion, take some decisions and the problems will be solved. If problems exist and are not placed on the table, they will remain unsolved for a long time and even drag on for years. The "squad leader" and the committee members should show understanding in their relations with each other.

Nothing is more important than mutual understanding, support and friendship between the secretary and the committee members, between the Central Committee and its bureaus and between the bureaus and the area Party committees. In the past this point received little attention, but since the Seventh Party Congress much progress has been made in this respect and the ties of friendship and unity have been greatly strengthened. We should continue to pay constant attention to this point in the future.

3. "Exchange information." This means that members of a Party committee should keep each other informed and exchange views on matters that have come to their attention. This is of great importance in achieving a common language. Some fail to do so and, like the people described by Lao Tzu, "do not visit each other all their lives, though the crowing of their cocks and the barking of their dogs are within hearing of each other".[1] The result is that they lack a common language. In the past some of our high-ranking cadres did not have a common language even on basic theoretical problems of Marxism-Leninism, because they had not studied enough. There is more of a common language in the Party today, but the problem has not yet been fully solved. For instance, in the land reform there is still some difference in the understanding of what is meant by "middle peasants" and "rich peasants".

4. Ask your subordinates about matters you don't understand or don't know, and do not lightly express your approval or disapproval. Some documents, after having been drafted, are withheld from circulation for a time because certain questions in them need to be clarified and it is necessary to consult the lower levels first. We should never pretend to know what we don't know, we should "not feel ashamed to ask and learn from people below"[2] and we should listen carefully to the views of the cadres at the lower levels. Be a pupil before you become a teacher; learn from the cadres at the lower levels before you issue orders. In handling problems, this should be the practice of all bureaus of the Central Committee and Party committees of the fronts, except in military emergencies or when the facts of the matter are already clear. To do this will not lower one's prestige, but can only raise it. Since our decisions incorporate the correct views of the cadres at the lower levels, the latter will naturally support them. What the cadres at the lower levels say may or may not be correct; we must analyse it.

---

* This was part of Comrade Mao Tse-tung's concluding speech at the Second Plenary Session of the Seventh Central Committee of the Communist Party of China.

We must heed the correct views and act upon them. The reason why the leadership of the Central Committee is correct is chiefly that it synthesizes the material, reports and correct views coming from different localities. It would be difficult for the Central Committee to issue correct orders if the localities did not provide material and put forward opinions. Listen also to the mistaken views from below; it is wrong not to listen to them at all. Such views, however, are not to be acted upon but to be criticized.

5. Learn to "play the piano". In playing the piano all ten fingers are in motion; it won't do to move some fingers only and not others. But if all ten fingers press down at once, there is no melody. To produce good music, the ten fingers should move rhythmically and in co-ordination. A Party committee should keep a firm grasp on its central task and at the same time, around the central task, it should unfold the work in other fields. At present, we have to take care of many fields; we must look after the work in all the areas, armed units and departments, and not give all our attention to a few problems, to the exclusion of others. Wherever there is a problem, we must put our finger on it, and this is a method we must master. Some play the piano well and some badly, and there is a great difference in the melodies they produce. Members of Party committees must learn to "play the piano" well.

6. "Grasp firmly." That is to say, the Party committee must not merely "grasp", but must "grasp firmly", its main tasks. One can get a grip on something only when it is grasped firmly, without the slightest slackening. Not to grasp firmly is not to grasp at all. Naturally, one cannot get a grip on something with an open hand. When the hand is clenched as if grasping something but is not clenched tightly, there is still no grip. Some of our comrades do grasp the main tasks, but their grasp is not firm and so they cannot make a success of their work. It will not do to have no grasp at all, nor will it do if the grasp is not firm.

7. "Have a head for figures." That is to say, we must attend to the quantitative aspect of a situation or problem and make a basic quantitative analysis. Every quality manifests itself in a certain quantity, and without quantity there can be no quality. To this day many of our comrades still do not understand that they must attend to the quantitative aspect of things – the basic statistics, the main percentages and the quantitative limits that determine the qualities of things. They have no "figures" in their heads and as a result cannot

help making mistakes. For instance, in carrying out the land reform it is essential to have such figures as the percentages of landlords, rich peasants, middle peasants and poor peasants among the population and the amount of land owned by each group, because only on this basis can we formulate correct policies. Whom to call a rich peasant, whom a well-to-do middle peasant, and how much income derived from exploitation makes a person a rich peasant as distinct from a well-to-do middle peasant – in all these cases too, the quantitative limits must be ascertained. In all mass movements we must make a basic investigation and analysis of the number of active supporters, opponents and neutrals and must not decide problems subjectively and without basis.

8. "Notice to Reassure the Public." Notice of meetings should be given beforehand; this is like issuing a "Notice to Reassure the Public", so that everybody will know what is going to be discussed and what problems are to be solved and can make timely preparations. In some places, meetings of cadres are called without first preparing reports and draft resolutions, and only when people have arrived for the meeting are makeshifts improvised; this is just like the saying, "Troops and horses have arrived, but food and fodder are not ready", and that is no good. Don't call a meeting in a hurry if the preparations are not completed.

9. "Fewer and better troops and simpler administration." Talks, speeches, articles and resolutions should all be concise and to the point. Meetings also should not go on too long.

10. Pay attention to uniting and working with comrades who differ with you. This should be borne in mind both in the localities and in the army. It also applies to relations with people outside the Party. We have come together from every corner of the country and should be good at uniting in our work not only with comrades who hold the same views as we but also with those who hold different views. There are some among us who have made very serious mistakes; we should not be prejudiced against them but should be ready to work with them.

11. Guard against arrogance. For anyone in a leading position, this is a matter of principle and an important condition for maintaining unity. Even those who have made no serious mistakes and have achieved very great success in their work should not be arrogant. Celebration of the birthdays of Party leaders is forbidden. Naming places, streets and enterprises after Party leaders is likewise forbidden. We must keep to our style of plain living and hard work and put a stop to flattery and exaggerated praise.

12. Draw two lines of distinction. First, between revolution and counter-revolution, between Yenan and Sian.[3] Some do not understand that they must draw this line of distinction. For example, when they combat bureaucracy, they speak of Yenan as though "nothing is right" there and fail to make a comparison and distinguish between the bureaucracy in Yenan and the bureaucracy in Sian. This is fundamentally wrong. Secondly, within the revolutionary ranks, it is necessary to make a clear distinction between right and wrong, between achievements and shortcomings and to make clear which of the two is primary and which secondary. For instance, do the achievements amount to 30 per cent or to 70 per cent of the whole? It will not do either to understate or to overstate. We must have a fundamental evaluation of a person's work and establish whether his achievements amount to 30 per cent and his mistakes to 70 per cent, or vice versa. If his achievements amount to 70 per cent of the whole, then his work should in the main be approved. It would be entirely wrong to describe work in which the achievements are primary as work in which the mistakes are primary. In our approach to problems we must not forget to draw these two lines of distinction, between revolution and counter-revolution and between achievements and shortcomings. We shall be able to handle things well if we bear these two distinctions in mind; otherwise we shall confuse the nature of the problems. To draw these distinctions well, careful study and analysis are of course necessary. Our attitude towards every person and every matter should be one of analysis and study.

The members of the Political Bureau and I personally feel that only by using the above methods can Party committees do their work well. In addition to conducting Party congresses well, it is most important for the Party committees at all levels to perform their work of leadership well. We must make efforts to study and perfect the methods of work so as to raise further the Party committees' level of leadership.

NOTES

[1] The quotation is from *Lao Tzu*, Chapter LXXX.

[2] The quotation is from the *Confucian Analects*, Book V, "Kungyeh Chang".

[3] Yenan was the headquarters of the Central Committee of the Communist Party of China from January 1937 to March 1947; Sian was the centre of the reactionary rule of the Kuomintang in northwestern China. Comrade Mao Tse-tung cited the two cities as symbols of revolution and counter-revolution.

WHITHER THE NANKING GOVERNMENT?

April 4, 1949

Two roads are open to the Nanking Kuomintang government and its military and administrative personnel. Either they cling to the Chiang Kai-shek clique of war criminals and its master, U.S. imperialism, that is, continue to be the enemy of the people and so perish together with the Chiang Kai-shek clique of war criminals in the People's War of Liberation. Or they come over to the people, that is, break with the Chiang Kai-shek clique of war criminals and U.S. imperialism, perform meritorious service in the People's War of Liberation to atone for their crimes and so obtain clemency and understanding from the people. There is no third road.

There are three different groups of people in the government of Li Tsung-jen and Ho Ying-chin at Nanking.[1] One group stubbornly persist in following the first road. No matter how plausible they are in words, in deeds they are continuing to prepare for war, to betray the nation and to oppress and massacre the people who are demanding genuine peace. They are Chiang Kai-shek's followers even unto death. Another group want to follow the second road but have not yet been able to take any decisive action. The third group are hesitating at the crossroads, and it is uncertain which way they will go. They do not want to offend Chiang Kai-shek and the U.S. government, yet they hope that they will be understood and admitted by the camp of people's democracy. But this is an illusion and is impossible.

The Nanking government of Li Tsung-jen and Ho Ying-chin is mainly a mixture of people from the first and third groups, with only a handful from the second. To this day, this government remains a tool of Chiang Kai-shek and the U.S. government.

The massacre which occurred in Nanking on April 1[2] was no accident. It was the inevitable result of the actions taken by the government of Li Tsung-jen and Ho Ying-chin to protect Chiang Kai-shek, his sworn followers and the forces of U.S. aggression. It was the result of the absurd trumpeting about "honourable peace on an equal footing" by the government of Li Tsung-jen and Ho Ying-chin and by the sworn followers of Chiang Kai-shek, which had the purpose of countering the Chinese Communist Party's eight terms for peace, and particularly the punishment of war criminals. Now that the government of Li Tsung-jen and Ho Ying-chin has sent its delegation to Peiping to negotiate peace with the Communist Party of China and has indicated its willingness to accept the Communist Party's eight terms as the basis for negotiations, it should, if it has the slightest good faith, start by dealing with the Nanking Massacre, arrest and severely punish the chief criminals, Chiang Kai-shek, Tang En-po and Chang Yao-ming, arrest and severely punish the thugs of the secret police in Nanking and Shanghai and arrest and severely punish the chief counter-revolutionaries, who are obstinately opposing peace, actively disrupting the peace negotiations and actively preparing to resist the advance of the People's Liberation Army to the south of the Yangtse River. "Until Ching Fu is done away with, the crisis in the state of Lu will not be over."[3] Until the war criminals are eliminated, there will be no peace in the country. Isn't this truth clear enough by now?

We should like to speak plainly to the Nanking government. If you are unequal to this job, you should at least help the People's Liberation Army do it, as our army will soon cross the Yangtse River and advance south. At this late hour, you should not indulge in idle talk and had better do some real work to atone for your crimes. In that case you will not have to flee for your lives, you will not have to submit to the bullying of Chiang Kai-shek's sworn followers, and you will not be spurned for ever by the people. This is your last chance. Don't lose it. The People's Liberation Army will soon advance south of the Yangtse River. We are not bluffing. The People's Liberation Army will advance, whether or not you sign the agreement accepting the eight terms. An agreement signed before our army advances, will be advantageous to many – to the people, to the People's Liberation Army, to all those in the Kuomintang government who wish to atone for their crimes by performing meritorious service, and to the broad ranks of officers and men in the Kuomintang army; it will be disadvantageous only to Chiang Kai-shek, his sworn followers and the imperialists. If the agreement is not signed, the situation will be about the same; solutions can be achieved by local negotiations. There may yet be some fighting, but not much. Over the vast area and long front extending from Sinkiang to Taiwan, the Kuomintang has only about 1,100,000 combat troops left, and so there will not be much fighting. Whether a general agreement is signed, or whether no such agreement is signed but instead many local agreements are signed, it will be all the same for Chiang Kai-shek, for his sworn followers and for U.S. imperialism, in a word, for all those reactionaries who will not change even unto death; they are irrevocably doomed. Perhaps it will be slightly more advantageous to Nanking, as well as to ourselves, to sign rather than not to sign a general agreement, and that is why we are still striving to conclude it. But if a general agreement is to be signed, we must be prepared as a consequence to deal with many messy matters. It would be very much neater for us not to sign a general agreement but instead to sign many local agreements. Nevertheless, we are still ready to sign a general agreement. If the Nanking government and its delegation are also willing to do so, they must make up their minds in the next few days; all illusions and all empty talk should be discarded. We are not forcing you to make up your minds. The Nanking government and its delegation are free to make up their minds or not to. That is to say, you may either listen to Chiang Kai-shek and Leighton Stuart and side with them irrevocably, or listen to us and side with us; you are free to choose. But there is not much time for you to make your choice. The People's Liberation Army will soon start its march, and there is no opportunity left for hesitation.

NOTES

[1] After Sun Fo's resignation, Li Tsung-jen appointed Ho Ying-chin to succeed him as president of the bogus Executive Yuan on March 12, 1949.

[2] On April 1, 1949, over six thousand students from eleven colleges and universities in Nanking demonstrated, demanding that the reactionary Kuomintang government should accept the eight peace terms of the Chinese Communist Party. On the instructions of Chiang Kai-shek, Chang Yao-ming, commander-in-chief of the Kuomintang garrison forces at Nanking, ordered soldiers, policemen and secret agents to beat the students brutally; two were killed and more than a hundred wounded.

[3] According to Tso Chuan, an ancient Chinese historical work dealing with the important events of the Spring and Autumn Era (770-475 B.C.), Ching Fu, a noble in the state of Lu, repeatedly stirred up internal strife and murdered two reigning princes of that state. The saying in the text was then current among the people of Lu, and Ching Fu's name has since become a byword for those who stir up internal strife.

ORDER TO THE ARMY
FOR THE COUNTRY-WIDE ADVANCE*

April 21, 1949

Comrade commanders and fighters of all field armies, comrades of
the People's Liberation Army in the guerrilla areas of the south!

The Agreement on Internal Peace, drafted after long negotiations
between the delegation of the Communist Party of China and the
delegation of the Nanking Kuomintang government, has been rejected
by that government.[1] The responsible members of the Nanking Kuomintang government have rejected the agreement because they are
still obeying the orders of U.S. imperialism and Chiang Kai-shek, the
chieftain of the Kuomintang bandit gang, and because they are trying
to block the progress of the cause of the Chinese people's liberation
and prevent the internal problem from being solved by peaceful
means. The Agreement on Internal Peace, comprising eight sections
with twenty-four articles formulated by the two delegations in the
negotiations, is lenient on the problem of war criminals, is lenient
towards the Kuomintang officers, soldiers and government personnel
and provides appropriate solutions for other problems, all proceeding
from the interests of the nation and the people. The rejection of this
agreement shows that the Kuomintang reactionaries are determined
to fight to the finish the counter-revolutionary war which they started.
The rejection of this agreement shows that in proposing peace negotiations on January 1 of this year the Kuomintang reactionaries were
only trying to check the advance of the People's Liberation Army
and thus gain a breathing space for a later comeback to crush the
revolutionary forces. The rejection of this agreement shows that
the Li Tsung-jen government at Nanking was utterly hypocritical in
professing to accept the Chinese Communist Party's eight terms for
peace as the basis for negotiations. Inasmuch as the Li Tsung-jen
government had already accepted such fundamental terms as the

punishment of war criminals, the reorganization of all the reactionary Kuomintang troops on democratic principles and the handing over of all power and authority by the Nanking government and its subordinate governments at all levels, it had no reason to reject the specific measures which were drawn up on the basis of these fundamental terms and which are most lenient.   In these circumstances, we order you as follows:

1.   Advance bravely and annihilate resolutely, thoroughly, wholly and completely all the Kuomintang reactionaries within China's borders who dare to resist. Liberate the people of the whole country. Safeguard China's territorial integrity, sovereignty and independence.

2.   Advance bravely and arrest all the incorrigible war criminals. No matter where they may flee, they must be brought to justice and punished according to law.   Pay special attention to arresting the bandit chieftain Chiang Kai-shek.

3.   Proclaim to all Kuomintang local governments and local military groups the final amended version of the Agreement on Internal Peace.   In accordance with its general ideas, you may conclude local

---

* This order was drafted by Comrade Mao Tse-tung.   After the reactionary Kuomintang government refused to sign the Agreement on Internal Peace, the People's Liberation Army acted on this order issued by Chairman Mao Tse-tung and Commander-in-Chief Chu Teh and embarked upon a general advance, unprecedented in scale, into the vast areas which had not yet been liberated.   On the morning of April 21, 1949, the Second Field Army led by Liu Po-cheng, Teng Hsiao-ping and other comrades and the Third Field Army led by Chen Yi, Su Yu, Tan Chen-lin and other comrades, forced the Yangtse River on a front extending more than five hundred kilometres from Hukou (northeast of Kiukiang) in the west to Kiangyin in the east and completely destroyed the defence line along the Yangtse which the enemy had painstakingly built in three and a half months.   On April 23 these forces liberated Nanking, which had been the centre of the counter-revolutionary rule of the Kuomintang for twenty-two years, and proclaimed the downfall of the reactionary Kuomintang regime.   Then they thrust south along separate routes, liberated Hangchow on May 3 and Nanchang on May 22 and captured Shanghai, China's biggest city, on May 27. In June they began their march into Fukien Province; they liberated Foochow on August 17 and Amoy on October 17.   On May 14 the Fourth Field Army led by Lin Piao, Lo Jung-huan and other comrades forced the Yangtse on a front of more than one hundred kilometres in the Tuanfeng-Wuhsueh sector east of Wuhan.   On May 16 and 17 it liberated Wuchang, Hanyang and Hankow, cities of strategic importance in central China.   Then it marched south into Hunan.   Cheng Chien, Kuomintang governor of Hunan Province, and Chen Ming-jen, Commander of the 1st Army, renounced their allegiance to the Kuomintang on August 4, and Hunan Province was peacefully liberated.   The Fourth Field Army fought the Hengyang-Paoching campaign in September and October, wiped out the main force of the Kuomintang troops under Pai Chung-hsi and then pushed on to Kwangtung and Kwangsi Provinces.

agreements with those who are willing to cease hostilities and to settle matters by peaceful means.

4. After the People's Liberation Army has encircled Nanking, we are willing to give the Li Tsung-jen government at Nanking another opportunity to sign the Agreement on Internal Peace, if that government has not yet fled and dispersed and desires to sign it.

Mao Tse-tung

Chairman of the Chinese People's
Revolutionary Military Commission

Chu Teh

Commander-in-Chief of the Chinese
People's Liberation Army

It liberated Canton on October 14, Kweilin on November 22 and Nanning on December 4. While the Second and Third Field Armies were forcing the Yangtse River, the armies in northern China led by Nieh Jung-chen, Hsu Hsiang-chien and other comrades captured Taiyuan on April 24, 1949. The First Field Army led by Peng Teh-huai, Ho Lung and other comrades, after liberating Sian on May 20, continued its march into the Kuomintang areas in the Northwest together with two armies from northern China. They captured Lanchow on August 26, liberated Sining on September 5 and Yinchuan on September 23 and completely annihilated the Kuomintang troops under Ma Pu-fang and Ma Hung-kuei. Late in September Tao Chih-yueh, Kuomintang Garrison Commander-in-Chief of Sinkiang Province, and Burhan, the governor, renounced their allegiance to the Kuomintang, and Sinkiang was peacefully liberated. At the beginning of November the Second Field Army led by Liu Po-cheng, Teng Hsiao-ping and other comrades, together with the 18th Army of the Northern China Field Army and part of the First Field Army led by Ho Lung, Li Ching-chuan and other comrades, began their march into southwestern China. They liberated Kweiyang on November 15 and Chungking on November 30. On December 9 Lu Han, Kuomintang governor of Yunnan Province, Liu Wen-hui, Kuomintang governor of Sikang Province, and Teng Hsi-hou and Pan Wen-hua, deputy directors of the Kuomintang Bureau of Military and Administrative Affairs in the Southwest, renounced their allegiance to the Kuomintang, and the two provinces of Yunnan and Sikang were peacefully liberated. In late December the People's Liberation Army which had entered the Southwest fought the Chengtu campaign, completely wiped out the Kuomintang troops under Hu Tsung-nan and liberated Chengtu on December 27. By the end of December 1949 the People's Liberation Army had wiped out all the Kuomintang troops on China's mainland and liberated the entire mainland except Tibet.

NOTES

[1] On April 1, 1949, the Kuomintang government delegation headed by Chang
Chih-chung arrived in Peiping to negotiate peace with the delegation of the Communist Party of China. An Agreement on Internal Peace was drafted after a half
month of negotiations. The agreement (final amended version) was handed to the
Nanking government delegation by the delegation of the Communist Party of China
on April 15 and was rejected by the Nanking government on April 20. The full text
of the agreement (final amended version) is as follows:

In the 35th year of the Republic of China, the National Government at Nanking,
with the aid of the Government of the United States of America, defied the will of the
people, wrecked the truce agreement and the resolutions of the Political Consultative
Conference and, on the pretext of opposing the Communist Party of China, launched
a country-wide civil war against the Chinese people and the Chinese People's Liberation
Army. This war has lasted two years and nine and a half months. It has brought
untold disaster to the people throughout the country. The country has suffered
tremendous losses of financial and material resources, and its sovereignty has been
further infringed. The people of the whole country have always expressed dissatisfaction
with the National Government at Nanking for its violation of Dr. Sun Yat-sen's
revolutionary Three People's Principles and of his correct policies of alliance with
Russia, co-operation with the Communist Party and assistance to the peasants and workers, and for its violation of his revolutionary testament. In particular, the whole
people have voiced their opposition to the launching of the present unprecedented
large-scale civil war by the National Government at Nanking and to the erroneous
political, military, financial, economic, cultural and foreign policies and measures which
that government has adopted in its pursuit of the civil war. The National Government
at Nanking has completely forfeited the confidence of the entire people. In the present
civil war its troops have already been defeated by the People's Liberation Army led
by the Communist Party of China and commanded by the Chinese People's Revolutionary Military Commission. Finding itself in this situation, the National Government at Nanking proposed to the Communist Party of China on January 1 of the
38th year of the Republic of China that negotiations should be held for the cessation
of the civil war and the restoration of peace. On January 14 of the same year, the
Communist Party of China issued a statement agreeing to this proposal of the Kuomintang government at Nanking and putting forward eight terms as the basis for the
peace negotiations between the two sides. These terms are as follows: punish the
war criminals; abolish the bogus constitution; abolish the bogus "constituted
authority"; reorganize all reactionary troops on democratic principles; confiscate
bureaucrat-capital; reform the land system; abrogate treasonable treaties; convene
a New Political Consultative Conference without the participation of reactionary
elements and form a democratic coalition government to take over all the power
and authority of the reactionary Nanking Kuomintang government and of its subordinate governments at all levels. These eight basic terms were agreed to by the
National Government at Nanking. Thereupon, the Communist Party of China and
the National Government at Nanking appointed their respective delegations, fully
empowered to conduct negotiations and to sign an agreement. The delegates of
both parties met in Peiping, have affirmed first of all that the National Government
at Nanking should bear the full responsibility for the present civil war and for all its
erroneous policies and have agreed to conclude this agreement.

SECTION ONE

Article 1. In order to distinguish between right and wrong and to establish responsibility, the delegation of the Communist Party of China and the delegation of the National Government at Nanking (hereinafter referred to as both sides) affirm that, as a matter of principle, punishment shall be meted out to the war criminals of the National Government at Nanking who are held responsible for launching and prosecuting the present civil war, but that they will be dealt with on the merits of each case in accordance with the following conditions:

Item 1. All war criminals, no matter who they are, may be cleared of the charge of being war criminals and treated with leniency, provided they show by actual deeds that they are really sincere in distinguishing right from wrong and are determined to make a clean break with their past, thus facilitating the progress of the cause of the Chinese people's liberation and the peaceful settlement of the internal problem.

Item 2. All incorrigible war criminals, no matter who they are, shall be severely punished if they obstruct the progress of the cause of the people's liberation, hinder the peaceful settlement of the internal problem, or go so far as to instigate rebellion. The Chinese People's Revolutionary Military Commission will be responsible for suppressing the ringleaders of rebellion.

Article 2. Both sides affirm that the National Government at Nanking was wrong in pronouncing General Yasuji Okamura, war criminal in the Japanese aggression against China, not guilty and releasing him on January 26 of the 38th year of the Republic of China and in granting permission on January 31 of the same year for the repatriation to Japan of 260 other Japanese war criminals. The cases of all these Japanese war criminals shall be reopened as soon as the Democratic Coalition Government of China, the new central government representing the people throughout China, is formed.

SECTION TWO

Article 3. Both sides affirm that the "Constitution of the Republic of China", adopted by the "National Assembly" convened by the National Government at Nanking in November of the 35th year of the Republic of China, shall be abolished.

Article 4. After the abolition of the "Constitution of the Republic of China", the fundamental law to be observed by the state and the people shall be determined in accordance with the resolutions of the New Political Consultative Conference and the Democratic Coalition Government.

SECTION THREE

Article 5. Both sides affirm that the entire legally constituted authority of the National Government at Nanking shall be abolished.

Article 6. After the Democratic Coalition Government is formed, the people's democratic constituted authority shall be established, and all reactionary laws and decrees shall be annulled in all places entered and taken over by the People's Liberation Army.

SECTION FOUR

Article 7. Both sides affirm that all armed forces under the Nanking National Government (all the ground, naval and air forces, gendarmerie, communications police corps, local troops, all military institutions, academies, factories, rear-service establishments, etc.) shall be reorganized into the People's Liberation Army on democratic principles. After the signing of the Agreement on Internal Peace, a national reorganization committee shall be established at once to take charge of this work of reorganization. The reorganization committee is to consist of seven to nine members, four to five of whom shall be appointed by the People's Revolutionary Military Commission, and three to four by the National Government at Nanking, with one of the members appointed by the People's Revolutionary Military Commission serving as chairman and one of the members appointed by the National Government at Nanking serving as vice-chairman. In places entered and taken over by the People's Liberation Army, regional sub-committees of the reorganization committee may be established as required. The proportion of the members of both sides in the sub-committees and the allocation of the posts of chairmen and vice-chairmen shall be the same as in the national reorganization committee. A reorganization committee shall be established for the navy and another for the air force. All matters relating to the People's Liberation Army's entry into, and taking over of, the areas at present administered by the National Government at Nanking shall be decided by orders issued by the Chinese People's Revolutionary Military Commission. The armed forces of the National Government at Nanking must not resist the entry of the People's Liberation Army.

Article 8. Both sides agree that the reorganization plan in each region shall be carried out in two stages:

Item 1. The first stage – assembling and regrouping.

Point 1. All the armed forces under the Nanking National Government (ground, naval and air forces, gendarmerie, communications police corps, local troops, etc.) shall be assembled and regrouped. The principle of regrouping shall be as follows: the reorganization committee shall, on the basis of the actual local conditions, order such armed forces in the areas entered and taken over by the People's Liberation Army to move, area by area and stage by stage, to the designated places for assembling and regrouping, according to their original designations, formations and numerical strength.

Point 2. Before the People's Liberation Army enters and takes over, all the armed forces under the Nanking National Government shall be held responsible for maintaining local order and preventing any acts of sabotage where they are stationed: in all large and small cities, along important lines of communication and rivers, at seaports and in the villages.

Point 3. In the above-mentioned places, when the People's Liberation Army enters and takes over, the armed forces under the Nanking National Government shall, in accordance with the orders of the reorganization committee and its sub-committees, hand over peacefully and move to the designated places. While moving to the designated places and after arriving there, the armed forces under the Nanking National Government shall observe strict discipline and shall not disturb local order.

Point 4. When, in compliance with the orders of the reorganization committee and its sub-committees, the armed forces under the Nanking National Government leave their original stations, the local police or peace preservation corps stationed in those places shall not withdraw, but shall be responsible for maintaining local peace and order and shall obey the directions and orders of the People's Liberation Army.

Point 5. The reorganization committee, its sub-committees and the local governments shall be responsible for providing all the armed forces of the Nanking National Government which are being moved or assembled with necessary supplies, such as grain, fodder, bedding and clothing.

Point 6. The reorganization committee and its sub-committees shall, according to the actual conditions in various areas, order the authorities of the Nanking National Government to hand over, area by area and stage by stage, all its military establishments (institutions, schools, factories, storehouses and the like, belonging to all its organizations ranging from the Ministry of National Defence to the Combined Rear-Service Headquarters), all its military installations (naval ports, forts, air bases and the like) and all its military supplies to the People's Liberation Army and the latter's Military Control Commissions in various places.

Item 2. The second stage – reorganization area by area.

Point 1. After the ground forces under the Nanking National Government (infantry, cavalry, special arms, gendarmerie, communications police corps and local troops) have moved to the designated places and have been assembled and regrouped, area by area and stage by stage, the reorganization committee shall, according to the actual conditions in different areas, draw up plans for their reorganization area by area and carry out these plans at specified times. The principle of reorganization shall be that all the above-mentioned ground forces, after being assembled and regrouped, shall be reorganized into regular units of the People's Liberation Army in conformity with its democratic system and regular structure. The reorganization committee and its sub-committees shall be responsible for handling the cases of those soldiers who have been found eligible for retirement because of age or disability and who wish to retire, as well as the cases of those officers and non-commissioned officers who wish to retire or take up other occupations; the committees shall provide them with facilities to return home and with means of livelihood, so that everyone will be properly placed and no one will commit misdeeds because he lacks means of support.

Point 2. After the naval and air forces under the Nanking National Government have moved to the designated places and been assembled and regrouped, area by area and stage by stage, they shall be reorganized according to their original designations, formations and numerical strength by the navy and air force reorganization committees, in conformity with the democratic system of the People's Liberation Army.

Point 3. All the armed forces under the Nanking National Government, after being reorganized into the People's Liberation Army, must strictly observe the Three Main Rules of Discipline and the Eight Points for Attention of the People's Liberation Army and loyally abide by the military and political systems of the People's Liberation Army, without any violation.

Point 4. The officers and men who have retired after reorganization must respect the local people's governments and obey the laws and decrees of the People's Government. The people's governments and the people of various localities shall be considerate of these retired officers and men and shall not discriminate against them.

Article 9. After the signing of the Agreement on Internal Peace, all the armed forces under the Nanking National Government must cease conscripting or recruiting soldiers or other personnel. They must be responsible for protecting all their arms and ammunition, equipment, military institutions and installations and military matériel, and must not destroy, conceal, transfer or sell any of them.

Article 10. After the signing of the Agreement on Internal Peace, the National Government at Nanking must, in case any of its armed forces refuses to carry out the reorganization plan, assist the People's Liberation Army to enforce the reorganization plan and ensure its thorough execution.

SECTION FIVE

Article 11. Both sides agree that all bureaucrat-capitalist enterprises and property (including banks, factories, mines, vessels, companies and shops) acquired or seized during the rule of the National Government at Nanking through the use of political prerogatives and the influence of wealth and position shall be confiscated and become the property of the state.

Article 12. In areas not yet entered and taken over by the People's Liberation Army, the National Government at Nanking shall be held responsible for supervising the bureaucrat-capitalist enterprises and property mentioned in Article 11 so that no theft or concealment, damage, transfer or secret sale shall occur. Assets which have already been moved shall be frozen wherever found, and their being subsequently removed, transported abroad or damaged shall not be permitted. Bureaucrat-capitalist enterprises and property located abroad shall be declared the property of the state.

Article 13. In areas already entered and taken over by the People's Liberation Army, the bureaucrat-capitalist enterprises and property mentioned in Article 11 shall be confiscated by the local Military Control Commissions or institutions authorized by the Democratic Coalition Government. Private shares in them, if any, shall be investigated; after they have been verified as being in fact private and not secretly transferred bureaucrat-capital, they shall be recognized, and their owners shall be permitted to remain shareholders or to withdraw their shares.

Article 14. Bureaucrat-capitalist enterprises dating from the period prior to the rule of the National Government at Nanking, as well as those dating from the period of the rule of the National Government at Nanking, which are neither large nor harmful to the national economy and the people's livelihood, shall not be confiscated. But among these, the enterprises and property of certain persons who have committed criminal offences, such as reactionaries guilty of heinous crimes which have been reported by the people and confirmed, shall be confiscated.

Article 15. In cities not yet entered and taken over by the People's Liberation Army, the provincial, municipal and county governments under the National Government at Nanking shall be responsible for protecting the people's democratic forces and their activities in the locality and must not suppress or injure them.

SECTION SIX

Article 16. Both sides affirm that the feudal system of landownership in the rural areas of China shall be reformed step by step. After the entry of the People's Liberation Army, reduction of rent and interest shall generally be carried out first and distribution of land later.

Article 17. In areas not yet entered and taken over by the People's Liberation Army, the local governments under the National Government at Nanking shall be responsible for protecting the organizations of the peasant masses and their activities and must not suppress or damage them.

SECTION SEVEN

Article 18. Both sides agree that all treaties and agreements concluded with foreign states during the rule of the National Government at Nanking and other diplomatic documents and archives, open or secret, shall be handed over by the National Government at Nanking to the Democratic Coalition Government and examined by the Democratic Coalition Government. All treaties or agreements which are detrimental to the Chinese people and their state, especially those which are in the nature of selling out the rights of the state, shall be either abrogated, or revised, or new treaties and agreements shall be concluded instead, as the case may be.

SECTION EIGHT

Article 19.   Both sides agree that after the signing of the Agreement on Internal Peace and before the formation of the Democratic Coalition Government, the National Government at Nanking and its *yuan*, ministries, commissions and other organs shall temporarily continue to function but must consult the Chinese People's Revolutionary Military Commission in the conduct of affairs and assist the People's Liberation Army in matters relating to the taking over and handing over of the various areas.   After the formation of the Democratic Coalition Government, the National Government at Nanking shall immediately hand over to the Democratic Coalition Government and proclaim its own termination.

Article 20.   Upon the handing over of the National Government at Nanking and its local governments at various levels and all their subordinate organs, the People's Liberation Army, the local people's governments and the Democratic Coalition Government of China shall take care to enlist all the patriotic and useful persons among the former's personnel, give them democratic education and assign them to suitable posts so that they will not become destitute and homeless.

Article 21.   Before the People's Liberation Army enters and takes over, the National Government at Nanking and its subordinate local governments in the provinces, cities and counties shall be responsible for maintaining peace and order in their respective areas, looking after and protecting all government organizations and state-owned enterprises (including banks, factories, mines, railways, postal and telegraph offices, aircraft, vessels, companies, warehouses and all communications facilities) and other movable and immovable properties belonging to the state; and no destruction, loss, removal, concealment, or sale is permitted.   Books, archives, antiques, valuables, bullion, foreign currencies and all properties and assets which have been removed or concealed shall be frozen at once wherever they are found, pending their take-over.   As for those properties which have been sent abroad or were originally abroad, the National Government at Nanking shall be responsible for their recovery and safekeeping and be prepared to hand them over.

Article 22.   All the powers as well as the properties and assets of the state in areas already entered and taken over by the People's Liberation Army shall be taken over by the local Military Control Commissions, the local people's governments or institutions authorized by the Coalition Government.

Article 23.   After the Agreement on Internal Peace has been signed by the delegation of the National Government at Nanking and carried out by that government, the delegation of the Communist Party of China will take the responsibility of proposing to the preparatory committee of the New Political Consultative Conference that the National Government at Nanking should be permitted to send a number of patriotic persons as representatives to the Conference; after securing the approval of its preparatory committee, the representatives of the National Government at Nanking may attend the New Political Consultative Conference.

Article 24.   After the National Government at Nanking has sent its representatives to the New Political Consultative Conference, the Communist Party of China will take the responsibility of proposing to the Conference that in the interests of co-operation there should be included in the Democratic Coalition Government a number of patriotic persons from the National Government at Nanking.

The delegations of both sides declare: We hereby assume the responsibility of signing this agreement for the sake of the liberation of the Chinese people and the independence and freedom of the Chinese nation and for the sake of an early conclusion of the war and the restoration of peace so that the commencement of the great task of production and construction on a nation-wide scale will be facilitated and so that our country and people will steadily attain prosperity, strength and well-being. It is hoped that the people of the entire country will unite as one to struggle for the complete fulfilment of this agreement. This agreement shall enter into force immediately upon signature.

PROCLAMATION OF
THE CHINESE PEOPLE'S LIBERATION ARMY

April 25, 1949

The Kuomintang reactionaries have rejected the terms for peace and persist in their stand of waging a criminal war against the nation and the people. The people all over the country hope that the People's Liberation Army will speedily wipe out the Kuomintang reactionaries. We have ordered the People's Liberation Army to advance courageously, wipe out all reactionary Kuomintang troops who dare to resist, arrest all the incorrigible war criminals, liberate the people of the whole country, safeguard China's territorial integrity, sovereignty and independence, and bring about the genuine unification of the country, which the whole people long for. We earnestly hope that people in all walks of life will assist the People's Liberation Army wherever it goes. We hereby proclaim the following eight-point covenant by which we, together with the whole people, shall abide.

1. Protect the lives and property of all the people. People in all walks of life, irrespective of class, belief or occupation, are expected to maintain order and adopt a co-operative attitude towards the People's Liberation Army. The People's Liberation Army on its part will adopt a co-operative attitude towards people in all walks of life. Counter-revolutionaries or other saboteurs who seize the opportunity to create disturbances, loot or sabotage shall be severely dealt with.

2. Protect the industrial, commercial, agricultural and livestock enterprises of the national bourgeoisie. All privately owned factories, shops, banks, warehouses, vessels, wharves, farms, livestock farms and other enterprises will without exception be protected against any encroachment. It is hoped that workers and employees in all

occupations will maintain production as usual and that all shops will remain open as usual.

3. Confiscate bureaucrat-capital. All factories, shops, banks and warehouses, all vessels, wharves and railways, all postal, telegraph, electric light, telephone and water supply services, and all farms, livestock farms and other enterprises operated by the reactionary Kuomintang government and the big bureaucrats shall be taken over by the People's Government. In such enterprises the private shares held by national capitalists engaged in industry, commerce, agriculture or livestock raising shall be recognized, after their ownership is verified. All personnel working in bureaucrat-capitalist enterprises must remain at their posts pending the take-over by the People's Government and must assume responsibility for the safekeeping of all assets, machinery, charts, account books, records, etc., in preparation for the check-up and take-over. Those who render useful service in this connection will be rewarded; those who obstruct or sabotage will be punished. Those desiring to go on working after the take-over by the People's Government will be given employment commensurate with their abilities so that they will not become destitute and homeless.

4. Protect all public and private schools, hospitals, cultural and educational institutions, athletic fields and other public welfare establishments. It is hoped that all personnel in these institutions will remain at their posts; the People's Liberation Army will protect them from molestation.

5. Except for the incorrigible war criminals and counter-revolutionaries who have committed the most heinous crimes, the People's Liberation Army and the People's Government will not hold captive, arrest or subject to indignity any officials, whether high or low, in the Kuomintang's central, provincial, municipal and county governments, deputies to the "National Assembly", members of the Legislative and Control Yuans, members of the political consultative councils, police officers and district, township, village and *pao-chia*[1] officials, so long as they do not offer armed resistance or plot sabotage. All these persons are enjoined, pending the take-over, to stay at their posts, abide by the orders and decrees of the People's Liberation Army and the People's Government and assume responsibility for the safekeeping of all the assets and records of their offices. The People's Government will permit the employment of those among them who can make themselves useful in some kind of work and have not committed

any grave reactionary act or other flagrant misdeed. Punishment shall be meted out to those who seize the opportunity to engage in sabotage, theft or embezzlement, or abscond with public funds, assets or records, or refuse to give an accounting.

6. In order to ensure peace and security in both cities and rural areas and to maintain public order, all stragglers and disbanded soldiers are required to report and surrender to the People's Liberation Army or the People's Government in their localities. No action will be taken against those who voluntarily do so and hand over their arms. Those who refuse to report or who conceal their arms shall be arrested and investigated. Persons who shelter stragglers and disbanded soldiers and do not report them to the authorities shall be duly punished.

7. The feudal system of landownership in the rural areas is irrational and should be abolished. To abolish it, however, preparations must be made and the necessary steps taken. Generally speaking, the reduction of rent and interest should come first and land distribution later; only after the People's Liberation Army has arrived at a place and worked there for a considerable time will it be possible to speak of solving the land problem in earnest. The peasant masses should organize themselves and help the People's Liberation Army to carry out the various initial reforms. They should also work hard at their farming so as to prevent the present level of agricultural production from falling and should then raise it step by step to improve their own livelihood and supply the people of the cities with commodity grain. Urban land and buildings cannot be dealt with in the same way as the problem of rural land.

8. Protect the lives and property of foreign nationals. It is hoped that all foreign nationals will follow their usual pursuits and observe order. All foreign nationals must abide by the orders and decrees of the People's Liberation Army and the People's Government and must not engage in espionage, act against the cause of China's national independence and the people's liberation, or harbour Chinese war criminals, counter-revolutionaries or other law-breakers. Otherwise, they shall be dealt with according to law by the People's Liberation Army and the People's Government.

The People's Liberation Army is highly disciplined; it is fair in buying and selling and is not allowed to take even a needle or a piece of thread from the people. It is hoped that the people throughout the country will live and work in peace and will not give credence to rumours or raise false alarms. This proclamation is hereby issued in all sincerity and earnestness.

Mao Tse-tung

Chairman of the Chinese People's
Revolutionary Military Commission

Chu Teh

Commander-in-Chief of the Chinese
People's Liberation Army

NOTES

[1] *Pao chia* was the administrative system by which the Kuomintang reactionary clique enforced its fascist rule at the primary level. On August 1, 1932, Chiang Kai-shek promulgated the "Regulations for the Organization of *Pao* and *Chia* and for a Population Census in the Counties" covering the provinces of Honan, Hupeh and Anhwei. The "Regulations" provided that "the *pao* and *chia* are to be organized on the basis of households; there is to be a head of each household, of each *chia*, which is made up of ten households, and of each *pao*, which is made up of ten *chia*". Neighbours were required to watch and report each other's activities to the authorities, and all were punishable when one was found guilty; various counter-revolutionary measures for exacting compulsory labour were also laid down. On November 7, 1934, the Kuomintang government officially announced that this system of fascist rule was to be established in all the provinces and municipalities under its rule.

ON THE OUTRAGES BY BRITISH WARSHIPS[1] — STATEMENT BY THE SPOKESMAN OF THE GENERAL HEADQUARTERS OF THE CHINESE PEOPLE'S LIBERATION ARMY*

April 30, 1949

We denounce the preposterous statement of the warmonger Churchill.[2] In the British House of Commons on April 26, Churchill demanded that the British government should send two aircraft carriers to the Far East for "effective power of retaliation". What are you "retaliating" for, Mr. Churchill? British warships together with Kuomintang warships intruded into the defence area of the Chinese People's Liberation Army and fired on the People's Liberation Army, causing no less than 252 casualties among our loyal and gallant fighters. Since the British have trespassed on Chinese territory and committed so great a crime, the People's Liberation Army has good reason to demand that the British government admit its wrongdoing, apologize and make compensation. Isn't this what you should do, instead of dispatching forces to China to "retaliate" against the Chinese People's Liberation Army? Prime Minister Attlee's statement is also wrong.[3] Britain, he said, has the right to send her warships into China's Yangtse River. The Yangtse is an inland waterway of China. What right have you British to send in your warships? You have no such right. The Chinese people will defend their territory and sovereignty and absolutely will not permit encroachment by foreign governments. Attlee said that the People's Liberation Army "would be prepared to allow the ship [the *Amethyst*] to proceed to Nanking but only on condition that she should assist the People's Liberation Army to cross the Yangtse". Attlee lied. The People's Liberation Army gave no permission to the *Amethyst* to proceed to Nanking. The People's Liberation Army does not want the armed forces of any foreign country to help it cross the Yangtse or to

401

do anything else.   On the contrary, the People's Liberation Army demands that Britain, the United States and France quickly withdraw their armed forces – their warships, military aircraft and marines stationed in the Yangtse and Whangpoo Rivers and other parts of China – from China's territorial inland waters, seas, land and air and that they refrain from helping the enemy of the Chinese people to wage civil war.   The Chinese People's Revolutionary Military Commission and the People's Government have so far not established diplomatic relations with any foreign government.   The Chinese People's Revolutionary Military Commission and the People's Government will protect those foreign nationals in China who are engaged in legitimate pursuits.   They are willing to consider the establishment of diplomatic relations with foreign countries; such relations must be based on equality, mutual benefit, mutual respect for sovereignty and territorial integrity and, first of all, on no help being given to the Kuomintang reactionaries.   They will tolerate no act of intimidation by any foreign government.   A foreign government which wishes to consider establishing diplomatic relations with us must sever relations with the remnant Kuomintang forces and withdraw its armed forces from China.   Attlee complained that the Communist Party of China, having no diplomatic relations with foreign countries, was unwilling to have contacts with the old diplomatic personnel of foreign governments (consuls recognized by the Kuomintang).   Such complaints are groundless.   In the past few years, the governments of the United States, Britain, Canada, etc. have helped the Kuomintang to oppose us.   Can Mr. Attlee have forgotten this?   Can it also be that Mr. Attlee does not know which country gave the Kuomintang the *Chungking*,[4] the heavy cruiser which was recently sunk?

---

* This statement was drafted by Comrade Mao Tse-tung for the spokesman of the General Headquarters of the Chinese People's Liberation Army.   It expressed the solemn stand of the Chinese people who fear no threats and resolutely oppose imperialist aggression; it also set forth the foreign policy of the new China which was soon to be established.

NOTES

[1] On April 20-21, 1949, while the People's Liberation Army was fighting its way across the Yangtse, the *Amethyst* and three other British warships intruded into the river, an inland waterway of China, and, together with Kuomintang warships, fired on our army, causing 252 casualties. The People's Liberation Army returned the fire; the *Amethyst* was disabled and forced to anchor near Chinkiang; the other three British warships escaped. The British authorities requested that the *Amethyst* should be allowed to leave, and its captain, acting on the orders of Brind, Commander-in-Chief of the British Far Eastern Fleet, conducted negotiations with the representative of our army. During these negotiations, the British side consistently prevaricated and refused to admit its criminal acts of aggression. While the negotiations were continuing, on the night of July 30, the *Amethyst* forced her way alongside a passenger ship, the *Liberated Chiangling*, which was going downstream off Chinkiang, and escaped by using that ship as a shield. When our army signalled a warning to the *Amethyst* to stop, she opened fire, collided with and sank a number of junks and escaped from the Yangtse River.

[2] On April 26, 1949, speaking in the British House of Commons, Churchill, the chieftain of the British Conservative Party, slandered as an "atrocious outrage" the action taken by the Chinese People's Liberation Army in counter-attacking the British warships which had fired on our army, and demanded that the British government "get in Chinese waters one aircraft carrier, if not two, capable of . . . effective power of retaliation".

[3] On April 26, 1949, British Prime Minister Attlee declared in the House of Commons that British naval vessels had been within their rights in going up the Yangtse on their "peaceful missions", because they had the permission of the Kuomintang government of China. At the same time, when speaking about the negotiations which the British representative was holding with the representative of the Chinese People's Liberation Army, Attlee lied, saying that the Chinese People's Liberation Army "would be prepared to allow the ship [the *Amethyst*] to proceed to Nanking but only on condition that she should assist the People's Liberation Army to cross the Yangtse".

[4] It was the British government which in February 1948 gave the Kuomintang the heavy cruiser *Chungking*, the largest cruiser in the Kuomintang navy. On February 25, 1949, the officers and men of the cruiser revolted, renounced their allegiance to the reactionary Kuomintang government and joined the Chinese People's Navy. On March 19 the U.S. imperialists and the Kuomintang bandits sent heavy bombers and sank the *Chungking* off Hulutao, in Liaotung Gulf in northeastern China.

ADDRESS TO THE PREPARATORY MEETING OF THE NEW POLITICAL CONSULTATIVE CONFERENCE

June 15, 1949

Fellow Delegates,

Today we are holding the inaugural session of the Preparatory Meeting of the New Political Consultative Conference.[1] The task of this meeting is to complete all necessary preparations and speedily convene the New Political Consultative Conference, which will form a democratic coalition government in order to lead the people of the whole country in eliminating the remnant forces of Kuomintang reaction and unifying all China as swiftly as possible, and in carrying out, systematically and step by step, country-wide construction in the political, economic and cultural fields and in national defence. This is what the people of the whole country expect us to do, and we must do it.

The convening of the New Political Consultative Conference was proposed to the people of the whole country by the Communist Party of China on May 1, 1948.[2] The proposal obtained a quick response from the democratic parties, people's organizations, democratic personages in all walks of life throughout China, the country's minority nationalities and the overseas Chinese. The Communist Party of China, the democratic parties, people's organizations, democratic personages in all walks of life, minority nationalities and overseas Chinese all hold that we must overthrow the rule of imperialism, feudalism, bureaucrat-capitalism and the Kuomintang reactionaries, convene a Political Consultative Conference of representatives of all the democratic parties, people's organizations, democratic personages in all walks of life, minority nationalities and overseas Chinese, proclaim the founding of the People's Republic of China and elect a democratic coalition government to represent it. Only thus can our great motherland free herself from a semi-colonial and semi-feudal fate and take the road of independence, freedom, peace, unity, strength and prosperity. This is a common political basis. It is the common political basis for the united struggle of the Communist Party of China, the democratic parties, people's organizations, democratic personages in all walks of life, minority nationalities and overseas Chinese; it is also the common political basis for the united struggle of the whole people. So firm is this political basis that no serious-minded democratic party, people's organization or democratic personage has expressed any differences of opinion, and all hold that this is the only road which leads in the right direction for solving all China's problems.

The people of the whole country supporting their own People's Liberation Army have won the war. This great People's War of Liberation, begun in July 1946, has now lasted three years. The war was launched by the Kuomintang reactionaries with the help they received from foreign imperialism. In unleashing this civil war against the people the Kuomintang reactionaries perfidiously and unscrupulously tore up the truce agreement and the resolutions of the Political Consultative Conference of January 1946. But in three short years they have been defeated by the heroic People's Liberation Army. Not long ago, after the Kuomintang reactionaries' peace plot was exposed, the People's Liberation Army bravely advanced and crossed the Yangtse River. Nanking, the capital of the Kuomintang reactionaries, is now in our hands. Shanghai, Hangchow, Nanchang, Wuhan and Sian have been liberated. At this very moment, the field armies of the People's Liberation Army are conducting a great march unprecedented in Chinese history into the southern and north-western provinces. In three years the People's Liberation Army has wiped out a total of 5,590,000 of the reactionary Kuomintang troops. Now the remnants of the Kuomintang forces number only about 1,500,000, including regulars, irregulars and those in the military establishments and academies in the rear. It will still take some time to mop up these enemy remnants, but not long.

This is a victory for the people of all China, and also a victory for the peoples of the whole world. The whole world, except the imperialists and the reactionaries in various countries, is elated and inspired by this great victory of the Chinese people. The struggle of the Chinese people against their own enemies and the struggles of the peoples of the world against their own enemies have the same meaning. The people of China and the peoples of the world have all witnessed the fact that the imperialists have directed the Chinese reactionaries ruthlessly to oppose the Chinese people by means of a counter-revolutionary war and that the Chinese people have triumphantly overthrown the reactionaries by means of a revolutionary war.

Here, I think it is necessary to call people's attention to the fact that the imperialists and their running dogs, the Chinese reactionaries, will not resign themselves to defeat in this land of China. They will continue to gang up against the Chinese people in every possible way. For example, they will smuggle their agents into China to sow dissension and make trouble. That is certain; they will never neglect these activities. To take another example, they will incite the Chinese reactionaries, and even throw in their own forces, to blockade China's ports. They will do this as long as it is possible. Furthermore, if they still hanker after adventures, they will send some of their troops to invade and harass China's frontiers; this, too, is not impossible. All this we must take fully into account. Just because we have won victory, we must never relax our vigilance against the frenzied plots for revenge by the imperialists and their running dogs. Whoever relaxes vigilance will disarm himself politically and land himself in a passive position. In view of these circumstances, the people all over the country must unite to smash resolutely, thoroughly, wholly and completely every plot against the Chinese people by the imperialists and their running dogs, the Chinese reactionaries. China must be independent, China must be liberated, China's affairs must be decided and run by the Chinese people themselves, and no further interference, not even the slightest, will be tolerated from any imperialist country.

The Chinese revolution is a revolution of the broad masses of the whole nation. Everybody is our friend, except the imperialists, the feudalists and the bureaucrat-capitalists, the Kuomintang reactionaries and their accomplices. We have a broad and solid revolutionary united front. This united front is so broad that it includes the working class, the peasantry, the urban petty bourgeoisie and the national bourgeoisie. This united front is so solid that it possesses the resolute will and the inexhaustible capacity to defeat every enemy and overcome every difficulty. The epoch we are living in is an epoch in which the imperialist system is heading for total collapse, the imperialists have fallen inextricably into crisis and, no matter how they continue to oppose the Chinese people, the Chinese people will always have a way to win final victory.

At the same time, we proclaim to the whole world that what we oppose is exclusively the imperialist system and its plots against the Chinese people. We are willing to discuss with any foreign government the establishment of diplomatic relations on the basis of the principles of equality, mutual benefit and mutual respect for territorial integrity and sovereignty, provided it is willing to sever relations with the Chinese reactionaries, stops conspiring with them or helping them and adopts an attitude of genuine, and not hypocritical, friendship towards People's China. The Chinese people wish to have friendly co-operation with the people of all countries and to resume and expand international trade in order to develop production and promote economic prosperity.

Fellow Delegates, all the conditions are ripe for us to convene the New Political Consultative Conference and to form a democratic coalition government. The people throughout the country are most eagerly expecting us to convene the conference and form the government. I believe the work we have now begun will fulfil this hope, and do so before long.

Upon the formation of China's democratic coalition government, its central tasks will be: (1) to mop up the remnants of the reactionaries and suppress their trouble-making; and (2) to do everything possible and make the utmost effort to restore and develop the people's economy and, at the same time, to restore and develop the people's culture and education.

The Chinese people will see that, once China's destiny is in the hands of the people, China, like the sun rising in the east, will illuminate every corner of the land with a brilliant flame, swiftly clean up the mire left by the reactionary government, heal the wounds of war and build a new, powerful and prosperous people's republic worthy of the name.

Long live the People's Republic of China!

Long live the democratic coalition government!

Long live the great unity of the people of the whole country!

NOTES

[1] The meeting was held at Peiping from June 15 to 19, 1949. It was attended by 134 representatives from twenty-three organizations and groups, including the Communist Party of China, the various democratic parties, the people's organizations, democratic personages in all walks of life, the minority nationalities of the country

and the overseas Chinese. It adopted the "Organic Rules of the Preparatory Committee of the New Political Consultative Conference" and the "Provisions Regarding the Organizations and Groups Participating in the New Political Consultative Conference and the Size of Their Delegations" and elected a Standing Committee headed by Chairman Mao Tse-tung. The Conference was called the New Political Consultative Conference to distinguish it from the Political Consultative Conference which had opened at Chungking on January 10, 1946. Its name was changed to the Chinese People's Political Consultative Conference at its first plenary session on September 21, 1949.

[2] See "On the September Meeting – Circular of the Central Committee of the Communist Party of China", Note 4, p. 276 of this volume.

ON THE PEOPLE'S DEMOCRATIC DICTATORSHIP

In Commemoration of the Twenty-eighth Anniversary of the Communist Party of China

June 30, 1949

The first of July 1949 marks the fact that the Communist Party of China has already lived through twenty-eight years. Like a man, a political party has its childhood, youth, manhood and old age. The Communist Party of China is no longer a child or a lad in his teens but has become an adult. When a man reaches old age, he will die; the same is true of a party. When classes disappear, all instruments of class struggle – parties and the state machinery – will lose their function, cease to be necessary, therefore gradually wither away and end their historical mission; and human society will move to a higher stage. We are the opposite of the political parties of the bourgeoisie. They are afraid to speak of the extinction of classes, state power and parties. We, on the contrary, declare openly that we are striving hard to create the very conditions which will bring about their extinction. The leadership of the Communist Party and the state power of the people's dictatorship are such conditions. Anyone who does not recognize this truth is no communist. Young comrades who have not studied Marxism-Leninism and have only recently joined the Party may not yet understand this truth. They must understand it – only then can they have a correct world outlook. They must understand that the road to the abolition of classes, to the abolition of state power and to the abolition of parties is the road all mankind must take; it is only a question of time and conditions. Communists the world over are wiser than the bourgeoisie, they understand the laws governing the existence and development of things, they understand dialectics and they can see farther. The bourgeoisie does not welcome this

411

truth because it does not want to be overthrown.   To be overthrown
is painful and is unbearable to contemplate for those overthrown, for
example, for the Kuomintang reactionaries whom we are now overthrowing and for Japanese imperialism which we together with other
peoples overthrew some time ago.   But for the working class, the
labouring people and the Communist Party the question is not one of
being overthrown, but of working hard to create the conditions in which
classes, state power and political parties will die out very naturally
and mankind will enter the realm of Great Harmony.[1] We have
mentioned in passing the long-range perspective of human progress in
order to explain clearly the problems we are about to discuss.

As everyone knows, our Party passed through these twenty-eight
years not in peace but amid hardships, for we had to fight enemies,
both foreign and domestic, both inside and outside the Party.   We
thank Marx, Engels, Lenin and Stalin for giving us a weapon.   This
weapon is not a machine-gun, but Marxism-Leninism.

In his book *"Left-Wing" Communism, an Infantile Disorder* written in 1920, Lenin described the quest of the Russians for revolutionary
theory.[2]   Only after several decades of hardship and suffering did
the Russians find Marxism.   Many things in China were the same as,
or similar to, those in Russia before the October Revolution.   There
was the same feudal oppression.   There was similar economic and
cultural backwardness.   Both countries were backward, China even
more so.   In both countries alike, for the sake of national regeneration progressives braved hard and bitter struggles in their quest for
revolutionary truth.

From the time of China's defeat in the Opium War of 1840,[3]
Chinese progressives went through untold hardships in their quest for
truth from the Western countries.   Hung Hsiu-chuan,[4] Kang Yu-wei,[5]
Yen Fu[6] and Sun Yat-sen were representative of those who had looked
to the West for truth before the Communist Party of China was born.
Chinese who then sought progress would read any book containing
the new knowledge from the West.   The number of students sent
to Japan, Britain, the United States, France and Germany was
amazing.   At home, the imperial examinations[7] were abolished and
modern schools sprang up like bamboo shoots after a spring rain;
every effort was made to learn from the West.   In my youth, I too
engaged in such studies.   They represented the culture of Western
bourgeois democracy, including the social theories and natural sciences
of that period, and they were called "the new learning" in contrast to

Chinese feudal culture, which was called "the old learning". For quite a long time, those who had acquired the new learning felt confident that it would save China, and very few of them had any doubts on this score, as the adherents of the old learning had. Only modernization could save China, only learning from foreign countries could modernize China. Among the foreign countries, only the Western capitalist countries were then progressive, as they had successfully built modern bourgeois states. The Japanese had been successful in learning from the West, and the Chinese also wished to learn from the Japanese. The Chinese in those days regarded Russia as backward, and few wanted to learn from her. That was how the Chinese tried to learn from foreign countries in the period from the 1840s to the beginning of the 20th century.

Imperialist aggression shattered the fond dreams of the Chinese about learning from the West. It was very odd – why were the teachers always committing aggression against their pupil? The Chinese learned a good deal from the West, but they could not make it work and were never able to realize their ideals. Their repeated struggles, including such a country-wide movement as the Revolution of 1911,[8] all ended in failure. Day by day, conditions in the country got worse, and life was made impossible. Doubts arose, increased and deepened. World War I shook the whole globe. The Russians made the October Revolution and created the world's first socialist state. Under the leadership of Lenin and Stalin, the revolutionary energy of the great proletariat and labouring people of Russia, hitherto latent and unseen by foreigners, suddenly erupted like a volcano, and the Chinese and all mankind began to see the Russians in a new light. Then, and only then, did the Chinese enter an entirely new era in their thinking and their life. They found Marxism-Leninism, the universally applicable truth, and the face of China began to change.

It was through the Russians that the Chinese found Marxism. Before the October Revolution, the Chinese were not only ignorant of Lenin and Stalin, they did not even know of Marx and Engels. The salvoes of the October Revolution brought us Marxism-Leninism. The October Revolution helped progressives in China, as throughout the world, to adopt the proletarian world outlook as the instrument for studying a nation's destiny and considering anew their own problems. Follow the path of the Russians – that was their conclusion. In 1919, the May 4th Movement took place in China. In 1921, the Communist Party of China was founded. Sun Yat-sen, in the depths of despair, came across the October Revolution and the Communist Party of China. He welcomed the October Revolution, welcomed Russian help to the Chinese and welcomed co-operation of the Communist Party of China. Then Sun Yat-sen died and Chiang Kai-shek rose to power. Over a long period of twenty-two years, Chiang Kai-shek dragged China into ever more hopeless straits. In this period, during the anti-fascist Second World War in which the Soviet Union was the main force, three big imperialist powers were knocked out, while two others were weakened. In the whole world only one big imperialist power, the United States of America, remained uninjured. But the United States faced a grave domestic crisis. It wanted to enslave the whole world; it supplied arms to help Chiang Kai-shek slaughter several million Chinese. Under the leadership of the Communist Party of China, the Chinese people, after driving out Japanese imperialism, waged the People's War of Liberation for three years and have basically won victory.

Thus Western bourgeois civilization, bourgeois democracy and the plan for a bourgeois republic have all gone bankrupt in the eyes of the Chinese people. Bourgeois democracy has given way to people's democracy under the leadership of the working class and the bourgeois republic to the people's republic. This has made it possible to achieve socialism and communism through the people's republic, to abolish classes and enter a world of Great Harmony. Kang Yu-wei wrote *Ta Tung Shu*, or the *Book of Great Harmony*, but he did not and could not find the way to achieve Great Harmony. There are bourgeois republics in foreign lands, but China cannot have a bourgeois republic because she is a country suffering under imperialist oppression. The only way is through a people's republic led by the working class.

All other ways have been tried and failed. Of the people who hankered after those ways, some have fallen, some have awakened and some are changing their ideas. Events are developing so swiftly that many feel the abruptness of the change and the need to learn anew. This state of mind is understandable and we welcome this worthy desire to learn anew.

The vanguard of the Chinese proletariat learned Marxism-Leninism after the October Revolution and founded the Communist Party of China. It entered at once into political struggles and only now, after a tortuous course of twenty-eight years, has it won basic victory. From our twenty-eight years' experience we have drawn a conclusion similar to the one Sun Yat-sen drew in his testament from his "experience of forty years"; that is, we are deeply convinced that to win victory, "we must arouse the masses of the people and unite in a common struggle with those nations of the world which treat us as equals". Sun Yat-sen had a world outlook different from ours and started from a different class standpoint in studying and tackling problems; yet, in the 1920s he reached a conclusion basically the same as ours on the question of how to struggle against imperialism.

Twenty-four years have passed since Sun Yat-sen's death, and the Chinese revolution, led by the Communist Party of China, has made tremendous advances both in theory and practice and has radically changed the face of China. Up to now the principal and fundamental experience the Chinese people have gained is twofold:

(1) Internally, arouse the masses of the people. That is, unite the working class, the peasantry, the urban petty bourgeoisie and the national bourgeoisie, form a domestic united front under the leadership of the working class, and advance from this to the establishment of a state which is a people's democratic dictatorship under the leadership of the working class and based on the alliance of workers and peasants.

(2) Externally, unite in a common struggle with those nations of the world which treat us as equals and unite with the peoples of all countries. That is, ally ourselves with the Soviet Union, with the People's Democracies and with the proletariat and the broad masses of the people in all other countries, and form an international united front.

"You are leaning to one side." Exactly. The forty years' experience of Sun Yat-sen and the twenty-eight years' experience of the Communist Party have taught us to lean to one side, and we are firmly convinced that in order to win victory and consolidate it we must lean to one side. In the light of the experiences accumulated in these forty years and these twenty-eight years, all Chinese without exception must lean either to the side of imperialism or to the side of socialism. Sitting on the fence will not do, nor is there a third road. We oppose the Chiang Kai-shek reactionaries who lean to the side of imperialism, and we also oppose the illusions about a third road.

"You are too irritating." We are talking about how to deal with domestic and foreign reactionaries, the imperialists and their running dogs, not about how to deal with anyone else. With regard to such reactionaries, the question of irritating them or not does not arise. Irritated or not irritated, they will remain the same because they are reactionaries.   Only if we draw a clear line between reactionaries and revolutionaries, expose the intrigues and plots of the reactionaries, arouse the vigilance and attention of the revolutionary ranks, heighten our will to fight and crush the enemy's arrogance can we isolate the reactionaries, vanquish them or supersede them.   We must not show the slightest timidity before a wild beast.   We must learn from Wu Sung[9] on the Chingyang Ridge.   As Wu Sung saw it, the tiger on Chingyang Ridge was a man-eater, whether irritated or not.   Either kill the tiger or be eaten by him – one or the other.

"We want to do business."   Quite right, business will be done. We are against no one except the domestic and foreign reactionaries who hinder us from doing business.   Everybody should know that it is none other than the imperialists and their running dogs, the Chiang Kai-shek reactionaries, who hinder us from doing business and also from establishing diplomatic relations with foreign countries.   When we have beaten the internal and external reactionaries by uniting all domestic and international forces, we shall be able to do business and establish diplomatic relations with all foreign countries on the basis of equality, mutual benefit and mutual respect for territorial integrity and sovereignty.

"Victory is possible even without international help."   This is a mistaken idea.   In the epoch in which imperialism exists, it is impossible for a genuine people's revolution to win victory in any country without various forms of help from the international revolutionary forces, and even if victory were won, it could not be consolidated. This was the case with the victory and consolidation of the great October Revolution, as Lenin and Stalin told us long ago.   This was also the case with the overthrow of the three imperialist powers in World War II and the establishment of the People's Democracies. And this is also the case with the present and the future of People's China.   Just imagine!   If the Soviet Union had not existed, if there had been no victory in the anti-fascist Second World War, if Japanese imperialism had not been defeated, if the People's Democracies had not come into being, if the oppressed nations of the East were not rising in struggle and if there were no struggle of the masses of the people against their reactionary rulers in the United States, Britain, France, Germany, Italy, Japan and other capitalist countries – if not for all these in combination, the international reactionary forces bearing down upon us would certainly be many times greater than now. In such circumstances, could we have won victory?   Obviously not.

And even with victory, there could be no consolidation. The Chinese people have had more than enough experience of this kind. This experience was reflected long ago in Sun Yat-sen's death-bed statement on the necessity of uniting with the international revolutionary forces.

"We need help from the British and U.S. governments." This, too, is a naive idea in these times. Would the present rulers of Britain and the United States, who are imperialists, help a people's state? Why do these countries do business with us and, supposing they might be willing to lend us money on terms of mutual benefit in the future, why would they do so? Because their capitalists want to make money and their bankers want to earn interest to extricate themselves from their own crisis – it is not a matter of helping the Chinese people. The Communist Parties and progressive groups in these countries are urging their governments to establish trade and even diplomatic relations with us. This is goodwill, this is help, this cannot be mentioned in the same breath with the conduct of the bourgeoisie in the same countries. Throughout his life, Sun Yat-sen appealed countless times to the capitalist countries for help and got nothing but heartless rebuffs. Only once in his whole life did Sun Yat-sen receive foreign help, and that was Soviet help. Let readers refer to Dr. Sun Yat-sen's testament; his earnest advice was not to look for help from the imperialist countries but to "unite with those nations of the world which treat us as equals". Dr. Sun had experience; he had suffered, he had been deceived. We should remember his words and not allow ourselves to be deceived again. Internationally, we belong to the side of the anti-imperialist front headed by the Soviet Union, and so we can turn only to this side for genuine and friendly help, not to the side of the imperialist front.

"You are dictatorial." My dear sirs, you are right, that is just what we are. All the experience the Chinese people have accumulated through several decades teaches us to enforce the people's democratic dictatorship, that is, to deprive the reactionaries of the right to speak and let the people alone have that right.

Who are the people? At the present stage in China, they are the working class, the peasantry, the urban petty bourgeoisie and the national bourgeoisie. These classes, led by the working class and the Communist Party, unite to form their own state and elect their own government; they enforce their dictatorship over the running dogs of imperialism – the landlord class and bureaucrat-bourgeoisie, as well as the representatives of those classes, the Kuomintang reactionaries and their accomplices – suppress them, allow them only to behave themselves and not to be unruly in word or deed. If they speak or act in an unruly way, they will be promptly stopped and punished. Democracy is practised within the ranks of the people, who enjoy the rights of freedom of speech, assembly, association and so on. The right to vote belongs only to the people, not to the reactionaries. The combination of these two aspects, democracy for the people and dictatorship over the reactionaries, is the people's democratic dictatorship.

Why must things be done this way? The reason is quite clear to everybody. If things were not done this way, the revolution would fail, the people would suffer, the country would be conquered.

"Don't you want to abolish state power?" Yes, we do, but not right now; we cannot do it yet. Why? Because imperialism still exists, because domestic reaction still exists, because classes still exist in our country. Our present task is to strengthen the people's state apparatus – mainly the people's army, the people's police and the people's courts – in order to consolidate national defence and protect the people's interests. Given this condition, China can develop steadily, under the leadership of the working class and the Communist Party, from an agricultural into an industrial country and from a new-democratic into a socialist and communist society, can abolish classes and realize the Great Harmony. The state apparatus, including the army, the police and the courts, is the instrument by which one class oppresses another. It is an instrument for the oppression of antagonistic classes; it is violence and not "benevolence". "You are not benevolent!" Quite so. We definitely do not apply a policy of benevolence to the reactionaries and towards the reactionary activities of the reactionary classes. Our policy of benevolence is applied only within the ranks of the people, not beyond them to the reactionaries or to the reactionary activities of reactionary classes.

The people's state protects the people. Only when the people have such a state can they educate and remould themselves by democratic methods on a country-wide scale, with everyone taking part, and shake off the influence of domestic and foreign reactionaries (which is still very strong, will survive for a long time and cannot be quickly destroyed), rid themselves of the bad habits and ideas acquired in the old society, not allow themselves to be led astray by the reactionaries, and continue to advance – to advance towards a socialist and communist society.

Here, the method we employ is democratic, the method of persuasion, not of compulsion. When anyone among the people breaks the law, he too should be punished, imprisoned or even sentenced to death; but this is a matter of a few individual cases, and it differs in principle from the dictatorship exercised over the reactionaries as a class.

As for the members of the reactionary classes and individual reactionaries, so long as they do not rebel, sabotage or create trouble after their political power has been overthrown, land and work will be given to them as well in order to allow them to live and remould themselves through labour into new people. If they are not willing to work, the people's state will compel them to work. Propaganda and educational work will be done among them too and will be done, moreover, with as much care and thoroughness as among the captured army officers in the past. This, too, may be called a "policy of benevolence" if you like, but it is imposed by us on the members of the enemy classes and cannot be mentioned in the same breath with the work of self-education which we carry on within the ranks of the revolutionary people.

Such remoulding of members of the reactionary classes can be accomplished only by a state of the people's democratic dictatorship under the leadership of the Communist Party. When it is well done, China's major exploiting classes, the landlord class and the bureaucrat-bourgeoisie (the monopoly capitalist class), will be eliminated for good. There remain the national bourgeoisie; at the present stage, we can already do a good deal of suitable educational work with many of them. When the time comes to realize socialism, that is, to nationalize private enterprise, we shall carry the work of educating and remoulding them a step further. The people have a powerful state apparatus in their hands – there is no need to fear rebellion by the national bourgeoisie.

The serious problem is the education of the peasantry. The peasant economy is scattered, and the socialization of agriculture, judging by the Soviet Union's experience, will require a long time and painstaking work. Without socialization of agriculture, there can be no complete, consolidated socialism. The steps to socialize agriculture must be co-ordinated with the development of a powerful industry having state enterprise as its backbone.[10] The state of the people's democratic dictatorship must systematically solve the problems of industrialization. Since it is not proposed to discuss economic problems in detail in this article, I shall not go into them further.

In 1924 a famous manifesto was adopted at the Kuomintang's
First National Congress, which Sun Yat-sen himself led and in which
Communists participated. The manifesto stated:

> The so-called democratic system in modern states is usually
> monopolized by the bourgeoisie and has become simply an instru-
> ment for oppressing the common people. On the other hand, the
> Kuomintang's Principle of Democracy means a democratic system
> shared by all the common people and not privately owned by
> the few.

Apart from the question of who leads whom, the Principle of Democracy stated above corresponds as a general political programme to
what we call People's Democracy or New Democracy. A state system
which is shared only by the common people and which the bourgeoisie
is not allowed to own privately – add to this the leadership of the
working class, and we have the state system of the people's democratic
dictatorship.

Chiang Kai-shek betrayed Sun Yat-sen and used the dictatorship
of the bureaucrat-bourgeoisie and the landlord class as an instrument
for oppressing the common people of China. This counter-revolutionary
dictatorship was enforced for twenty-two years and has only now been
overthrown by the common people of China under our leadership.

The foreign reactionaries who accuse us of practising "dictatorship"
or "totalitarianism" are the very persons who practise it. They practise the dictatorship or totalitarianism of one class, the bourgeoisie,
over the proletariat and the rest of the people. They are the very
persons Sun Yat-sen spoke of as the bourgeoisie of modern states
who oppress the common people. And it is from these reactionary
scoundrels that Chiang Kai-shek learned his counter-revolutionary
dictatorship.

Chu Hsi, a philosopher of the Sung Dynasty, wrote many books
and made many remarks which are now forgotten, but one remark
is still remembered, "Deal with a man as he deals with you."[11] This
is just what we do; we deal with the imperialists and their running
dogs, the Chiang Kai-shek reactionaries, as they deal with us. That
is all there is to it!

Revolutionary dictatorship and counter-revolutionary dictatorship
are by nature opposites, but the former was learned from the latter.
Such learning is very important. If the revolutionary people do not
master this method of ruling over the counter-revolutionary classes,

they will not be able to maintain their state power, domestic and foreign reaction will overthrow that power and restore its own rule over China, and disaster will befall the revolutionary people.

The people's democratic dictatorship is based on the alliance of the working class, the peasantry and the urban petty bourgeoisie, and mainly on the alliance of the workers and the peasants, because these two classes comprise 80 to 90 per cent of China's population. These two classes are the main force in overthrowing imperialism and the Kuomintang reactionaries. The transition from New Democracy to socialism also depends mainly upon their alliance.

The people's democratic dictatorship needs the leadership of the working class. For it is only the working class that is most far-sighted, most selfless and most thoroughly revolutionary. The entire history of revolution proves that without the leadership of the working class revolution fails and that with the leadership of the working class revolution triumphs. In the epoch of imperialism, in no country can any other class lead any genuine revolution to victory. This is clearly proved by the fact that the many revolutions led by China's petty bourgeoisie and national bourgeoisie all failed.

The national bourgeoisie at the present stage is of great importance. Imperialism, a most ferocious enemy, is still standing alongside us. China's modern industry still forms a very small proportion of the national economy. No reliable statistics are available, but it is estimated, on the basis of certain data, that before the War of Resistance Against Japan the value of output of modern industry constituted only about 10 per cent of the total value of output of the national economy. To counter imperialist oppression and to raise her backward economy to a higher level, China must utilize all the factors of urban and rural capitalism that are beneficial and not harmful to the national economy and the people's livelihood; and we must unite with the national bourgeoisie in common struggle. Our present policy is to regulate capitalism, not to destroy it. But the national bourgeoisie cannot be the leader of the revolution, nor should it have the chief role in state power. The reason it cannot be the leader of the revolution and should not have the chief role in state power is that the social and economic position of the national bourgeoisie determines its weakness; it lacks foresight and sufficient courage and many of its members are afraid of the masses.

Sun Yat-sen advocated "arousing the masses of the people" or "giving assistance to the peasants and workers". But who is to "arouse" them or "give assistance" to them? Sun Yat-sen had the petty bourgeoisie and the national bourgeoisie in mind. As a matter of fact, they cannot do so. Why did forty years of revolution under Sun Yat-sen end in failure? Because in the epoch of imperialism the petty bourgeoisie and the national bourgeoisie cannot lead any genuine revolution to victory.

Our twenty-eight years have been quite different. We have had much valuable experience. A well-disciplined Party armed with the theory of Marxism-Leninism, using the method of self-criticism and linked with the masses of the people; an army under the leadership of such a Party; a united front of all revolutionary classes and all revolutionary groups under the leadership of such a Party – these are the three main weapons with which we have defeated the enemy. They distinguish us from our predecessors. Relying on them, we have won basic victory. We have travelled a tortuous road. We have struggled against opportunist deviations in our Party, both Right and "Left". Whenever we made serious mistakes on these three matters, the revolution suffered setbacks. Taught by mistakes and setbacks, we have become wiser and handle our affairs better. It is hard for any political party or person to avoid mistakes, but we should make as few as possible. Once a mistake is made, we should correct it, and the more quickly and thoroughly the better.

To sum up our experience and concentrate it into one point, it is: the people's democratic dictatorship under the leadership of the working class (through the Communist Party) and based upon the alliance of workers and peasants. This dictatorship must unite as one with the international revolutionary forces. This is our formula, our principal experience, our main programme.

Twenty-eight years of our Party are a long period, in which we have accomplished only one thing – we have won basic victory in the revolutionary war. This calls for celebration, because it is the people's victory, because it is a victory in a country as large as China. But we still have much work to do; to use the analogy of a journey, our past work is only the first step in a long march of ten thousand *li*. Remnants of the enemy have yet to be wiped out. The serious task of economic construction lies before us. We shall soon put aside some of the things we know well and be compelled to do things we don't know well. This means difficulties. The imperialists reckon that we will not be able to manage our economy; they are standing by and looking on, awaiting our failure.

We must overcome difficulties, we must learn what we do not know. We must learn to do economic work from all who know how, no matter who they are. We must esteem them as teachers, learning from them respectfully and conscientiously. We must not pretend to know when we do not know. We must not put on bureaucratic airs. If we dig into a subject for several months, for a year or two, for three or five years, we shall eventually master it. At first some of the Soviet Communists also were not very good at handling economic matters and the imperialists awaited their failure too. But the Communist Party of the Soviet Union emerged victorious and, under the leadership of Lenin and Stalin, it learned not only how to make the revolution but also how to carry on construction. It has built a great and splendid socialist state. The Communist Party of the Soviet Union is our best teacher and we must learn from it. The situation both at home and abroad is in our favour, we can rely fully on the weapon of the people's democratic dictatorship, unite the people throughout the country, the reactionaries excepted, and advance steadily to our goal.

NOTES

[1] Also known as the world of Great Harmony. It refers to a society based on public ownership, free from class exploitation and oppression – a lofty ideal long cherished by the Chinese people. Here the realm of Great Harmony means communist society.

[2] See V. I. Lenin, *"Left-Wing" Communism, an Infantile Disorder*, Chapter 2. Lenin said: "For nearly half a century – approximately from the 'forties to the 'nineties – advanced thinkers in Russia, under the oppression of an unparalleled, savage and reactionary tsardom, eagerly sought for the correct revolutionary theory and followed each and every 'last word' in Europe and America in this sphere with astonishing diligence and thoroughness. Russia achieved Marxism, the only correct revolutionary theory, veritably through *suffering*, by half a century of unprecedented torment and sacrifice, of unprecedented revolutionary heroism, incredible energy, devoted searching, study, testing in practice, disappointment, verification and comparison with European experience."

[3] Faced with the opposition of the Chinese people to her traffic in opium, Britain sent forces in 1840-42 to invade Kwangtung and other coastal regions of China under the pretext of protecting trade. The troops in Kwangtung, led by Lin Tse-hsu, fought a war of resistance.

[4] Hung Hsiu-chuan (1814-64), who was born in Kwangtung, was the leader of a peasant revolutionary war in the middle of the 19th century. In 1851 he led a mass uprising in Kwangsi and proclaimed the establishment of the Taiping Heavenly Kingdom, which held many provinces and fought the Ching Dynasty for fourteen years. In 1864 this revolutionary war failed and Hung Hsiu-chuan committed suicide by poison.

[5] Kang Yu-wei (1858-1927), of Nanhai County, Kwangtung Province. In 1895, after China had been defeated by Japanese imperialism in the previous year, he led thirteen hundred candidates for the third grade in the imperial examinations at Peking in submitting a "ten thousand word memorial" to Emperor Kuang Hsu, asking for "constitutional reform and modernization" and asking that the autocratic monarchy be changed into a constitutional monarchy. In 1898, in an attempt to introduce reforms, the emperor promoted Kang Yu-wei together with Tan Sze-tung, Liang Chi-chao and others to key posts in the government. Later, the Empress Dowager Tzu Hsi, representing the die-hards, again took power and the reform movement failed. Kang Yu-wei and Liang Chi-chao fled abroad and formed the Protect-the-Emperor Party, which became a reactionary political faction in opposition to the bourgeois and petty bourgeois revolutionaries represented by Sun Yat-sen. Among Kang's works were *Forgeries in the Classics of the Confucian Canon, Confucius as a Reformer*, and *Ta Tung Shu* or the *Book of Great Harmony*.

[6] Yen Fu (1853-1921), of Foochow, Fukien Province, studied at a naval academy in Britain. After the Sino-Japanese War of 1894, he advocated constitutional monarchy and reforms to modernize China. His translations of T. H. Huxley's *Evolution and Ethics*, Adam Smith's *The Wealth of Nations*, J. S. Mill's *System of Logic*, Montesquieu's *L'Esprit des Lois*, and other works were vehicles for the spread of European bourgeois thought in China.

[7] A system of examinations adopted by China's autocratic dynasties. It was a method used by the feudal ruling class for selecting personnel to govern the people and also for enticing the intellectuals. The system, dating from the 7th century, persisted into the early 20th century.

[8] The Revolution of 1911 overthrew the autocratic regime of the Ching Dynasty. On October 10 of that year, a section of the New Army, at the urging of the revolutionary societies of the bourgeoisie and petty bourgeoisie, staged an uprising in Wuchang. This was followed by uprisings in other provinces, and very soon the rule of the Ching Dynasty crumbled. On January 1, 1912, the Provisional Government of the Republic of China was set up in Nanking, and Sun Yat-sen was elected Provisional President. The revolution achieved victory through the alliance of the bourgeoisie, peasants, workers and urban petty bourgeoisie. But because the group which led the revolution was compromising in nature, failed to bring real benefits to the peasants and yielded to the pressure of imperialism and the feudal forces, state power fell into the hands of the Northern warlord Yuan Shih-kai, and the revolution failed.

[9] A hero in the novel, *Shui Hu Chuan (Heroes of the Marshes)*, who killed a tiger with his bare hands on the Chingyang Ridge. This is one of the most popular episodes in that famous novel.

[10] For the relation between the socialization of agriculture and the industrialization of the country, see *On the Question of Agricultural Co-operation* (Sections 7 and 8), a report made by Comrade Mao Tse-tung on July 31, 1955 at the Conference of the Secretaries of the Provincial, Municipal and Autonomous Region Committees of the Chinese Communist Party. In this report Comrade Mao Tse-tung, on the basis of Soviet experience and our own country's practice, greatly developed the thesis that socialization of agriculture should proceed in step with socialist industrialization.

[11] The quotation is from Chu Hsi's commentary on the *Confucian Doctrine of the Mean*, Chapter 13.

CAST AWAY ILLUSIONS,
PREPARE FOR STRUGGLE*

August 14, 1949

It is no accident that the U.S. State Department's White Paper on China-U.S. Relations and Secretary of State Acheson's Letter of Transmittal to President Truman[1] have been released at this time. The publication of these documents reflects the victory of the Chinese people and the defeat of imperialism, it reflects the decline of the entire world system of imperialism. The imperialist system is riddled with insuperable internal contradictions, and therefore the imperialists are plunged into deep gloom.

Imperialism has prepared the conditions for its own doom. These conditions are the awakening of the great masses of the people in the colonies and semi-colonies and in the imperialist countries themselves. Imperialism has pushed the great masses of the people throughout the world into the historical epoch of the great struggle to abolish imperialism.

Imperialism has prepared the material as well as the moral conditions for the struggle of the great masses of the people.

The material conditions are factories, railways, firearms, artillery, and the like. Most of the powerful equipment of the Chinese People's Liberation Army comes from U.S. imperialism, some comes from Japanese imperialism and some is of our own manufacture.

The British aggression against China in 1840[2] was followed by the wars of aggression against China by the Anglo-French allied forces,[3] by France,[4] by Japan,[5] and by the allied forces of the eight powers (Britain, France, Japan, tsarist Russia, Germany, the United States, Italy and Austria);[6] by the war between Japan and tsarist Russia on Chinese territory;[7] by Japan's war of aggression against China in China's Northeast, which began in 1931; by Japan's war of aggression against all China, which began in 1937 and lasted eight long years; and, finally, by the latest war of aggression against the Chinese people, which has gone on for three years, waged to all appearances by Chiang Kai-shek but in reality by the United States. As stated in Acheson's Letter, the United States in this last war has given the Kuomintang government material aid to the value of "more than 50 percent" of the latter's "monetary expenditures" and "furnished the Chinese armies" (meaning the Kuomintang armies) with "military supplies". It is a war in which the United States supplies the money and guns and Chiang Kai-shek supplies the men to fight for the United States and slaughter the Chinese people. All these wars of aggression, together with political, economic and cultural aggression and oppression, have caused the Chinese to hate imperialism, made them stop and think, "What is all this about?" and compelled them to bring their revolutionary spirit into full play and become united through struggle. They fought, failed, fought again, failed again and fought again and accumulated 109 years of experience, accumulated the experience of hundreds of struggles, great and small, military and political, economic and cultural, with bloodshed and without bloodshed – and only then won today's basic victory. These are the moral conditions without which the revolution could not be victorious.

To serve the needs of its aggression, imperialism created the comprador system and bureaucrat-capital in China. Imperialist aggression stimulated China's social economy, brought about changes in it and created the opposites of imperialism – the national industry and national bourgeoisie of China, and especially the Chinese proletariat working in enterprises run directly by the imperialists, those run by bureaucrat-capital and those run by the national bourgeoisie. To serve the needs of its aggression, imperialism ruined the Chinese peasants by exploiting them through the exchange of unequal values and thereby created great masses of poor peasants, numbering hundreds of millions and comprising 70 per cent of China's rural population. To serve the needs of its aggression, imperialism created for China

---

* This article and the four that follow – "Farewell, Leighton Stuart!", "Why It Is Necessary to Discuss the White Paper", " 'Friendship' or Aggression?" and "The Bankruptcy of the Idealist Conception of History" – were commentaries written by Comrade Mao Tse-tung for the Hsinhua News Agency on the U.S. State Department's White Paper and Dean Acheson's Letter of Transmittal. They exposed the imperialist nature of United States policy towards China, criticized the illusions about U.S. imperialism harboured by some of the bourgeois intellectuals in China and gave a theoretical explanation of the reasons for the rise of the Chinese revolution and for its victory.

millions of big and small intellectuals of a new type, differing from the old type of *literatus* or scholar-bureaucrat. But imperialism and its running dogs, the reactionary governments of China, could control only a part of these intellectuals and finally only a handful, such as Hu Shih, Fu Sze-nien and Chien Mu;[8] all the rest got out of control and turned against them. Students, teachers, professors, technicians, engineers, doctors, scientists, writers, artists and government employees, all are revolting against or parting company with the Kuomintang. The Communist Party is the party of the poor and is described in the Kuomintang's widespread, all-pervasive propaganda as a band of people who commit murder and arson, who rape and loot, who reject history and culture, renounce the motherland, have no filial piety or respect for teachers and are impervious to all reason, who practise community of property and of women and employ the military tactics of the "human sea" – in short, a horde of fiendish monsters who perpetrate every conceivable crime and are unpardonably wicked. But strangely enough, it is this very horde that has won the support of several hundred million people, including the majority of the intellectuals, and especially the student youth.

Part of the intellectuals still want to wait and see. They think: the Kuomintang is no good and the Communist Party is not necessarily good either, so we had better wait and see. Some support the Communist Party in words, but in their hearts they are waiting to see. They are the very people who have illusions about the United States. They are unwilling to draw a distinction between the U.S. imperialists, who are in power, and the American people, who are not. They are easily duped by the honeyed words of the U.S. imperialists, as though these imperialists would deal with People's China on the basis of equality and mutual benefit without a stern, long struggle. They still have many reactionary, that is to say, anti-popular, ideas in their heads, but they are not Kuomintang reactionaries. They are the middle-of-the-roaders or the right-wingers in People's China. They are the supporters of what Acheson calls "democratic individualism". The deceptive manoeuvres of the Achesons still have a flimsy social base in China.

Acheson's White Paper admits that the U.S. imperialists are at a complete loss as to what to do about the present situation in China. The Kuomintang is so impotent that no amount of help can save it from inevitable doom; the U.S. imperialists are losing grip over things and feel helpless. Acheson says in his Letter of Transmittal:

The unfortunate but inescapable fact is that the ominous result of the civil war in China was beyond the control of the government of the United States. Nothing that this country did or could have done within the reasonable limits of its capabilities could have changed that result; nothing that was left undone by this country has contributed to it. It was the product of internal Chinese forces, forces which this country tried to influence but could not.

According to logic, Acheson's conclusion should be, as some muddle-headed Chinese intellectuals think or say, to act like "the butcher who lays down his knife and at once becomes a Buddha" or "the robber who has a change of heart and becomes a virtuous man", that is, he should treat People's China on the basis of equality and mutual benefit and stop making trouble. But no, says Acheson, trouble-making will continue, and definitely so. Will there be any result? There will, says he. On what group of people will he rely? On the supporters of "democratic individualism". Says Acheson:

> . . . ultimately the profound civilization and the democratic individualism of China will reassert themselves and she will throw off the foreign yoke. I consider that we should encourage all developments in China which now and in the future work toward this end.

How different is the logic of the imperialists from that of the people! Make trouble, fail, make trouble again, fail again . . . till their doom; that is the logic of the imperialists and all reactionaries the world over in dealing with the people's cause, and they will never go against this logic. This is a Marxist law. When we say "imperialism is ferocious", we mean that its nature will never change, that the imperialists will never lay down their butcher knives, that they will never become Buddhas, till their doom.

Fight, fail, fight again, fail again, fight again . . . till their victory; that is the logic of the people, and they too will never go against this logic. This is another Marxist law. The Russian people's revolution followed this law, and so has the Chinese people's revolution.

Classes struggle, some classes triumph, others are eliminated. Such is history, such is the history of civilization for thousands of years. To interpret history from this viewpoint is historical materialism; standing in opposition to this viewpoint is historical idealism.

The method of self-criticism can be applied only within the ranks of the people; it is impossible to persuade the imperialists and the Chinese reactionaries to show kindness of heart and turn from their evil ways.   The only course is to organize forces and struggle against them, as in our People's War of Liberation and the agrarian revolution, to expose the imperialists, "irritate"[9] them, overthrow them, punish them for offences against the law and "allow them only to behave themselves and not to be unruly in word or deed".   Only then will there be any hope of dealing with imperialist foreign countries on the basis of equality and mutual benefit.   Only then will there be any hope that those landlords, bureaucrat-capitalists, members of the reactionary Kuomintang clique and their accomplices, who have laid down their arms and surrendered, can be given education for transforming the bad into the good and be transformed, as far as possible, into good people.   Many Chinese liberals – the old-type democratic elements, *i.e.*, the supporters of "democratic individualism", whom Truman, Marshall, Acheson, Leighton Stuart and the like count on and have been trying to win over – often find themselves in a passive position and are often wrong in their judgements on the U.S. rulers, on the Kuomintang, on the Soviet Union and also on the Communist Party of China.   The reason is precisely that they do not look at, or disapprove of looking at, problems from the standpoint of historical materialism.

It is the duty of progressives – the Communists, members of the democratic parties, politically conscious workers, the student youth and progressive intellectuals – to unite with the intermediate strata, middle-of-the-roaders and backward elements of various strata, with all those in People's China who are still wavering and hesitating (these people will waver for a long time to come and, even after they have once become steady, will waver again as soon as they meet difficulties), give them sincere help, criticize their wavering character, educate them, win them over to the side of the masses, prevent the imperialists from pulling them over and tell them to cast away illusions and prepare for struggle.   Let no one think that there is no more work to do now that victory is won.   We still have to work, to do a great deal of patient work, before we can truly win these people over.   When they are won over, imperialism will be entirely isolated, and Acheson will no longer be able to play any of his tricks.

The slogan, "Prepare for struggle", is addressed to those who still cherish certain illusions about the relations between China and the

imperialist countries, especially between China and the United States.
With regard to this question, they are still passive, their minds are
still not made up, they are still not determined to wage a long struggle
against U.S. (and British) imperialism because they still have illusions
about the United States. There is still a very wide, or fairly wide,
gap between these people and ourselves on this question.

The publication of the U.S. White Paper and Acheson's Letter of
Transmittal is worthy of celebration, because it is a bucket of cold
water and a loss of face for those who have ideas of the old type of
democracy or democratic individualism, who do not approve of, or do
not quite approve of, or are dissatisfied with, or are somewhat dissatisfied with, or even resent, people's democracy, or democratic collectiv-
ism, or democratic centralism, or collective heroism, or patriotism
based on internationalism – but who still have patriotic feelings and
are not Kuomintang reactionaries. It is a bucket of cold water particularly for those who believe that everything American is good and
hope that China will model herself on the United States.

Acheson openly declares that the Chinese democratic individualists
will be "encouraged" to throw off the so-called "foreign yoke". That
is to say, he calls for the overthrow of Marxism-Leninism and the
people's democratic dictatorship led by the Communist Party of China.
For this "ism" and this system, it is alleged, are "foreign", with no
roots in China, imposed on the Chinese by the German, Karl Marx
(who died sixty-six years ago), and the Russians, Lenin (who died
twenty-five years ago) and Stalin (who is still alive); this "ism" and
this system, moreover, are downright bad, because they advocate the
class struggle, the overthrow of imperialism, etc.; hence they must be
got rid of. In this connection, it is alleged, "the democratic individualism of China will reassert itself" with the "encouragement" of
President Truman, the backstage Commander-in-Chief Marshall, Secretary of State Acheson (the charming foreign mandarin responsible
for the publication of the White Paper) and Ambassador Leighton
Stuart who has scampered off. Acheson and his like think they are
giving "encouragement", but those Chinese democratic individualists
who still have patriotic feelings, even though they believe in the United
States, may quite possibly feel this is a bucket of cold water thrown
on them and a loss of face; for instead of dealing with the authorities
of the Chinese people's democratic dictatorship in the proper way,
Acheson and his like are doing this filthy work and, what is more,
they have openly published it. What a loss of face! What a loss

of face! To those who are patriotic, Acheson's statement is no "encouragement" but an insult.

China is in the midst of a great revolution. All China is seething with enthusiasm. The conditions are favourable for winning over and uniting with all those who do not have a bitter and deep-seated hatred for the cause of the people's revolution, even though they have mistaken ideas. Progressives should use the White Paper to persuade all these persons.

NOTES

[1] The U.S. White Paper, *United States Relations with China*, was published by the U.S. State Department on August 5, 1949. Acheson's Letter of Transmittal to Truman was dated July 30, 1949. The main body of the White Paper, divided into eight chapters, deals with Sino-U.S. relations in the period from 1844, when the United States forced China to sign the "Treaty of Wanghia", to 1949, when victory was basically won throughout the country in the Chinese people's revolution. The White Paper goes into particular detail about how, in the five years from the last part of the War of Resistance Against Japan to 1949, the United States pursued a policy of support for Chiang Kai-shek and of anti-communism, opposed the Chinese people by every possible means and finally met with defeat. The White Paper and Acheson's Letter of Transmittal are full of distortions, omissions and fabrications, and also of venomous slanders and deep hatred against the Chinese people. In the quarrel within the U.S. reactionary camp over its policy towards China, imperialists like Truman and Acheson were compelled to reveal publicly through the White Paper some of the truth about their counter-revolutionary activities in an attempt to convince their opponents. Thus, in its objective effect, the White Paper became a confession by U.S. imperialism of its crimes of aggression against China.

[2] See "On the People's Democratic Dictatorship", Note 3, p. 423 of this volume.

[3] From 1856 to 1860 Britain and France jointly carried on a war of aggression against China, with the United States and tsarist Russia supporting them from the side-lines. The government of the Ching Dynasty was then devoting all its energy to suppressing the peasant revolution of the Taiping Heavenly Kingdom and adopted a policy of passive resistance towards the foreign aggressors. The Anglo-French allied forces occupied such major cities as Canton, Tientsin and Peking, plundered and burned down Yuan Ming Yuan Palace in Peking and forced the Ching government to conclude the "Treaty of Tientsin" and the "Treaty of Peking". The main provisions of these treaties included the opening as treaty ports of Tientsin, Newchwang, Tengchow, Taiwan, Tanshui, Chaochow, Chiungchow, Nanking, Chinkiang, Kiukiang and Hankow and the granting to foreigners of the special privileges of travel and missionary activities in China's interior and of inland navigation. From then on foreign forces of aggression extended over all China's coastal provinces and penetrated deep into the hinterland.

[4] In 1884-85 the French aggressors invaded Vietnam and the Chinese provinces of Kwangsi, Fukien, Taiwan and Chekiang. Chinese troops resisted vigorously and won a series of victories. Notwithstanding the victories in the war, the corrupt

Ching government signed the humiliating "Treaty of Tientsin", which recognized the occupation of Vietnam by the French and permitted their forces of aggression to penetrate southern China.

[5] The Sino-Japanese War of 1894. The war broke out as a result of Japan's aggression against Korea and her provocations to the Chinese land and naval forces. In this war the Chinese forces put up a heroic fight, but China suffered defeat owing to the corruption of the Ching government and its lack of preparation for resistance. As a result, the Ching government concluded the shameful "Treaty of Shimonoseki" with Japan, under which it ceded Taiwan and the Penghu Islands, paid war reparations of 200 million taels of silver, permitted the Japanese to set up factories in China, opened Shasi, Chungking, Soochow and Hangchow as treaty ports and recognized Japan's domination over Korea.

[6] In 1900 eight imperialist powers, Britain, France, Japan, tsarist Russia, Germany, the United States, Italy and Austria, sent a joint force to attack China in an attempt to suppress the Yi Ho Tuan Uprising of the Chinese people against aggression. The Chinese people resisted heroically. The allied forces of the eight powers captured Taku and occupied Tientsin and Peking. In 1901 the Ching government concluded a treaty with the eight imperialist countries; its main provisions were that China had to pay those countries the enormous sum of 450 million taels of silver as war reparations and grant them the special privilege of stationing troops in Peking and in the area from Peking to Tientsin to Shanhaikuan.

[7] This was the imperialist war fought between Japan and tsarist Russia in 1904-05 to grab China's Northeast and Korea. As the war was fought mainly in the area of Fengtien (now Shenyang) and Liaoyang and around the port of Lushun in China's Northeast, it caused enormous losses to the Chinese people. As a result of the war tsarist Russia was defeated and supplanted by Japanese imperialism in the dominant role in China's Northeast. Under the peace treaty (the Treaty of Portsmouth) concluded at the end of this war tsarist Russia also recognized Japan's exclusive control over Korea.

[8] Hu Shih, who was formerly a university professor, university president and ambassador of the Kuomintang government to the United States, is a well-known apologist for U.S. imperialism among Chinese bourgeois intellectuals. Fu Sze-nien and Chien Mu, also university professors, were scholars serving the reactionary Kuomintang government.

[9] See "On the People's Democratic Dictatorship", pp. 415-16 of this volume.

FAREWELL, LEIGHTON STUART!

August 18, 1949

It is understandable that the date chosen for the publication of the U.S. White Paper was August 5, a time when Leighton Stuart[1] had departed from Nanking for Washington but had not yet arrived there, since Leighton Stuart is a symbol of the complete defeat of the U.S. policy of aggression. Leighton Stuart is an American born in China; he has fairly wide social connections and spent many years running missionary schools in China; he once sat in a Japanese gaol during the War of Resistance; he used to pretend to love both the United States and China and was able to deceive quite a number of Chinese. Hence, he was picked out by George C. Marshall, was made U.S. ambassador to China and became a celebrity in the Marshall group. In the eyes of the Marshall group he had only one fault, namely, that the whole period when he was ambassador to China as an exponent of their policy was the very period in which that policy was utterly defeated by the Chinese people; that was no small responsibility. It is only natural that the White Paper, which is designed to evade this responsibility, should have been published at a time when Leighton Stuart was on his way to Washington but had not yet arrived.

The war to turn China into a U.S. colony, a war in which the United States of America supplies the money and guns and Chiang Kai-shek the men to fight for the United States and slaughter the Chinese people, has been an important component of the U.S. imperialist policy of world-wide aggression since World War II. The U.S. policy of aggression has several targets. The three main targets are Europe, Asia and the Americas. China, the centre of gravity in Asia, is a large country with a population of 475 million; by seizing China, the United States would possess all of Asia. With its Asian front consolidated, U.S. imperialism could concentrate its forces on attacking Europe. U.S. imperialism considers its front in the Americas relatively secure. These are the smug over-all calculations of the U.S. aggressors.

But in the first place, the American people and the peoples of the world do not want war. Secondly, the attention of the United States has largely been absorbed by the awakening of the peoples of Europe, by the rise of the People's Democracies in Eastern Europe, and particularly by the towering presence of the Soviet Union, this unprecedentedly powerful bulwark of peace bestriding Europe and Asia, and by its strong resistance to the U.S. policy of aggression. Thirdly, and this is most important, the Chinese people have awakened, and the armed forces and the organized strength of the people under the leadership of the Communist Party of China have become more powerful than ever before. Consequently, the ruling clique of U.S. imperialism has been prevented from adopting a policy of direct, large-scale armed attacks on China and instead has adopted a policy of helping Chiang Kai-shek fight the civil war.

U.S. naval, ground and air forces did participate in the war in China. There were U.S. naval bases in Tsingtao, Shanghai and Taiwan. U.S. troops were stationed in Peiping, Tientsin, Tangshan, Chinwangtao, Tsingtao, Shanghai and Nanking. The U.S. air force controlled all of China's air space and took aerial photographs of all China's strategic areas for military maps. At the town of Anping near Peiping, at Chiutai near Changchun, at Tangshan and in the Eastern Shantung Peninsula, U.S. troops and other military personnel clashed with the People's Liberation Army and on several occasions were captured.[2] Chennault's air fleet took an extensive part in the civil war.[3] Besides transporting troops for Chiang Kai-shek, the U.S. air force bombed and sank the cruiser *Chungking*, which had mutinied against the Kuomintang.[4] All these were acts of direct participation in the war, although they fell short of an open declaration of war and were not large in scale, and although the principal method of U.S. aggression was the large-scale supply of money, munitions and advisers to help Chiang Kai-shek fight the civil war.

The use of this method by the United States was determined by the objective situation in China and the rest of the world, and not by any lack of desire on the part of the Truman-Marshall group, the ruling clique of U.S. imperialism, to launch direct aggression against China. Moreover, at the outset of its help to Chiang Kai-shek in fighting the civil war, a crude farce was staged in which the United

States appeared as mediator in the conflict between the Kuomintang and the Communist Party; this was an attempt to soften up the Communist Party of China, deceive the Chinese people and thus gain control of all China without fighting. The peace negotiations failed, the deception fell through and the curtain rose on the war.

Liberals or "democratic individualists" who cherish illusions about the United States and have short memories! Please look at Acheson's own words:

> When peace came the United States was confronted with three possible alternatives in China: (1) it could have pulled out lock, stock and barrel; (2) it could have intervened militarily on a major scale to assist the Nationalists to destroy the Communists; (3) it could, while assisting the Nationalists to assert their authority over as much of China as possible, endeavor to avoid a civil war by working for a compromise between the two sides.

Why didn't the United States adopt the first of these policies? Acheson says:

> The first alternative would, and I believe American public opinion at the time so felt, have represented an abandonment of our international responsibilities and of our traditional policy of friendship for China before we had made a determined effort to be of assistance.

So that's how things stand: the "international responsibilities" of the United States and its "traditional policy of friendship for China" are nothing but intervention against China. Intervention is called assuming international responsibilities and showing friendship for China; as to non-intervention, it simply won't do. Here Acheson defiles U.S. public opinion; his is the "public opinion" of Wall Street, not the public opinion of the American people.

Why didn't the United States adopt the second of these policies? Acheson says:

> The second alternative policy, while it may look attractive theoretically and in retrospect, was wholly impracticable. The Nationalists had been unable to destroy the Communists during the 10 years before the war. Now after the war the Nationalists were, as indicated above, weakened, demoralized, and unpopular. They had quickly dissipated their popular support and prestige in the areas liberated from the Japanese by the conduct of their civil

and military officials.   The Communists on the other hand were
much stronger than they had ever been and were in control of
most of North China.   Because of the ineffectiveness of the Na-
tionalist forces which was later to be tragically demonstrated, the
Communists probably could have been dislodged only by American arms.   It is obvious that the American people would not have
sanctioned such a colossal commitment of our armies in 1945 or
later.   We therefore came to the third alternative policy. . . .

What a splendid idea!   The United States supplies the money
and guns and Chiang Kai-shek the men to fight for the United States
and slaughter the Chinese people, to "destroy the Communists" and
turn China into a U.S. colony, so that the United States may fulfil its
"international responsibilities" and carry out its "traditional policy
of friendship for China".

Although the Kuomintang was corrupt and incompetent, "demor-
alized and unpopular", the United States nevertheless supplied it
with money and guns and made it fight.   Direct armed intervention
was all right, "theoretically".   It also seems all right "in retrospect"
to the rulers of the United States.   For direct armed intervention
would really have been interesting and it might "look attractive".
But it would not have worked in practice, for "it is obvious that the
American people would not have sanctioned" it.   Not that the imperialist group of Truman, Marshall, Acheson and their like did not
desire it – they very much desired it – but the situation in China, in
the United States and in the world as a whole (a point Acheson does
not mention) did not permit it; they had to give up their preference
and take the third way.

Let those Chinese who believe that "victory is possible even
without international help" listen.   Acheson is giving you a lesson.
Acheson is a good teacher, giving lessons free of charge, and he is
telling the whole truth with tireless zeal and great candour.   The
United States refrained from dispatching large forces to attack China,
not because the U.S. government didn't want to, but because it had
worries.   First worry: the Chinese people would oppose it, and the
U.S. government was afraid of getting hopelessly bogged down in a
quagmire.   Second worry: the American people would oppose it, and
so the U.S. government dared not order mobilization.   Third worry:
the people of the Soviet Union, of Europe and of the rest of the
world would oppose it, and the U.S. government would face universal

condemnation. Acheson's charming candour has its limits and he is unwilling to mention the third worry. The reason is he is afraid of losing face before the Soviet Union, he is afraid that the Marshall Plan in Europe,[5] which is already a failure despite pretences to the contrary, may end dismally in total collapse.

Let those Chinese who are short-sighted, muddle-headed liberals or democratic individualists listen. Acheson is giving you a lesson; he is a good teacher for you. He has made a clean sweep of your fancied U.S. humanity, justice and virtue. Isn't that so? Can you find a trace of humanity, justice or virtue in the White Paper or in Acheson's Letter of Transmittal?

True, the United States has science and technology. But unfortunately they are in the grip of the capitalists, not in the hands of the people, and are used to exploit and oppress the people at home and to perpetrate aggression and to slaughter people abroad. There is also "democracy" in the United States. But unfortunately it is only another name for the dictatorship of the bourgeoisie by itself. The United States has plenty of money. But unfortunately it is willing to give money only to the Chiang Kai-shek reactionaries, who are rotten to the core. The United States, it is said, is and will be quite willing to give money to its fifth column in China, but is unwilling to give it to the ordinary run of liberals or democratic individualists, who are much too bookish and do not know how to appreciate favours, and naturally it is even more unwilling to give money to the Communists. Money may be given, but only conditionally. What is the condition? Follow the United States. The Americans have sprinkled some relief flour in Peiping, Tientsin and Shanghai to see who will stoop to pick it up. Like Chiang Tai Kung fishing,[6] they have cast the line for the fish who want to be caught. But he who swallows food handed out in contempt[7] will get a bellyache.

We Chinese have backbone. Many who were once liberals or democratic individualists have stood up to the U.S. imperialists and their running dogs, the Kuomintang reactionaries. Wen Yi-to rose to his full height and smote the table, angrily faced the Kuomintang pistols and died rather than submit.[8] Chu Tse-ching, though seriously ill, starved to death rather than accept U.S. "relief food".[9] Han Yu of the Tang Dynasty wrote a "Eulogy of Po Yi",[10] praising a man with quite a few "democratic individualist" ideas, who shirked his duty towards the people of his own country, deserted his post and opposed the people's war of liberation of that time, led by King Wu. He

lauded the wrong man.   We should write eulogies of Wen Yi-to and
Chu Tse-ching who demonstrated the heroic spirit of our nation.

What matter if we have to face some difficulties?   Let them
blockade us!   Let them blockade us for eight or ten years!   By that
time all of China's problems will have been solved.   Will the Chinese
cower before difficulties when they are not afraid even of death?
Lao Tzu said, "The people fear not death, why threaten them with
it?"[11] U.S. imperialism and its running dogs, the Chiang Kai-
shek reactionaries, have not only "threatened" us with death but
actually put many of us to death.   Besides people like Wen Yi-to,
they have killed millions of Chinese in the last three years with U.S.
carbines, machine-guns, mortars, bazookas, howitzers, tanks and bombs
dropped from aeroplanes.   This situation is now coming to an end.
They have been defeated.   It is we who are going in to attack them,
not they who are coming out to attack us.   They will soon be finished.
True, the few problems left to us, such as blockade, unemployment,
famine, inflation and rising prices, are difficulties, but we have already
begun to breathe more easily than in the past three years.   We have
come triumphantly through the ordeal of the last three years, why
can't we overcome these few difficulties of today?   Why can't we
live without the United States?

When the People's Liberation Army crossed the Yangtse River,
the U.S. colonial government at Nanking fled helter-skelter.   Yet
His Excellency Ambassador Stuart sat tight, watching wide-eyed,
hoping to set up shop under a new signboard and to reap some profit.
But what did he see?   Apart from the People's Liberation Army
marching past, column after column, and the workers, peasants and
students rising in hosts, he saw something else – the Chinese liberals
or democratic individualists turning out in force, shouting slogans and
talking revolution together with the workers, peasants, soldiers and
students.   In short, he was left out in the cold, "standing all alone,
body and shadow comforting each other".[12]   There was nothing
more for him to do, and he had to take to the road, his briefcase
under his arm.

There are still some intellectuals and other people in China who
have muddled ideas and illusions about the United States.   Therefore we should explain things to them, win them over, educate them
and unite with them, so they will come over to the side of the people
and not fall into the snares set by imperialism.   But the prestige of
U.S. imperialism among the Chinese people is completely bankrupt,

and the White Paper is a record of its bankruptcy.   Progressives should make good use of the White Paper to educate the Chinese people.

Leighton Stuart has departed and the White Paper has arrived. Very good.   Very good.   Both events are worth celebrating.

NOTES

[1] John Leighton Stuart, who was born in China in 1876, was always a loyal agent of U.S. cultural aggression in China. He started missionary work in China in 1905 and in 1919 became president of Yenching University, which was established by the United States in Peking.   On July 11, 1946, he was appointed U.S. ambassador to China. He actively supported the Kuomintang reactionaries in prosecuting the civil war and carried out various political intrigues against the Chinese people.   On August 2, 1949, because all the efforts of U.S. imperialism to obstruct the victory of the Chinese people's revolution had completely failed, Leighton Stuart had to leave China quietly.

[2] Following the Japanese surrender in 1945, the armed forces of the United States, with the purpose of aggression against China's territory and sovereignty and of interference in her domestic affairs, landed in China and stationed themselves at Peiping, Shanghai, Nanking, Tientsin, Tangshan, Kaiping, Chinwangtao, Chinghai, Tsingtao and other places.   In addition, they repeatedly invaded the Liberated Areas.   On July 29, 1946, U.S. troops in Tientsin, in co-ordination with Chiang Kai-shek's bandit troops, assaulted the town of Anping, Hsiangho County, Hopei Province; this is the Anping Incident referred to in the text.   On March 1, 1947, U.S. troops made a military reconnaissance of the position of the People's Liberation Army at Hohsipao, situated between Changchun and Chiutai in northeastern China. On June 16, 1946, U.S. troops at Tangshan, Hopei Province, raided Sungchiaying and other places; in July they raided Sanho Village, Luanhsien County, and Hsihonan Village, Changli County, both near Tangshan.   Of the numerous attacks on the Eastern Shantung Peninsula, the most widely-known were two, one by U.S. aircraft and warships on Langnuankou and Hsiaoli Island, Mouping County, on August 28, 1947, and the other by U.S. forces on Wanglintao Village, north of Chimo County, on December 25, 1947 in co-ordination with Chiang Kai-shek's bandit troops.   In all these cases in which the U.S. forces committed acts of aggression by invading the Liberated Areas, the Chinese People's Liberation Army or the local people's armed forces took just action in self-defence.

[3] Claire Lee Chennault was at one time U.S. adviser to the Kuomintang government's air force.   After the Japanese surrender, he organized a group of the U.S. 14th Air Force personnel into an air transport corps to help the Kuomintang fight the civil war.   His air transport corps took a direct part in the criminal reconnoitring and bombing of the Liberated Areas.

[4] See "On the Outrages by British Warships – Statement by the Spokesman of the General Headquarters of the Chinese People's Liberation Army", Note 4, p. 403 of this volume.

[5] On June 5, 1947, U.S. Secretary of State George C. Marshall made a speech at Harvard University, putting forward a plan for so-called U.S. "aid" to rehabilitate Europe. The "European Recovery Programme" subsequently drawn up by the U.S. government on the basis of the speech was known as the "Marshall Plan".

[6] Chiang Tai Kung lived in the Chou Dynasty. According to a legend, he once fished in the Weishui River, holding a rod without hook or bait three feet above the water, and saying, "The fish that is destined to be caught will come up." (From *Stories About King Wu's Expedition Against the Yin Dynasty.*)

[7] "Food handed out in contempt" refers to alms handed out as an insult. It is an allusion to a story in the *Book of Rites*, which tells of a hungry man in the State of Chi, who would rather starve to death than accept food given him insultingly.

[8] Wen Yi-to (1899-1946), famed Chinese poet, scholar and university professor. In 1943 he began to take an active part in the struggle for democracy out of bitter hatred for the reaction and corruption of the Chiang Kai-shek government. After the War of Resistance Against Japan, he vigorously opposed the Kuomintang's conspiracy with U.S. imperialism to start civil war against the people. On July 15, 1946, he was assassinated in Kunming by Kuomintang thugs.

[9] Chu Tse-ching (1898-1948), Chinese man of letters and university professor. After the War of Resistance, he actively supported the student movement against the Chiang Kai-shek regime. In June 1948 he signed a declaration protesting against the revival of Japanese militarism, which was being fostered by the United States, and rejecting "U.S. relief" flour. He was then living in great poverty. He died in Peiping on August 12, 1948, from poverty and illness, but even on his death-bed he enjoined his family not to buy the U.S. flour rationed by the Kuomintang government.

[10] Han Yu (768-824) was a famous writer of the Tang Dynasty. "Eulogy of Po Yi" was a prose piece written by him. Po Yi, who lived towards the end of the Yin Dynasty, opposed the expedition of King Wu of Chou against the House of Yin. After the downfall of the House of Yin, he fled to the Shouyang Mountain and starved to death rather than eat of Chou grain.

[11] A quotation from *Lao Tzu*, Chapter LXXIV.

[12] A quotation from Li Mi's "Memorial to the Emperor".

WHY IT IS NECESSARY TO DISCUSS
THE WHITE PAPER

August 28, 1949

We have criticized the U.S. White Paper and Acheson's Letter of Transmittal in three articles ("A Confession of Helplessness",[1] "Cast Away Illusions, Prepare for Struggle" and "Farewell, Leighton Stuart!"). Our criticism has aroused widespread attention and discussion in all democratic parties, people's organizations, the press, universities and schools, and among democratic personages in all walks of life throughout the country; they have issued many correct and useful declarations, statements and comments. Forums on the White Paper are being held and the entire discussion is still developing. The discussion covers Sino-U.S. relations, Sino-Soviet relations, China's foreign relations in the past hundred years, the mutual relation between the Chinese revolution and the revolutionary forces of the world, the relation between the Kuomintang reactionaries and the Chinese people, the proper attitude to be adopted by the democratic parties, people's organizations and democratic personages in all walks of life in the struggle against imperialism, the proper attitude to be adopted by liberals or so-called democratic individualists on the country's internal and external relations as a whole, the ways of dealing with new imperialist intrigues, and so on. All this is very good and is of great educational value.

The whole world is now discussing the Chinese revolution and the U.S. White Paper. This is no accident, this shows the great significance of the Chinese revolution in world history. As for us Chinese, though we have basically won victory in our revolution, we have had no opportunity for a long time to discuss thoroughly the interrelations of this revolution and various forces at home and abroad. Such a discussion is necessary, and now an opportunity has been found in the discussion of the U.S. White Paper. We had no opportunity for this kind of discussion before because we had not won basic victory in the revolution, because Chinese and foreign reactionaries had cut off the big cities from the People's Liberated Areas and because some aspects of the contradictions had not yet been fully revealed by the development of the revolution. Now the situation is different. The greater part of China has been liberated, all aspects of the internal and external contradictions have been fully revealed, and just at this moment the United States has published the White Paper. Thus the opportunity for the discussion has been found.

The White Paper is a counter-revolutionary document which openly demonstrates U.S. imperialist intervention in China. In this respect, imperialism has departed from its normal practice. The great, victorious Chinese revolution has compelled one section or faction of the U.S. imperialist clique to reply to attacks from another by publishing certain authentic data on its own actions against the Chinese people and drawing reactionary conclusions from the data, because otherwise it could not get by. The fact that public revelation has replaced concealment is a sign that imperialism has departed from its normal practice. Until a few weeks ago, before the publication of the White Paper, the governments of the imperialist countries, though they engaged in counter-revolutionary activities every day, had never told the truth in their statements or official documents but had filled or at least flavoured them with professions of humanity, justice and virtue. This is still true of British imperialism, an old hand at trickery and deception, as well as of several other smaller imperialist countries. Opposed by the people on the one hand and by another faction in their own camp on the other, the newly arrived, upstart and neurotic U.S. imperialist group – Truman, Marshall, Acheson, Leighton Stuart and others – have considered it necessary and practicable to reveal publicly some (but not all) of their counter-revolutionary doings in order to argue with opponents in their own camp as to which kind of counter-revolutionary tactics is the more clever. In this way they have tried to convince their opponents so that they can go on applying what they regard as the cleverer counter-revolutionary tactics. Two factions of counter-revolutionaries have been competing with each other. One said, "Ours is the best method." The other said, "Ours is the best." When the dispute was at its hottest, one faction suddenly laid its cards on the table and revealed many of its treasured tricks of the past – and there you have the White Paper.

And so the White Paper has become material for the education of the Chinese people. For many years, a number of Chinese (at one time a great number) only half-believed what we Communists said on many questions, mainly on the nature of imperialism and of socialism, and thought, "It may not be so." This situation has undergone a change since August 5, 1949. For Acheson gave them a lesson and he spoke in his capacity as U.S. Secretary of State. In the case of certain data and conclusions, what he said coincides with what we Communists and other progressives have been saying. Once this happened, people could not but believe us, and many had their eyes opened – "So that's the way things really were!"

Acheson begins his Letter of Transmittal to Truman with the story of how he compiled the White Paper. His White Paper, he says, is different from all others, it is very objective and very frank:

> This is a frank record of an extremely complicated and most unhappy period in the life of a great country to which the United States has long been attached by ties of closest friendship. No available item has been omitted because it contains statements critical of our policy or might be the basis of future criticism. The inherent strength of our system is the responsiveness of the Government to an informed and critical public opinion. It is precisely this informed and critical public opinion which totalitarian governments, whether Rightist or Communist, cannot endure and do not tolerate.

Certain ties do exist between the Chinese people and the American people. Through their joint efforts, these ties may develop in the future to the point of the "closest friendship". But the obstacles placed by the Chinese and U.S. reactionaries were and still are a great hindrance to these ties. Moreover, because the reactionaries of both countries have told many lies to their peoples and played many filthy tricks, that is, spread much bad propaganda and done many bad deeds, the ties between the two peoples are far from close. What Acheson calls "ties of closest friendship" are those between the reactionaries of the two countries, not between the peoples. Here Acheson is neither objective nor frank, he confuses the relations between the two peoples with those between the reactionaries. For the peoples of the two countries the victory of the Chinese revolution and the defeat of the Chinese and U.S. reactionaries are the most joyful events that have ever happened, and the present period is the happiest of their lives. Conversely, it is only for Truman, Marshall, Acheson, Leighton Stuart and other U.S. reactionaries and for Chiang Kai-shek, H. H.

Kung, T. V. Soong, Chen Li-fu, Li Tsung-jen, Pai Chung-hsi and other Chinese reactionaries that it is truly "an extremely complicated and most unhappy period" in their lives.

In considering public opinion, the Achesons have mixed up the public opinion of the reactionaries with that of the people. Towards the public opinion of the people, the Achesons have no "responsiveness" whatsoever and are blind and deaf. For years they have turned a deaf ear to the opposition voiced by the people of the United States, China and the rest of the world to the reactionary foreign policy of the U.S. government. What does Acheson mean by "informed and critical public opinion"? Nothing but the numerous instruments of propaganda, such as the newspapers, news agencies, periodicals and broadcasting stations which are controlled by the two reactionary parties in the United States, the Republicans and the Democrats, and which specialize in the manufacture of lies and in threats against the people. Of these things Acheson says rightly that the Communists "cannot endure and do not tolerate" them (nor do the people). That is why we have closed down the imperialist offices of information, stopped the imperialist news agencies from distributing their dispatches to the Chinese press and forbidden them the freedom to go on poisoning the souls of the Chinese people on Chinese soil.

To say that a government led by the Communist Party is a "totalitarian government" is also half true. It is a government that exercises dictatorship over domestic and foreign reactionaries and does not give any of them any freedom to carry on their counter-revolutionary activities. Becoming angry, the reactionaries rail: "Totalitarian government!" Indeed, this is absolutely true so far as the power of the people's government to suppress the reactionaries is concerned. This power is now written into our programme; it will also be written into our constitution. Like food and clothing, this power is something a victorious people cannot do without even for a moment. It is an excellent thing, a protective talisman, an heirloom, which should under no circumstances be discarded before the thorough and total abolition of imperialism abroad and of classes within the country. The more the reactionaries rail "totalitarian government", the more obviously is it a treasure. But Acheson's remark is also half false. For the masses of the people, a government of the people's democratic dictatorship led by the Communist Party is not dictatorial or autocratic but democratic. It is the people's own government. The working personnel of this government must respectfully heed the voice of the people. At the same time, they are teachers of the people, teaching the people by the method of self-education or self-criticism.

As to what Acheson calls a "Rightist totalitarian government", the U.S. government has ranked first in the world among such governments since the downfall of the fascist governments of Germany, Italy and Japan. All bourgeois governments, including the governments of the German, Italian and Japanese reactionaries which are being shielded by imperialism, are governments of this type. The Tito government of Yugoslavia has now become an accomplice of this gang. The U.S. and British governments belong to the type in which the bourgeoisie, and this class alone, exercises dictatorship over the people. Contrary in all respects to the people's government, this type of government practises so-called democracy for the bourgeoisie but is dictatorial towards the people. The governments of Hitler, Mussolini, Tojo, Franco and Chiang Kai-shek discarded the veil of democracy for the bourgeoisie or never used it because the class struggle in their countries was extremely intense and they found it advantageous to discard, or not to use, this veil lest the people too should make use of it. The U.S. government still has a veil of democracy, but it has been cut down to a tiny patch by the U.S. reactionaries and become very faded, and is not what it used to be in the days of Washington, Jefferson and Lincoln.[2] The reason is that the class struggle has become more intense. When the class struggle becomes still more intense, the veil of U.S. democracy will inevitably be flung to the four winds.

As everybody can see, Acheson makes a great many mistakes the moment he opens his mouth. This is inevitable because he is a reactionary. As to how much of a "frank record" the White Paper is, we think it is frank and not frank at the same time. The Achesons are frank where they imagine that frankness will benefit their party or faction. Otherwise, they are not. To feign frankness is a ruse of war.

NOTES

[1] A commentary by the editorial department of the Hsinhua News Agency published on August 12, 1949.

[2] George Washington (1732-99), Thomas Jefferson (1743-1826) and Abraham Lincoln (1809-65) were well-known bourgeois statesmen in the early days of the

United States. Washington was the commander-in-chief of the revolutionary army
of the colonies during the American War of Independence (1775-83) and the first
president of the United States. Jefferson drafted the American Declaration of
Independence and became president of the United States. Lincoln advocated the
abolition of Negro slavery in the United States and during his presidency led the
war against the slave-owners of the southern states (1861-65); he issued the
"Emancipation Proclamation" in 1862.

"FRIENDSHIP" OR AGGRESSION?

August 30, 1949

Seeking to justify aggression, Dean Acheson harps on "friendship" and throws in lots of "principles".

Acheson says:

> The interest of the people and the Government of the United States in China goes far back into our history. Despite the distance and broad differences in background which separate China and the United States, our friendship for that country has always been intensified by the religious, philanthropic and cultural ties which have united the two peoples, and has been attested by many acts of good will over a period of many years, including the use of the Boxer indemnity for the education of Chinese students, the abolition of extraterritoriality during the Second World War, and our extensive aid to China during and since the close of the War. The record shows that the United States has consistently maintained and still maintains those fundamental principles of our foreign policy toward China which include the doctrine of the Open Door, respect for the administrative and territorial integrity of China, and opposition to any foreign domination of China.

Acheson is telling a bare-faced lie when he describes aggression as "friendship".

The history of the aggression against China by U.S. imperialism, from 1840 when it helped the British in the Opium War to the time it was thrown out of China by the Chinese people, should be written into a concise textbook for the education of Chinese youth. The United States was one of the first countries to force China to cede extraterritoriality[1] – witness the Treaty of Wanghia[2] of 1844, the first treaty ever signed between China and the United States, a treaty to which the White Paper refers. In this very treaty, the United States

447

compelled China to accept American missionary activity, in addition to imposing such terms as the opening of five ports for trade. For a very long period, U.S. imperialism laid greater stress than other imperialist countries on activities in the sphere of spiritual aggression, extending from religious to "philanthropic" and cultural undertakings. According to certain statistics, the investments of U.S. missionary and "philanthropic" organizations in China totalled 41,900,000 U.S. dollars, and 14.7 per cent of the assets of the missionary organizations were in medical service, 38.2 per cent in education and 47.1 per cent in religious activities.[3] Many well-known educational institutions in China, such as Yenching University, Peking Union Medical College, the Huei Wen Academies, St. John's University, the University of Nanking, Soochow University, Hangchow Christian College, Hsiangya Medical School, West China Union University and Lingnan University, were established by Americans.[4] It was in this field that Leighton Stuart made a name for himself; that was how he became U.S. ambassador to China. Acheson and his like know what they are talking about, and there is a background for his statement that "our friendship for that country has always been intensified by the religious, philanthropic and cultural ties which have united the two peoples". It was all for the sake of "intensifying friendship", we are told, that the United States worked so hard and deliberately at running these undertakings for 105 years after the signing of the Treaty of 1844.

Participation in the Eight-Power Allied Expedition to defeat China in 1900, the extortion of the "Boxer indemnity" and the later use of this fund "for the education of Chinese students" for purposes of spiritual aggression – this too counts as an expression of "friendship".

Despite the "abolition" of extraterritoriality, the culprit in the raping of Shen Chung was declared not guilty and released by the U.S. Navy Department on his return to the United States[5] – this counts as another expression of "friendship".

"Aid to China during and since the close of the War", totalling over 4,500 million U.S. dollars according to the White Paper, but over 5,914 million U.S. dollars according to our computation, was given to help Chiang Kai-shek slaughter several million Chinese – this counts as yet another expression of "friendship".

All the "friendship" shown to China by U.S. imperialism over the past 109 years (since 1840 when the United States collaborated with Britain in the Opium War), and especially the great act of "friendship" in helping Chiang Kai-shek slaughter several million Chinese in the last few years – all this had one purpose, namely, it "consistently maintained and still maintains those fundamental principles of our foreign policy toward China which include the doctrine of the Open Door, respect for the administrative and territorial integrity of China, and opposition to any foreign domination of China".

Several million Chinese were killed for no other purpose than first, to maintain the Open Door, second, to respect the administrative and territorial integrity of China and, third, to oppose any foreign domination of China.

Today, the only doors still open to Acheson and his like are in small strips of land, such as Canton and Taiwan, and only in these places is the first of these sacred principles "still maintained". In other places, in Shanghai for instance, the door was open after liberation, but now some one is using U.S. warships and their big guns to enforce the far from sacred principle of the Blockaded Door.

Today, it is only in small strips of land, such as Canton and Taiwan, that thanks to Acheson's second sacred principle administrative and territorial "integrity" is "still maintained". All other places are out of luck, and administration and territory have fallen to pieces.

Today, it is only in places such as Canton and Taiwan that thanks to Acheson's third sacred principle all "foreign domination", including U.S. domination, has been successfully done away with through the "opposition" of Acheson and his like; therefore such places are still dominated by the Chinese. The rest of the land of China – the mere mention makes one weep – is all gone, all dominated by foreigners, and the Chinese there have one and all been turned into slaves. Up to this point in his writing, His Excellency Dean Acheson did not have time to indicate what country these foreigners came from, but it becomes clear as one reads on, so there is no need to ask.

Whether non-interference in China's domestic affairs also counts as a principle, Acheson didn't say; probably it does not. Such is the logic of the U.S. mandarins. Anyone who reads Acheson's Letter of Transmittal to the end will attest to its superior logic.

NOTES

[1] "Extraterritoriality" here refers to consular jurisdiction. It was one of the special privileges for aggression which the imperialists wrested from China. Under the so-called consular jurisdiction, nationals of imperialist countries residing in China

were not subject to the jurisdiction of Chinese law; when they committed crimes or became defendants in civil lawsuits, they could be tried only in their respective countries' consular courts in China, and the Chinese government could not intervene.

[2] The "Treaty of Wanghia" was the first unequal treaty signed as a result of U.S. aggression against China. The United States, taking advantage of China's defeat in the Opium War, compelled the Ching Dynasty to sign this treaty, also called the "Sino-American Treaty on the Opening of Five Ports for Trade", in Wanghia Village near Macao in July 1844. Its thirty-four articles stipulated that whatever rights and privileges, including consular jurisdiction, were gained by Britain through the Treaty of Nanking and its annexes would also accrue to the United States.

[3] See C. F. Remer, *Foreign Investments in China*, Chapter 15.

[4] Yenching University was in Peiping; the Huei Wen Academies, in Peiping and Nanking; St. John's University, in Shanghai; Hsiangya Medical School (Yale in China), in Changsha; West China Union University, in Chengtu; and Lingnan University, in Canton.

[5] William Pierson, a corporal, and other U.S. marines raped Shen Chung, a girl student of Peking University, in Peiping on December 24, 1946. This aroused the great indignation of the people throughout the country against the atrocities of the U.S. forces. In January 1947, brushing aside the people's protests, the Kuomintang government handed over the chief criminal, Pierson, to the Americans to be dealt with at their discretion. In August the U.S. Navy Department set this criminal free with a verdict of "not guilty".

THE BANKRUPTCY OF
THE IDEALIST CONCEPTION OF HISTORY

September 16, 1949

The Chinese should thank Acheson, spokesman of the U.S. bourgeoisie, not merely because he has explicitly confessed to the fact that the United States supplied the money and guns and Chiang Kai-shek the men to fight for the United States and slaughter the Chinese people and because he has thus given Chinese progressives evidence with which to convince the backward elements. You see, hasn't Acheson himself confessed that the great, sanguinary war of the last few years, which cost the lives of millions of Chinese, was planned and organized by U.S. imperialism? The Chinese should thank Acheson, again not merely because he has openly declared that the United States intends to recruit the so-called "democratic individualists" in China, organize a U.S. fifth column and overthrow the People's Government led by the Communist Party of China and has thus alerted the Chinese, especially those tinged with liberalism, who are promising each other not to be taken in by the Americans and are all on guard against the underhand intrigues of U.S. imperialism. The Chinese should thank Acheson also because he has fabricated wild tales about modern Chinese history; and his conception of history is precisely that shared by a section of the Chinese intellectuals, namely, the bourgeois idealist conception of history. Hence, a refutation of Acheson may benefit many Chinese by widening their horizon. The benefit may be even greater to those whose conception is the same, or in certain respects the same, as Acheson's.

What are Acheson's wild fabrications about modern Chinese history? First of all, he tries to explain the occurrence of the Chinese revolution in terms of economic and ideological conditions in China. Here he has recounted many myths.

Acheson says:

The population of China during the eighteenth and nineteenth centuries doubled, thereby creating an unbearable pressure upon the land. The first problem which every Chinese Government has had to face is that of feeding this population. So far none has succeeded. The Kuomintang attempted to solve it by putting many land-reform laws on the statute books. Some of these laws have failed, others have been ignored. In no small measure, the predicament in which the National Government finds itself today is due to its failure to provide China with enough to eat. A large part of the Chinese Communists' propaganda consists of promises that they will solve the land problem.

To those Chinese who do not reason clearly the above sounds plausible. Too many mouths, too little food, hence revolution. The Kuomintang has failed to solve this problem and it is unlikely that the Communist Party will be able to solve it either. "So far none has succeeded."

Do revolutions arise from over-population? There have been many revolutions, ancient and modern, in China and abroad; were they all due to over-population? Were China's many revolutions in the past few thousand years also due to over-population? Was the American Revolution against Britain 174 years ago[1] also due to over-population? Acheson's knowledge of history is nil. He has not even read the American Declaration of Independence. Washington, Jefferson and others made the revolution against Britain because of British oppression and exploitation of the Americans, and not because of any over-population in America. Each time the Chinese people overthrew a feudal dynasty it was because of the oppression and exploitation of the people by that feudal dynasty, and not because of any over-population. The Russians made the February Revolution and the October Revolution because of oppression and exploitation by the tsar and the Russian bourgeoisie, not because of any over-population, for to this day in Russia there is a great abundance of land as compared with people. In Mongolia, where the land is so vast and the population so sparse, a revolution would be inconceivable according to Acheson's line of reasoning, yet it took place some time ago.[2]

According to Acheson, China has no way out at all. A population of 475 million constitutes an "unbearable pressure" and, revolution or no revolution, the case is hopeless. Acheson pins great hope on this; although he has not voiced this hope, it has often been revealed by a number of American journalists – through the allegation that the Communist Party of China will not be able to solve its economic problems, that China will remain in perpetual chaos and that her only way out is to live on U.S. flour, in other words, to become a U.S. colony.

Why did the Revolution of 1911 not succeed and why did it not solve the problem of feeding the population? Because it overthrew only the Ching Dynasty but did not overthrow imperialist and feudal oppression and exploitation.

Why did the Northern Expedition of 1926-27 not succeed and why did it not solve the problem of feeding the population? Because Chiang Kai-shek betrayed the revolution, surrendered to imperialism and became the chieftain of the counter-revolution which oppressed and exploited the Chinese.

Is it true that "so far none has succeeded"? In the old Liberated Areas in northwestern, northern, northeastern and eastern China, where the land problem has already been solved, does the problem of "feeding this population", as Acheson puts it, still exist? The United States has kept quite a number of spies or so-called observers in China. Why have they not ferreted out even this fact? In places like Shanghai, the problem of unemployment, or of feeding the population, arose solely because of cruel, heartless oppression and exploitation by imperialism, feudalism, bureaucrat-capitalism and the reactionary Kuomintang government. Under the People's Government, it will take only a few years for this problem of unemployment, or of feeding the population, to be solved as completely as in the northern, northeastern and other parts of the country.

It is a very good thing that China has a big population. Even if China's population multiplies many times, she is fully capable of finding a solution; the solution is production. The absurd argument of Western bourgeois economists like Malthus[3] that increases in food cannot keep pace with increases in population was not only thoroughly refuted in theory by Marxists long ago, but has also been completely exploded by the realities in the Soviet Union and the Liberated Areas of China after their revolutions. Basing itself on the truth that revolution plus production can solve the problem of feeding the population, the Central Committee of the Communist Party of China has issued orders to Party organizations and the People's Liberation Army throughout the country not to dismiss but to retain all former Kuomintang personnel, provided they can make themselves useful and are not confirmed reactionaries or notorious scoundrels. Where things are very difficult, food and housing will be shared. Those who have been dismissed and have no means of support will be reinstated and provided with a living. According to the same principle, we shall maintain all Kuomintang soldiers who have revolted and come over to us or been captured. All reactionaries, except the major culprits, will be given a chance to earn their living, provided they show repentance.

Of all things in the world, people are the most precious. Under the leadership of the Communist Party, as long as there are people, every kind of miracle can be performed. We are refuters of Acheson's counter-revolutionary theory. We believe that revolution can change everything, and that before long there will arise a new China with a big population and a great wealth of products, where life will be abundant and culture will flourish. All pessimistic views are utterly groundless.

"The impact of the West" is given by Acheson as the second reason why the Chinese revolution occurred. Acheson says:

> For more than three thousand years the Chinese developed their own high culture and civilization, largely untouched by out-side influences. Even when subjected to military conquest the Chinese always managed in the end to subdue and absorb the invader. It was natural therefore that they should come to look upon themselves as the center of the world and the highest expression of civilized mankind. Then in the middle of the nineteenth century the heretofore impervious wall of Chinese isolation was breached by the West. These outsiders brought with them aggressiveness, the unparalleled development of Western technology, and a high order of culture which had not accom-panied previous foreign incursions into China. Partly because of these qualities and partly because of the decay of Manchu rule, the Westerners, instead of being absorbed by the Chinese, intro-duced new ideas which played an important part in stimulating ferment and unrest.

To those Chinese who do not reason clearly, what Acheson says sounds plausible – the influx of new ideas from the West gave rise to the revolution.

Against whom was the revolution directed? Because there was "decay of Manchu rule" and because it is the weak point that is attacked, it would seem that the revolution was directed against the Ching Dynasty. But what Acheson says here is not quite right. The Revolution of 1911 was directed against imperialism. The Chinese directed the revolution against the Ching regime because it was the running dog of imperialism. The war against Britain's opium aggression, the war against the aggression of the Anglo-French allied forces, the war against the Ching regime, the running dog of imperialism, by the Taiping Heavenly Kingdom,[4] the war against French aggression, the war against Japanese aggression and the war against the aggression of the allied forces of the eight powers – all ended in failure; hence the Revolution of 1911 broke out against the running dog of imperialism, the Ching Dynasty. That is modern Chinese history up to 1911. What is the "impact of the West", as Acheson calls it? It is the effort of the Western bourgeoisie, as Marx and Engels said in the *Manifesto of the Communist Party* of 1848,[5] to remould the world after its own image by means of terror. In the process of this impact or remoulding, the Western bourgeoisie, which needed compradors and flunkeys familiar with Western customs, had to let countries like China open schools and send students abroad, and thus "new ideas were introduced" into China. Concurrently the national bourgeoisie and the proletariat were born in countries like China. At the same time, the peasantry was bankrupted, and a huge semi-proletariat was brought into existence. Thus the Western bourgeoisie created two categories of people in the East, a small minority, the flunkeys of imperialism, and a majority which is opposed to imperialism and consists of the working class, the peasantry, the urban petty bourgeoisie, the national bourgeoisie and the intellectuals coming from these classes. Those in the majority group are all grave-diggers of imperialism, who were created by imperialism itself, and the revolution originates from them. It was not that the so-called influx of ideas from the West stirred up "ferment and unrest", but that imperialist aggression provoked resistance.

For a long time in the course of this resistance movement, that is, for over seventy years from the Opium War of 1840 to the eve of the May 4th Movement of 1919, the Chinese had no ideological weapon with which to defend themselves against imperialism. The ideological weapons of the old die-hard feudalism were defeated, had to give way and were declared bankrupt. Having no other choice, the Chinese were compelled to arm themselves with such ideological weapons and political formulas as the theory of evolution, the theory of

natural rights and of the bourgeois republic, which were all borrowed
from the arsenal of the revolutionary period of the bourgeoisie in the
West, the native home of imperialism.   The Chinese organized political parties and made revolutions, believing that they could thus resist
foreign powers and build a republic.   However, all these ideological
weapons, like those of feudalism, proved very feeble and in their
turn had to give way and were withdrawn and declared bankrupt.

The Russian Revolution of 1917 awakened the Chinese, and they
learned something new, Marxism-Leninism.   In China, the Communist Party was born, an epoch-making event.   Sun Yat-sen, too,
advocated "learning from Russia" and "alliance with Russia and the
Communist Party".   In a word, from that time China changed her
orientation.

Being the spokesman of an imperialist government, Acheson naturally does not want to breathe even a word about imperialism.   He
describes imperialist aggression thus: "These outsiders brought with
them aggressiveness. . . ."   "Aggressiveness" – what a beautiful name!
Having learned this "aggressiveness", the Chinese did not aggress
into Britain or the United States but only created "ferment and
unrest" inside China, *i.e.*, carried out revolutions against imperialism
and its running dogs.   But unfortunately they never once succeeded;
each time, they were defeated by the imperialists, the inventors of
"aggressiveness".   The Chinese therefore turned around to learn
something else and, strangely enough, they immediately found that
it worked.

The Chinese Communist Party "had been organized in the early
twenties under the ideological impetus of the Russian revolution".
Here Acheson is right.   This ideology was none other than Marxism-
Leninism.   This ideology is immeasurably superior to that of the
Western bourgeoisie, which Acheson calls a "high order of culture
which had not accompanied previous foreign incursions into China".
The clinching proof of the effectiveness of this ideology is that Western
bourgeois culture, which the Achesons can boast of as a "high order of
culture" compared with China's old feudal culture, was defeated the
moment it encountered the new Marxist-Leninist culture, the scientific
world outlook and the theory of social revolution, which the Chinese
people had acquired.   In its first battle, this scientific and revolutionary new culture acquired by the Chinese people defeated the Northern
warlords, the running dogs of imperialism; in the second, it defeated
the attempts by another running dog of imperialism, Chiang Kai-shek,

to intercept the Chinese Red Army during its 25,000-*li* Long March;[6] in the third, it defeated Japanese imperialism and its running dog, Wang Ching-wei; and in the fourth, it finally put an end to the domination of China by the United States and all other imperialist powers as well as to the rule of their running dogs, Chiang Kai-shek and all the other reactionaries.

The reason why Marxism-Leninism has played such a great role in China since its introduction is that China's social conditions call for it, that it has been linked with the actual practice of the Chinese people's revolution and that the Chinese people have grasped it. Any ideology – even the very best, even Marxism-Leninism itself – is ineffective unless it is linked with objective realities, meets objectively existing needs and has been grasped by the masses of the people. We are historical materialists, opposed to historical idealism.

Oddly enough, "Soviet doctrine and practice had a measurable effect upon the thinking and principles of Dr. Sun Yat-sen, particularly in terms of economics and Party organization". What was the effect produced on Dr. Sun by the "high order of culture" of the West, of which Acheson and his like are so proud? Acheson doesn't say. Was it an accident that Dr. Sun, who devoted the greater part of his life to seeking from Western bourgeois culture the truth that would save the nation, was finally disappointed and turned to "learning from Russia"? Obviously not. Of course it was no accident that Dr. Sun and the long suffering Chinese people he represented were all infuriated by the "impact of the West" and resolved to form an "alliance with Russia and the Communist Party" in order to wage a life-and-death struggle against imperialism and its running dogs. Acheson dare not say here that the Soviet people are imperialist aggressors and that Sun Yat-sen learned from aggressors. Well, then, if Sun Yat-sen could learn from the Soviet people and the Soviet people are not imperialist aggressors, why can't his successors, the Chinese who live after him, learn from the Soviet people? Why are the Chinese, Sun Yat-sen excepted, described as "dominated by the Soviet Union" and as "the fifth column of the Comintern" and "lackeys of Red imperialism" for learning the scientific world outlook and the theory of social revolution through Marxism-Leninism, linking these with China's specific characteristics, starting the Chinese People's War of Liberation and the great people's revolution and founding a republic of the people's democratic dictatorship? Can there be such superior logic anywhere in the world?

Since they learned Marxism-Leninism, the Chinese people have ceased to be passive in spirit and gained the initiative. The period of modern world history in which the Chinese and Chinese culture were looked down upon should have ended from that moment. The great, victorious Chinese People's War of Liberation and the great people's revolution have rejuvenated and are rejuvenating the great culture of the Chinese people. In its spiritual aspect, this culture of the Chinese people already stands higher than any in the capitalist world. Take U.S. Secretary of State Acheson and his like, for instance. The level of their understanding of modern China and of the modern world is lower than that of an ordinary soldier of the Chinese People's Liberation Army.

Up to this point, Acheson, like a bourgeois professor lecturing on a tedious text, has pretended to trace the causes and effects of events in China. Revolution occurred in China, first, because of over-population and, second, because of the stimulus of Western ideas. You see, he appears to be a champion of the theory of causation. But in what follows, even this bit of tedious and phoney theory of causation disappears, and one finds only a mass of inexplicable events. Quite unaccountably, the Chinese fought among themselves for power and money, suspecting and hating each other. An inexplicable change took place in the relative moral strength of the two contending parties, the Kuomintang and the Communist Party; the morale of one party dropped sharply to below zero, while that of the other rose sharply to white heat. What was the reason? Nobody knows. Such is the logic inherent in the "high order of culture" of the United States as represented by Dean Acheson.

NOTES

[1] The bourgeois revolution of 1775-83, known as the War of Independence, in which the people of North America opposed British colonial rule.

[2] In their struggle for liberation in 1921-24 the Mongolian people, under the leadership of the Mongolian People's Revolutionary Party, drove out the Russian Whiteguard bandit troops and the armed forces of the Northern warlords of China, both of which were backed by Japanese imperialism, overthrew Mongolian feudal rule and founded the Mongolian People's Republic.

[3] T. R. Malthus (1766-1834), Anglican clergyman and reactionary economist. In his *Essay on Population* (1798), he wrote that "population unchecked . . . increases in

geometrical ratio . . . [while] the means of subsistence . . . could not possibly be made to increase faster than in an arithmetical ratio". Basing himself on this arbitrary assumption, he came to the conclusion that all poverty and all evils in human society are permanent phenomena of nature. According to him, the only ways to solve the problem of poverty of the working people were to shorten their life-span, reduce the population or stop its increase. He regarded famine, pestilence and war as means to cut down population.

[4] The War of the Taiping Heavenly Kingdom was a peasant revolutionary war waged against the feudal rule and national oppression of the Ching Dynasty in the middle of the 19th century. Hung Hsiu-chuan, Yang Hsiu-ching and others, the leaders of this revolution, staged an uprising in Kwangsi in January 1851 and proclaimed the founding of the Taiping Heavenly Kingdom. In 1852 the peasant army proceeded northward from Kwangsi and marched through Hunan, Hupeh, Kiangsi and Anhwei and in 1853 it captured Nanking, the main city on the lower Yangtse. Part of its forces then continued the drive north and pushed to the vicinity of Tientsin, a major city in northern China. Because the Taiping army failed to build stable base areas in the places it occupied and also because, after establishing its capital in Nanking, the leading group in the army committed many political and military errors, it could not withstand the joint attack of the counter-revolutionary troops of the Ching government and the aggressors, Britain, the United States and France, and suffered defeat in 1864.

[5] See *Manifesto of the Communist Party*, Chapter I, "Bourgeois and Proletarians". The bourgeoisie "compels all nations, on pain of extinction, to adopt the bourgeois mode of production; it compels them to introduce what it calls civilization into their midst, *i.e.*, to become bourgeois themselves. In one word, it creates a world after its own image".

[6] In October 1934 the First, Third and Fifth Army Groups of the Chinese Workers' and Peasants' Red Army (that is, the First Front Army of the Red Army, also known as the Central Red Army) set out from Changting and Ninghua in western Fukien and from Juichin, Yutu and other places in southern Kiangsi and started a major strategic movement. In traversing the eleven provinces of Fukien, Kiangsi, Kwangtung, Hunan, Kwangsi, Kweichow, Szechuan, Yunnan, Sikang, Kansu and Shensi, crossing perpetually snow-capped mountains and trackless grasslands, sustaining untold hardships and frustrating the enemy's repeated encirclements, pursuits, obstructions and interceptions, the Red Army covered 25,000 *li* (12,500 kilometres) on this march and finally arrived triumphantly at the revolutionary base area in northern Shensi in October 1935.

毛 泽 东 选 集

第 四 卷

＊

外文出版社出版（北京）

一九六一年第一版

一九六九年第三次印刷

编号：（英）1050—169

00330（精）

00220（平）

1—E—444

49797